The Peopling of Newfoundland

The Peopling of Newfoundland

Essays in Historical Geography

John J. Mannion, Editor

Social and Economic Papers No. 8

**Institute of Social and Economic Research,
Memorial University of Newfoundland**

© Memorial University of Newfoundland 1977
ISBN 0-919666-17-5

Second Printing 1986
Third Printing 1990

Canadian Cataloguing in Publication Data

Main entry under title:

The Peopling of Newfoundland

(Social and economic papers; no. 8)

Bibliography: p.
Includes index.
ISBN 0-919666-17-5

1. Migration, Internal – Newfoundland.
2. Newfoundland – Emigration and immigration.
3. Newfoundland – Population.   I. Mannion, John J.,
1941–   II. Memorial University of Newfoundland.
Institute of Social and Economic Research.
III. Series: Newfoundland social and economic
papers; no. 8.

HB1990.N4P46   301.32′6′09718   C78-001007-8

Contents

Figures

Plates (Trinity Bay)

Tables

Preface

This collection of essays has its origins in a series of seminars on historical geography held at Memorial University during the academic year 1972–73. It incorporates some of the research of graduate students and faculty from the Department of Geography in progress at that time. In April 1974, the authors met for a final one-week seminar at Memorial's branch campus in Old Harlow, near London, to discuss pre-circulated essay drafts. Revision of the papers has continued since then.

The main objective of this volume is to analyse the process of the peopling of Newfoundland. Each essay examines the initial inflow of migrants and settlers to a particular area or areas and then considers the subsequent growth of population there and the expansion of permanent settlement. Beyond the common theme of migration and settlement formation, each author focuses on a specific topic pertinent to the historical geography of Newfoundland. A variety of approaches has been employed, from detailed demographic analyses to interpretations through evidence gleaned from the cultural landscape, and a wide range of source material has been consulted, from census data, government papers and reports, newspapers, travellers' accounts, parish registers, merchants' letter books, ledgers and old diaries to gravestone evidence, interviews and observation and measurement in the field.

Despite its importance for any investigation of Newfoundland society and culture, there is little in print, in the geographical literature or elsewhere, on the main theme of this volume. Indeed there is not much comparable detail yet for most other provinces in Canada. Newfoundland is one of Europe's oldest areas of colonial settlement in North America and these essays are intended as a contribution towards an understanding of its complex evolution.

We wish to express our thanks to the Institute of Social and Economic Research for funding the Harlow seminar and for supporting some of us in our field and archival research. Our thanks also to the staff at the Institute, particularly Shirley Fraize for supervising the initial typing of the manuscript, Sonia Kuryliw Paine for editorial work, and Jeanette Gleeson for final typing and production. We are indebted to Mrs. Joan Lloyd of the Harlow campus for making our stay there such a pleasant one. Thanks are due to Dr. C. Grant Head and Dr. John Warkentin for reading the manuscript and making helpful suggestions. Our principal debt is to our cartographer, Gary McManus, for undertaking the considerable task of drafting and producing seventy maps for the volume. Finally, I would like to record my personal appreciation to all authors for their continued faith in this project, and for their patience and understanding through the protracted process of bringing these essays to fruition.

This book has been published with the help of a grant from the Social Science Federation of Canada, using funds provided by the Canada Council.

September, 1977   *John Mannion*
St. John's

Notes on Contributors

W. GORDON HANDCOCK is Associate Professor of Geography at Memorial University. His principal research is on the migrations to Newfoundland from England's West Country, Newfoundland settlement and toponomy.

ALAN G. MACPHERSON is Professor of Geography at Memorial University. He has done detailed work on the historical geography and demography of Scots Highlanders in Scotland and on environmental perception and geographical change in Newfoundland.

JOHN J. MANNION is Professor of Geography at Memorial University and is currently working on the Irish migrations to Newfoundland.

GARY MCMANUS is Associate Director of Cartography in the Department of Geography, Memorial University and specializes in thematic cartography and design.

DAVIS S. MILLS is Assistant Director of the Historic Resources Division of the Department of Culture, Recreation and Youth in Newfoundland and is a specialist in heritage conservation.

ROSEMARY E. OMMER is Associate Professor of History at Memorial University. Her research includes the study of Jersey Island merchants and settlement in the Gulf of St. Lawrence, shipping, and the fisheries in 19th century Atlantic Canada.

FRANK W. REMIGGI is Professeur Régulier Département de géographie, Université du Québec à Montreal. He is presently working on the geography of religion in rural Quebec in the 19th century.

CHESLEY W. SANGER is Associate Professor of Geography at Memorial University. His research includes the historical geography of Scottish northern whaling, and sealing in Newfoundland.

MICHAEL STAVELEY is Professor of Geography and Dean of Arts at Memorial University. His major research interests are social and historical geography, with an emphasis on Newfoundland population studies.

PATRICIA A. THORNTON is Associate Professor of Geography at McGill University and is currently investigating demographic aspects of settlement in Eastern Canada.

Introduction

John J. Mannion

The central theme of this volume is the gradual spread of settlement in Newfoundland in the 19th century. By 1800 the permanent population was still largely confined to the Avalon Peninsula and the northeast coast to Notre Dame Bay, with only a scattering of settlements in the remaining areas of the island to the north and west, and in Labrador. A century later this vast area was settled, with twelve times as many people; the Newfoundland maritime frontier was finally closed.

The unifying theme of the following chapters is related to the inflow of migrants and settlers to different parts of Newfoundland or neighbouring areas, the establishment and growth of a permanent population and the concomitant spread of permanent settlement. There is a shared emphasis also on the source areas of the migrants, their social and economic background, and the adaptations made to a new environment as manifested by the patterns of resource use and settlement. Beyond this, each author focuses on a specific topic and almost all deal with a specific part of Newfoundland or its adjacent areas.

In a rigorously conceptualized study of the English migrations to Newfoundland, Handcock introduces a rich store of fresh data and outlines new methods for measuring the expansion of English population and settlement on the island over more than two centuries. For much of its early history, Newfoundland had a highly transient, fluctuating population, and it is difficult to measure the growth of the permanent population. Handcock's index of permanency hinges on the proportion of women and children resident on the island, and on the incidence of marriage. By means of these parameters existing notions of the timing and extent of English emigration are revised. Perhaps more important is his delimitation of the source area to southwest England, and the relationship of human migration to specific paths of transatlantic mercantile trade. In the extensive literature on the European origins of the Atlantic migrations, few studies present comparable detail on the source area of the immigrants, or treat the areas of origin and destination in so balanced and integrated a manner. In Chapter 2, Staveley, using different parameters, extends and deepens Handcock's discourse through a macro-quantitative assessment, based on detailed census data, of migration, circulation, and population growth in Newfoundland during the 19th century. The emerging regional patterns of age structures, fertility, and mortality are described, and the relative contributions of natural increase and in-migration to demographic growth measured. Newfoundland's 19th century population can be seen as progressing through a stage sequence somewhat similar to that found in other marginal frontier areas and there is a striking and persistent contrast over the century, in terms of the population parameters considered here, between the old core and the 19th century Newfoundland frontier.

The remaining studies are less quantitative, focusing on particular areas within the island or nearby mainland (Fig. 1). They are presented in a rough regional order following the paths of advancing settlement from the old core to the northern and western frontiers. Newfoundland's cultural landscape is unique in contemporary North America, not just because the population is predominantly restricted to a necklace of communities around the coast, but also because of its historic isolation from the mainland; the landscape and the technology that helped create it have preserved until recently much of an Old World character. Folk housing is one of the diagnostic elements of this landscape, and in Chapter 3 Mills explores its development over two centuries in a predominantly West Country culture area in Trinity Bay. Most studies of North American folk architecture tend to simplify the complexity of Old World antecedents, implying stability and homogeneity, and simplify also the evolution of house forms in the New World. Mills attempts to relate the construction of New World dwellings not just to homeland antecedents but to the larger and ultimately more fundamental context of the peopling and development of a frontier. The author rejects the notion of general and abrupt changes in style as implied in the concept of sequential stages, and emphasizes instead the continuing innovative character of the Trinity Bay architectural tradition. Even in Newfoundland, the notion of stability or continuity of folk cultural elements can be over-drawn.

In Chapter 4 Macpherson returns to the theme of initial formation of sedentary settlement and the growth of a permanent population in an area in central Bonavista Bay. He refines the existing indices of residency and by examining population returns beginning as early as the 1670s, church registers, and contemporary observations, succeeds in reconstituting detailed family profiles of the migrants and immigrants; settlement by settlement he outlines the timing, volume, and specific channels of movement (both from the Old World and from longer settled parts of Newfoundland), and the social structure of the migrant streams. The fleeting nature and radically fluctuating social composition of the temporary population is unfolded, and the author's conclusion that there is no evidence of progressive population growth in this long-exploited territory until the 19th century provides a sound basis for comparison with other areas of the old English shore.

Although cod was the commercial staple in virtually all parts of Newfoundland, sedentary settlement would have been extremely precarious, indeed probably impossible, without large-scale dependence on other locally exploitable resources. More important in the context of the growth and expansion of permanent settlement was the availability of resources that could be exploited commercially and at a time of year not conflicting with the summer fishery. Early in the 18th century sealing became an important commercial winter activity in the more northerly areas of the island and, as Sanger shows in Chapter 5, it was important in the expansion of permanent settlement in northeast Newfoundland, in areas adjacent to the migratory route of the harp seal. This enterprise was initially conducted inshore by "landsmen," and for some emerging communities in the northern areas seal became a leading source of income. Later in the 18th century a more capital-intensive seal hunt developed offshore, somewhat analogous in scale to the Banks cod fishery which in fact it partially replaced. Sanger examines the shifting regional patterns of participation as the industry grew throughout the 19th century.

The relationship between an integrated economy based on the year-round exploitation of a combination of resources and the formation of permanent settlement in marginal areas is further developed by Thornton (Chapter 6) in a broad and detailed study of the emerging economy and demography in the Strait of Belle Isle. For centuries Europeans had migrated annually to this area to fish for cod, but it was not

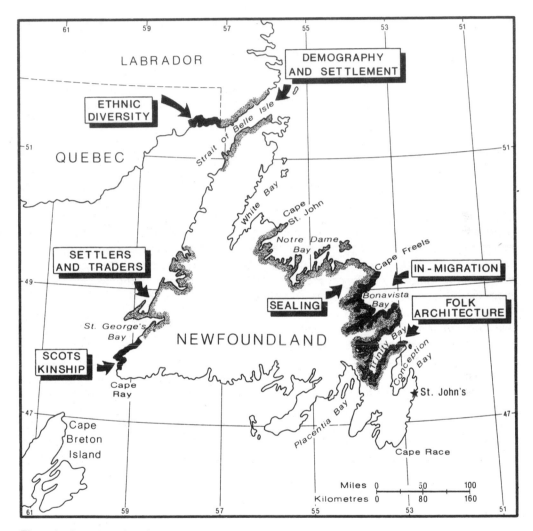

Figure 1 *Location of Study Areas*

until other resources, notably salmon, seals and fur, were exploited commercially in conjunction with cod that permanent settlement developed. The Strait was part of Newfoundland's last maritime frontier and is a laboratory in the sense that the processes of settlement formation there were largely an extension of those evinced on the Old English shore more than a century before. By analysing detailed genealogical data the author reinforces Handcock's conclusions on the importance of the availability of women for the creation and growth of settlement on the frontier. As in the peopling of central Bonavista Bay, there were highly specific migrant flows in terms of areas of origin and destination, and the social composition of the migrating streams changed through the 19th century. Thornton examines the nature and extent of mercantile and metropolitan control over these migrations, the changing relationship between merchant and settler and its implications in the context of the commercial organization and the expansion, distribution, and pattern of settlement on the Strait. In Chapter 7, using similar data, Remiggi considers ethnic diversity and residential segregation in a small area adjoining the north coast of the Strait, but within the modern province of Quebec. This isolated area attracted settlers from diverse sources, including a Newfoundland and French Canadian component. Despite its current relevancy, there have been few micro-studies by historical geographers on the roots of conflict between French and English speakers in Quebec, or Canada, and the author attempts to reconstruct inter-ethnic relationships as manifested in the residential location of settlers from the early 19th century on. Language and religion are selected as the diagnostic elements of ethnicity and marriage as the main mechanism in the assimilation or exclusion of members of different groups. Religion emerges as a more inhibiting force than language in the integrative process and the author's analysis of the gradual contraction of French-speaking settlement in this remote part of Quebec warrants comparative investigation.

Residential segregation existed not only between ethnic groups, but within them, as demonstrated by Ommer in her study of kinship and the selectivity of Highland Scottish migrations to Cape Breton and southwest Newfoundland. It is generally maintained in the literature that migration implies a sundering of kinship ties. In Chapter 8 the author argues that intricate elements of Scots kinship persisted despite movement. The traditional Scottish clan system was still an important, if declining, element in the Highlands at the beginning of Scottish migrations across the Atlantic. The social composition of this migration stream stands in contrast to the other highly selective migrations, largely dominated by merchants, considered elsewhere in this volume.

Some Scots settled north of Codroy, mainly in St. George's Bay, but the 19th century migrations to this part of the western shore were culturally far more heterogeneous and were drawn from a wide diversity of source areas. In the final chapter of this volume Mannion describes the ethnic composition of these latter settlers and their dispersions along the west coast as far north as Bonne Bay. Different combinations of resources were exploited at different times throughout the century, stimulating movement to particular parts of the coast. Most of the goods produced commercially were destined for distant overseas markets. A distinctive system of exchange evolved between settlers and traders, and an elaborate network of external trading links were established. This essay examines the background of merchants and traders on the coast, the changing system of mercantile commerce, and the relationship between the location of mercantile operations and the emergence of central places.

What follows is a statement on the general conditions which form the background of these essays. The vast majority of contemporary Newfoundlanders are descended from immigrants who came originally from highly localized source areas in the southwest of England and the southeast of Ireland. There were three modes of migration from these places to Newfoundland: seasonal, temporary and permanent. There was a long period of seasonal and temporary movement, extending roughly for the English from the late 16th (and for the Irish from the late 17th) to the early 19th century, and an almost equally long period of permanent migration or immigration with its apogee between 1780 and 1830, in the wake of the declining seasonal and temporary migrations. A seasonal move meant an individual left the homeland in the spring, fished through the summer in Newfoundland, and returned home in the fall. A temporary move implied over-wintering: migrants stayed on for a winter or two or more before returning home. There was, of course, a close relationship between these temporary migrations and immigration. In the simplest terms, some of the men coming out temporarily to fish decided to bring out their womenfolk, and children if any, and settle, so that over-wintering spawned immigration and the formation of permanent settlement. Alternatively, single women were sometimes brought out, married in Newfoundland, and remained there.

For more than two centuries the volume of immigration remained a mere trickle in comparison to the seasonal and temporary flows, and was a desultory phenomenon. Hundreds of ships and thousands of men annually crossed the Atlantic, not just from the British Isles but from various other pockets of coastal Europe, from Portugal to northeast France, to prosecute the summer cod fishery. Yet by 1775 about twelve thousand persons – no more than half the total British summer population – wintered in Newfoundland, and in no way could all of them be considered permanent settlers. For more than two centuries the average annual intake of settlers from the temporary sector was less than 5 percent of the total number of British migrants fishing in Newfoundland waters. This sluggish rate of immigration and population growth is one of the salient themes of Newfoundland historiography.

The first year-round or permanent British settlements in Newfoundland, established early in the 17th century, did not emanate from the ranks of the traditional migratory fishermen, however, but were the result of plans by British merchants and others to colonize the island and tap local resources besides the staple cod. In the long run these tiny colonies in Conception Bay and on the Southern Shore of the Avalon Peninsula contributed little to the growth of permanent settlement, and by the end of the century there were still no more than three thousand inhabitants occupying some thirty settlements from Trepassey to Bonavista Bay (the English shore). The pace of immigration, and concomitant expansion of settlement quickened somewhat in the second quarter of the 18th century. In the southern Avalon the English pushed west into the traditional French fishing areas of St. Mary's and Placentia Bays after the Treaty of Utrecht (1713), and a decade or two thereafter began their slow expansion northwards towards Fogo and Twillingate and into Notre Dame Bay. This two-pronged extension of English settlement was, in part, occasioned by the availability of commercially exploitable resources ancillary to cod, including salmon, furs, and (in the north only) seals. The latter two resources could be exploited in winter and, when linked to the summer cod fishery, made year-round occupancy more feasible. Later in the century shipbuilding developed as another commercial winter activity. The gradual diversification of resource use and associated expansion of settlement represent a significant development in 18th century Newfoundland. Expansion proceeded at an inordinately slow pace on Newfoundland's northern and southern maritime frontiers, however, and large areas of the coast remained sparsely settled even at the end of the century.

Much more impressive was the relative growth of population in the old English core. The winter population at least quadrupled between 1725 and 1775, a period of rising European demand for cod. This increase reflected an even greater expansion of the migratory ship fishery and striking increases in the cod catch. Overcrowding of inshore waters in this area was partly responsible for the development of an offshore fishery on the Grand Banks which, in turn, resulted in increasing yields and stimulated population growth. Within the old English shore the rise of a permanent population was clearly evident in the growing proportion of women and young children. Yet, despite this increase in the last two decades of the century, there was still an excess of unattached adult males in the population, reflecting the continuous if diminishing presence of a temporary and seasonal sector. Demographic maturity came slowly to Newfoundland.

The formative phase in the growth of population and expansion of permanent settlement came during the Napoleonic Wars, especially after 1800 and in the two decades that followed the peace. This period of transition was marked by a dramatic increase in the rate of immigration from southwest England and southeast Ireland and the virtual collapse of the transatlantic migratory fishery. For more than a century the migratory ship fishery had outstripped the residents in terms of catch, and particularly so with the growth of the Banks fishery about the middle of the 18th century. It had reached its peak in the years immediately preceding the American Revolution when British ships brought out up to ten thousand men annually across the Atlantic, rallied again after the war-time hiatus to attain an all-time high in terms of catch, and then decline rapidly about 1790 when fish prices fell. The drop in price was due, in part, to a glutted market and also to the inferior quality of fish processed offshore. West Country merchants, who had prospered for decades on the expanding migratory fishery, were suddenly bankrupt or withdrew their capital: and the Napoleonic Wars resulted in its virtual demise. Unlike the situation following other conflicts in the 18th century, there was no major post-war reflux of migratory personnel or economic recovery offshore. But the migratory fishery was a long time dying, and vestiges of this ancient mode of mercantilist exploitation survived in remoter parts of Newfoundland and Labrador until the second half of the 19th century.

The decline of the migratory fishery in the first decade of the war did result in a proportionate increase in the resident population, but not in absolute terms. Early in the new century, however, the demographic structure of the island changed dramatically: in about three decades the population almost quadrupled, from 19,000 persons in 1803 to 75,000 in 1836, mainly as a consequence of in-migration (Appendix 1). In Chapter 1 of this volume, Handcock estimates that the rate of immigration during this period was twelve times greater than in the second quarter of the 18th century, itself a period of substantial demographic advance. During the three peak decades of immigration about 45,000 persons were recorded as passengers to Newfoundland on British ships, of whom some 75 percent were Irish, 23 percent English, and 2 percent from Jersey. It is impossible to determine how many of these migrants settled permanently on the island, how many moved to the mainland, how many may have returned to their homelands as part of the residual transient fishery, or indeed how accurate or comprehensive the returns are. Certainly the more voluminous Irish Catholic influx was not reflected in the Protestant:Catholic ratio (virtually synonymous with English:Irish) in Newfoundland throughout this period. In 1830 there were 30,766 Protestants to 27,322 Catholics, or 53:47, a ratio that had changed only slightly in favour of the Irish throughout the early 19th century. Either there was a considerable influx of English immigrants who went unrecorded, as Handcock suggests, or a rapid natural increase among the more mature Newfoundland-English population occurred; in fact, it is likely that both processes contributed to the continuing English edge over the Irish. There is also the possibility of considerable out-migration of the Irish to the mainland. Although the flow of people from both homelands remained high almost every season during the first third of the century, there were two major waves of migration, each overwhelmingly Irish, between 1811 and 1816 and again between 1825 and 1833. Subsequently, the volume of Irish immigration declined dramatically. The massive movement of Irish during the famine in the 1840s bypassed Newfoundland almost completely. The volume of English emigration remained lower than the Irish, but persisted longer through the 19th century.

In terms of the growth of a permanent population, and the expansion of sedentary settlement, the actual volume of the 19th century migrations was not as important in the long run as the modified sex ratio of the migrants. In contrast to the predominance of single adult males and boys in the 18th century seasonal and temporary migrations, the subsequent influx was marked by an increase in the number of women and even young children, although their percentage was still exceedingly low. However, the resulting increase in the availability of female spouses had a profound impact on natural demographic growth in Newfoundland through the 19th century.

One of the interesting unanswered questions on the derivation of Newfoundland's immigrant population is the extent to which the 19th century influx is a transfer from the migratory population of the late 18th century – transient fishermen who decided to come out and stay – or to what extent the emigration was one of people with no former experience of Newfoundland. Certainly the 19th century movement emanated from the traditional 18th century source areas of temporary migrants in southwest England and southeast Ireland. It is unlikely that any other province or state in contemporary North America drew such an overwhelming proportion of its immigrants from such localized source areas in the European homeland over so substantial a period of time. Handcock has delimited the area of origin of the English emigrants to the two contiguous counties of Dorset and Devon and to the neighbouring border areas of Somerset and Hampshire. The extent of the source areas is closely related to the hinterlands of those West Country Channel ports involved in the Newfoundland migratory cod fishery, particularly Dartmouth, Teignmouth, Topsham, Poole, and Bristol, and St. Aubin and St. Helier in Jersey. Similarly, the territorial extent of the Irish source area was restricted to a pocket in the southeast. From the late 17th century onwards, ships from southwest England called into ports in southeast Ireland each spring to recruit cheap labour and collect provisions for the summer fishery. Although there was competition from other neighbouring ports – notably New Ross, Youghal, and Cork – the port of Waterford emerged early as the pivot of Ireland's

Newfoundland trade; the majority of Irish involved in the cod fishery and in the 19th century migration came from within thirty miles radius of Waterford city, specifically from southwest Wexford, south Kilkenny, southeast Tipperary, southeast Cork, and County Waterford.

Any explanation for the localized nature of these source areas must take into account the role of British, and later Irish, merchants and their agents in organizing the annual flow of people and provisions across the Atlantic. Because of the distance separating Newfoundland from its European bases of exploitation, and the high capital costs of equipping a crew for a transatlantic fishing venture, Newfoundland trade, from the beginning, was controlled by merchants in the ports of Europe rather than by individual fishermen. Each winter and early spring these merchants and their agents hired young men and boys on a contract basis to fish in Newfoundland, usually for one to three summers, and sometimes advanced cash as security to the young fishermen or their parents. Recruiting was generally conducted locally in taverns or at fairs or other gatherings, or through advertisements in local newspapers. A wide range of supplies for the fishery was also collected by the merchants, who used an elaborate network of communications between their home port and hinterland in organizing the trade. Initially the men were employed directly by the merchants to fish on ships owned by the merchants and their business colleagues. But gradually, as the resident fishery grew in Newfoundland in the 18th century, and as the prices of provisions and labour increased, the merchants found it more profitable to carry out passengers and provisions for the planters and byeboatmen in exchange for cash or a portion of the cod catch than to fish on their own account. This transition from a mercantile ship fishery to a supply trade was first evidenced in the old English shore and diffused slowly over a century or more to the more recently settled parts of the island. Individual merchants in the Old World traded with specific areas in Newfoundland, and channeled people and provisions from certain areas in the homeland to specific parts of the island. This mercantile influence over the migrations, which endured at least up to the exodus of the early 19th century, resulted in even greater localization regarding the place of origin of Newfoundland immigrants.

Since Irish, as well as English, migrants were transported to Newfoundland almost exclusively on English ships owned by English merchants, and sometimes as mixed crews, until the last third of the 18th century there was a considerable intermingling of both groups on the island, especially among the temporary population. In the 17th century the English had occupied almost all the main harbours from Trepassey to Bonavista Bay, and in the following century the Irish also dispersed along this shore. Mixed communities gradually developed and some persist to this day. From the beginning, however, the Irish tended to concentrate on the Avalon, particularly from St. John's to Placentia, and were also prominent in some of the more populous centres of summer settlement in the bays north of St. John's to Fogo Island; elsewhere the English dominated. This pattern is still clearly discernible today.

Much of the early distribution pattern of both groups may be explained in the context of individual mercantile nodes of labour recruitment in the homelands, and of individual mercantile areas of exploitation in Newfoundland. In the case of the Irish, Waterford and its neighbouring ports in the southeast were ideally placed for vessels from southwest England bound for, or returning from, Newfoundland on the Westerlies route, especially the Bristol Channel ports such as Bideford, Barnstaple, and Bristol, which were much closer to the Irish ports than were those of south Devon. In the late 17th century the Bristol Channel ports had close commercial ties with Waterford and its neighbouring ports primarily through the wool trade. Merchants from these ports began to collect provisions and cheap labour in the Irish ports for the Newfoundland fishery and directed the Irish toward the southern Avalon and other specific areas of the Bristol Channel fishery in Newfoundland. Later other ports, such as Poole in Dorset, captured much of the Irish-Newfoundland trade and consolidated and extended the pattern of Irish settlement on the island. Similarly, the English migrations to the northeast and south coasts were, to a great degree, channeled from particular parts of southwest England by individual West Country mercantile houses (see Handcock, this vol.).

Little is yet known about the relationship between the organization of the old temporary migrations and the flood of immigration in the early 19th century. Certainly the extent of Old World mercantile control over the volume and direction of the Newfoundland migrations declined with the demise of the migratory fishery, but to what extent we do not know. Indeed, control had begun to decline even earlier, with the waning of the ship fishery, as byeboatmen or planters supplied by the merchants began to influence the inflow of people and the expansion of settlement (see Thornton, this vol.). In the case of the English immigration to Newfoundland's expanding 19th century frontier, however, it is likely that the merchant's organizational role was maintained. This is less likely in the case of the heavy Irish influx, especially to St. John's, but it is interesting to note that the broad channels of Irish migration from the traditional source area in the southeast to the established areas of 18th century Irish summer and over-wintering settlement in Newfoundland persisted.

The reasons for these migrations, both temporary and permanent, are far too complex to be considered in detail here. Probably the principal motivation for out-migration was over-population and growing social and economic distress in the homelands. In Ireland the population had jumped from four to eight million during the main period of the Newfoundland migrations. Rapid population growth was least evident in the east and southeast, but even here dramatic increases occurred in the second half of the 18th century so that by the end of the Napoleonic Wars parts of this area were heavily overpopulated. Population growth was not as striking in England's West Country, but was substantial enough to cause considerable distress with the economic recession following the Napoleonic Wars. In the second half of the 18th century both areas experienced impressive economic and population growth; however, the gradual mechanization of production due to centralized industrialization resulted in rising regional unemployment, especially among the artisan class as a wide range of traditional cottage crafts became obsolete. This was particularly true in southwest England, and it is likely that the majority of English emigrants to Newfoundland were displaced artisans (or their sons) from the towns. The collapse of Devonshire's staple serge trade with the continent during the Napoleonic Wars increased unemployment among clothiers and ancillary trades throughout the country; some drifted into seasonal farm work in nearby counties, some moved to the industrial midlands, and still others emigrated.

In Ireland, too, the failure of the domestic textile industry in the southeast, especially in the towns, influenced out-migration. Following the Napoleonic Wars, the prohibition on subdividing and on subletting to undertenants reduced the alternatives for the sons of small holders, and the non-renewal of long leases by landlords made farming less attractive. Far more important in the southeast was the drop in post-war farm prices and in the market for provisions which made small farms less viable. In both countries, but especially in southwest England, advances in farm technology since the mid-18th century resulted in a rising surplus of farm labourers unable to find permanent work. There was no increase in manufacturing in the towns to absorb this surplus, and with retrenchment in most other local resource-based industries, out-migration was one of the few viable alternatives.

Despite economic distress in the homelands, the common assumption that the majority of the Newfoundland migrants were impoverished on departure is erroneous. There is a dearth of quantifiable data on the social origins of the temporary migrants or immigrants in Newfoundland, but from the sparse documentation extant we know that they came from a broader spectrum of society than traditionally postulated in the literature. Some of the Irish were the surplus sons of small but comfortable farmers unwilling to subdivide the land; others worked plots too small to be economically viable under the changing market conditions; others were fishermen-farmers, farm labourers or cottiers; and still others were engaged in a wide variety of crafts in the towns and countryside of the southeast. The English were probably more urban than the Irish, coming predominantly from an artisan background in the towns, or from the ranks of farm labourers. Certainly some of these people were close to poverty in their own land, but others were attracted to Newfoundland because they perceived they could better their economic lot, and were not forced to leave solely because of economic distress in their homelands. Indeed, in th. 18th century the majority of migrants returned home and some, such as the English byeboatmen, planters, merchants or their agents often brought back considerable capital to continue with their Old World occupations or develop new enterprises. In Ireland, well-to-do farmers sent sons out to help earn the rent, and others returned with capital to rent their own farms. Even the early 19th century influx, which was almost certainly composed of poorer people – a reflection of the gradual impoverishment of the homelands at this time – was probably as much a consequence of the 'pull' of attractive conditions in Newfoundland as enforced emigration due to distress in the homeland. Newfoundland enjoyed a monopoly over the world salt cod markets during the war, and hence, an economic boom. Fish prices rose rapidly and wages for fishermen reached unprecedented levels while remaining static or increasing only slightly in the homelands. This boom coincided with the Irish influx of 1811–15, despite the fact that soaring prices for Irish farm goods, also as a result of the war, meant high profits even for the small tenant farmers of the southeast. Newfoundland shared in the post-war recession of the homelands, and it is more difficult to explain the continuing emigration of English and Irish to the island over the two decades following peace; there was still considerable room for expansion in the inshore fishery, albeit at the cost of a reduction in the overall standard of living, whereas opportunities for expansion in the homelands were far more limited.

The Newfoundland migrations were numerically of no great consequence to the homelands, although the broad impact of the Newfoundland trade on the commercial economies of these Old World areas was profound. In southeast Ireland, and to a much greater extent in southwest England, the transatlantic cod fishery and concomitant supply trade ranked as the leading commercial ventures over a considerable period of time, employing great numbers of people in related activities in the ports, in the inland towns and villages, and on the farms. Fish caught in Newfoundland waters fetched good prices in the Mediterranean markets where local and exotic goods could be procured for the British import trade. The temporary migrations and overseas cod fishery suited the then-popular colonial mercantilism of Britain, with the profits flowing back to base in goods or in bullion. Emigration and the growth of permanent settlement in Newfoundland were seen by some British merchants and politicians as a threat to the colonial mercantilist philosophy; but for a variety of reasons settlement was established and continued to grow, especially after 1800.

In the early part of the century, much of this growth was a result of high immigration, but after the 1830s natural increase accounted for a large part of it (see Staveley, this vol.). Settlement expanded in three basic ways: by intensive subdivision of ancestral properties among heirs; by the gradual occupation of habitable sites, usually coves and poorer harbours within the old core; and by the extension of settlement along the northern, southern, and ultimately western frontiers. Partible inheritance of paternal properties by sons became the dominant system of land succession and sometimes resulted in a patchwork of kin-group clusters within a single harbour. As the traditional foci of settlement in the harbours of the old core became crowded, and the limits of locally exploitable resources, capable of supporting a community, were reached, surplus sons and daughters tended to move out and re-locate nearby, if possible. These processes of internal proliferation of households and short-distance dispersion became the salient modes of settlement expansion in 19th century Newfoundland. Others moved much greater distances, from Conception Bay to northern Newfoundland and Labrador, for example, at first seasonally, and then permanently, a pattern not unlike the older transatlantic migrations. As in the early 18th century, movement to the frontier implied the exploitation of a range of resources ancillary to cod.

The rapid growth of population in the 19th century had important implications not just in the context of the territorial extension of sedentary settlement, but in the economic and social structure of Newfoundland communities. During and after the Napoleonic Wars, the high cost of labour and provisions forced the old planter class to rely less on contracted labour from the Old World, and more on their families, other kin, and sometimes sharemen, and to develop subsistence household production as a means of lessening the importation of provisions. The traditional class of indentured servants disappeared, and the planter was gradually reduced to the status of an ordinary fisherman largely dependent on family rather than migratory labour. Whenever labour was recruited outside the family, it was usually in return for a share of the catch, and not for wages as in the case of the 18th century servants. As the 19th century progressed there was a regression also in the system of commercial exchange between fishermen and merchant. Supplies were advanced by the merchants to the fishermen each spring, in return for a promise of the fishermens' catch in the fall, largely eliminating cash in favour of barter as a medium of exchange. In the flagging fishery of the 19th century, fishermens' debts accumulated and the credit system was greatly extended.

Throughout the 19th century mercantile activity gradually became centralized in St. John's, and a concomitant decline of the outport merchant firms with their specialized personnel and services occurred. With this fundamental social change, the basic structure of modern outport society began to emerge, socially more egalitarian and occupationally less specialized than in the previous century. Labour and production were now almost completely organized around the family household unit which aimed towards a greater degree of self-sufficiency and engaged in a wide range of self-supporting domestic activities. This was reflected in the rise of subsistence agriculture during and after the Napoleonic Wars, the development of household crafts such as boat-building and barrel-making, previously executed by a specialized class of artisans, and the elimination of the old specialized units of labour (replaced by the family) involved in catching and curing fish.

Population growth was not accompanied by any major diversification of commercial production, at least not until the end of the century. Cod remained the staple export, and indeed, increased in overall importance. Labour in the fishery rose almost in proportion to general population growth until the 1880s when incipient industrialization and out-migration helped reverse the trend. Technology in the traditional fishery became much more labour intensive, as smaller boats and crews replaced larger ones. One of the underlying problems of outport society was the fact that by the 1880s the annual average production of fish per fisherman had declined to roughly one quarter the early 19th century catch. Nor was there much compensation in terms of a stable increase in fish prices or substantial reductions in the cost of imported supplies. To ward off impoverishment, Newfoundlanders turned more and more to locally exploitable resources. With the collapse of the migratory fishery and the associated Old World mercantile system of trade, and the subsequent periods of economic stagnation and underdevelopment within the confines of a colonial economy, the burgeoning Newfoundland outports became increasingly introverted and isolated from the outside world. Throughout most of the 19th century the development of transportation and communications even within the island was sluggish, and as the St. John's merchants tightened their control over commerce, dispatching their trading vessels to the bays, the range of external contacts of many outports contracted.

Research on the historical geography of Newfoundland is still in its infancy. The only other major work is C. Grant Head's *Eighteenth Century Newfoundland* (1976). No attempt is made in this present volume to write a general historical geography. It is a collection of specialized essays united under the common theme of the peopling of the province. Nor is there any effort within this limited theme to cover comprehensively all areas of the province, or even the basic immigrant groups. There is no detailed treatment of the Irish, the nuclear areas of settlement on the Avalon, nor the expansion of settlement along the south coast. There is a bias instead towards the more northern and western areas, part of Newfoundland's 19th century settlement frontier. Much work remains to be done before any definitive historical geography of Newfoundland can be written.

APPENDIX 1

Population of Newfoundland: 1803–1901[1]

Year	Number	Year	Number
1803	19,034	1821	47,083
1804	20,380	1822	47,530
1805	21,975	1823	49,503
1806	—	1824	—
1807	25,234	1825	55,504
1808	24,625	1826	—
1809	25,157	1827	53,238
1810	—	1828	59,101
1811	25,985	1829	59,035
1812	30,772	1830	60,088
1813	32,749	1836	74,993
1814	35,952	1845	96,296
1815	40,568	1857	124,228
1816	41,898	1869	146,536
1817	43,409	1874	161,374
1818	40,854	1884	197,335
1819	40,937	1891	202,040
1820	42,535	1901	220,249

[1]S. Ryan, 1973, "The Newfoundland Cod Fishery in the Nineteenth Century." Paper presented to the Canadian Historical Association, Kingston.

English Migration to Newfoundland

W. Gordon Handcock

1

Spatial Concepts of Migration

One of the most basic concepts in the study of migration is that of migration streams –
the movement of a body of migrants from any area of origin to any area of destination
during an interval. This concept provides the basic spatial framework required for the
analysis of any aspects of migration such as volume, direction, and other characteristics, and allows questions to be scaled according to the exigencies of a problem posed
and the nature of available data. Origins and destinations, for example, may be
conceived at national, regional, or local scales, and the migration channels that link
them as the population movements occurring between given areal units or locations.
In his theory of migration, Lee adopts origins and destinations as the basic framework
in which to summarize the migration process and to identify factors associated with it
(1966:47–57). Olsson also uses a set theoretical framework of origins and destinations
to analyse population movements (1965:3–43), and Harvey asserts that migration can
be defined only by a set of spatial co-ordinates (origins and destinations) and temporal
co-ordinates (migration periods) (1969:96).

In most migration studies there are no problems defining origins and destinations
because data are obtained from official censuses in which origins and destinations are
usually those of the censal recording units and the migration interval – the intercensal
period. In order to examine pre-censal migrations, particularly those such as European migrations overseas from the 16th century onwards, the reconstruction of the
patterns of origins and destinations, and the major regularities of the population
movements may be considered an end in itself, or at least a necessary first stage in a
research progression that leads to some of the issues relevant to understanding the
migrations. Previous studies demonstrating methods and techniques of reconstructing
earlier migration patterns and data sets, which can be adapted for this purpose,
include those of Hägerstrand (1957), Morrill and Pitts (1967:401–22), and Randell
(1971). Sources such as church registers, maps, and the social columns of early
newspapers are used in order to reconstruct migration fields. Morrill and Pitts, for
example, suggest that when church registers and other sources such as newspapers
record the birth-places of marriage partners and deceased persons for many individuals over a long period, it becomes possible to reconstruct the total migration field and
to recognize the general empirical regularities of sources, flows, and destinations.

This paper uses data materials suggested by Morrill and Pitts and a set-theoretical
framework in reconstituting the source areas, regional destinations, and the migration
channels between the British Isles – mainly southwest England – and Newfoundland
during the 18th and 19th centuries. It is necessary to review first of all some of the
general historical features of the migration system that promoted the growth of a
permanent population of British origins in Newfoundland.

Migration and the Growth of Permanent Population

Migration is usually defined as a move that involves a "substantial" period of time or

one that is "permanent" or "temporary" (Goldscheider, 1971:59). Since, in reality,
the migration process does not have any upper or lower temporal limits, it is necessary
to use some criteria, however arbitrary, to define permanence. Normally seasonal
movements and labour movements are included as migration types, particularly when
such movements have an important impact on the structure of communities in the
areas of origin and destination.

In the case of Newfoundland, seasonal or transient movers dominated the population structure from the early 17th to the late 18th century. The seasonal movement of
fishermen to Newfoundland for the summer fishing season and back to Europe for the
winter was the standard mode of mercantilist exploitation.

One of the chief difficulties in tracing the growth of permanent population in
Newfoundland stems from the fact that the seasonal migrations and the permanent
population were related, with the former being the main contributing agency to the
latter. Thus, the process of migration cannot be viewed as an instantaneous detach-
ment from one location with a new beginning at another. Rather, it should be considered from an historical perspective to facilitiate the analytical distinction between a
moving or semi-permanent population with the aid of such criteria as moves associated with marriage, with the establishment of independent nuclear family residences, and indigenous settlement expansion.

In the long run, although the transfer of seasonal labourers into the inhabitant sector
was the main dynamic in the growth of Newfoundland's population, the initial establishment of a permanent population appears to have stemmed from a small migration
not associated with the summer fishery, but with English colonizing ventures in the
early 17th century. Cell (1969:53–78) judges that one of the few successes achieved by
Guy's Conception Bay Colony (1610) was the establishment of a few families. Similar
settlements may have been established at Bristol's Hope a few years after, at Ferryland by Baltimore (1621) and Kirke (1637), at St. John's (c. 1622) and at Renews (1623)
(Lounsbury, 1934:128). Throughout the 17th century the settled population was
augmented by men from the English shipping fleets, "men from Bristol, Bideford,
Barnstaple, Falmouth, Truro, Fowey, Plymouth, Dartmouth, Exeter, Weymouth,
Southampton, and many other places who, for one reason or another, decided to
remain in Newfoundland rather than return to England" (Seary et al., 1968:9–10).

The 1675 and 1677 censuses provide comprehensive data of the extent of English
settlement in that period. These records show that over thirty sites were occupied
along the east coast of the island between Salvage in the north and Trepassey in the
south[1] (Fig. 1–1). Of these, however, eight settlements contained only a single nuclear
family each and twenty-four had less than five families. These features indicated the
relative recency of settlement as well as the instability of the population. Indeed, these
censuses were taken by English officials to assess the numbers of settlers to be
removed, either to England or to other colonies, with the intention of discouraging
further colonization in Newfoundland. However, this proposal was never imple-
mented because of French activity on the island. The establishment of a French
settlement at Placentia in 1662 raised the possibility of England's forfeiting her
sovereignty over the English Shore in default of occupation and of the additional
possibility of English settlers, who wished to remain in Newfoundland, defecting to
the French.[2] Others who were influential in undermining attempts to prevent colonization were certain West Country merchants and ships' masters who found economic
advantages in transporting servants to Newfoundland inhabitants and supplying the

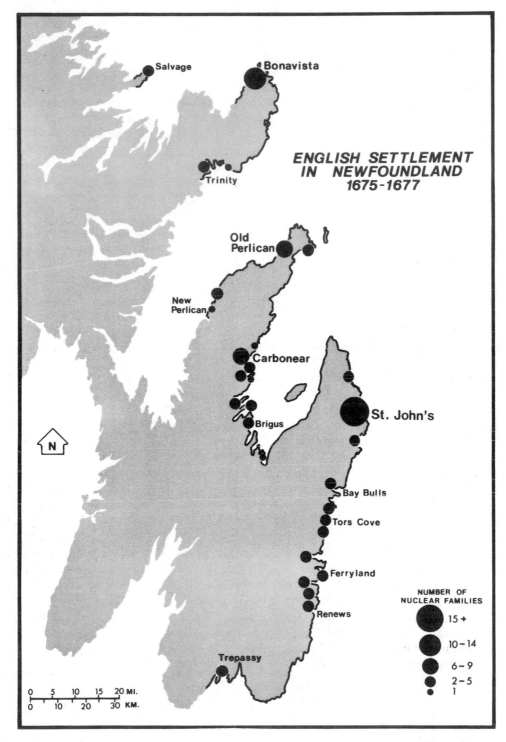

ENGLISH SETTLEMENT
IN NEWFOUNDLAND
1675-1677

Salvage

Bonavista

Trinity

Old
Perlican

New
Perlican

Carbonear

Brigus

St. John's

Bay Bulls

Tors Cove

Ferryland

Renews

Trepassy

N

0   5   10   15   20 MI.
0   10   20   30 KM.

NUMBER OF
NUCLEAR FAMILIES

15 +

10 - 14

6 - 9

2 - 5

1

Figure 1-1

latter with provisions at exorbitant prices. One report in 1715 described these so-called "abuses" and "disorders" as being occasioned by "inhabitants of the western counties," who dominate "the management of the Fishery, ... and keep the planters, who are their relations and belong to the same counties, in a continual dependence on them."[3]

The indirect intervention of the French in English settlement in Newfoundland during the 1670s was followed several decades later by more direct intervention. During the late 1690s, and early 18th century, French forces raided and plundered every English settlement in Newfoundland (for more details, see Prowse, 1896). Some settlers were deported to England, some taken prisoner to Placentia and Quebec, while others were killed. A single successful defence raised by some inhabitants of Conception Bay on Carbonear Island spared them a similar fate, but it seems reasonable that in many settlements the establishment of a permanent population had to assume new beginnings. The continuity of permanent settlement over the period of Queen Anne's War can be evaluated to some degree by comparing surnames recorded in the Censuses of 1675, 1676, and 1677 with those which appear in various sources (petitions, wills, and censuses) for the early 18th century within the same districts. For example, Hefford, Hopkins, Newell, Petten, Taverner, and Warren in Trinity Bay and Batten, Butler, Butt, Davis, Garland, Guy, Parsons, Pike, and Pynn in Conception Bay represent nominal links between the 1670s and the post-Queen-Anne-War period, even though the French raids probably bankrupted all. In the St. John's and Ferryland districts the impact of the French attacks appear to have been more complete in altering the population, as hardly any surnames of the post-war period can be paired with those of the pre-war censuses.

The 18th century in Newfoundland was marked by the imposition of English supremacy over the Newfoundland fishery and a concomitant territorial expansion over the Newfoundland coast (see Head, 1976, especially chapter IV). Until the latter half of the century seasonal migration continued to dominate the population; however, before the end of the century the transition towards a permanently settled community was well advanced. The two chief factors commonly attributed to this change were (1) the development of winter industries such as furring, sealing, and ship-building which increased the attractions of year-round habitation, and (2) the trend by English merchants, particularly those of the West Country ports of Poole, Dartmouth, and Teignmouth towards an increasing reliance upon the resident population for cod, oil, and furs, at the same time becoming specialized as traders, suppliers, and dealers (together with the emerging island-based merchants in St. John's and Conception Bay) to the permanent population. Clearly these two trends were related since winter activities were encouraged by the English merchants who, however, had no intention of promoting the growth of a permanent population. According to a Poole merchant, giving evidence before a Parliamentary committee on the Newfoundland trade in 1793,

Independently of this country, or some other, no Trade or Fishery can be carried on in Newfoundland – the very idea is absurd; a certain number of people must necessarily remain there during the winter season, to prosecute the different employments of the Seal Fishery, a concern of considerable importance, of the fur trade, of building ships and boats, erecting and repairing the plantations, houses, wharfs, fishing stages and flakes, and preparing for the ensuing fishing season ... .

It is the wish of the generality of the merchants to keep no more men in the island of Newfoundland than the interest of their particular concerns and employments require; and so far from its being the desire of the merchants to incline at all to make that Fishery more a residence than can be avoided, their distresses arising from a great number of families already on the island ... calls for the intervention and assistance of the Government of this country to prevent it and bring them home.[4]

The message contained in this evidence echoes British mercantilist policy toward Newfoundland of more than a century earlier.

Another more fundamental factor affecting the permanent population was identified by a Dartmouth merchant before the same committee. He complained that the increase in the population of St. John's was due mainly to the practice of customs, court, and army officers importing female domestics "who marry with residents and settle at St. John's, so that a number are annually carried out to replace them."[5] As early as 1684, a naval Captain attempted to dispel official fears of an increasing winter population in Newfoundland by observing that "soe long as there comes noe women they are not fixed."[6] The simple principal framed in the words of Emigration Commissioners in England in 1847 when they announced that "for the permanent growth of a colonial population every single man who is sent out in excess of the number of single women is absolutely useless" (Cowan, 1961:223) had not gone unnoticed by those who wished to prevent colonization in Newfoundland.

These examples illustrate a logic that can aid the analysis of changes in the permanent sector of a colonial population: the parameters derived from the number of females and children in the population provided a more objective means of evaluation of what is 'permanent' than total numbers of seasonal populations. Thus, for a given year the permanent population may be defined in a socio-biological formula expressed as $2F + C$, where F is the number of females and C the number of children. Implicitly T $- (2F + C)$ defines the 'temporary' population where T is the total. (For discussion, see MacPherson.)

The assumption that females and children provide the best expression of permanence in a colonizing context implies also that (i) families are less likely to return to origin or undertake second-stage migrations than individuals; (ii) families with children are less likely to migrate than families without children; (iii) single females are more likely to remain than single males; and (iv) the number of single males that can be absorbed into the colonial community will vary according to the number of females available as spouses. These migration differentials, having both temporal and spatial implications for the patterns of demographic structure that develop in early colonies, will most likely adumbrate population structure of later colonies or frontier regions.

In the population statistics of Newfoundland for the 1670s discussed above, females account for only about 12 percent of the total population, and the permanent population comprises about 25 percent, with little regional variation between the Southern Shore, St. John's Area, Conception Bay, and Trinity Bay. Long-term trends in the permanent population of Newfoundland can be determined for the period 1698 to 1833 by using statistics contained in the Colonial Office 194 Series for 89 years during which they are reportedly complete.[7] These statistics record the winter population under the following categories: masters were men who employed servants; men-servants were men fifteen years or older including the sons of "planters" (in 1788 the category of "dieters" was introduced to distinguish lodgers from winter servants); mistresses were wives of masters, and women who owned houses and employed servants; women servants were females fifteen years and older, including daughters of planters; and children were males and females under fifteen years. Although the accuracy of these statistics may be questioned for a given year – some figures are contradictory in totals, others contain slightly different results in two sets of statistics for the same year – single-year aggregate errors can be lessened by concentrating on the trends revealed and by calculating the permanent population in ten-year running means using the formula:

$$\frac{1}{10} \sum_{t=1}^{i+9} 2(Mt + Wt) + Ct = Ri \qquad i = i, \ldots, n$$

where M is the number of mistresses, W the number of women-servants and C the number of children. Similarly the 'semi-permanent' population can be determined from the formula:

$$\frac{1}{10} \sum_{t=1}^{i+9} T - \sum^{i+9} 2(Mt + Wt) + Ct \qquad i = i, \ldots, n.$$

The results obtained are plotted in Figure 1–2 in absolute values on a semi-logarithmic scale against an even-scaled time distribution, and in Figure 1–3 in relative values. Figure 1–2 shows that except for a brief period from 1728 to 1733 the 'semi-permanent' population, or excess male population, exceeded the permanent population until the 1780s. Indeed, until that time both sections of the population appear to have grown at much the same rate. Thus, besides becoming absorbed into the permanent population, the temporary population appears to have been increased in another way by the growing permanent sector, which in turn provided increased opportunities for winter employment and accommodation. On the other hand, it is reasonable to assume that the actual composition of the semi-permanent population varied considerably between one period and another and from year to year, since the general terms of employment throughout this period was two summers and a winter, or three summers and two winters. From the 1780s the permanent population exceeded the temporary and increased at a much more rapid rate than in any previous period (Fig. 1–2). In absolute terms, however, the permanent population did not reach 10,000 until the 1790s, a growth which had taken almost two centuries to achieve, despite the fact that during the same period, hundreds of thousands of individuals were engaged for a season or more in the Newfoundland summer fishery. Within two decades the permanent population had doubled and within four decades, quadrupled. By 1832, when the island achieved official recognition as a colony, about 80 percent of the population could be considered permanent (Fig. 1–3) and the demographic structure approached that of an established community.

The relative decrease in the temporary population from the 1780s (Fig. 1–3) was not accompanied by a reduction in absolute numbers. Figure 1–2 indicates that a slight decrease in the period 1795–1815 was followed by an absolute increase from 1815 to 1830. For a ten-year period after 1815, the semi-permanent population averaged about 11,000 per year, a figure which exceeds, by about one thousand, that frequently quoted for the total movement from England and Ireland during the 18th century. Although the rate of population change – which is affected by the cumulative factors of balance between births, deaths, out-migration, and in-migration – is at best a crude parameter of population change caused by any single factor, the trends revealed in these statistics suggest that in-migration was a major factor in increasing the permanent population of Newfoundland from the 1780s onwards, but that it was predominantly a phenomenon of the early 19th century, particularly after 1815. This conclusion is supported by other evidence, including that of statistical evidence of influxes of Irish emigrants to St. John's,[8] by parish record information on emigrant marriages discussed later in this paper, and from statistics on the number of births and deaths recorded for certain years in the Colonial Office 194 Series (1698–1833).

From this last source the net immigration for selected periods can be calculated

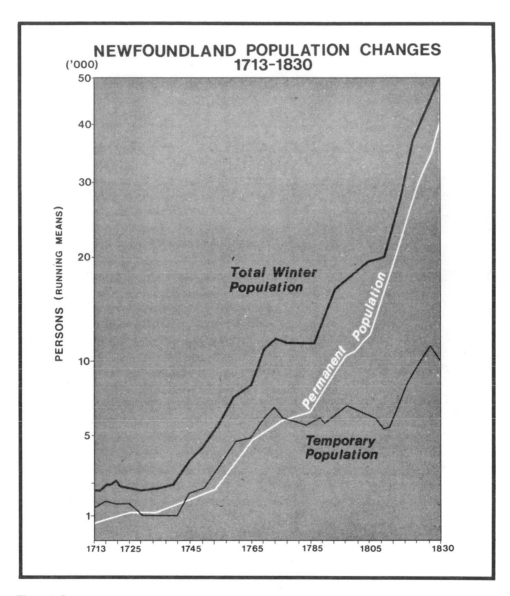

Figure 1–2

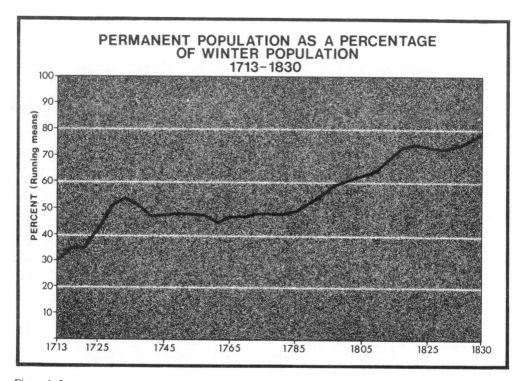

Figure 1-3

from the formula $(P_2 - P_1) - (B - D)$ where P_1 and P_2 represent the total winter population for successive years, and B and D the number of births and deaths for the given years, respectively, and reads as follows:

Period	Number of Years	Total Immigration	Annual Rate
1723–1749	18	1,732	96
1750–1791	16	8,045	502
1804–1823	13	15,510	1,193

The values derived here are less important than the comparative trends indicated: that is, that the rate of immigration after 1800 was twelve times greater than the rate during the first half of the 18th century and two and a half times greater than that of the late 18th century.

The expansion of the permanent population in Newfoundland throughout the 18th century occurred mostly within settlements and coastal areas along the traditional English Shore – the region between Cape Bonavista and Cape Race. Territorial concessions by the French arranged by the Treaties of Utrecht (1713) and Versailles (1783) opened up frontier regions for the extension of an English fishery and settlements along the south and northwest coasts. Although the Treaty of Utrecht conferred concurrent fishing and shore-cutting rights to the French and English between Cape Bonavista and Point Riche, and although the Treaty of Paris (1763) renewed them, English families settled at many sites along the coast, for example at Fogo and Twillingate as early as 1732. The readjusted French Shore after 1783 (between Cape St. John and Cape Ray) contained at least two English settlements, at Sops Arm in White Bay and another in St. George's Bay (see Rogers, 1911:130–35; also Mannion, Ommer, and Thornton in this vol.). Before the end of the century English settlers were established in many more sites along the French Shore. Together with the coast of Labrador and the South Coast, these 18th century additions formed the frontier regions of English colonization. Like the regions settled earlier it can be assumed that in the initial stages of settlement the population was dominated by adult males and that the period of adjustment in the sex-structure would take a longer time to bridge than in the older regions. An examination of regional statistics for part of Newfoundland for the year 1825, computed by the author in percentage values of the permanent population by the formula $2F + C$ (Table 1), confirms this assumption. The values in Table 1 show that the older regions (the Southern Shore, Conception Bay, and Trinity Bay) contain a relatively higher proportion of permanent population than Newfoundland as a whole, and also than the more recently settled regions (Bonavista Bay, Notre Dame Bay, Placentia Bay and Burin-Mortier-St. Lawrence).

Two major anomalies in the expected pattern of the permanent population shown in Table 1–1 occur: the low ranking of St. John's and the high proportion of the permanent population in Fortune Bay. It seems that St. John's, as the major point of disembarkation for recent influxes of Irish emigrants, reflects a male dominance in these movements. In 1815, for example, over 3,000 of the 3,400 Irish arrivals in St. John's were males. The relatively high proportion of permanent population in Fortune Bay is difficult to explain, for compared with other regions settled earlier, it contained a much larger proportion of women and children in its population than older settled areas.

TABLE 1-1

Permanent Population as a Proportion of Total Population, Newfoundland 1825

Regions	Permanent Population (%)	Difference (+ or −)
	74.2	
St. John's	74.1	− 0.1
Southern Shore (Avalon)	83.4	+ 9.2
Conception Bay	82.9	+ 8.7
Trinity Bay	81.7	+ 7.5
Bonavista Bay	77.5	+ 3.3
Notre Dame Bay	63.7	−10.5
Placentia Bay	61.1	−13.1
Burin-Mortier-St. Lawrence	62.5	−11.7
Fortune Bay	80.4	+ 6.2

Generally, the growth of a permanent population in Newfoundland can be attributed to a mercantilist system of migration. Seasonal migration, a surrogate factor of mercantilist exploitation, contributed progressively to emigration and colonization through the establishment of year-round economic activities. The retarding factor in the initial rate of growth was the lack of females in the population, a major characteristic of the Newfoundland population until the late 18th century. Although historical records show that merchants – at least officially – opposed permanent settlement in Newfoundland, further analysis strongly suggests that they were the activating agents in promoting settlement by providing the economic opportunities, the transportation and communication channels, and the supply and market support for permanent occupation. Within this system, however, settlement in Newfoundland appears to have been free and voluntary. Indeed, given the restrictions against colonization, the behaviour might more properly be classified as defiant. The significance of early colonization attempts appear not to lie in their success or size, but in the example set, an example repeated at many other locations throughout the 17th and 18th centuries.

Assumptions of Origins: Old and New

The existing literature on Newfoundland immigrant origins may be said to assume two basic generalizations: firstly that immigrants stemmed from southwest England (Devon, Dorset, and Cornwall), southeastern Ireland (Wexford, Waterford), and the Channel Islands, areas from which the English merchants drew their labour to conduct the Newfoundland fishery; and secondly, that the structure of the population by religious affiliation indicates the source areas of forebears. (See Prowse, 1896:18; Rogers, 1911:139 ff., 166, 213, 215; but particularly Matthews, 1968a:184–86 and Head, 1976:82–92.) The latter may be called the 'Tocque formula' expressed in the dictum: "The Roman Catholics are Irish and descendants of Irish; the Episcopalians, Methodists and Congregationalists are English and the descendants of English and Jersey; the Presbyterians are principally Scotch and their descendants" (Tocque, 1878:366). While there is little reason to doubt the validity of these generalizations, the empirical evidence presented to support them has been scant and no systematic attempt has been made to define the channels of emigration, to describe the emigrant source areas of particular parts of Newfoundland, or to measure differences between emigration patterns from these source areas.

An examination of sources such as the early church registers of Newfoundland indicates, where origins are specified, that it might be possible to reconsider the question of immigrant origins and to attempt the reconstruction of the spatial patterns in source areas together with regularities of movement between origins and destinations. The use of such data assumes as valid the previous discussion on the role of females, marriage, and the nuclear family in colonization; that is, that migrants who married were less likely to return to their place of origin or undertake second migrations than migrants who did not marry. Information gained from burial records and tombstones are equally or more valid, particularly for the more elderly, since propensity to migrate is also a function of age.

The Source Materials and Problems of Analysis

Data of the birth places of marriage partners or deceased persons were collected from Newfoundland church registers[9] and from the social columns (obituaries and marriage announcements) of 19th century newspapers. The single common element for selecting an entry was the specification of a place of origin outside Newfoundland. Other information included (in the case of marriage entries) occupations, ages, place of origin of spouse, and date and location of marriage. The newspapers, although less yielding numerically than the church records, often provided useful biographical notes such as the number of years resident in Newfoundland, occupational sketch, the year of immigration, other places of residence, and the names of relatives.

A number of problems in using such materials stem both from the nature of the source materials themselves and their application to the migration question. Among these problems are the validity of the immigrant population (data set) as a representative sample of total origins and the adequacy of the set for defining spatial and temporal coverage by origins and destinations. A scarcity of extant entries and records for certain important parts of Newfoundland such as Twillingate, the Burin Peninsula, and Placentia Bay add to the problems of fragmentation caused by gaps in the registers, lack of standardized forms of entry (both within a single register and between the registers of different denominations), illegibility, and variability of specific information which entries yield. For example, on the question of origins, some entries stated country, only; others recorded only the county. Most entries (88 percent) specified origin by county and settlement (usually parish); this is assumed to be the place of birth. The analysis of temporal variations in immigration is rendered difficult both by the gaps in the sources and by the fact that dates associated with specific events do not conform necessarily to the year of immigration.

Most of these weaknesses, however, can be minimized by dividing the population into appropriate sub-sets according to given assumptions. For example, a spatial definition of origins can be attempted by mapping all parishes recorded from all source materials with time held as a constant, on the assumption that the total of all specific origins will reconstruct the field of emigration most accurately. Spatial coverage by destination can be generalized by dividing Newfoundland into regions, or conversely, composing such regions by combining the data from several adjacent settlements and analysing the results on a more general scale. To some extent aggregation tends to overcome the problem of temporary coverage as well, since the individual records cover different periods and since time gaps in one source are often covered by the continuity of another. Nevertheless, the major biases in temporal coverage can be reduced by analysing the immigration frequencies in time aggregates (decades, units of decades), in running-means, and by using only the dates of marriage data on the assumption that these indicate more reliably the approximate year of immigration.

Most techniques developed to analyse the movement of individuals between origins and destinations tend to focus upon one part of the migration field. Usually either the origin or destination is reduced to a constant and the analysis focuses upon the distributional pattern of the other. Relating a large number of origins and destinations simultaneously has proven more problematic. For example, in the data set of approximately 3,000 emigrants collected for this study, the subset of origins included more than 600 separate parishes and the subset of destinations over 200 Newfoundland settlements. In reality, each individual movement between a point of origin and destination constitutes a migration channel. However, to avoid an analytical maze one could identify the main channels of migration by combining origins and destinations into larger units.

One such technique to isolate the larger or 'important' flows between pairs of places has been developed in econometrics by Savage and Deutsch (1960:59–66), and more recently Roseman has demonstrated its utility in identifying channels of migration.[10] Called "transaction flow analysis," this technique is particularly adaptable to the data used in this study as it allows the use of all references where origins are specified and analysed at the county level. On the other hand, it is less useful for defining the 'emigration fields' or source areas of various Newfoundland regions, since it is evident that emigration was not uniformly distributed by county and was unaffected by county boundaries. In order to reduce this defect the more traditional techniques can be employed of focusing upon origins related to a specific Newfoundland region and mapping the emigration field associated with it.

A recent appraisal of Irish emigration to Newfoundland has been made by Mannion (1973:1–12) using similar data and a somewhat parallel analysis to that considered here. Besides reassessing some aspects of Irish emigration, it remains to consider emigration from elsewhere in the British Isles, particularly from southwest England.

Distributions of Emigrants by Origin and Destination
The statistics presented in Tables 1–2 and 1–3 represent the geographical distributions for 2,124 emigrants whose origins were specified by county. The dominance of English (89.3 percent) and the high proportion of emigrants from the southern and southwestern regions confirm previous assumptions. Devon, Dorset, Somerset, and Hampshire account for more than three-quarters of all English emigrants. Cornwall, with a contribution of less than 2 percent, ranks very low as a source area. In fact, emigration from Bristol, London, and Liverpool seems to be more important than either Cornwall or the Channel Islands (Table 1–2). The matrix of origins (rows) and destinations (columns) in Table 1–2 shows the distributional connections of separate movement. The more distinctive geographical patterns indicated here include:

(i) The attraction of the St. John's region to immigrants from all origins, but more particularly to those from Devon, Cornwall, London, Liverpool, other English regions, Scotland, and Wales.

(ii) A basic similarity between the immigrant structure of St. John's and Conception Bay, except that St. John's attracted more Devonians and relatively fewer individuals from Dorset, Somerset, Hampshire, and Bristol than did Conception Bay.

TABLE 1-2

Migration Links Between Origins and Destinations

British Origins	St. John's	Conception Bay	Trinity Bay	Bonavista Bay	Notre Dame Bay	Northern Newfoundland Labrador	South Coast	West Coast	Total by origin
				Newfoundland Destinations					
English									
Devon	493	111	25	6	—	10	25	2	672
Dorset	90	122	134	69	36	11	83	15	560
Somerset	27	26	46	14	1	9	21	5	149
Hampshire (IW)	24	34	70	25	9	4	3	5	174
Cornwall	16	4	—	—	1	2	—	—	23
Bristol	14	29	—	2	—	—	—	—	45
London	40	10	2	—	—	—	—	1	53
Liverpool	23	4	3	—	1	—	—	—	31
Other English	120	33	15	7	1	2	10	3	191
Scottish									
Edinburgh	8	1	—	—	—	—	—	—	9
Glasgow	13	5	—	—	—	—	—	—	18
Greenock	13	4	—	1	—	—	—	—	18
Other Scots	92	18	8	3	1	1	2	—	125
Wales	7	1	2	1	—	—	—	—	11
Channel Islands	10	14	—	—	1	3	12	5	45
Total, by destination	990	416	305	128	51	42	156	36	2,124

(iii) The widespread and relatively even distribution of Dorset, Hampshire, and Somerset immigrants in all regions of Newfoundland – with greater concentration in Trinity Bay, Bonavista Bay, Notre Dame Bay, the South Coast, and Northern Newfoundland/Labrador.

(iv) A concentration of Channel Islanders in St. John's, Conception Bay, and the South Coast.

Main Channels of Emigration

An empirical regularity stressed in migration studies dealing with migration streams led Lee to the conclusion that "migration tends to take place within well-defined streams not only because of the dictates of opportunity and available transport, but also because migrants follow the flow of information established by earlier migrants" (1966:47–57). A similar but more explanatory view is contained in Vance's observation that "one of the critical facts of American historical geography is that a system of mercantilism was well-established before that of emigration" (1970:69). In the particular circumstances of Newfoundland, Matthews (1968a) proposed that the broad outlines of settlement were determined from the late 17th century onwards by the trade patterns established by English merchants from ports in the West of England (Dartmouth, Teignmouth, Topsham, Poole, Bristol, and others) to coastal regions in Newfoundland.

Before examining some of the relationships between mercantilist trade areas and emigration, it is useful first to attempt a more objective definition of emigration channels than is possible from inspecting the statistics. A useful technique for this purpose is the transaction flow analysis mentioned above. It is based upon an 'indifference model' which assumes that the proportion of total migrants from any origin to any destination will be equal to the proportion of all migrants at that destination. For example, in Table 3 we observe that the St. John's region received 46.6 percent of all the immigrants in the data set; thus the model assumes that each source area will send 46.6 percent of its migrants to St. John's. The difference between observed values and expected values produces 'salience' measures, which can be calculated as relative or absolute indices. The Relative Acceptance (RA) index is computed by

$$RAij = \frac{Aij - Eij}{Eij}$$

where Aij is the observed number of emigrants from origin i to destination j, and Eij is the expected number of emigrants calculated from the 'indifference model.'

The Absolute Difference (D) index is derived from Dij = Aij − Eij. The measures of salience are indicated by the positive values of the two indices; and the greater the positive values the more strongly channelled or biased are the movements. The positive measures of salience calculated from the data in Tables 1–2 and 1–3 are presented in summary form in Table 1–4. The interpretation of the results contained in Table 1–4 must be cautioned by two important reflections: firstly, the use of a statistical model assumes reliability of the data set; secondly, the small numbers of observed values in certain origin/destination sets provide measures that would be substantially altered by the addition of small numbers of similar data.

The RA indices indicate that (i) some of the less numerically-important source areas (Channel Islands, Bristol, London, and Scotland) produced more strongly channelled movements than the more important areas (Devon, Dorset), and (ii) that emigration from Dorset, Somerset, and Hampshire dominated movements in all regions outside St. John's and Conception Bay. The D indices, in assessing the absolute measures of

TABLE 1–3

Proportional Distributions by Origin and Destination

Origins	%	English	%		%
England	89.3	Devon	35.2	Bristol	2.5
Scotland	8.0	Dorset	29.0	London	2.8
Wales	0.5	Somerset	7.9	Liverpool	1.7
Channel Islands	2.2	Hampshire	8.2	Other	10.1
	100.0	Cornwall	1.3		

Destinations	%		%
St. John's	46.6	Notre Dame Bay	2.4
Conception Bay	19.6	Northern Nfld./Labrador	2.0
Trinity Bay	14.3	South Coast	7.4
Bonavista Bay	6.0	West Coast	1.7

salience in particular channels, show the strong bias toward St. John's as the destination for Devonians, Scots, and other English emigrants; they also show the attraction to Conception Bay of Bristolians, and as with the RA indices, the geographical diversity of destinations in Newfoundland of the emigration channels from Dorset, Somerset, and Hampshire.

Perhaps the most remarkable feature revealed, however, is the degree to which the immigrant structure of Conception Bay reflects the diversity of the immigrant structure of Newfoundland as a whole. Despite this, a close analysis by settlement within Conception Bay demonstrates striking local differences. For example, Dorset emigrants appear to dominate in places such as Carbonear and Brigus, and together with settlers from Somerset and Hampshire, emerge prominently in most settlements between Carbonear and Bay de Verde. On the other hand, Devonshire and Jersey settlers tend to concentrate in places such as Harbour Grace, Port de Grave, Bay Roberts, and Cupids. Bell Island, Portugal Cove, and harbours adjacent to St. John's were planted by Devonshiremen, whereas Bristolians focused almost entirely upon Harbour Grace. The main emigration streams derived from the indices in Table 1–4, together with some of the minor streams, are used in the construction of Figure 1–4.

The sample of 820 Irish/Newfoundland emigrants reveals that 64 percent originated in the three southeastern counties of Waterford, Wexford, and Kilkenny. Mannion, using the much larger sample of 6,410, calculated 69 percent from the same three counties, and concluded that the majority of these persons settled on the southern Avalon, dominating the ethnic composition of the population from St. John's to Placentia. This tendency of the Irish to settle on the southern Avalon was established as early as the 18th century. In 1720 Commodore Percy reported to the Council of Trade and Plantations that "here are brought over every year by the Bristol, Biddiford and Bastable ships great numbers of Irish Roman Catholic servants, who all settle to the southward in our Plantations ... ."[11] Though Bideford and Barnstaple ceased trading with Newfoundland in the 1780s, the continued influx of Irish emigrants in the late 18th century and early 19th century was largely directed toward St. John's and the southern Avalon. During this period at least, it was the pattern of settlement established by previous immigrants, rather than the mercantilist trade areas, that appears to have affected the choice of destination. Indeed, it is evident that a large proportion of Irish arrivals in Newfoundland during the period 1811–1830, which McLintock states

TABLE 1-4

Relative Acceptance and Absolute Difference Indices of Emigration Channels

Emigration Channel		RA Index >0.5	D Index (ranking)
Origin	Destination		
Channel Islands	South Coast	3.0	9 (15)
Bristol	Conception Bay	2.6	21 (10)
Somerset	N. Nfld./Labrador	2.0	6 (16)
Hampshire	Trinity Bay	1.9	46 (4)
Dorset	Notre Dame Bay	1.7	23 (9)
Somerset	West Coast	1.5	3 (22)
Hampshire	Bonavista Bay	1.5	15 (12)
Hampshire	Notre Dame Bay	1.2	5 (21)
Somerset	Trinity Bay	1.2	25 (8)
Dorset	Bonavista Bay	1.1	36 (6)
Somerset	South Coast	1.1	11 (13)
Dorset	South Coast	1.0	42 (5)
Liverpool	St. John's	0.7	10 (14)
Scotland	St. John's	0.7	47 (3)
Channel Islands	Conception Bay	0.7	6 (17)
Dorset	Trinity Bay	0.7	54 (2)
Somerset	Bonavista Bay	0.7	6 (18)
Dorset	West Coast	0.7	6 (19)
Hampshire	West Coast	0.7	2 (24)
Devon	St. John's	0.6	180 (1)
Cornwall	St. John's	0.6	6 (20)
London	St. John's	0.6	16 (11)
'Other English'	St. John's	0.5	31 (7)
Devon	Conception Bay	<0.5	Null hypothesis accepted
Dorset	Conception Bay	"	" " "
Somerset	Conception Bay	"	" " "
Hampshire	Conception Bay	"	" " "
Cornwall	Conception Bay	"	" " "
London	Conception Bay	"	" " "
Liverpool	Conception Bay	"	" " "
'Other English'	Conception Bay	"	" " "
Scotland	Conception Bay	"	" " "
Dorset	N. Nfld./Labrador	"	" " "
Hampshire	N. Nfld./Labrador	"	" " "
Devon	N. Nfld./Labrador	"	" " "

exceeded 24,000, disembarked at St. John's as genuine emigrants – responding to negative socio-economic conditions in the homeland – rather than answering specific labour demands in the Newfoundland economy afforded by the merchants and settlers.[12]

Outside the St. John's and the southern Avalon Peninsula, scattered Irish settlements did emerge in most regions of Newfoundland otherwise dominated by the English. Principal among them were the main centres of settlement in Conception Bay (Harbour Grace and Carbonear) and other settlements at the head of Conception Bay (Holyrood, Conception Harbour, and Harbour Main); Tilting Harbour and Fogo in Notre Dame Bay; Bonavista and King's Cove in Bonavista Bay; Trinity in Trinity

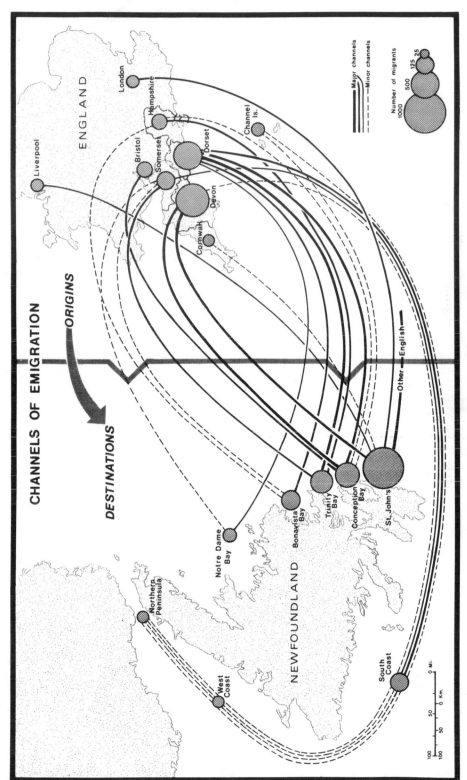

CHANNELS OF EMIGRATION

ORIGINS

DESTINATIONS

Figure 1-4

Bay; St. Lawrence on the Burin Peninsula and Harbour Breton on the South Coast. For the most part these migrations, though originating in the same source area, were quite independent from the main channels of Irish movements, being associated primarily with trade channels generated through the port of Poole. During the late 18th and early 19th centuries, merchants based in Poole, among other places, maintained trading establishments at Trinity, Bonavista, Greenspond, Fogo, Tilting Harbour, Carbonear, Brigus, Burin, St. Mary's, Placentia, Oderin, Grand Bank, and Harbour Breton. The diaries in the collected papers of the Lester-Garland family, deposited in the Dorset Record Office, contain numerous references to the movement of ships of all Poole firms engaged in the trade and in the transportation of fishermen, servants, and passengers.[13] Numerous entries in these diaries report ships calling at Waterford, Cork, and Youghal regularly en route from Poole to embark passengers for Newfoundland, while other entries record both the arrival and departure of ships in Newfoundland ports with Irish servants. They were then generally distributed from the mercantile centres to planters and boat-keepers at various outharbours. Undoubtedly, Bristol ships carried some of the Irish who settled at Harbour Grace, the main seat in Newfoundland of the Bristol merchants (Matthews, 1968b:1–12), while Dartmouth and other Devon ports offered transport to Conception Bay, St. John's, and the Southern Avalon.

Temporal Variations in Emigration Channels
The trends shown in the growth rate of the permanent population and the comparative rates of net migration discussed above indicate that a major period of emigration began by the 1780s, but that the main influxes occurred after 1800. Contemporary documentary evidence of emigration during this period is characterized mainly by reference to a steady flow of Irish. Mannion states that Irish emigration in the late 18th century was completely dwarfed by the influx after 1800 when 30–35,000 persons arrived, with two peaks in the flow during 1811–1816 and 1825–1831.

Emigration from other source areas over this period received little attention in the extant documents and no comparable estimates of volume of emigration seem available. But since the estimate of Irish emigration is based upon total arrivals and not the net emigration which resulted in permanent settlement, it is possible to compare the approximate balance of Irish/other British emigrants by using the Tocque formula in which the Roman Catholics and Protestants are calculated as proportions of the total population over the period 1790–1830. Statistics show that over the main period of Irish emigration, Roman Catholics constituted slightly less than 50 percent of the total Newfoundland population. In other words, it seems that the net emigration from other parts of the British Isles (mainly southwest England) was no less than that from Ireland, and indeed perhaps greater. It is possible that greater notice had been paid to Irish emigrants partly because the majority disembarked at St. John's or in nearby harbours where English officials viewed their growing numbers with some alarm. By contrast the English were apparently settling and being absorbed into the permanent population, not only in St. John's and in Conception Bay, but also in greater numbers than the Irish at destinations all around the coast of Newfoundland. English emigration was not only less obtrusive to English observers but also apparently less well-known.

Some official statistics of emigration from the British Isles to Newfoundland cover the period 1842–1863. They record the landing of 6,975 persons of whom 4,725 were

TABLE 1–5

Roman Catholics as a Proportion of
Total Population 1790–1830

Period	Mean Proportion
1790–95	48
1815–20	45
1825–30	47

Irish and 2,250 English and Scottish.[14] These figures, compiled by officials at ports of embarkation, refer to those individuals who declared themselves 'emigrants.' Examination of the yearly returns from these reports reveals several features which make it difficult to draw any clear conclusion from them regarding the temporal pattern of emigration, or indeed the origins of the emigrants involved. For example, few emigrants embarked from West of England Ports: only five emigrants embarked from Dartmouth in 1843; reports from Teignmouth record fourteen and from Exeter five; no emigrants were reported from Poole. Of the total of 1,361 emigrants embarking from all English ports, 808 sailed from Liverpool – and given the strong association of this port with Irish emigration, it may be assumed that many of those destined for Newfoundland were Irish. Other sources indicate that the West of England ports were still active in sending passenger ships to Newfoundland during this period and that some firms were still engaged in Newfoundland trade. The parish records indicate that many West Countrymen were still being absorbed into the permanent sector of the Newfoundland population. These obviously slipped through the emigration check-out. Two conclusions, however, may be drawn from the official emigration statistics for the period 1842–1862: first, the volume of emigration from Scotland is probably fairly accurate; secondly, that emigration from the British Isles continued well into the 19th century. But they cannot be used to support the claims by Rogers that population increase in Newfoundland in the preceding period was due to natural increase or that immigration played little part in population changes during the 19th century. The evidence from marriage records indicates otherwise.

Emigration Trends from the Marriage Record
The use of marriage-frequency data involving immigrants presents some difficulties in indicating temporal variations in movements. On the other hand, lacking other information, such data are particularly useful not only in detecting general trends, but also in identifying temporal variations in specific emigration channels. The main period of emigration from the British Isles to Newfoundland, as defined by marriage frequencies of emigrants was from 1795 to 1845 (Fig. 1–5). But this and other temporal variations contained in Table 6 (calculated by time series analysis using decadal running means from the aggregation of all emigrant marriages in all sources for the period 1755–1894) may be advanced at least a decade or more to estimate the actual main migration period. Even if the data available were complete and accurate the parameter derived would still need to be advanced since they would relate to the period of immigrant absorption rather than the periods of movement. The conditions of colonization were such that few, if any, of the pioneer families in any region would have been recorded locally, since the marriages occurred elsewhere – in the British Isles or in older settled regions of Newfoundland – or were contracted locally by common-law. The mission-

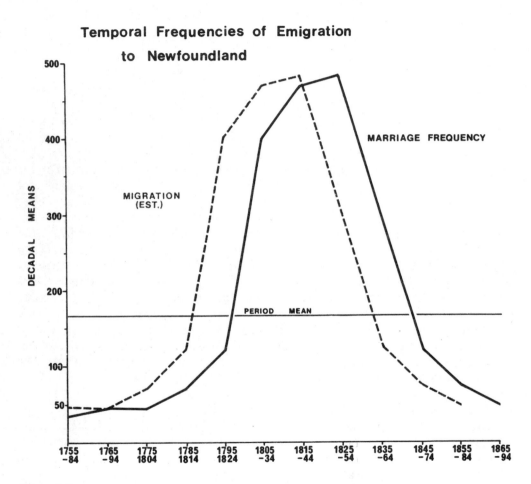

Figure 1–5

TABLE 1-6

Temporal Variations in Selected Emigration-Channels (from marriage records in decadal units)

Emigration-Channels Origin–Destination	Period Covered[1]	Period > Decadal Mean[2]	Peak Decade[3]
British Isles –Newfoundland	1755–1894	1795–1845	1825–1834
Devon –Newfoundland	1755–1894	1815–1854	1835–1844
Devon –St. John's	1755–1894	1815–1854	1835–1844
Dorset –Newfoundland	1765–1894	1805–1854	1835–1844
Dorset –Trinity Bay	1765–1864	1795–1834	1805–1814
Dorset –Bonavista Bay	1805–1874	1835–1854	1845–1854
Dorset –Conception Bay	1775–1874	1815–1854	1825–1834
Dorset –South Coast	1825–1894	1865–1884	1865–1874
Other English–Newfoundland	1755–1894	1845–1894	1875–1884

[1]Includes period covered by the records.
[2]The period of a positive variance from decadal mean of the period covered by the records.
[3]The decade of greatest positive variance from decadal mean of the period covered.

ary at Bay Bulls and Ferryland in 1793 "found it a prevailing custom for persons to live together in a state of matrimony, without ever coming to church."[15]

Until the mid-18th century, missionary contact with Newfoundland inhabitants was scant and irregular, so that "... the custom with respect to marriage there is for the Lord of the Harbour ... to perform the ceremony in the same way as it is performed in England by clergymen, and that in the Winter when they have no Lord of the Harbour, it is performed by any common man that can read."[16] St. John's, Harbour Grace, and Trinity were served by missionaries funded by the Society for the Propagation of the Gospel from the mid-18th century onwards; however, only Trinity (from 1757) and Harbour Grace (from 1776) have had complete marriage registers. A gap in the St. John's register, which begins in 1755, for the vital period 1784–1809 creates a temporal bias which even levelling techniques fail to correct. Similarly, the marriage records for other regions are biased temporally toward the 19th century, and are most accurate as indicators of the spatio-temporal patterns of emigration only from the 1820s onwards. Based upon these qualifications, each of the periods shown in Table 1–6 may be advanced at least one decade and some, such as Devon-St. John's and Dorset-Conception Bay, by at least two decades. Thus the main period of emigration from the British Isles to Newfoundland appears to have spanned the years 1785 to 1835, and the main decade of absorption of immigrants was from 1815 to 1825 (Fig. 1–5).

Among the more important trends demonstrated in Table 1-6 are regional variations in certain channels of emigration in the temporal pattern of Newfoundland as a whole, but particularly of Dorset. For example, it can be seen that immigration from Dorset to Trinity and Conception Bays peaked earlier than in Bonavista Bay and the South Coast. A similar pattern of regional/temporal alteration to that of Dorset can also be demonstrated in the direction of Somerset and Hampshire emigrants, though few emigrants from Hampshire appear to have settled on the South Coast. Emigration from Devonshire maintained a main directional attraction to the St. John's region and areas particularly from 1785 to 1834.

The marriage records reveal that emigration from the British Isles to Newfoundland continued until the mid-19th century, at least until emigration officials began to keep statistics in 1842. Most revealing, however, are that (i) during the second half of the 19th century the flow from traditional source areas seems to have been less important than emigration from "other English" source areas, particularly to St. John's (Tables 1–2, and 1–6); and (ii) that emigration from Dorset to the South Coast of Newfoundland seems to have been still active.

The marriage records from the south coast of Newfoundland indicate that this was one of the last regions outside St. John's to experience a late 19th century immigration. This evidence is based upon the observation that settlements such as Gaultois, Harbour Breton, Harbour le Cou, Pass Island, Pushthrough, La Poile, Rose Blanche, Hermitage, and Isle la Morte were still absorbing not only Dorset emigrants but also others from Somerset and the Channel Islands. The Channel Islanders – mostly from Jersey – appear to represent an emigration generated by Jersey firms who maintained trading houses at such places as Jersey Harbour and La Poile throughout most of the century (see Rogers, 1911:212, and Fay, 1961:28). The migrations from Dorset and Somerset are less obvious from the point of view of English mercantilist connections with South Coast 'trading' establishments for, apart from the Jersey firms, the other main trading posts in this region were operated by the Dartmouth firm of Newmans. Although it might be expected that Dorset and Somerset emigrants – following other emigration patterns – would have embarked with Poole merchants, there is no evidence to indicate that Poole maintained trading establishments in this region at this time. The lack of evidence of Devonians, who might be expected to have emigrated on Dartmouth ships, presents an additional anomaly in the pattern of immigrant structure.

To explain these anomalies, several suggestions have been or might be advanced, including that by Rogers that settlers came from Fortune Bay or else from Dorsetshire. It would appear more likely that the major reasons lie concealed in a complexity of merchant, family, and labour recruitment relationships. Matthews claims that Newmans of Dartmouth acquired their South Coast trading establishments originally operated by the Bird family of Sturminster Newton (Dorset) and Poole during the late 18th century, but continued to use the Bird connection in north Dorset/south Somerset to recruit fishermen and servants (Matthews, personal communication). The Bird family, itself, continued the Newfoundland trade and opened up trading establishments in southern Labrador. Another source suggests that the Bird family continued to maintain direct contact with the South Coast, for as late as the 1840s, the movement of the firm's vessels from Poole to Labrador can be traced to regular calls at Harbour Breton, as well as to the Bay of Islands and Bonne Bay to discharge supplies and servants ordered by the settlers.[17] This evidence is supported by an extant letter dated 3 February, 1841, written to Thomas S. Bird at Poole by his solicitor at Sturminster Newton. It reads, "Lots of boys and men today and yesterday called as candidates for Newfoundland and are anxious to know when they are likely to be put into commission."[18] Another letter from Jersey, February 16, 1844, by the firm of Nicolle, then trading with the South Coast, suggests that it was using the firm of Wm. Balston and Son, a Poole net and twine manufacturer, to recruit labour both for Newfoundland planters and for its own needs. The quotation "... you anticipate more difficulty in providing them than in former years," clearly indicates that Jersey recruitment in Dorset was an established practice. This letter is of particular interest because it documents a Jersey/Dorset/South Coast Newfoundland migration connection, and contains the names of thirty-four Newfoundland planters requesting servants, and the names of thirty-four servants assigned to each, together with four others hired by Nicolle. Among the planters, we find some distinctive regional South Coast surnames such as Buffett, Le Moine, Farrell, Hickman, May, and Forsey.

Three decades later a migratory fisherman from Dorset writes of his experiences which again reveal the Dorset/Somerset connection with the South Coast through the port of Dartmouth. "A man called Phillip Francis who lived at Hinton St. Mary advertised in the Western Gazette for men to go to Newfoundland for Newman, Hunt and Company. Forty-two men went, these five from Marnhull: Harry Lewis, Tom Curtis, Alfred Drew, Albert Hann, Harry Haskett. There were already several Marnhull men out there. They went on April 8th, 1878, to Yeovil Old Castle and from there to Dartmouth, where they had to stay for a week awaiting the boat ..." (Roscoe, 1952:146). The "several Marnhull men" probably include Henry John Moore, Nathaniel Hatcher, Robert Lewis, Frances Kendall, and George Guy whose marriages are registered at South Coast settlements between 1850 and 1877. Whether there is any significance in the fact that Newman's agent, Phillip Francis, married an Elizabeth Newman of Sturminster Newton in 1830, is not clear. What is clear, however, is that the Newman family was, together with the families of Bird, Colbourne, and Forward, among the wealthiest and more prominent of Sturminster families during the period 1750–1850, and the latter three all had trade connections with Newfoundland. Indeed, at least two Forwards (Ambrose and John) took themselves and their families to Grand Bank, while George Forward settled in Carbonear (Buffett, n.d.). The Birds and Colbournes of Sturminster Newton both operated ships from Poole and it seems possible that the Newmans may have developed a similar trade connection through the family namesake firm at Dartmouth.[19]

On the evidence of marriage frequencies the major period of emigration from the British Isles to Newfoundland occurred during the period 1795–1835, with the main influx during the late 1810s and early 1820s. Within emigration channels, however, particularly those from Dorset/Hampshire/Somerset source areas, the temporal pattern varied, and on the South Coast of Newfoundland the main immigration occurred during the second half of the century. In the last quarter of the century 'Other English' emigrants, that is, emigrants from non-traditional source areas, exceeded those from the areas formerly associated with the Newfoundland trade.

Emigration Fields

In the discussion on emigration channels, it was convenient to employ the county as the unit of British origins to maximize the use of available data on that scale. For example, of the 670 Devonians in the population, some 106 were specified merely as originating in Devon. If we employ the smaller sub-sets defined by settlement or parish of origin, we can attempt to reconstruct the total 'emigration field' of British/Newfoundland emigrants and to identify more precisely the spatial characteristics of 'emigration fields' of particular Newfoundland regions.

In a study of Irish emigration to Newfoundland, Mannion (1973) found that the movements were confined to particular parts of the contributing counties: "Roughly 90 percent of the Wexford immigrants come from the south western corner of the county and the same percentage applies to South Kilkenny, Southeast Tipperary, and Southeast Cork." Since these areas of Ireland represent the parts of the respective counties nearest to the main port of embarkation, Waterford, it would seem that

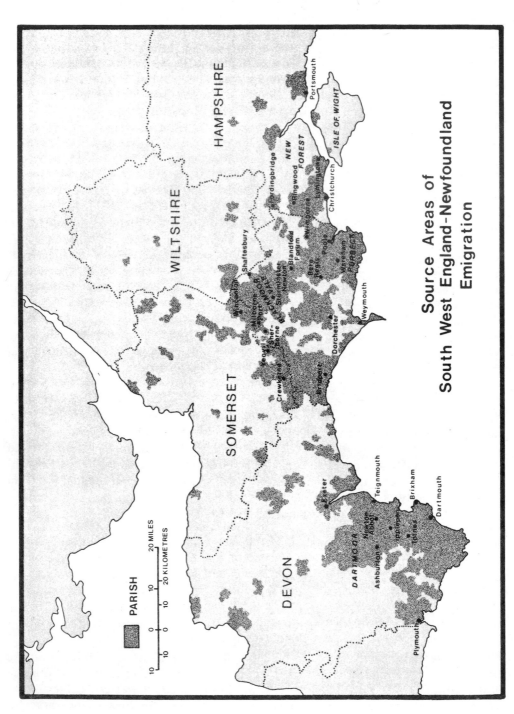

Source Areas of
South West England–Newfoundland
Emigration

Figure 1–6

distance from the port played some role in the selective process. On the other hand, it does not seem that emigration declined with increasing distance alone but varied according to the size of place origins; that is, larger inland settlements sent more emigrants, and smaller settlements nearer Waterford sent fewer. Generally, this same basic principle of distance from the ports and size of place of origin seems to have been a factor in the amount of emigration from southwest and southern England. The pattern of geographical origins in the main source areas of England is shown in Figure 1–6. These areas were derived by allowing the parish boundaries of origin – where contiguous – to coalesce. Generally, it can be seen that a triangular-shaped zone with apexes at Plymouth, Bristol, and Portsmouth defines the major source area of New-foundland as a whole. Within this zone there are numerous vacant areas indicating little or no emigration and some regions indicating intense movement. In Devon, for example, the source areas included some eighty-eight civil parishes, of which seventy-four form a contiguous region in south Devon adjacent to the ports engaged in the Newfoundland trades: Dartmouth, Plymouth, Teignmouth, and Exeter. Although the ports appear to have been the main centres of emigration numerically, inland market towns such as Totnes and Newton Abbott, together with their neighbouring rural parishes such as Berry Pomeroy, Little Hempston, Broadhempston, Staverton, Ipplepin, and Abbotskerswell seem to have been of equal importance, at least relative to their own population sizes. Indeed, in this respect the most significant emigration of all seems to have been from the coastal village of Shaldon near Teignmouth, from which twenty-five families moved to St. John's (and this figure is most likely just a fraction of the total).

Figure 1–6 suggests that only in Dorset was the pattern of origins widespread. Some regions in the southern and eastern sections of the county do not appear to have been important. Outside Poole and its immediate environs, a major source area appears to follow a northern axis oriented with the Stour Valley into the Blackmore Vale, where it assumes a northwest/southeast orientation encompassing parishes in north Dorset and south Somerset and also a few in southwest Wiltshire. Another major region of emigration is indicated in the immediate Poole region with western extensions in central Dorset and the Isle of Purbeck, and a similar eastern symmetrical counterpart including the western coastal and inland regions of Hampshire. While it can be assumed that the emigration fields were more closely associated with Newfoundland opportunities at the port of Poole, the evidence already presented indicates some overlap of emigration from Dartmouth. It is also likely that some emigrants, particularly from north Dorset and south Somerset, found Newfoundland destinations in Conception Bay through the port of Bristol.

The source areas of Scottish and 'other English' emigrants are indicated in Figure 1–7. The representation of Scottish origins indicate a lowland and coastal set of source areas; however, it disguises the fact that more than 80 percent originated in the coastal ports and that more than 90 percent came from the Scottish Lowlands. Thus it would seem that there was virtually no connection between the Scottish emigrants to Newfoundland and the influx of Highland Scots to Nova Scotia. 'Other English' source areas – areas outside southwest England – as Figure 1–7 shows, may be associated with a widespread set of geographical locations, although as already stated, London and Liverpool appear as emigration centres of some importance. Many of the individuals emigrating outside the main source areas appear to have been associated with specialized roles or occupations assumed in the Newfoundland setting. Mis-

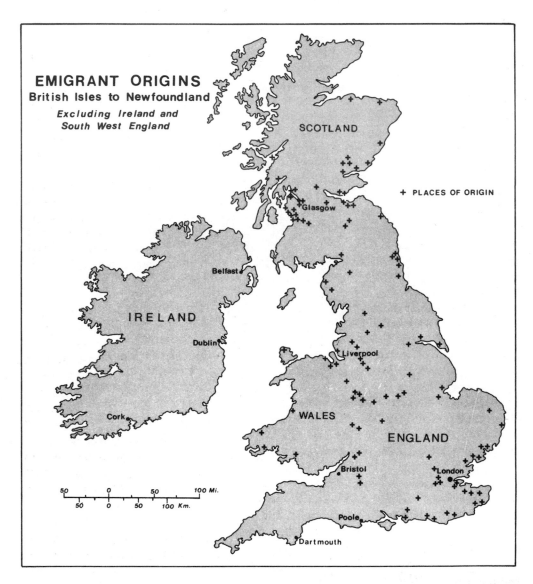

Figure 1–7

sionaries and clergymen, for instance, are identified in parochial records with places such as Warwick in Warwickshire, Boreham in Sussex, Thornton Rush in Yorkshire, Madeley in Shropshire, and Macclesfield in Cheshire. A sergeant-major came from Newcastle-Upon-Tyne, a school-teacher from Eckford in Roxburghshire, a medical doctor from Oxford, and merchants from such places as Birmingham, Lapworth, and Southport. Selectivity in the emigration process by specialized occupational types, however, was by no means confined to 'Other English' source areas; it was a factor in all regions including Scotland, southwest England, and Ireland.

The series of maps comprising Figure 1–8 attempts to relate emigration fields in southwest England with selected Newfoundland regional destinations. Generally the emigration fields of both St. John's and Conception Bay appear to have spatial patterns similar to those of the whole of Newfoundland, with the exceptions that St. John's settlers can be more closely linked with South Devon and Conception Bay settlers with Dorset, Hampshire, and Somerset. However, Figure 1–8 disguises the distinctive relationship between Bristol and Harbour Grace (see p. 29). The emigration fields of Trinity, Bonavista, and Notre Dame Bays appear to be very similar and associated with widespread place-origins in Dorset and a scatter of Dorset border places in south Somerset and west Hampshire. By contrast, the south coast of Newfoundland can be closely linked with emigration from north Dorset and south Somerset parishes. Although the evidence is scant, a pattern similar to the south coast source areas emerges for the English who settled in certain ports along the west coast, along the northwest coast, and in southern Labrador. These indications are gained from both parochial records (Table 1–2) and other sources (see Mannion, Ommer, and Thornton, this vol.).

Since some of the parishes of origin are identified from a single reference or parish registration, it is impractical to attempt any detailed quantitative assessment of emigration intensities. We may, nevertheless, examine this question generally by relating the number of observed immigrants to the population size of their places of origin. The most important emigration centre appears to have been Poole, which accounted for more than 20 percent of all Dorset emigrants, contributing one and a half times as many emigrants as Dartmouth, the second most important centre. Indeed, it seems that emigration from Poole was three times that of the Channel Islands and more than four times that of the whole of Cornwall.

Table 1–7 shows the proportion of emigrants coming from their places of origin in Devon, Dorset, Hampshire and Somerset, in association with emigration frequencies. These figures reveal several main features. Firstly, if it is assumed that the larger-sized settlements (those over 1,000 population) are more urban and the smaller-sized parishes are more rural, it is evident that the greater proportion of emigrants originated in the more urban centres: the ports, market-towns, and manufacturing settlements. This is most vividly illustrated in the case of Hampshire, where more than 40 percent of the emigrants seem to have originated in Christchurch. Christchurch, together with the inland market town of Ringwood, account for more than half of all Hampshire origins. Among the 33 places listed in Table 1–7, only 9 had early 19th century populations of less than 2,500 and only 7 had less than 1,000. It must be recognized, however, that the statistics in Table 1–7 do not consider those entries where settlement of origin was unspecified; but even if the total of these derived from settlements of less than one thousand population, the proportion of emigration from the more rural areas of southwest England would still barely comprise one third of the total. Hence,

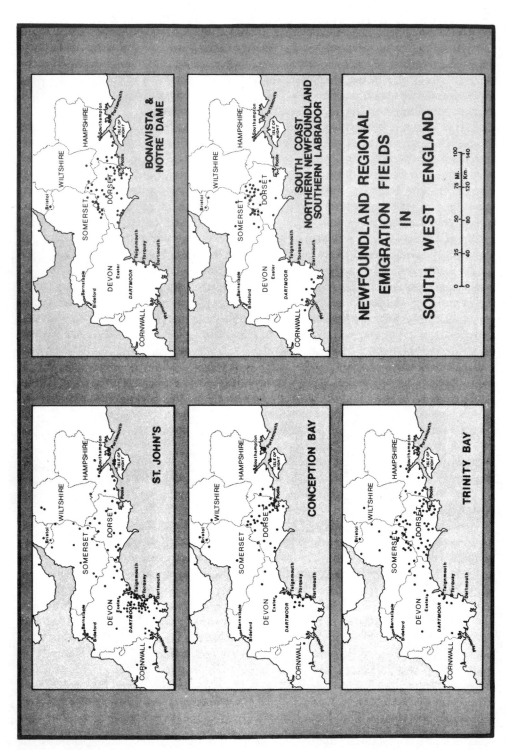

Figure 1-8

TABLE 1–7a

Proportion of Emigrants by Population Size[1] of Place Origins

Population	Devon	Dorset	Somerset	Hampshire	Average
over 5,000	14	32	15	12	18
2,501–5,000	27	23	33	58	35
1,000–2,500	29	20	27	24	25
less than 1,000	30	25	25	6	22

[1]Calculated from the mean population of civil parishes 1801–1841.

TABLE 1-7b

Number of Emigrants[2] by Selected Place Origins

Number of Emigrants	Places	
over 100	Dorset:	Poole.
50–99	Devon:	Dartmouth, Teignmouth.
	Hampshire:	Christchurch; London.
40–49	Bristol	
30–39	Devon:	Plymouth, Torquay, Liverpool.
	Dorset:	Sturminster Newton, Bridport.
20–29	Devon:	Exeter, Newton Abbot, Shaldon.
	Dorset:	Wimborne Minster.
	Somerset:	Crewkerne.
	Hampshire:	Ringwood.
10–19	Devon:	Abbotskerswell, Ashburton, Brixham, Broadhempston, Ipplepin, Kingskerswell, Paignton, Staverton, Stokeintinhead, St. Mary Church, Torbryan, Totnes.
	Dorset:	Bere Regis, Blandford Forum, Dorchester, Sherborne, Shaftesbury, Wareham.
	Hampshire:	Lymington.
	Somerset:	Yeovil.

[1]From Newfoundland parochial records.

the English came predominantly from the 'labouring poor' of the larger towns and villages; they were mainly artisans, craftsmen, and labourers. Yet about 60 percent of the emigrants from Devon derived from parishes of less than 2,500 in population. Certain inland agricultural parishes such as Abbotskerswell, Broadhempston, Ipplepin, Kingskerswell, Staverton, and Torbryan appear to have been as important sources as some of the market towns of Dorset, western Hampshire, and south Somerset (Table 1–7).

Summary

This paper has attempted to reconsider the question of migration from the British Isles to Newfoundland during the 18th and 19th centuries, and to explore the temporal and spatial patterns in that movement, which resulted in the establishment of permanent settlements. The nature of the migration process, primarily seasonal or semi-permanent, which contributed to the growth of the permanent population, makes it difficult to assess changing trends in any particular population sector. However, the use of parameters relating to the proportions of females and children in the population made it possible to define and separate the permanent population and to isolate temporal trends. It was revealed that the permanent population was well-established by the late 18th century and grew rapidly after 1800, largely as a result of an increase in the volume of immigration. Other evidence indicates that the balance of net migration from the two major source areas, southeastern Ireland and southwest England, remained about the same from the late 18th century onwards. Statistics relating to mid-19th century emigration have been shown to be erroneous both in terms of the source areas indicated and the volume of emigration. These statistics, however, indicate that emigration from the British Isles continued well into the 19th century. Temporal trends in the frequency of emigration from marriage records are shown to be similar to those indicated by the changing growth rates of the permanent population and the rates of emigration, as far as can be assessed. Immigrant marriages indicate that the main period of immigrant absorption occurred in the period 1795–1845 with the peak influxes occurring in the 1820s and 1830s, but also that regional differences in flows occurred in emigration channels. The St. John's region attracted emigrants throughout the whole of the 18th and 19th centuries, but in the latter half of the 19th century the larger numbers arrived from 'Other English' source areas, with emigration from the traditional areas, particularly Devon and southern Ireland, virtually ceasing. The most spatially and temporally diverse emigration patterns appear to have stemmed from Dorset, Somerset, and Hampshire and these counties seem to have been the major population components helping to shape the human geography of Newfoundland outside the Avalon Peninsula.

Examination of the main channels of emigration in relation to trade patterns established by the West Country merchants indicates that in some cases the flow of emigration followed the expected pattern; for example, Dorset/Somerset/Hampshire settlers dominated within the Newfoundland trading regions of Poole. On the other hand, there were clearly many exceptions to this rule, the more obvious being the destination patterns of the Irish who settled in most regions, but predominantly in the Southern Avalon: major flows of Irish emigrants in the early 19th century were directed to what had become the Irish areas from the early 18th century. A similar leader/follower relationship in the pattern of emigration seems to have occurred on the South Coast of Newfoundland, where initial colonization by Dorset and Somerset settlers in the late 18th and early 19th centuries continued to attract emigrants from these counties until the late 19th century, despite the fact that Dartmouth and Jersey Island replaced Poole as the main entrepôts of the South Coast trade in the interim.

It has been shown by Mannion that Irish emigration to Newfoundland originated in the county of Waterford and parts of adjacent counties (southwest Wexford, south Kilkenny, southeast Tipperary and southeast Cork). The volume of emigration in this case appears to have been governed to some degree by the population size of the sending settlements and the distance from the port of Waterford. A similar pattern emerged in southwest England with relation to the main ports of embarkation: Dartmouth, Plymouth, Teignmouth, Bristol, and Poole. The English emigration fields of St. John's and Conception Bay appear to have been as geographically diverse as the whole of Newfoundland, but the former were focused mainly in south Devon, and the latter in Dorset, Somerset, and Hampshire. In Dorset, Somerset, and Hampshire, destinations can be associated with Conception Bay, Trinity Bay, Bonavista Bay, Notre Dame Bay, the South Coast, and with early settlement along the west coast, the northwest coast, and southern Labrador. In all these cases the emigration fields overlapped spatially and only emigration to the South Coast and the northwest coast appears to have been distinctively associated with a particular origin – that of north Dorset and south Somerset.

The territorial expansions of the English shore throughout the 18th century represented, for the most part, extensions to the coastal trading territories of merchants based in Poole. These areas were settled by Dorset, Somerset, and Hampshire pioneers upon the establishment of mercantile posts; indeed, in some instances the advent of both the Poole merchants and settlers upon the changing French Shore, fixed by Anglo-French treaties, preceded political adjustments.

Although dominated by English settlements, the Poole/Newfoundland regions also experienced some Irish emigration. In Placentia Bay, for example, mercantile ties between Poole and Waterford promoted an almost exclusive Irish movement. The Sweetman firm of Newbaun (Wexford) and Waterford City succeeded the Poole family of Saunders; initially trading in Placentia was controlled by Saunders, and then jointly by Saunders and Sweetman. The lack of male heirs in the Saunders line and the marriage of a daughter to a Sweetman sealed the Sweetman succession. In the mercantile system of migration, which became one of emigration, the relationship of Ireland to the ports of the West of England, as illustrated by Poole but by no means peculiar to it, assumed a role not dissimilar to that of the English source areas. In this scheme the spatial relationships between the port of Waterford with respect to Waterford county, west Wexford, and south Kilkenny mirror similar relationships to Poole of Dorset, west Hampshire, and south Somerset.

The role of the port of Poole in shaping the ethnic structure of Newfoundland settlements is expressed not only through the spatial spheres of its merchants' activities, but also in its role as the chief centre of English emigration. Indeed, the parochial registers of Newfoundland indicate that most of the ports (Dartmouth, Teignmouth, Plymouth, Bristol, London, and Poole) involved in the Newfoundland trade were important as emigration centres, followed by the market towns, manufacturing centres, and larger villages in southwest England (Newton Abbot, Totnes, Bridport, Sturminster Newton, Christchurch, Ringwood, and Crewkerne). These (and other) centres account for more than two thirds of all emigrants, whereas the smaller, more rural areas – though more numerous in total number of place origins – account for less than one-third.

SOURCES ON HOMELAND ORIGINS

Parish Registers
1. Deposited in Newfoundland Archives
    Anglican Cathedral, St. John's: Baptisms 1752–1828, Marriages 1752–1879, Burials 1752–1879 (11 vols.); Trinity (C. of E.) Baptisms and Marriages 1757–1839, Burials 1757–1820, (microfilm); King's Cove (R.C.) Marriages 1815–1855; Brigus (Methodist) Marriages 1822–1831.
2. Transcripts formerly deposited and examined by the author in Vital Statistics Division, Dept. of Public Health and Welfare, Confederation Building, St. John's, now held by the Newfoundland Archives, St. John's, include
    Church of England Marriage Records St. Thomas, St. John's 1802–1891, King's Cove 1834–1891, Trinity North (Catalina) 1833–1891, Bonavista 1786–1891, Greenspond 1815–1891, White Bay

1864–1890, Port de Grave and Clarke's Beach 1837–1890, Fogo 1841–1849, Rose Blanche 1860–1891, Hermitage 1867–1877, Harbour Grace 1776–1871.

Methodist/Wesleyan Marriage Records Bonavista (W) 1822–1890, St. Anthony (M) 1873–1890, Burin (M) 1850–1880, St. George's (M) 1862–1891, Carbonear (M) 1794–1891, Brigus-Cupids (M) 1837–1891, Blackhead (M) 1816–1891.

Congregational/Presbyterian Marriage Records St. John's (P) 1842–1891, St. John's (C) 1802–1891.

3. *Register of Marriages 1825–1828* (a manuscript of marriages, mostly Roman Catholic/Irish, performed at numerous places throughout Newfoundland during the period)

Marriage Certificates (a loose-leaf collection of original certificates, some fire-charred, covering the period 1825–1879)

Social and Obituary Columns of Newspapers deposited at the Newfoundland Archives: *The Royal Gazette and Newfoundland Advertiser*, 1810–16; the *Mercantile Journal*, 1816–24; *The Carbonear Star and Conception Bay Journal*, 1833–35; *The Harbour Grace Standard*, 1879–1886; *The Harbour Grace Weekly Journal*, 1828; *The Weekly Herald*, 1849–56; *The Newfoundlander* 1830–82; *The Newfoundland Patriot* 1840–8; *The Times*, 1829–44; *The Evening Telegram*, 1879–90; *The Mercury*, 1889.

Other Sources included tombstone surveys of the *General Protestant Cemetery*, St. John's; *United Church Cemetery*, Brigus; *Harbour Grace C/E Cemetery*; *Topsail C/E Cemetery*, Topsail (per Mr. Howard Brown, Department of Geography, Memorial University); *Bay Bulls C/E Cemetery* (per Mrs. Margaret Chang, Provincial Archives, St. John's); and entries transcribed from parish records and cemeteries relating to *St. Barbe and Southern Labrador* (per Prof. Patricia Thornton, Department of Geography, McGill University).

NOTES

1   C.O.I./35 (1675), Census by Sir John Berry. See: Prowse, 1896:699, for a published version of the 1677 census.

2   Calendar of State Papers, Colonial Series, American and the West Indies, 1675–76, items 470, 475, 477, 499, 550, 612 and 628 (1675) and 731, 769, 1015, 1120, and 1160 (1776).

3   Calendar of State Papers, Colonial Series, American and the West Indies (1715) item 179:77.

4   Great Britain, House of Commons, 10 (1785–1801), *Report from the Committee on the State of the Newfoundland Trade* (1793), Testimony of John Jeffrey, pp. 394–96.

5   *Ibid.*, Testimony of Peter Ougier, p. 405.

6   C.O.I./55:241 (1684), Report of Captain Wheeler.

7   The C.O. 194 statistics relating to Newfoundland trade and population have been compiled by S. Ryan, Department of History, Memorial University of Newfoundland, under *Abstract of Returns for the Newfoundland Fishery 1698–1833* (1969).

8   McLintock (1941:126) claims that Irish immigration between 1811 and 1830, "the only years for which reliable figures are available," exceeded 24,000.

9   Parish registers and other sources examined are listed at the end of this chapter.

10   For the application of the model of migration see, Roseman, 1970:140–46.

11   Calendar of State Papers, Colonial Series, American and West Indies, (1720:177–8).

12   Great Britain, House of Commons, *Report from Select Committee on Newfoundland Trade*, London, 1817.

13   "Records of the Lester and Garland Families," D365, Dorset Record Office, Dorchester. See particularly Diaries of Benjamin Lester 1761–1764, 1767–1771, 1779–1786, 1786–1796 and 1796–1802, Diaries of Isaac Lester 1765–1770, 1770–1774, 1774–1776 and 1776–1779, for ship movements of Poole Merchants.

14   *British Parliamentary Papers*. Emigration: Appendices to Reports of the Colonial Land and Emigration Commissioners, 10 (1842–48), 11 (1849–52), 12 (1853–55), 13 (1856–58), 14 (1859–64).

15   Calendar of Letters, 1721–1793, United Society for the Propagation of the Gospel, Archives, London.

16   Dorset Record Office, Easter Kiley, November 6, 1788. P227/OV11. Rev. Lawrence Coughlan, Harbour Grace, 1769, complained that "Common fishermen, English and Irish, in this parish marry and baptize"; Rev. James Balfour of Trinity, 1764 noted that "Marriage [is] sometimes dispensed with," and Mr. Cole, Missionary at Ferryland and Bay Bulls, 1793, "found it to be a prevailing custom for persons to live together in a state of matrimony, without ever coming to church." Calendar of Letters, 1721–1793, United Society for the Propagation of the Gospel, Archives, London.

17   The author is grateful for this information on the Bird family given by P. Thornton from *Accounts and Letter Books of Joseph Bird and Thomas Street (1824–48) C/108/71*, National Archives of Canada, Ottawa.

18   In the possession of Dr. E. F. J. Mathews of Poole, a noted Poole-historian, by whose kind permission the author was permitted to examine and copy.

19   Information on the Colbourne family gained from parish records of Sturminster Newton and Poole, and family wills in the Dorset Record Office, from various documents in the possession of Dr. E. F. J. Mathews of Poole and personal correspondence with a descendant of the Sturminster Newton family of Colbournes, Colonel Peter Harrison of Chichester, Sussex, who has conducted intensive genealogical research.

REFERENCES: SECONDARY SOURCES

BUFFET, A. F.
   n.d. "Records of Births, Deaths and Marriages, Grand Bank." St. John's, Centre for Newfoundland Studies, Memorial University Library.
CELL, G. T.
   1969 *English Enterprize in Newfoundland 1577–1660.* Toronto, University of Toronto Press.
COWAN, H. I.
   1961 *British Emigration to British North America.* Toronto, University of Toronto Press.
FAY, C. R.
   1961 *Channel Islands and Newfoundland.* Cambridge, Heffer and Sons.
GOLDSCHEIDER, C.
   1971 *Population Modernization and Social Structure.* Boston, Little, Brown & Co.
HAGERSTRAND, T.
   1957 "Migration and Area." In D. Hannerberg et al. (eds)., *Migration in Sweden: A Symposium.* Lund, C. W. K. Gleerup.
HARVEY, D.
   1969 *Explanation in Geography.* London, E. Arnold.
HEAD, C. G.
   1976 *Eighteenth Century Newfoundland: A Geographers Perspective.* Toronto, McClelland and Stewart.
LEE, E. S.
   1966 "A Theory of Migration." *Demography,* 3:47–57.
LOUNSBURY, R. G.
   1934 *The British Fishery at Newfoundland 1634–1763.* New Haven, Yale University Press.
MANNION, J.
   1973 "The Irish Migrations to Newfoundland." Newfoundland Historical Society Lecture, 1–12.
MATTHEWS, K.
   1968a "A History of the West of England – Newfoundland Fishery." Unpublished Ph.D. thesis, University of Oxford.
MATTHEWS, K.
   1968b "The West Country Merchants in Newfoundland." Newfoundland Historical Society Lecture, 1–12.
MORRILL, R. L. and F. R. PITTS
   1967 "Marriage, Migration and the Mean Information Field: A Study in Uniqueness and Generality." *Annals, Association of American Geographers,* 57 (4):401–22.
McLINTOCK, A. H.
   1941 *The Establishment of Constitutional Government in Newfoundland,* 1783–1832. London, Longmans, Green and Co.
OLSSON, G.
   1965 "Distance and Human Interaction: A Migration Study." *Geografiska Annaler,* 47B(1):3–43.
PROWSE, D. W.
   1896 *A History of Newfoundland.* Second Edition. London, Eyre and Spottiswoode.
RANDELL, R. A.
   1971 "Some Aspects of Population Geography in Certain Rural Areas of England During the Eighteenth and Early Nineteenth Centuries." Unpublished Ph.D. Thesis, Department of Geography, University of Newcastle-Upon-Tyne.

ROGERS, J. D.
   1911 "Newfoundland." In H. J. Herbertson and D. J. Howarth (eds.), *A Historical Geography of the British Colonies*, vol. 4. Oxford, Clarendon Press.
ROSCOE, E. (ed.)
   1952 *The Marn'll Book*. Gillingham, Blackmore Press.
ROSEMAN, C. C.
   1970 "Channelization of Migration Flows from the Rural South to the Industrial Midwest." *Annals, Association of American Geographers*, 60(1):140–46.
SAVAGE, R. and K. W. DEUTSCH
   1960 "A Statistical Model of the Gross Analysis of Transaction Flows." *Econometrica*, 39:59–66.
SEARY, E. R. et al.
   1968 *The Avalon Peninsula of Newfoundland: An Ethno-linguistic Study*. Ottawa, National Museum of Canada, Bulletin 219.
TOCQUE, P.
   1878 *Newfoundland as it Was and as it is in 1877*. Toronto, J. B. Magnum.
VANCE, J. E.
   1970 *The Merchant's World: The Geography of Wholesaling*. Englewood Cliffs, N.J., Prentice Hall.

Population Dynamics in Newfoundland: The Regional Patterns

2

Michael Staveley

The process by which a country is settled is interesting on at least two separate counts. In the first place, it may represent a fascinating, even exhilarating saga which constitutes an important element in the iconography of the nation. Secondly, it may influence subsequent patterns of social and economic development. For both these reasons, it is important that the process of settlement, together with its associated phenomena of migration, population growth, and personal mobility, be objectively described and understood.

Settlement is a process essentially operating in two dimensions, space and time, though many accounts of settlement have tended to emphasize one of these aspects at the expense of the other. For example, we commonly see population growth examined largely as a function of time, or the expansion of settlement studied as a spatial function. Rarely are these two dimensions perceived as operating in close interdependence, perhaps because until recently no adequate conceptual base has been provided for their joint consideration.

One attempt to describe and explain the development of population in terms of both space and time has been made by the Finnish geographer Naukkarinen. Building on studies done by Kirk (1946) and Webb (1963), Naukkarinen examined the dynamic components of population growth (natural increase and net migration) and suggested certain sequences which he considered basic to what he calls "a theory of population development characteristic ... of fringe settlement areas in general" (1969:1–149). He postulated that settlement and population development should follow a regular and logical sequence which he summed up in the model reproduced in Figure 2–1. During the initial settlement of a region, the components of population increase should intersect in Sector C of the model, indicating a condition in which net in-migration is greater than natural increase. The growth of a settled population and the slackening of in-migration would be represented by a shift from Sector C to Sector B as natural increase grew to exceed net in-migration. In the third stage of development, population would grow at a rate more than sufficient to fill all available niches in a spatial-economic system functioning at equilibrium. Some relief from surplus population would derive from a developing net out-migration, but in this third phase natural increase would still exceed net out-migration. At a later stage, however, in Sector H, net out-migration would begin to exceed natural increase, and the sequence is continued logically through Sectors G and F.

This model follows the conventional assumption that frontiers or settlement fringes have distinct and swiftly changing population structures which differentiate them from more settled cores. Eblen has challenged this view, basing his hypothesis on a close examination of American statistics for the period 1840 to 1860 (1965:399–413).

The thrust towards a more ordered and conceptual comprehension of settlement and mobility has been further advanced by Zelinsky (1971:219–49). In essence his hypothesis of "mobility transition" attempts to comprehend the redistribution of population as a process in both space and time described by the useful term,

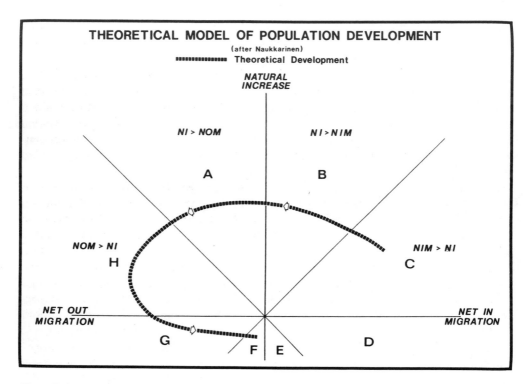

Figure 2–1

"spatiotemporal."[1] The gist of the hypothesis is contained in the assertion that "There are definite patterned regularities in the growth of personal mobility through space-time during recent history, and these regularities comprise an essential component of the modernization process" (p. 221–22).

The notion of the mobility transition is weaned from the more celebrated concept of the "demographic transition" and, of course, is interdependent with it. For example, just as in the demographic transition the development of populations in various nations passes from a pre-modern near-equilibrium to a modern near-equilibrium by changes in the schedules of fertility and mortality, so the schedules of mobility (migration and circulation) shift also. Equally important, perhaps, the progression of the mobility transition is said to be "irreversible" (p. 249).

Zelinsky postulates five phases of territorial mobility. Phase I, "The Pre-modern Traditional Society," is characterized by "a spatially stable peasant society" (p. 235): internal migration is negligible in periods and societies of this type. Phase II, "The Early Transitional Society," is characterized by "a great shaking loose of migrants from the countryside" (p. 236) and their relocation in cities and rural settlement frontiers both home and abroad. Phase III, "The Late Transitional Society," is marked by a slackening of rural-urban migration and emigration, with more emphasis being given to 'circulation' as a technologically derived substitute for migration. In Phase IV, "The Advanced Society," traditional forms of migration have all but disappeared and settlement frontiers are in retreat: inter-urban and intra-urban migration dominate the system of movement. In Phase V, "A Superadvanced Society," the trends of Phase IV are continued, with a possible diminution in actual personal mobility as systems of delivery and communication improve, and with a possibility of stricter political control on both internal and international movements. Zelinsky's schematic representation of various spatial sectors of mobility is portrayed in Figure 2–2.

Certain generalizations of a "spatiotemporal" character are adduced by Zelinsky in the course of his analysis. In brief he suggests that:

1. in countries experiencing Phase I, "a rapid massive build-up in rural numbers occurred well before any surge in the mobility rates" (p. 236).
2. the propensity to migrate begins in the more developed socio-economic zones "and then radiate(s) outward into less advanced, less accessible regions" (p. 238).
3. the role of the regional or national metropolis is to function as "the advanced outpost of the modernization process." Demographic innovations "flow outward" from the city to the "traditional (Phase I) countryside" (p. 243).
4. there is a growth through time of "non-economic motivations" for circulation and mobility (p. 247).

The significance of these two statements for an understanding of the geography of settlement is to be found in their combination. Zelinsky's hypothesis is stated entirely in qualitative terms; as such, it is bold, even sweeping, in its suggestive generalization. Naukkarinen, on the other hand, as befits an empirically and statistically grounded hypothesis, is more cautious. Taken together, these hypotheses form the basis of a more considered and conceptually organized examination of the settlement process than has yet been possible.

The Pattern of Newfoundland Immigration
The early settlement of Newfoundland does not lend itself readily to precise quantitative assessment. We know from the Governor's Returns that at the end of the 17th

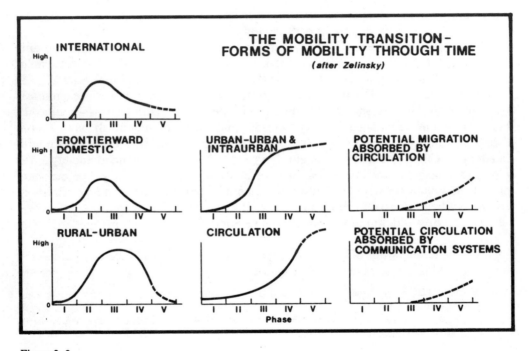

Figure 2–2

century, the resident population of the island was little more than 1,000 souls (see Handcock, this vol.). By the end of the 18th century, this figure had risen to about 15,000 and by the early years of the 19th century had exceeded 20,000 (Hatton and Harvey, 1883:72). But it was not until 1836 that detailed official censuses became available which allow a quantitative assessment of population dynamics in Newfoundland as a whole.

The most substantial influx of immigrants to Newfoundland took place, however, before these official censuses were recorded. English and Irish fishermen had been visiting and sporadically settling the island for over two hundred years when, after 1800, renewed and concentrated incursions took place (see Handcock). Social and economic upheavals in Ireland, together with high fish prices and high wages arising from the English monopoly over European markets during the Napoleonic Wars induced great numbers to emigrate. It was largely through the medium of immigration that the population rose steeply in the first few decades of the 19th century; in 1804 the resident population was computed at 20,380, but by 1827 this figure had risen to 59,571 (*op. cit.*:361), an increase of more than 8 percent per year.

Most of the attention given to immigration by contemporary observers was directed at the Irish, largely because the Irish inflow was more concentrated in both time and space. Moreover, the Irish were viewed by the authorities as a potentially dissident sector of the population and their growth in numbers was observed with care, not unmixed with alarm. This literary and official emphasis should not, however, obscure the fact that immigration from England, though less concentrated, was still an important element in the peopling of the country (see Handcock). This becomes clear from the census data (Table 2–1) on the proportion of foreign-born in the colony at mid-century: if the massive surplus of Irish-born in St. John's is ignored, the rest of the colony had roughly equal numbers of English-born and Irish-born immigrants. Those of Irish provenance dominated the Avalon only; the English held sway elsewhere.

The startling rates of population increase were not sustained, however, as immigration diminished in the face of a fluctuating economy on both sides of the Atlantic after the Napoleonic Wars, and particularly after the 1830s. This fact, together with interesting sidelights on the scale and mode of immigration to which Newfoundland was subject, is seen in an exchange of correspondence which took place in 1857–58 between the authorities in Newfoundland and the Colonial Office in London. The Governor of the day, Sir Alexander Bannerman, opened the official exchange by stating:

... it appears that since the year 1847, emigration from Ireland to Newfoundland has declined rapidly and is now nearly extinct, the cause of which is want of employment, and the inhabitants writing to their friends that many of them were in a state of extreme destitution; this was perfectly correct; but from one or two successful fisheries things have taken a very different turn; the want of labour, and the high price of wages, are now severely felt. The Board of Works here, and several respectable firms, have been obliged to authorize Messrs. James and Robert Kent of the City of Cork, to procure a number of labourers for Newfoundland; but which, they say, cannot be effected unless H.M. Government will allow some relaxations of the Passenger Act, which are pointed out in the enclosed Minute ... (*J.H.A.*, 1858:604–6).

The Governor's request was prompted by the concern of local merchants who could see in the recently passed Passenger Acts obstacles to the supply of Old Country immigrants who were so badly needed. They saw that these Acts, by raising the fixed costs incurred in shipping emigrants, made economies of scale all the more necessary in the passenger-carrying trade. This could not fail to discriminate against the interests

TABLE 2–1

Newfoundland—Population by Country of Birth as Percentage of Total Population, 1857 and 1869

District	1857 Born in:				1869 Born in:			
	Population	Newfoundland	England	Ireland	Population	Newfoundland	England	Ireland
St. John's E.	17,352	79.7	3.9	13.9	17,204	93.1	2.3	8.5
St. John's W.	13,124	79.2	3.3	16.1	11,646	87.4	1.9	9.8
Harbour Main	5,386	94.0	0.8	5.0	6,542	96.8	0.5	2.6
Port de Grave	6,489	94.2	1.9	3.6	7,536	96.2	1.2	2.0
Harbour Grace	10,067	93.0	1.3	5.1	12,740	96.4	0.7	2.1
Carbonear	5,233	90.6	1.7	7.6	5,633	94.2	1.0	4.4
Bay de Verde	6,221	97.4	1.2	1.3	7,057	98.6	0.6	0.8
Trinity Bay	10,736	97.2	1.8	0.9	13,817	98.3	1.2	0.4
Bonavista Bay	8,850	95.7	2.5	1.6	11,560	98.0	1.0	0.8
Fogo and Twillingate	9,717	93.8	4.8	1.1	13,067	95.7	3.2	0.8
French Shore	3,334		(no data)		5,387	89.4	1.8	0.5
Burgeo-LaPoile	3,545	89.4	7.9	0.1	5,119	91.6	6.8	0.1
Fortune Bay	3,493	89.8	7.7	0.3	5,233	93.6	5.2	0.2
Burin	5,529	90.2	6.1	3.0	6,731	95.0	3.0	1.3
Placentia and St. Mary's	8,334	92.6	1.5	5.7	8,794	95.8	0.7	3.3
Ferryland	5,228	91.8	1.3	6.8	5,991	96.1	0.5	3.3
Newfoundland	107,339	90.0	2.9	6.2	144,057	94.2	1.8	3.0

of Newfoundland because her need for labour, though considerable on the local scale, was small when compared to her more populous neighbours. Thus, the local pressure group complained that "The provisions of the present Act ... have had the effect of diverting the stream of Emigration from the smaller British North American colonies to the United States and Canada ... (*op. cit.*:607–8).

The submission met with a cool reception from the Colonial Office, however, and the reply of the Secretary for the Colonies is instructive both in its analysis of the real reasons emigration to Newfoundland had dwindled, and in the raw data on emigration he advanced to support his case:

The question moreover arises, whether there is any reason why Her Majesty's Government should stimulate Emigration to Newfoundland by exceptional arrangements. I annex a statement of the Emigration to the Island in the sixteen years ending in December 1856. It will be seen that in the six years preceding 1847, the Emigration averages 516 a year, while in the nine years following, it averaged only 197; – but the variations in the numbers appear to show that the falling off is rightly attributed by you to a failure of the demand for labour, and not to an increase in the cost of passage ... you state that 'from one or two successful fisheries' the Island has now become prosperous; but you add afterwards that 'fisheries are precarious and two or three bad seasons might bring along with them the same want of labour and its consequences which took place some years ago.' Under such circumstances it would not be desirable that Her Majesty's Government should interfere to give an unusual impulse to Emigration to Newfoundland, since they would thereby make themselves, to a certain extent, responsible for the employment of those who might proceed thither ...

(annexed Return of Emigration from Britain to Newfoundland)

1841	336	1849	87
1842	490	1850	345
1843	448	1851	241
1844	684	1852	209
1845	618	1853	173
1846	523	1854	95
1847	993	1855	94
1848	343	1856	215 (*op. cit.*:605–7)

Thus the scale of, and scope for immigration was diminished both by economic fluctuations and by official reluctance to promote more favourable conditions for emigrants. A trickle of emigrants did continue to arrive, but these were insufficient in number to form a significant element in population growth.

In addition to the diminishing *proportions* of non-native inhabitants, the *actual* numbers of foreign-born fell – the foreign population was not even being replaced by the modest immigration. Only two areas were exceptions to this trend: on the South Coast in Burgeo-LaPoile and in Fortune Bay the actual numbers of both English and Irish-born either rose or remained steady (Table 2–1). This is not surprising considering that these areas were undergoing the most dynamic population growth of the whole colony in this period, both through heavy in-migration and natural increase. However, though there was stability in the numbers of foreign-born, the actual increase in the numbers of foreign-born was negligible in the case of the Irish, and slight in the case of the English.

A second exception to this state of affairs, not noted in Table 2–1, was the French Shore in what later became the District of St. George's. In 1869, this area was inhabited by a significant minority group of neither direct English nor Irish antecedents, but rather of recent immigrants from Cape Breton and other parts of Nova Scotia. To their number, mostly Scottish and Acadian, could be added a smaller number of 'Foreign-Born,' deserters from French fishing ships. Together, these peoples comprised 8.3 percent of the population of the French Shore – in itself a small proportion of the total population on the shore – but it was concentrated in a relatively small area in southwestern Newfoundland in the most agriculturally productive part of the colony. Perhaps by reason of their isolation and their distinctiveness in origin and economy (they were the greatest proponents of subsistence agriculture), they imparted a persistently different scale of population dynamics to this corner of Newfoundland.

The diminution of immigration then, after the first third of the 19th century, can scarcely be questioned, and in any calculation of the dynamics of population growth, immigration appears negligible. As one near contemporary observer noted: "The increase of population has risen almost entirely from natural growth, as since 1814 the amount of immigration has been insignificant. The fisheries were barely sufficient to sustain the existing settlers and latterly have failed to expand so as to meet the wants of a rapidly growing population ..." (Hatton and Harvey, 1883:365). Nineteenth century Newfoundlanders were optimistic about the development of the island's resources which was, as yet (1883), only beginning. Mines, forests, and agriculture were on the verge of being opened up, mainly by the incipient building of the railroad on which great hopes were pinned: "We may now fairly expect that ere long a stream of thrifty immigrants will pour into the colony, and turn the fine natural resources to industrious account" (*op. cit.*:365).

Cognizant of the great trans-Atlantic migrations that were then reaching their peak, the writers were confident that when "... (the island's) attractions are thoroughly known, it can hardly fail to secure a considerable rill from the great stream of emigration now flowing from the Old World to the New" (*op. cit.*:365). But Newfoundland's attractions for the late 19th century emigrant were too few to compete with the more publicized virtues of Canada and particularly the United States. The trans-Atlantic stream passed by unbroken, and despite the optimism of Newfoundland's enthusiastic promoters, no significant rill came her way.

The Growth of Population

Even if Newfoundland's population was essentially and increasingly home grown, it was, at least in the earlier phases, a healthily growing one. Table 2–2 indicates the average annual population changes from 1836–1911 computed on the basis of intercensal periods. (The data from this table have been incorporated into the accompanying maps [Figs. 2–3, 2–4] depicting the spatial distribution of the population over the period.) From 1836–45 (Fig. 2–3) growth was rapid in nearly all districts. The longer established areas recorded the lowest growth, but even there, the advance was substantial: in both St. John's and the Conception Bay districts, the annual increase was over 2 percent.[2] It was in the developing frontier districts, however, that growth was strongest: on both the northeast coast and the south coast, average annual increases of over 3.5 percent were common, and in Burgeo-LaPoile, the increase averaged 7 percent per annum. Only in Ferryland was there no advance in population. The overall increase for the colony was approximately 3.5 percent per annum; this appears to represent a healthy natural increase *and* sustained in-migration. The declining trickle of immigration, noted previously, in the following period (1845–57) gave lower growth rates, but the pattern of growth was not substantially different. From 1857–69 (Fig. 2–3) many of the growth rates diminished, and in the St. John's

TABLE 2-2

Average Annual Percentage Population Increase/Decrease, Newfoundland and Districts, 1836–1911

District	1836–45	1845–57	1857–69	1869–74	1874–84	1884–91	1891–01	1901–11
St. John's E.	3.7	1.7	-0.1	0.7	2.5	-0.9	2.3	-0.2
St. John's W.			-0.9	1.9	2.5	-0.6	2.1	1.1
Harbour Main			1.8	1.9	2.5	0.4	0.3	-0.1
Port de Grave			1.3	1.0	1.0	-1.2	-0.7	-0.6
Harbour Grace	2.3	1.6	2.2	0.5	1.3	-0.8	-0.9	-0.6
Carbonear			0.6	-0.5	1.3	-1.0	-1.3	0.2
Bay de Verde			1.1	1.1	1.3	2.2	0.1	0.4
Trinity Bay	3.3	1.8	2.4	2.7	2.1	-0.1	1.0	0.5
Bonavista Bay	4.4	1.9	2.6	2.5	2.7	1.2	1.5	1.1
Fogo	4.2	3.7	2.9	3.2	3.4	2.2	1.3	0.9
Twillingate							1.6	1.7
St. Barbe	7.0	3.2	5.1	12.1	3.8	1.6	2.2	2.9
St. George's							3.7	3.0
Burgeo-LaPoile			3.7	-0.1	2.8	-0.2	0.8	1.1
Fortune Bay	4.3	1.7	4.2	2.1	2.0	1.6	1.4	1.4
Burin			1.8	2.8	1.1	0.9	1.5	1.2
Placentia and St. Mary's	4.2	2.4	0.5	2.4	2.0	1.2	2.4	0.1
Ferryland	-1.2	1.4	1.2	1.4	0.1	-1.4	-0.3	0.2
Newfoundland	3.5	2.3	1.5	2.1	2.1	0.4	1.0	1.0

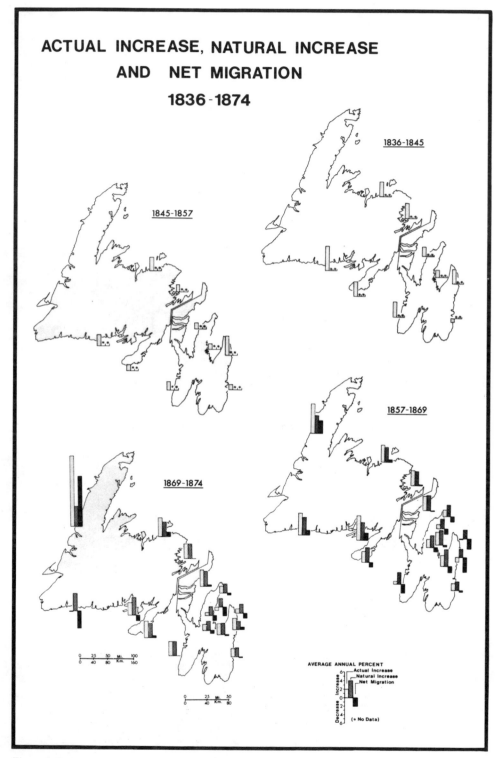

ACTUAL INCREASE, NATURAL INCREASE
AND   NET MIGRATION
1836-1874

Figure 2–3

districts an actual decrease was reported. Again the heaviest advances were made outside the old established centres, on the French Shore, in the west, on the south coast, and on the northeast coast. With few exceptions, this pattern was repeated throughout 1869–74 and 1874–84 (Fig. 2–4).

The period 1884–91 (Fig. 2–4) shows a sharp discontinuity in the pattern of population development. For the first time, total population advanced very slowly, by less than 0.4 percent per annum. Naturally the decline was widespread: in St. John's and the inlying Conception Bay districts actual decrease of population was universal, with only Harbour Main managing a fractional increase. Beyond Carbonear, increases were usually recorded, but even these were but a fraction of those recorded in previous periods. Ferryland lost population heavily.

The causes, or official interpretations, of this population stagnation are not difficult to find. They were succinctly outlined by Robert Bond, Colonial Secretary, in the Preface to the 1891 Census: "It will be noticed that in many of the Districts the increase has been small whilst in a few there has been a decrease. This may be accounted for by the large inducements held out to artisans and labourers in the United States."[3]

There were, doubtless, other reasons such as pressure on existing local resources for such a large apparent decrease in growth rates,[4] but it is worth noting that the areas of heaviest decline – St. John's, Ferryland, and to a lesser extent, the Conception Bay districts – were the strongholds of the Newfoundland Irish. The close links maintained by many amongst this group with relatives who had moved to the New England States gave them the information and incentive to migrate further. This movement began as early as 1850 and had profound long-term effects on the political ascendancy of the colony.[5] From 1884 the trend became especially pronounced.

The period from 1891–1901 (Fig. 2–4) showed a mild resurgence of demographic growth with an average annual increase of approximately 1 percent for the colony as a whole. Again, the west coast districts, which during this period became almost free of the pernicious French Shore Treaty restrictions, were growing the most vigorously, though St. John's also was experiencing rapid growth. The northeast coast showed steady, if unspectacular growth, generally above 1 percent per annum, but again Conception Bay and Ferryland were marked by decline. This pattern persisted, with mild variations, throughout the succeeding decade (Fig. 2–4).

Population Parameters
The analysis and description of regional patterns of growth and decline do not, themselves, tell us much about population structure and dynamics. Thus, for example, a 1 percent average annual growth in Carbonear may be similar to the figure for Burgeo-LaPoile, and yet the two districts are unlikely to have experienced the same complex of demographic processes. To introduce more precision to the analysis of the processes informing Newfoundland's population geography, several parameters have been calculated and comparative statistics are analysed to show secular and spatial shifts in the values for age structure and fertility. The role played by mortality in Newfoundland's demographic progression has also been calculated, and, utilizing these indices, inferences are drawn concerning patterns of migration and circulation.[6]

Age Structures. It is a commonplace of demography and population geography that the age distribution of a population is of fundamental importance in influencing the

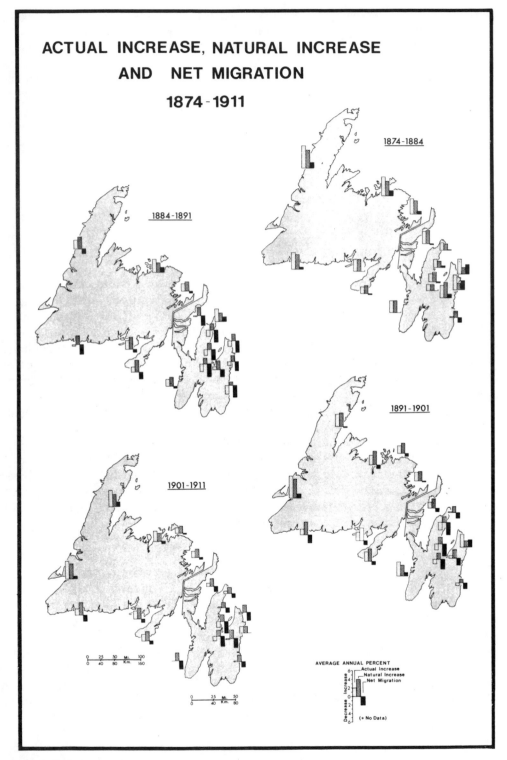

ACTUAL INCREASE, NATURAL INCREASE
AND NET MIGRATION
1874-1911

Figure 2–4

behavioural patterns in that group. Therefore an analysis of age structures was made for each district in Newfoundland for each census year. Coulson's method of computation was used, whereby the *beta* value or slope of the least squares line drawn to express the relationship between the mid-points of the age groups (x), and the percentage of the total population in each group (y) were simply transformed into an age structure index consisting of five digits (1968:155–76).

The results of the age structure analysis are given in Figure 2–5 from which it can be seen that the indices range from a value of 58,000 (the youngest) for one district in 1836, to a value of less than 36,000 (the oldest) in 1911. The overall picture is one of the steady aging of the population – each set of figures occupies a range slightly lower down the age axis than its predecessor. This, in itself, is not surprising. One would expect a youthful pioneer population to age over the decades – but the consistency of the Newfoundland data is impressive, not least because it suggests a reasonable level of veracity in the census data.

Although the population as a whole, and in its separate parts, exhibits a consistent aging trend, the index at the end of the period still denotes a 'young' population – young that is, when compared with some contemporary populations. The early age structures denote an excessively youthful series of populations – indeed one demographer would term them 'primitive' (Vielrose, 1965:40) – but even the 'oldest' age structures remain strongly 'progressive' in the sense of having more than enough potential for rapid replacement.

In order to assess the significance of the spatial and secular differences that appeared in the age structures, the indices were then graphed. The trends are depicted in Figure 2–6; for convenience, and to avoid too much graphic clutter, the districts were divided into three sets of contiguous units. Thus the data are set out separately for the area from Ferryland through St. John's to Conception Bay; then for the northeast coast and the French Shore; and finally for the South Coast.

Although this mode of subdivision is primarily one of convenience, it does appear, with hindsight, to reflect some intuitive realization that the three zones thus divided represent, to a degree, distinct demographic provinces. For when the districts of southeast Newfoundland are compared closely with those of the northeast coast, there is little overlap. The three districts of Carbonear, Port de Grave, and Ferryland appear consistently as the most aged, at least from 1884, and the districts of Trinity, Fogo, and Bonavista, decline steeply towards the end of the period to approach these low levels. Only Twillingate escapes dipping to the same levels, perhaps because of the injection of youthful recruits to the developing pulp and paper town of Grand Falls in its landward portion. Most significant is the level of the values for the French Shore, later to be known as St. Barbe and St. George: although they follow the same trend as the others, they lie consistently higher than any other group. The graph lines for the south coast districts follow essentially the same trends as the others, though they begin higher (younger) and finish higher than any other district with the exception of the French Shore.

Fertility. Fertility trends were assessed over the period by use of the child-woman ratio. Vital statistics for Newfoundland became available in 1901, but they are patchy in coverage for the early years; the use of the child-woman ratio makes possible a more comparative survey over the whole period. To make the comparison of the values even easier, an index was derived by averaging out all the raw values for all years.

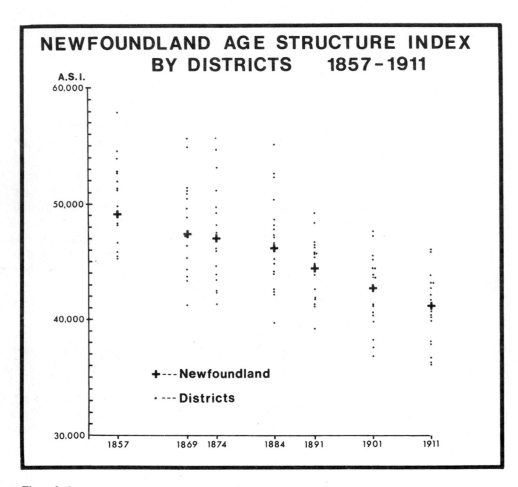

Figure 2–5

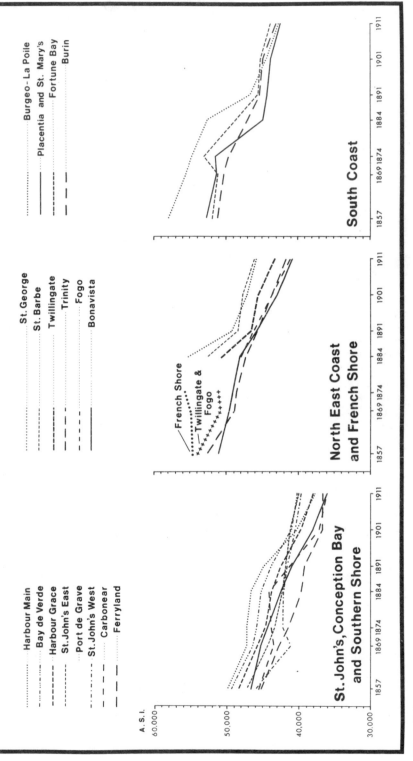

Figure 2-6

TABLE 2–3

Fertility Indices by Districts 1857–1911

District	1857	1869	1874	1884	1891	1901	1911
St. John's E.	89	87	80	79	67	68	65
St. John's W.	96	85	88	85	68	70	70
Harbour Main	124	98	110	124	94	79	85
Port de Grave	107	106	100	104	80	81	78
Harbour Grace	109	n.d.*	105	103	91	83	84
Carbonear	110	125	113	101	78	75	91
Bay de Verde	135	115	112	115	103	93	81
Trinity Bay	128	125	116	120	104	102	85
Bonavista Bay	120	121	119	119	97	88	83
Fogo	126	126	127	112	109	85	81
Twillingate				121	101	101	74
St. Barbe	142	140	148	141	128	118	102
St. George				124	128	127	102
Burgeo-LaPoile	147	169	141	130	98	102	95
Fortune Bay	132	140	125	114	94	103	89
Burin	124	127	122	113	95	100	89
Placentia and St. Mary's	130	141	106	100	99	101	84
Ferryland	102	110	122	103	81	78	90

*n.d. = no data.

Then each fertility value was expressed as a percentage of the overall mean (see Table 2–3). The data in Table 2–3 are then plotted in Figure 2–7 in the same groupings used to depict regional and temporal variations in age structures.

The fertility trends for southeast Newfoundland (including the St. John's Districts, the Southern Shore, and Conception Bay) demonstrate a fairly clear distinction between the values for St. John's and those for the other, more rural districts; almost without exception, the urban districts display lower fertility. In the other districts the fertility rates fluctuate widely in the earlier part of the period, but all decline steeply after 1884. Generally, this whole area is characterized by average or below average fertility for this period.

Fertility on the northeast coast was marginally higher than that in southeast Newfoundland over most of the period. The sharp decline in values noted after 1884 for the former region was less marked here, and generally did not become pronounced until after 1901. In all other respects, however, the fertility trends of the northeast coast districts were similar to those of the southeast districts, with the exception of the French Shore where, though the same trend occurred, fertility was always significantly higher. Similar fertility curves appeared for the South Coast districts. Here the decline in fertility came early, but from much higher levels. In general, levels of fertility were higher than in the other districts (except for the French Shore), with below-average fertility occurring during a relatively small part of the period.

This brief analysis of fertility trends, following that of age structures, prompts comment on the probable relationship between the two. It is clear from a comparison of both sets of graphs that levels of fertility and age structures in the various districts are positively associated, and that the association persists through time; that is, the younger the population, the higher the fertility and vice versa. The functional relation-

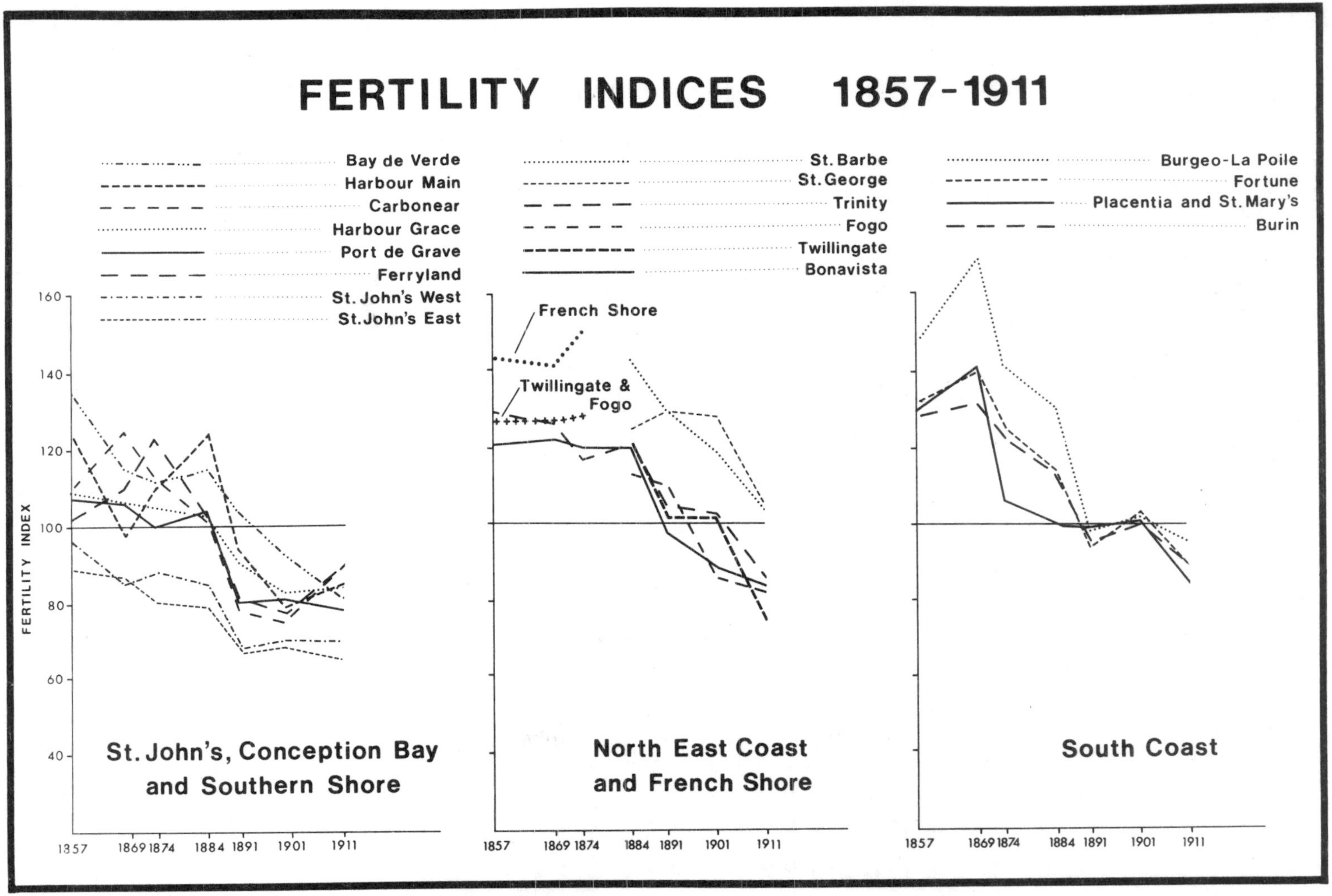
FERTILITY INDICES 1857-1911
Bay de Verde
Harbour Main
Carbonear
Harbour Grace
Port de Grave
Ferryland
St. John's West
St. John's East
St. Barbe
St. George
Trinity
Fogo
Twillingate
Bonavista
Burgeo-La Poile
Fortune
Placentia and St. Mary's
Burin
FERTILITY INDEX
160
140
120
100
80
60
40
French Shore
Twillingate & Fogo
St. John's, Conception Bay and Southern Shore
North East Coast and French Shore
South Coast
1357
1869
1874
1884
1891
1901
1911
1857

Figure 2–7

ship between the two, however, is likely to be more intricate. *Prima facie*, it might seem that young populations are more likely to express themselves in higher levels of fertility than are old populations, or to put it differently, age structure is the independent variable. This would certainly be true if the measure of fertility were a crude birth rate. In this case, however, the fertility indices were derived from a statistic, the child-woman ratio, which already reflected, to a degree, differences in age structure. Hence it would be reasonable to assume that in the Newfoundland case, fertility is more the independent variable, and that variations in fertility fluctuations explain the variations in age structure. This being the case, regional variations in the timing and level of fertility advance may be fundamental to prediction in many subsequent and dependent population dynamics.

Mortality. Mortality statistics for Newfoundland provide the most slender of all the demographic indices available, at least for the 19th century. Vital statistics for the colony were not available until 1901, and yet it is essential to get some idea of the mortality rates before this date to make reasoned inferences about early circulation patterns. The only source of comprehensive statistics for mortality in the early period is derived from responses to the census question put to the head of each household asking the "number of Deaths in the previous 12 months." Clearly, this question is imprecise – if only because it encourages the recording of innocent misinformation. Nevertheless, as it is the only source of evidence, the data were analysed and contrasted with the succeeding more formal and official rates to see what information could be gleaned (see Table 2–4).

Analysis of this table suggests that in most cases the sequences of values are not unreasonable: the range of values in any one district from year to year and the range from district to district are not improbable considering the size of the populations and the arbitrary nature of the cross-section. In general the statistics inferred from the cruder census data lose little by comparison with the official vital statistics. If these statistics can be taken at face value for the interpretation of broad trends, it will be seen that mortality tends to increase over the period as a whole. The year which appears most aberrant, indicating an unusually high death-rate compared with the general trend, is 1891. This may be partly due to error, but it can also be attributed to the steep decline in fertility in the most populous districts in the years leading up to 1891, and to the consequent aging of the population.

It remains to be explained why the mortality rate should increase steadily with the passage of time, as a diminution might be expected in the light of gradually improving conditions elsewhere. It may be suggested that this phenomenon is not an aberration, but a function of the age-structure of the population. The extremely low death rates of the earlier years are associated with the strikingly youthful populations (Vielrose's "primitive" populations) of that period. As the population aged, so the crude death rate grew.[7]

Natural Increase and Migration
Given the foregoing analyses of admittedly imperfect data on fertility and mortality, it is possible to compute statistics for intercensal natural increase. By comparing these latter figures with the more certain data for actual intercensal increase (see Table 2–2) it becomes possible to make calculations as to net migration and circulation (see Table 2–5). The calculations for the period 1891–1911 are nearly correct, as figures for

TABLE 2-4

Mortality by Districts 1857–1911 (0/00 population)

District	1857	1869*	1874	1884	1891	1901	1911
St. John's E.	9.3		14.5	17.1	23.7	22.7	22.1
St. John's W.	10.0		11.8	15.3	17.7		
Harbour Main	15.2		5.0	12.4	21.0	16.1	11.4
Port de Grave	8.6		14.0	17.6	18.0	20.8	19.3
Harbour Grace	11.5		8.8	11.1	18.6	18.8	16.0
Carbonear	11.2		8.7	9.2	14.6	19.7	17.8
Bay de Verde	11.0		13.1	20.2	20.6	18.6	18.4
Trinity Bay	9.6		16.5	13.6	30.4	15.8	17.1
Bonavista Bay	12.0		12.2	11.1	22.6	14.0	16.8
Fogo	8.6		7.1	18.2	20.3	12.0	13.0
Twillingate				8.7	29.7	13.3	11.1
St. Barbe	8.0		6.3	13.1	20.2	14.9	12.1
St. George				7.7	14.2	13.7	9.0
Burgeo-LaPoile	7.6		16.4	11.5	18.2	16.1	14.5
Fortune Bay	8.0		12.6	14.7	8.3	13.1	16.3
Burin	11.7		13.9	15.4	29.7	13.9	13.0
Placentia and St. Mary's	11.0		8.9	13.3	21.1	12.8	11.4
Ferryland	10.3		12.4	12.7	27.0	21.1	18.1
Newfoundland	10.3		11.5	13.6	22.0	17.0	16.0

*No data.

Sources: Newfoundland Census 1857, 1874, 1884, 1891—author's own calculations. Annual Reports of the Registrar of Births, Marriages, and Deaths. J.H.A., 1909:454; 1912:559–570.

natural increase are given in the appropriate censuses. Before 1891, no such data exist, and the figures in the table are reasoned estimates from the information available on fertility, mortality, and age structure.

When these data are incorporated into the maps depicting population change (Figs. 2–3, 2–4), a picture of the population movement which developed over the period becomes clear. It is apparent that as early as 1857–69 no district in southeast Newfoundland could maintain the whole of its own moderate growth. Even the vigorously expanding northeast coast, in Trinity and Bonavista Bays, was hard put to accommodate its own increase. Only the French Shore, and to a lesser extent, the south coast in Burgeo and Fortune attracted considerable numbers of in-migrants. This pattern, set early, remained fairly consistent, with few deviations. St. John's intermittently attracted as well as despatched net flows of migrants; the Conception Bay Districts continued to send out streams of surplus population, gradually to be joined by the surplus from the districts of the northeast coast as they too filled up their available space. The south coast districts, especially Ferryland, are a picture of unrelieved demographic gloom as most, if not all, of the natural increase is winnowed away.

It seems that the high rate of natural increase could not or would not be accommodated within the confines of the island colony. Since the second quarter of the 18th century the settlements on the Avalon Peninsula were sending out surplus population to the more thinly peopled outlying bays and peninsulas. But as these areas became full, a more drastic resort was to be had by permanent out-migration from the colony – sometimes to Canada, but more usually to the United States. If the statistics and

TABLE 2-5

Natural Increase, Actual Increase and Net Migration Newfoundland by Districts 1836–1911 (Average Annual %)

District	1836-45			1845-57			1857-69			1869-74			1874-84			1884-91			1891-01			1901-11		
	N.I.	A.I.	N.M.	N.I.	A.I.	N.M.	N.I.	A.I.	N.M.	N.I.	A.I.	N.M.	N.I.	A.I.	N.M.	N.I.	A.I.	N.M.	N.I.	A.I.	N.M.	N.I.	A.I.	N.M.
St. John's E.	*	3.7	*	*	1.7	*	1.5	-0.1	-1.6	1.5	0.7	-0.8	1.0	2.5	1.5	1.1	-0.9	-2.0	1.0	2.2	1.2	1.2	-0.2	-1.3
St. John's W.	*		*	*		*	1.5	-0.9	-2.4	1.5	1.9	0.4	1.0	2.5	1.5	1.0	-0.6	-1.6	1.1	1.4	0.3	1.1	1.1	0.0
Harbour Main							2.8	1.8	-1.0	2.0	1.9	-0.1	2.0	2.5	0.5	1.5	0.4	-1.1	1.4	0.3	-1.1	1.4	-0.1	-1.5
Port de Grave							2.0	1.3	-0.7	1.5	1.0	-0.5	1.0	1.0	0.0	1.0	-1.2	-2.2	1.0	-0.7	-1.7	0.9	-0.6	-1.5
Harbour Grace	*	2.3	*	*	1.6	*	2.5	2.2	-0.3	1.5	0.5	-1.0	1.5	1.3	-0.2	1.0	-0.8	-1.8	1.1	-0.9	-2.0	1.0	-0.6	-1.6
Carbonear							1.5	0.6	-0.9	1.0	-0.5	-1.5	1.0	1.3	0.3	1.0	-1.0	-2.0	0.9	-1.3	-2.2	0.9	0.2	-0.7
Bay de Verde							2.0	1.1	-0.9	1.5	1.1	-0.4	1.2	1.3	0.1	1.5	2.2	0.7	1.0	0.1	-0.9	1.0	0.4	-0.6
Trinity Bay	*	3.3	*	*	1.8	*	2.5	2.4	-0.1	2.5	2.7	0.2	2.2	2.1	-0.1	1.5	-0.1	-1.6	1.6	1.0	-0.6	1.3	0.5	-0.8
Bonavista Bay	*	4.4	*	*	1.9	*	2.5	2.6	0.1	2.5	2.5	0.0	2.2	2.7	0.5	1.5	1.2	-0.3	1.1	1.0	-0.1	1.4	1.1	-0.3
Fogo	*	4.2	*	*	3.7	*	2.5	2.9	0.4	2.5	3.2	0.7	2.8	3.4	0.6	1.7	0.1	-1.6	1.6	1.5	-0.1	1.2	0.9	-0.3
Twillingate										2.8	3.4	0.6				2.2	0.2	-2.0	1.7	1.3	-0.4	1.4	1.7	0.3
St. Barbe	*		*							3.5	12.1	8.6	3.0	3.8	0.8	2.3	3.0	0.7	2.3	2.2	-0.1	2.2	2.9	0.7
St. George							3.0	5.1	2.1	2.8	-0.1	-2.9	2.5	2.8	0.3	2.0	1.6	-0.4	3.1	3.7	0.6	2.6	3.0	0.4
Burgeo-LaPoile	*	7.0	*	*	3.2	*	3.0	3.7	0.7	3.0	2.1	-0.9	2.0	2.0	0.0	1.5	-0.2	-1.7	2.1	0.8	-1.3	2.1	1.1	-1.0
Fortune Bay	*	4.3	*	*	1.7	*	3.0	4.2	1.2	2.5	2.8	0.3	2.0	2.0	0.0	2.0	1.6	-0.4	2.1	1.4	-0.7	1.8	1.4	-0.4
Burin							2.5	1.8	-0.7				1.3	1.1	-0.2	2.0	0.9	-1.1	2.1	1.5	-0.6	1.6	1.2	-0.4
Placentia and St. Mary's	*	4.2	*	*	2.4	*	2.0	0.5	-1.5	2.4	2.4	0.0	1.5	2.0	0.5	1.5	1.2	-0.3	1.8	2.4	0.6	1.4	0.1	-1.3
Ferryland	*	-1.2	*	*	1.4	*	1.5	1.2	-0.3	1.5	1.4	-0.1	1.0	0.1	-0.9	0.5	-1.4	-1.9	0.6	-0.3	-0.9	1.1	0.2	-0.9

*no data

contemporary accounts are to be believed, this long slow trickle of emigrants became a flood after 1884. But many years before this flood took place, there developed a less painful strategy as a response to the problems of overpopulation: that of seasonal migration associated with the prosecution of the Labrador fishery.

The Labrador Migrations
In the face of increasing pressure on available resources, first felt in the old-established, spatially-restricted districts of the Avalon Peninsula, there developed a pattern of seasonal migration in which fishermen, with their families, would spend the summer fishing on the Labrador coast. This fishery was functionally divided into two parts: the 'floater' fishery and the 'stationer' fishery. In the former, schooners carrying local crews sailed each June or early July from Conception Bay and the northeast coast; their fishing was conducted from their 'floating' base, the schooner. The stationers were fishermen who went up to the Labrador and prosecuted the fishery from shore 'stations.'

The floater fishery has been analysed by Black (1960:267–95), who noted that the greatest activity in this sector was experienced from about 1875 to 1910. Early in the 20th century as many as 1400 vessels left Newfoundland each summer. In 1907, for example, "1192 vessels were engaged in fishing, their total crews numbering 8344 persons." In contrast, the stationer fishery was less closely analysed, possibly because records of the earlier period did not distinguish between stationer and floater. However, to gain some idea of the significance of the Labrador fishery as a whole in the maintenance of the population of Newfoundland, the available census data have been collated and are presented in Table 2–6 and Figure 2–8.

From the data presented we get an uncomplicated but, nonetheless, striking picture. The overall interest in the Labrador fishery, expressed both in real numbers and as a proportion of the population, declined over the period. Although the actual numbers of people going to the Labrador declined just a little, the proportion of a growing population represented by these numbers declined steeply. The Conception Bay districts, and to a lesser degree the northeast coast, were the heart of the Labrador venture: in 1884, for example, 44 percent of the total population of the district of Carbonear summered on the Labrador. This percentage was made up of 26.6 percent males and 17.4 percent women and children. If the male adult labour force comprised roughly one-third of the population, it can be seen that about 70–80 percent of the working males were migrant labourers. Admittedly this example was an exception, but in degree rather than in kind, for other Conception Bay districts exhibited similar concentrations of Labrador migrants.

This pattern persisted, though with more moderate levels of seasonal migration, until 1911 after which there was a marked decline. But even in 1935 (and later) the tradition continued and we see 5 percent or 7 percent of the population of certain districts in Conception Bay repeating their annual migration. If there was a shift that was both secular and spatial in this phenomenon, it was that the decline in migration from Conception Bay was not so emphatically repeated on the northeast coast; in essence, the people of Conception Bay found the Labrador migrations to be less and less of a salvation, and as their stake in the seasonal fishery dwindled, their only option was to leave the colony. This is reflected in the migration statistics presented previously. The northeast coast maintained its modest level of association with the Labrador fishery for a longer period, and its out-migration was less severe, though it cannot be asserted from this that these factors are causally associated.

TABLE 2-6

Population Engaged in the Labrador Fishery by Districts 1884–1911 (% of District Population)

District	1884				1891				1901				1911			
	Total Population	% Men	% Women and Children	Total	Total Population	% Men	% Women and Children	Total	Total Population	% Men	% Women and Children	Total	Total Population	% Men	% Women and Children	Total
St. John's E.	22,193	1.4	0.5	1.9	20,776	0.2	—	0.2	21,512	0.3	0.1	0.4	25,135	—	—	—
St. John's W.	15,962	6.7	1.8	8.5	15,251	—	—	—	18,483	0.1	—	—	20,550	—	—	—
Harbour Main	8,935	4.2	1.4	5.6	9,189	7.0	1.2	8.2	9,500	7.1	1.2	8.3	9,471	3.1	0.6	3.7
Port de Grave	8,698	15.7	10.8	26.5	7,896	19.0	7.2	26.2	7,445	23.4	8.5	31.9	6,986	13.6	4.7	18.3
Harbour Grace	14,727	15.9	9.9	25.8	13,881	14.3	7.3	21.5	12,671	14.5	4.3	18.8	11,925	9.8	2.4	12.2
Carbonear	6,206	26.6	17.4	44.0	5,765	13.1	7.0	20.1	5,023	13.1	6.9	20.0	5,114	14.9	6.0	20.9
Bay de Verde	8,403	8.2	4.7	12.9	9,708	9.7	3.8	13.5	9,827	4.9	1.4	6.3	10,213	3.1	1.0	4.1
Trinity Bay	19,005	7.1	1.5	8.6	18,872	6.0	0.5	6.5	20,695	8.5	0.4	8.9	21,788	9.3	0.7	10.0
Bonavista Bay	16,486	8.4	1.5	9.9	17,849	10.2	1.3	11.5	20,557	9.2	1.0	10.2	22,984	9.4	0.4	9.8
Fogo	6,264	0.3	0.1	0.4	6,700	5.7	0.7	6.4	7,570	4.9	0.1	5.0	8,257	4.4	0.1	4.5
Twillingate	14,058	10.9	0.6	11.5	16,780	6.7	0.3	7.0	19,453	5.1	0.3	5.4	22,705	3.4	0.1	3.5
St. Barbe	6,500	1.5	0.1	1.6	6,690	0.1	—	0.1	8,134	0.3	—	0.3	10,481	1.0	0.2	1.2
St. George	5,473	0.4	0.4	0.8	6,632	0.7	0.2	0.9	9,100	0.9	0.3	1.2	11,861	0.5	—	0.5
Burgeo-LaPoile	6,544	0.4	—	0.4	6,471	0.4	—	0.4	7,011	0.4	—	0.4	7,793	0.1	—	0.1
Fortune Bay	6,917	4.1	—	4.1	7,671	0.1	—	0.1	8,762	0.7	—	0.7	9,989	0.7	—	0.7
Burin	8,502	—	—	—	9,059	—	—	—	10,402	—	—	—	11,616	0.5	—	0.5
Placentia and St. Mary's	11,789	0.2	—	0.2	12,801	—	—	—	15,194	—	—	—	16,099	—	—	—
Ferryland	6,472	—	—	—	5,853	—	—	—	5,697	—	—	—	5,793	—	—	—
Newfoundland	193,124	6.5	2.6	9.1	197,934	5.3	1.4	6.7	217,037	4.9	1.0	5.9	238,670	3.8	0.6	4.4

% men = number of men going to Labrador as % of whole district population.
% women and children = number of women and children going to Labrador as % of whole district population.

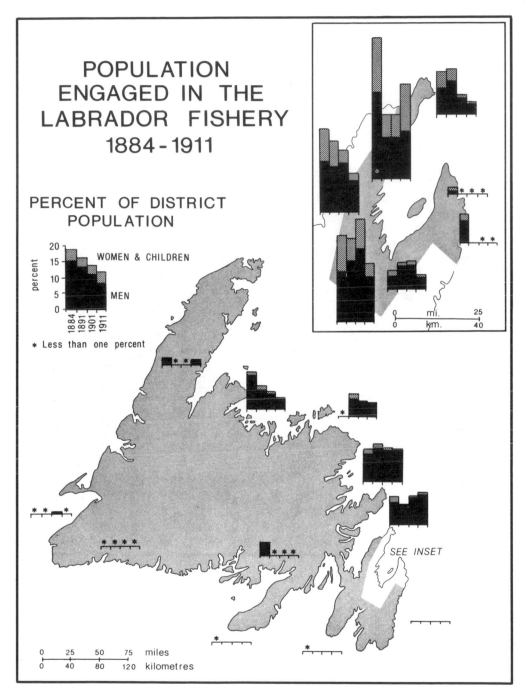

Figure 2–8

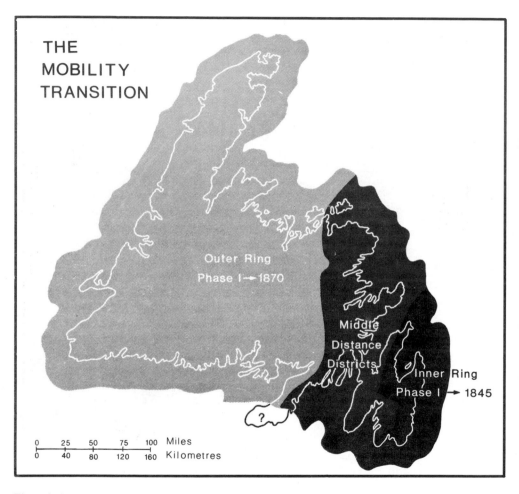

Figure 2–9

Nevertheless, the Labrador migrations played a crucial role in the emerging spatial dynamics of Newfoundland's population. Although the economic *raison d'être* of the Labrador fishery diminished, it remained an attractive outlet, in both social and economic terms, to many otherwise economically marginal family units, and the momentum developed in former, more prosperous times has continued to the present.

Summary and Conclusions

It is evident from the foregoing data on population dynamics that the colonization and settlement of Newfoundland was not a random or chance process, but may be interpreted along the lines of the schema outlined in Zelinsky's hypothesis of mobility transition. All the population parameters examined exhibited orders of regularity in the various districts which were consistent through space and time (see Fig. 2–9). The older-established districts, focused on the north and east of the Avalon (the Conception Bay districts and Ferryland), were the first to experience the Phase I condition of a "spatially stable peasant society" together with a "rapid massive build-up in rural numbers." It might be added, parenthetically, that this "build-up" was, to a degree, a function of their limited area or their spatially restricted nature. For most of this region, Phase I was over by 1845, and Phase II with its "great shaking loose of migrants from the countryside" had begun. Beyond the ring of these 'inner districts' was a group of 'middle distance districts' (Trinity, Bonavista, Placentia and St. Mary's, and perhaps Burin) in which Phase I was more protracted and in which Phase II did not commence until the 1850s. Finally, there occurred a ring of 'outer districts' (Fogo, Twillingate, St. Barbe, St. George, Burgeo-LaPoile, Fortune Bay) in which the "rapid massive build-up" persisted until the 1870s and in some cases, even later.

Three generalizations may be adduced from this analysis. Firstly, it can be seen that the propensity to migrate did radiate outward from the more developed socio-economic zones into the "less advanced, less accessible regions," as Zelinsky hypothesizes. Secondly, it is apparent that few, if any districts had passed completely through Phase II by the end of the period. If the Labrador fishery is accepted as an element of mobility taking the place of migration in the absolute sense, it will be seen that even by 1911, the "shaking loose" was still widespread; but compared to previous periods, it was slackening. Thirdly, the role of St. John's, the "national metropolis," in the suggested mobility transition, is more problematic. There is, however, some indication that St. John's functioned as the focus for some "demographic innovations" (see Figure 2–7 on fertility trends), and that the metropolis was a leader in the trend towards increased mobility instead of functioning simply as the urban terminus in an orthodox rural-urban migration system.

In order that this apparent regularity could be further examined, the data for natural increase and net migration were plotted according to the procedures followed by Naukkarinen. The patterns realized (Fig. 2–10) deviated substantially from the theoretical norm suggested. Although there is a general shift in accordance with the theoretical line in Figure 2–1 (most districts moving from upper right positions to lower left locations on the graph – see Fig. 2–10.a), the paths taken between the points of beginning and ending are anything but direct (Fig. 2–10.b). Perhaps we should not make too much of this finding, for the data utilized are rather general for such precise plotting. Furthermore, the period for which these data are available (post 1857), omits from consideration the incomplete data of the earlier settlement phases.

But one important generalization is clear from Figure 2–10 and Table 2–5: in few

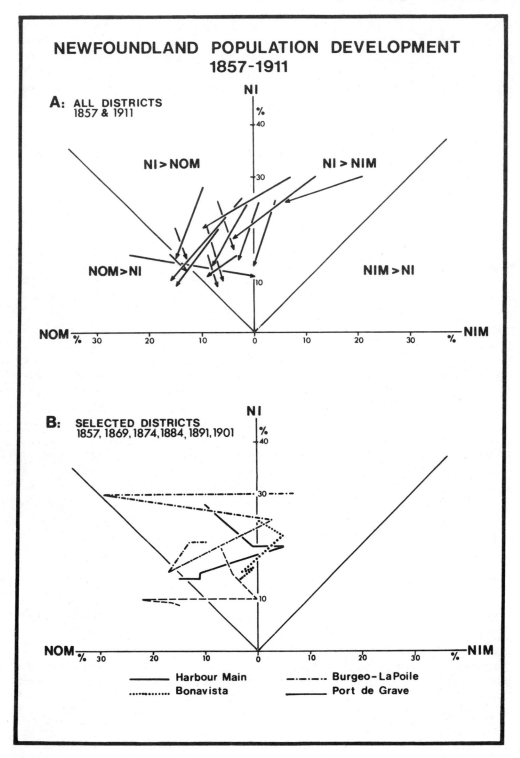

NEWFOUNDLAND POPULATION DEVELOPMENT
1857-1911

A: ALL DISTRICTS
1857 & 1911

NI
%
40

NI > NOM

NI > NIM

30

NOM > NI

NIM > NI

10

NOM % 30   20   10   0   10   20   30   % NIM

B: SELECTED DISTRICTS
1857, 1869, 1874, 1884, 1891, 1901

NI
%
40

30

10

NOM % 30   20   10   0   10   20   30   % NIM

Harbour Main   ____.____ Burgeo-LaPoile
Bonavista   Port de Grave

Figure 2–10

periods did in-migration exceed natural increase. From 1845–74 only Fogo-Twillingate (and perhaps Burgeo-LaPoile), and the French Shore (1857–74) were dominated by in-migration. On the contrary, after 1845 the normal source of colonization and settlement in any district appears *prima facie* to have been derived from the natural increase of those already in the district. It would perhaps be surprising if these data supported, without qualification, the abstract but simple model postulated by Naukkarinen, for this would suppose that all districts were characterized throughout the whole period by predominantly fringe or frontier characteristics. That this was far from the case is seen in the partial application of Zelinsky's hypothesis. Clearly, over such a wide area, and through such a lengthy period as treated here, there were considerable variations in population dynamics and evolving settlement structures. The complexity of population movement attendant on such a varied map is poorly depicted by a model pertaining to a simpler situation.[8]

It has been suggested recently that the conventional analysis of the settlement fringe, in which frontier population is markedly different in structure from that of longer established areas, has been overemphasized (Eblen, 1965:399–413). Thus, "by focusing on the core areas of expansion, it could be demonstrated that the population characteristics of the United States' frontiers varied far less from the national norms of the times than has been generally realized" (*op. cit.*:399). It would, however, be difficult to make a similar interpretation of the Newfoundland data. Not only do the statistics for Newfoundland demonstrate marked variations as between frontier and settled districts, but, perhaps more interesting, these differences tend to persist over at least half a century, and in some cases longer. This may be a further demonstration of the difficulties inherent in the use of the American frontier as the norm (Thistlethwaite, 1960:32–59).

NOTES

1   A contemporary work on a similar topic, though more narrowly conceived, is to be found in Roseman (1971:589–98).
2   A growth rate of 2 percent will double a population in 35 years.
3   Census of Newfoundland, 1891. Newfoundland, Department of Colonial Secretary, St. John's. Preface.
4   The discontinuity in population growth may be due to census error, either to over-enumeration (1884) or under-enumeration (1891), or both. Although this is not impossible, it is improbable that such a large discrepancy would be accounted for solely by errors which would have required the omission of some 10–15 percent of the 1891 population. In light of the care devoted to censuses of this period (see Prefaces for Censuses of 1891, 1901, 1911), and in view of the admitted cause of the decline (emigration), an error of this magnitude is improbable.
5   See Noel (1971:22); also *J.H.A.* (1872:645) "... Carbonear ... The Roman Catholics emigrate in large numbers to the States from this port."
6   The data used to describe regional growth and decline of population can be taken as reasonably accurate at the level of generalization here employed. The indices now being developed, however, being inferential, are less 'firm' and therefore many of the conclusions drawn must be broad enough to allow for error. They are, however, considerably more precise than any previously attempted.
7   This was probably a more complex function. The chief cause of death for a long period was infantile mortality. In 1912, a Commission on Public Health stated that "Infantile mortality again forms the largest single item in the mortality tables." As late as 1921, 33.7 percent of all deaths were of children 0–4 years of age. This might suggest that increased fertility would have the effect of raising mortality. But in fact an increase in fertility would result in a greater *margin* of live births, assuming that infantile mortality remained constant as it appears to have done. Thus the secular increase in mortality is consistent with the phenomenon of an aging population. In the early period much of the mortality would be concentrated in the earlier

years of life: with the aging of the population this would be progressively supplemented by higher death rates in the more populous older age categories. Thus, mortality would increase through time. See *J.H.A.* (1912:588, 1922:180–181).
8   More appropriate perhaps would be the situation suggested by Conzen (1974:339–61) who describes and analyses from Iowan data the welter of superimposed migratory patterns experienced in the frontier situation.

REFERENCES: SECONDARY SOURCES

BLACK, W. A.
  1960 "The Labrador Floater Cod Fishery." *Annals, Association of American Geographers*, 50(3):267–93.
CONZEN, M. P.
  1974 "Local Migration Systems in Nineteenth-Century Iowa." *Geographical Review*, 64(3):339–61.
COULSON, M. R. C.
  1968 "The Distribution of Population Age Structure in Kansas City." *Annals, Association of American Geographers*, 58(1):155–76.
EBLEN, J. E.
  1965 "An Analysis of Nineteenth Century Frontier Populations." *Demography*, 2:399–413.
HATTON, J. and M. HARVEY
  1883 *Newfoundland: Its History, its Present Condition, and its Prospects in the Future*. Boston, Doyle and Whittle.
KIRK, D.
  1946 *Europe's Population in the Interwar Years*. New York, Gordon and Breach.
NAUKKARINEN, A.
  1969 "Population Development in Northern Finland 1960–65." *Nordia*, 8:1–149.
NOEL, S.
  1971 *Politics in Newfoundland*. Toronto, University of Toronto Press.
PROWSE, D. W.
  1895 *A History of Newfoundland from the English Colonial and Foreign Records*. London, Eyre and Spottiswoode.
ROSEMAN, C. C.
  1971 "Migration as a Spatial and Temporal Process." *Annals, Association of American Geographers*, 61(3):589–98.
THISTLETHWAITE, F.
  1960 "Migration from Europe Overseas in the Nineteenth and Twentieth Centuries." *Rapports* V:32–59. Histoire Contemporaire Comité Internationale des Sciences Historique. Stockholm.
VIELROSE, E.
  1965 *Elements of the Natural Movement of Population*. Oxford, Pergamon.
WEBB, J. W.
  1963 "Natural and Migrational Components of Population Change in England and Wales 1921–31." *Economic Geography*, 39:130–47.
ZELINSKY, W.
  1971 "The Hypothesis of the Mobility Transition." *Geographical Review*, 61:219–49.

The Development of Folk Architecture in Trinity Bay, Newfoundland

3

David B. Mills

Introduction

The study of folk architecture in Newfoundland and in Canada is in its infancy compared to that in Europe, and even the United States, where cultural geographers, folklorists, and architectural historians have laboured for decades in this field. Their research has focused on the architectural traditions of rural areas where folk practices have been least affected by the more dominant, popular, urban culture. In rural societies ideas and practices are often passed on, little changed, from generation to generation.

The historic isolation of Newfoundland in North America, and its overwhelmingly rural nature, have allowed it to remain until recently a splendid laboratory for the study of folk architecture and, indeed, many aspects of folk culture. Hundreds of small Newfoundland outport communities remain basically rural in character and can still be described as outposts of English and Irish folk culture on the edge of North America. Customs, superstitions, songs, dialects, and a wide array of rural crafts, many no longer extant in their original homelands, are still part of the living traditions of the island. But as yet there are few analyses of the depth and longevity of these traditions, of which one of the most interesting manifestations is folk architecture. This paper will concentrate on the development of folk architecture in Trinity Bay, eastern Newfoundland, from the period of initial settlement in the 17th century to the 20th century.

The use of the term "folk," as defined by cultural geographers, presents particular problems when dealing with housing practices in 18th and early 19th century New-foundland. It presupposes the existence of a relatively homogeneous community, having a common cultural background and adhering to established traditions. "Folk" implies continuity, the passing on from generation to generation of accepted forms and practices which serve to characterize the group. Much of the American literature on folk architecture focuses, for example, on dwellings built by culturally distinctive groups: the Pennsylvanian Germans, the Dutch of the Hudson Valley, or the Swedes of the Delaware. There is a basic assumption that these groups were part of a homogeneous Old World culture which they transferred to the New World (Zelinsky, 1953; Wright, 1958; Jordan, 1964; Kniffen, 1965; Glassie, 1968a, 1968b; Evans, 1969; Wacker and Trindell, 1969; Wilson, 1970; Wilhelm, 1971). The sweeping scale of many of these studies and especially the lack of detailed historical data on exact Old World locations and the conditions from which many of these settlers emigrated often result in simplistic and generalized statements on the origins, transfer, and adaptation of architectural traditions in the New World.

It appears that the early English immigrants to Trinity Bay, although coming from an extremely restricted (compared with other Atlantic migrations) source area in the southwest of England, were far from culturally homogeneous. The majority arrived from Devon and Dorset between c. 1650 and 1850 (see Handcock, this vol.). Trinity also attracted a large number of Irish migratory labourers in the mid-18th century, but few settled permanently in the area. Both counties were predominantly agricultural, with land being held in large estates and farmed by tenants who relied on agricultural labourers. After 1750, the conditions of these labourers deteriorated steadily. In addition, a new farming technology and a general population increase created a surplus of farm labourers (Hoskins, 1954:63–6). The traditional practice of apprenticing the children of labour-class families to a farmer or village tradesman was continued until the 19th century, but the local economy was unable to absorb the increase in labourers and young tradesmen. Many had little choice but to seek employment in the industrial midlands or to emigrate (Kerr, 1963:159–77). Many of these emigrants arrived as transient labourers. They were young, single, adult males often indentured for two summers and a winter to work for one of the West Country merchant firms or for a local planter. Many returned home several times before settling permanently in Trinity Bay.

The West Country merchant firms recruited these young men for the Newfoundland fishery, even though they had little or no experience as fishermen. Their early apprenticeship may have been served with a local carpenter, cooper, blacksmith, butcher, tailor, textile worker, or with other tradesmen. Many had little experience building houses or other structures in their homeland; apprentices and farm labourers were either accommodated in the homes or outbuildings of their employers, or the latter built small cottages for them (Barley, 1961; Brunskill, 1970; Kerr, 1964). Without land or capital, the poor were often unable to provide housing for themselves. Some labourers did build cottages on small allotments, and some squatted on the commons; but they were a minority.

In contrast to the homeland, conditions in Trinity Bay were relatively homogeneous. Carpenters and coopers might have preserved their crafts, but the majority of immigrants were employed in the summer fishery and in winter lumbering work and boat-building. As in the homeland housing was often initially provided by the merchant or local planters. After two or more years in Trinity Bay, these recruits were familiarized with local architectural traditions and after making a commitment to settle permanently as self-employed fishermen, readily accepted the folk process of building established by earlier settlers.

The population of Trinity Bay grew slowly during the 17th and 18th centuries. In 1772 the permanent population was just over 1,500 people and 600 of these lived in or near Trinity Harbour (Head, 1971:264). The remaining immigrants chose such sites as Catalina, Old Bonaventure, Ireland's Eye, Old Perlican, Hant's Harbour, New Perlican, and Hearts Content because of their proximity to the productive fishing grounds at the mouth of the Bay (Fig. 3–1). Trinity Bay received a major influx of Englishmen between 1800 and 1830. The permanent population of the Bay jumped by more than 130 percent between 1804 and 1815 (Ryan, 1971:241). By then virtually all of the contemporary hamlets in the outer bay area were established and a seasonal cycle of work, focusing on a summer cod fishery, subsistence agriculture, and a winter logging operation was followed.

From the outset, men from all parts of the Bay were employed in the woods. Some received their orders directly from West Country mercantile firms at Trinity or indirectly through their agents in smaller communities such as Hant's Harbour or New Perlican; others operated independently, moving to various parts of the Bay in the late fall to cut firewood and to saw logs which would later be used for boat building, house construction or general maintenance of their own property, bartering only their surplus to the commercial firms. Before they came to Trinity Bay, many of the West

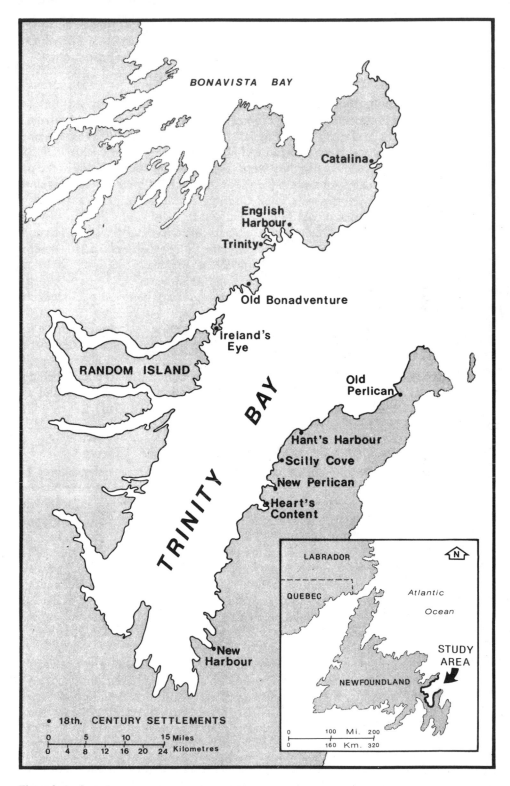

Figure 3-1 *Location.*

Countrymen had little experience working with wood, but local timber became the dominant – indeed virtually exclusive – medium of house construction from the very inception of settlement and winter logging often served as a useful introduction.

The Study Area

In contrast to the bulk of research on folk architecture conducted by cultural geographers, this study is conceived on a micro-scale. Intensive field work was carried out in four communities in Trinity Bay: English Harbour and Old Bonaventure on the north side of the Bay and New Perlican and Hant's Harbour on the south side (Fig. 3–1). They were selected because they were typical fishing communities in the older nuclear area of settlement and were suitable for the study of house styles developing over more than two centuries in a West Country culture area. The availability of numerous extant examples of old houses and a rich local oral tradition were also important in their selection. The principal objectives of the study were: (i) to collect data on as many traditional houses as possible in the four settlements, (ii) to establish a typology and delineate stages in the evolution of house forms in this area, (iii) to study the effect of architectural innovation on existing folk structures, (iv) to establish the chronological range for each house type and analyse architectural persistence and change.

Archival references relating to buildings or construction techniques for the early period of settlement are sparse. Oral tradition supplied some reliable data but folk memory of an object as complex as a house rarely extends past four generations. It is difficult to obtain any detailed descriptions of houses built before the mid-nineteenth century. Local timber was the predominant construction material used, and since wooden structures have a relatively short life span[2] (Faris, 1972:50–1), it is rare to find houses over one hundred years old still standing. The availability of timber and the relatively modest size of most outport houses often made replacement of an old house a more attractive alternative than extensive renovation.

Table 3–1 shows the number of houses in each of the four communities from 1836–1935.[3] There is no indication of how many houses in the table are replacements for houses previously recorded. Nor do the census data provide any information on the size or style of individual buildings. Since data-collecting depended on the memory and availability of informants, coverage of the four communities is uneven. In English Harbour there were several sources of detailed information for the period prior to 1880, but comparable information from New Perlican was unavailable. It was also difficult to establish accurate dates for the construction of many houses. Informants were uncertain of dates before 1900 and the frequent appearance of houses constructed in decennial of quiquennial years after 1860 indicates a rounding-off in the dating of individual houses. Each date was carefully checked, however, and may be considered accurate to a tolerance of plus or minus two years.

Information provided by the older inhabitants in the four communities was recorded on both existing structures and extinct structures still remembered. Information was collected on the basic floor plan, window and door locations, the pitch of the roof, chimney location, appendages, renovations, and construction techniques. Ultimately, all elements of the house must be recorded, but those which prove to be the most persistent or least changing are considered the most important by cultural geographers in establishing a typology. In Trinity Bay, the basic floor plan was the most persistent element in the architectural tradition; yet it changed as the initial house developed from a two-room, one-storey structure into a seven or eight room, two-storey struc-

TABLE 3-1

Number of Houses 1836–1935

Settlement	1836	1845	1857	1869	1874	1884	1891	1901	1911	1921	1935
Hant's Harbour	49	75	99	120	112	131	124	142	141	143	142
New Perlican	36	49	71	74	89	96	108	108	133	153	141
Old Bonaventure	29	30	20	21	20	22	28	27	35	33	29
English Harbour	21	38	45	53	59	74	76	77	84	79	72

ture. Other elements such as height and pitch of roof, floor space, window placement, chimney type, and location were less stable but were, nevertheless, important criteria in the classification.

Complete information was collected for 258 houses. Analysis of this information suggests that it is possible to establish an evolutionary sequence of styles involving four distinct stages, the first preceded by a temporary dwelling called a *tilt*. Stage one, or the first-generation house, was a small one-storey cottage with a loft, and it persisted as the basic house type probably throughout the period 1650–1850. The last half of the 19th century was characterized by rapid change. The Trinity Bay house passed through three stages: a one-and-a-half storey saltbox, a full two-storey house with peaked roof and a flat rear extension, and finally a full two-storey house with a low-pitched roof, the last true folk house to be constructed in the area. The following section treats each stage in turn.

The Tilt

All groups attempting to establish themselves in a frontier environment resort to some type of temporary shelter. In Trinity Bay such structures were called tilts (Pl. 3–1). They were constructed, initially, by transient West Country fishermen to provide shelter during the summer fishing season. The first permanent settlers also lived in tilts while sufficient timber could be cut and prepared for a more permanent home. Tilts varied somewhat in size and construction, but had some common characteristics. They were small, rectangular structures, perhaps no more than 10' × 14', covered with a low-pitched gable-end roof. Walls were constructed of vertically placed round sticks abutting each other. The interstices between the logs were stuffed or "chintzed" with moss, old rope, or other material. The vertical sticks forming the walls usually rested directly on the ground, but ground sills were occasionally used. Tilts usually contained only one room and access was by a centrally placed front door, or by a door in the shorter gable end. Windows, if present, were small and unglazed. Heat was provided by an open fire on a stone hearth located at the end of the house. The smoke escaped through a hole in the roof. In some tilts crude wooden chimneys were constructed but this practice was not widespread in Trinity Bay. The roof was formed of logs or rough boards resting on a ridge pole and then covered with birch bark, old sail cloth, or any other suitable material. Tree branches were sometimes placed on the roof to encourage an accumulation of snow which acted as insulation against wind and frost. Workmanship varied. Some tilts were extremely crude, without wooden floor or windows; others were more carefully constructed. Similar structures were used extensively by settlers during the winter months when they moved from their permanent homes to hunt, trap, cut timber, or build boats (see Anspach, 1819:468; Wix, 1836:23; Jukes, 1842).

Tilts were constructed in Newfoundland from the early 17th century on. The

Plate 3–1 *The Tilt*

rectangular floor plan, single room, and gable-end hearth were similar to crude cottages built in the west of England from at least medieval times to the 18th century by squatters and landless labourers in both Devon and Dorset (Kerr, 1964; Alcock, 1969). In Trinity Bay vertical logs replaced turf or cob as the exclusive building material. Whatever the formal parallels, it is difficult to establish that the West Country huts are linked conceptually to the Newfoundland tilt. Both Old and New World structures were a product of pioneer expediency, and the similarity of such a basic form was probably more fortuitous than designed. As previously noted, many of the settlers had little experience of building in the homeland.

Tilts persisted in Trinity Bay because they provided adequate temporary shelter to migratory fishermen and permanent settlers when they moved from their homes for extended periods of time. They could be built quickly of local material, and it was easy to abandon them when no longer needed. The tilt was the equivalent of a modern-day tent, useful for temporary shelter, but hardly adequate for a permanent home.

The First-Generation House

By 1800 there were some 1500 people in Trinity Bay and at least 250 houses. For more than a century these settlers had been solving the problems of house construction in a novel environment: the climate, available building materials, as well as changes in daily work and living patterns necessitated adapting English housing models to meet these new conditions. The result was the first-generation Trinity Bay house which set the style for the post-1800 wave of immigrants.

Field research has shown that the first-generation house was a small, single-storey, rectangular structure with a peaked roof and loft (Pl. 3–2). Although numerous examples of this house type were recorded from oral descriptions in all four communities under study, they were omitted from the data set because neither the date of construction nor accurate measurements were available. The first-generation house was modest in size. Calculations based on 65 examples, dating from 1835 to 1910, reveal that the average floor area was 21'8" wide and of 20'3" deep, totalling only 672 square feet.[4] The front of the house had two or three windows and sometimes a centrally placed door. In the older houses three windows were more common. The rear door, opening into the *linhay*, was the most frequently used. The linhay, an appendage which extended the full length of the rear of the house, provided extra storage space and acted as an air lock to prevent cold air from entering the kitchen when the exterior door was opened. It was usually subdivided into two compartments: a porch with a door leading to the outside and a pantry with an entrance to the kitchen (Fig. 3–2).

The floor space was divided into two rooms, usually a kitchen and a bedroom, although the second room was occasionally reserved as a parlour. Children slept in the loft which was reached by a wooden ladder or by a small enclosed corner stairway leading from the kitchen. The floor joists of the loft were usually placed three to four feet below the wall plate, allowing considerably more head-room in the loft. The loft area was sometimes partitioned by a light curtain wall and one or two gable windows let in daylight.

No definite pattern of chimney location could be established. Open fireplaces, although present in all of the earlier houses, were replaced by iron stoves after c. 1865 – the first stove recorded at English Harbour was in 1863 – and chimneys were often replaced by stove pipes. Only four open fireplaces were recorded from oral sources.

Plate 3–2a   *First Generation House*

Plate 3–2b   *First Generation House*

DEVELOPMENT OF HOUSE STYLES
1835-1960

FIRST GENERATION: One storey with loft and linhay.
1835-1910

SECOND GENERATION: One and a half storey.
1865-1920

  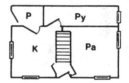

THIRD GENERATION: Two storey, full upstairs.
1880-1935

  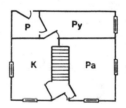

FOURTH GENERATION: Two storey with central hall and flat roof.
1870-1960

 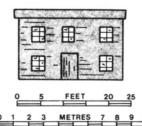 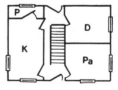

P — Porch
Py — Pantry
Pa — Parlour

0   5   FEET   20   25

0 1 2 3   METRES 7 8 9 10

B — Bedroom
K — Kitchen
D — Dining room

Figure 3–2

They were located at the gable end of the house inside the exterior wall. Three were of local stone and one was built of imported brick. They appear to have been considerably smaller than the large fireplaces of Irish immigrants in the southern Avalon (cf. Mannion, 1974:149–51).

The first-generation house was constructed of local spruce or fir boards usually pit-sawn, but in some cases prepared with an adze; it was either of "studded" or framed construction. Technically, studding is a form of frame construction, for "studding" refers primarily to the method of filling in the wall space between the vertical studs of a frame structure (Pl. 3–3). This construction technique, which also typified the tilt, is not unique to Newfoundland. Kniffen and Glassie state that "Building with closely set vertical members is so widespread in America and so varied in detail, as to suggest that any common origin must be in a remote European concept" (1966:43). In England also, this construction was once probably common. One observes that the older the wooden structure, the more closely the vertical studs were spaced; for example, in the 11th century example of the Greensted Church, Essex, the studs form a solid vertical wall of wood (Innocent, 1916:109–15). By the 16th century this technique was no longer used for external walls, but was retained until at least the 18th century for internal room partitions. Boards were set up vertically on a sill, each tongued and grooved to fit into its neighbour; this technique was called clapboarding (Wood, 1965:146). In North America clapboard refers to boards which are horizontally set, the English equivalent being weatherboard. Vertically placed planks were ubiquitous in Trinity Bay until the late 19th century for internal wall construction. Boards were not tongued and grooved, however, but merely grooved on both sides and joined by a lath or spline running the full length of the board. The external walls of studded houses were identical in form to these internal walls, the only difference being the larger scantling of the exterior studs. It is possible that studding represents the reintroduction of this Old World construction of the interior partition to the construction of external walls in the New World where wood was abundant.

Studding was the first technique of wall construction in Trinity Bay. Tilts were universally studded as were the majority of the first-generation houses. The practice persisted on the north side of the Bay into the 20th century but was not used for house construction, after c. 1870, on the south side of the Bay. For example, of the sixty-five first-generation houses recorded, forty-five were of studded construction, the remainder framed. All of these studded houses were recorded either in English Harbour or Old Bonaventure on the north side of the Bay. Usually every fourth stud was dovetailed or tenoned into the sill to form the frame and give the wall stability. The remaining studs were either dowelled into the sill or allowed to rest on top, forming, in effect, a wooden panel between the mortised studs. The studs varied in both width and length, depending on the timber used, but were usually $1^1/_2$ to $2^1/_2$ inches in thickness. The interstices of the studded wall were chintzed with moss, old rope, or wood shavings. Studded houses were usually clapboarded or shingled on the outside and sheathed on the inside with inch board. The houses were constructed of local timber; only the glass, bricks, and hardware were imported from Britain via the West Country merchants at Trinity.

In the original house there was a distinct break between the main roof and the roof of the linhay, but four examples were recorded with continuous rear rafters. The linhay, as an appendage, disappeared and the porch area became an integral part of the house, adding space on both the lower and upper floors. This roof line was a logical structural

Plate 3–3 *Studded Construction*

simplification of the first-generation house and provides a clear link between it and the development of the second-generation "saltbox" style. A second variation involved replacing the peaked roof with a hipped roof, a roof style found only in English Harbour where twelve examples were recorded. Other examples of this roof were recorded outside the study area in Melrose and Catalina. It was known in English Harbour as a "cottage" roof, and although the earliest example recorded was constructed in 1864, oral tradition indicates they were common in the community from c. 1830 on. The cottage-roof house differed visually from the peaked-roof house, although the floor plan and general dimensions were identical. The cottage-roof house in English Harbour subsequently passed through a similar series of morphological changes ending in a two-storey house with a low-pitched pyramid roof. It is doubtful that the cottage-roof style originated locally; similar cottage-roof houses exist in the environs of Dartmouth, Devon (personal observation, 1973), and they were common in Conception Bay, Newfoundland in the 19th century.

There are few contemporary descriptions in the literature of first-generation houses in Trinity Bay. Anspach, writing in 1819, provides a description of the "common dwellings" of the fishermen, which is basically in agreement with the first generation style in Trinity Bay:

The common dwellings consist only of ground floor, or at most of one-storey; the materials, except the shingles, are the produce of the Newfoundland woods; the best sorts are clapboard on the outside, others are built of logs left rough and uneven on the inside and outside; the interstices being filled up with moss, and generally lined with boards planed and tongued. This filling with moss the vacancies between the studs to keep out the weather, is there called chinsing ... . They have only one fireplace in a very large kitchen ... (p. 467–68).

These features are similar to those found in the earliest one-room cottages constructed elsewhere in the North American seaboard colonies by English immigrants (Shurtleff, 1939; Kimball, 1927; Kniffen, 1965). Antecedents for both the basic form and for the construction techniques of this cottage have been established in medieval rural England (Kerr, 1964; Alcock, 1969). This was the earliest type of house remembered in Trinity Bay. As in New England it formed the foundation for subsequent styles.

The Second-Generation House

By 1860 the first-generation one-storey house with loft had evolved into the second-generation saltbox house (Pl. 3–4). The saltbox was found extant in all four communities: 18 in English Harbour, 8 in Old Bonaventure, 15 in Hant's Harbour, and 16 in New Perlican. Calculations based on these examples, dating from 1865 to 1920, indicate it was somewhat larger in size than its predecessor. The mean average floor area measured 869 square feet and had an average width of 24'9" and an average depth of 22'11". Although the increase in floor space was not great, the second-generation house was considerably more spacious. The house had higher ceilings in the ground floor rooms and the raised front wall allowed for two full-size bedrooms on the second floor as well as two smaller storage rooms under the sloping roof. The older examples of this saltbox had only one door which was located at the gable end of the house. Later examples added a centrally placed front door leading to a small entry which gave access to the kitchen, the parlour, and the staircase leading to the second floor (Fig. 3–2). The front door was used only for formal occasions.

Sixteen examples of this second-generation house were studded while forty-one were of frame construction. In the Trinity Bay idiom, frame construction meant

Plate 3–4a *The Saltbox*

Plate 3–4b *The Saltbox*

"balloon-framing," or the building of exterior walls by means of evenly spaced light (usually "two by fours") timber studs, as opposed to heavy timber. Spacing of the vertical studs was standardized at sixteen inches, but in older houses it often varied. The earliest recorded use of this technique in Trinity Bay is 1870; some of the earlier houses, particularly merchant houses and stores, were of heavy frame construction, but this earlier technique was not found in smaller folk houses. In American seaboard states balloon-framing did not appear until after 1830, becoming popular only after 1850 (Kniffen and Glassie, 1966:42). Rempel gives a date of ±1880 for its introduction and adoption in Ontario (1967:117–26). The relatively late introduction of balloon-framing in Trinity Bay and the general lack of heavily framed structures give further evidence of the universal use of the studding technique in the earlier period of settlement.

The construction of these early frame houses followed a set pattern. First, ground posts, usually made of larch because of its resistence to moisture, were tamped into holes dug in the ground and then braced with rock fill. They were often placed in pairs, one post notched inward and one outward, to hold the "sleeper" which was laid on top. In the smaller houses there were only three sleepers, at the front, centre, and back, each squared on the top and bottom, but left round on the sides and running the full width of the house. On the top of the sleepers, and running in the opposite direction, were the joists which carried the floor. The joists, which were smaller than the sleepers, were trimmed on top and bottom with an axe. They were affixed to the sleepers with one-inch wooden "trunnels" which were hammered into holes drilled by an auger through the joists and into the sleepers. Trunnels (tree nails) were hand-made from pine. The floor was then laid on top of the joists with the boards running parallel to the front of the house. Floor boards varied in length but were usually joined to the centre joist. Pine flooring was preferred but was not always available. The sills were made of 4″ × 4″ spruce or fir boards laid directly on the joists. Usually, the sills merely abutted and were nailed to the joists. On the north side of the Bay, however, where studding persisted, corner-notching was a common practice even after the introduction of frame construction.

The second-storey floor rested on joists of 2″ × 6″ pine board set on two-foot centres and running the length of the house. On the second floor they were covered with inch-board, but were left exposed on the ground-floor rooms. Exterior walls were sheeted on the outside with inch board, then clapboard or shingled. Shingles were not often used because they were expensive to buy and time-consuming to apply. Inside, the walls were sheathed with a double thickness of half-inch board with the seams over-lapping. Exterior walls were approximately six inches thick and it was a common practice to insulate them with sawdust or wood shavings. If no insulation was used, the heat loss was significant. Interior walls, as noted earlier, were of vertical plank construction.

The roof rafters or "couples" rested on a wall plate, measuring 1″ × 4″, which was nailed to the top of the upright studs. Rafters were not usually braced but were nailed where they abutted at the peak for extra strength. Ridge poles were not used. The pitch of the roof was generally "six on twelve" indicating a rise of six feet for a horizontal run of twelve feet, although it was occasionally steeper. Rafters were sheathed on the outside with inch board placed side by side and running horizontally along the roof, then covered with pine shingles 18″ × 6″ with a 9″ to 13″ overlap. The peak of the roof was covered with a saddle board: two long pieces of plank running the length of the ridge and nailed together into a "V"-shape.

The second-generation Trinity Bay house was identical in external form to the New England saltbox. The latter, however, was usually much larger and was most popular between 1725 and 1775, one hundred years before the style developed in Trinity Bay. Pillsbury (1970) has suggested that the New England saltbox evolved from the two-storey garrison house which has no counterpart in outport Newfoundland. The Trinity Bay saltbox developed directly from the smaller one-storey rectangular house with extended rear rafters. The large central chimney characteristic of the New England saltbox was not used in Trinity Bay; instead, an iron stove with a small brick chimney or stove pipe, usually located at the gable end of the house, dominated.

In the last quarter of the 19th century many first-generation houses in Trinity Bay were enlarged to duplicate this saltbox form. Enlarging or "raising" a first- or second-generation house was a common practice. In all, sixty-six houses were raised to duplicate newer styles. The average age of the initial house at the time of enlargement was forty years, with a range of fifteen to seventy-five years. Raising a house to a full two-storey structure, rather than extending it horizontally, had two major advantages: (i) the second storey increased the floor space significantly but did not enlarge the area of the roof, an important consideration when shingles were either difficult to make or expensive to buy; (ii) the second-floor rooms could be easily and economically heated from a stove on the bottom floor.

The motives for raising a house are complex. The process may be viewed as a simple function of modernization and maintenance. After 40 years, most homes in Trinity Bay required major repairs, especially the roof which tended to sag and leak from exposure to the severe Newfoundland climate. When questioned about their motives, most informants replied that "the old roof was gone and we just raised her up while the roof was off." The fact that houses were usually raised when they were a little less than two generations old may suggest that it was the second-generation inhabitants of the original house who made the decision to enlarge. In Trinity Bay the youngest son traditionally inherited, not only the family home, but also the responsibility of looking after his parents. This extended family arrangement placed considerable pressure on living and private space in a small home. Raising the old house may have been a conscious effort to increase living space without the expense or bother of constructing a new home. The reluctance of older couples to leave the old family home and to move into a new house further encouraged renovation and repairs. No significant correlation could be found between the number of children in a family and the process of house-raising.

The Third-Generation House
By 1890 the third-generation house had developed from the earlier saltbox. It was a full two-storey structure with a peaked roof plus a flat rear extension (Pl. 3–5). Fifty-four examples of this house were recorded, dating from 1889 to 1935. The mean average floor area was 1106 square feet and was 24'6" wide and 22'1" deep.

This house evolved by raising the rear wall of the saltbox by five or six feet and covering it with a flat roof abutting the main slope of the roof. Given the form of the saltbox, this solution to the problem of increasing the living space of the house was economical in terms of both material and labour. Although it did not increase the floor

Plate 3–5a   *Two Storey with extension*

Plate 3–5b   *Two Storey and Linhay*

space, it did make the third-generation house considerably more spacious on the second floor which now contained four bedrooms and a central hall. Of the fifty-four second-generation houses recorded, sixteen were raised to duplicate this form.

The plan did present some structural problems. The weight of the roof was now carried on a ledger beam which extended the length of the house and rested on the interior upright studs. This arrangement made it difficult to move interior partitions thereby limiting the size of the upstairs rooms. It would have been impossible to develop this type of roof had not roofing felt been introduced to the area. The almost flat section of roof at the junction point with the peaked roof was difficult to keep watertight even with flexible felt. Shingles were totally inadequate for this rear section but continued to be used on the peaked section of the roof. In all other details the third-generation house and the saltbox were similar (Fig. 3–2).

The Fourth-Generation House

This was a two-storey, rectangular house with a central front door, five front windows, and a low pitched roof (Pl. 3–6), which became popular by 1900 in all four communities. Some structural difficulties inherent in the third-generation house were eliminated: the roof used less construction material than the older, more steeply pitched roof and was more accessible when repairs were needed. It was also less exposed to the wind. Eighty-six examples of this fourth-generation house were recorded, dating from 1872 to 1961. Three examples in Old Bonaventure predated the first recorded third-generation house and may represent the innovative trend of an individual family. The style, however, was not widely accepted until c. 1900 and is clearly a structural development from the third-generation form. Technically, the third-generation house was not "raised" although the term was usually employed when describing alterations to this house. It was re-roofed, but this did not increase the floor space or the height of the walls. It was somewhat smaller in size with a mean average floor area of 1,004 square feet and a mean average width of 24'3" and average depth of 22'2". A major innovation in the fourth-generation house was the introduction of a central hall to the basic floor plan (Fig. 3–2). (Some third-generation houses had a central hall but this was not common in the older homes.) The fourth-generation house became ubiquitous in Trinity Bay after 1900, but declined rapidly after 1940 in favour of the popular urban-inspired one-storey bungalow. Seven first-generation, twenty second-generation, and twenty-four third-generation houses were raised to duplicate the former style. Of the twenty-five examples of the fourth-generation house constructed after 1940, twenty-three were originally second or third-generation houses, re-roofed. It was, in effect, a catching-up process by those living in older houses to a style of construction which had already become obsolete.

Persistence and Innovation in Newfoundland Folk Architecture

Each of the four styles described above had a different chronological range (Fig. 3–3) and when data for the four communities are aggregated, the four house types fall into definite construction periods (Fig. 3–4). The terminal dates in Figure 3–4 indicate the time of the construction, not the demolition of a dwelling.

    (i) First generation cottage   1835–1910
   (ii) Second generation saltbox   1865–1920
  (iii) Third generation modified saltbox   1890–1935
  (iv) Fourth generation flat roof   1870–1960

Plate 3–6 *Two Storey Low Roof*

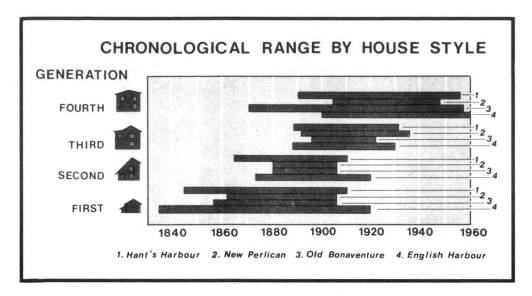

Figure 3–3

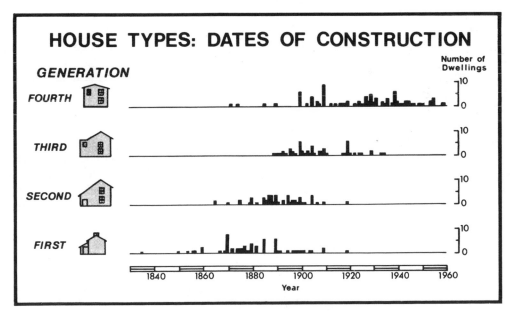

Figure 3–4

Both oral and archival references such as Anspach's 1819 description of the common dwellings of the fishermen suggest that the temporal range of the first-generation house extended back to at least the 18th century. But there is no full description of these early structures for the pre-1830 period and they are, therefore, excluded from the data set. However, no other house type was recorded for the period prior to 1860 and it is likely that the first generation house was the ubiquitous style. Only in Old Bonaventure was the chronological sequence of house styles disrupted (Fig. 3–4). There, the introduction of the fourth-generation house – of which there are three examples – preceded that of the third-generation by twenty-five years. This anomaly may simply reflect a lack of adequate data but it is more likely that it resulted from the early local development of this house style; the earliest fourth-generation house in Old Bonaventure predated all recorded third-generation houses in the study area. The date of initial acceptance and the ultimate displacement of each house style varied slightly from community to community as did the period of greatest popularity of any type. With the exception of the first-generation house, no style remained popular for more than forty years. The fourth generation house, appearing as early as 1870, did not become widely accepted until 1900 and was not popular after 1940, being replaced by the contemporary bungalow. Twenty-five examples of this fourth-generation house style were recorded after 1940 but twenty-three of them were renovated third-generation houses. The date for the introduction and general acceptance of the first-generation cottage in each of the four settlements is uncertain. However, the second- and third-generation house styles had diffused to all four settlements only fifteen years after being introduced to the area and the introduction of the fourth-generation house style – with the exception of the three early examples in Old Bonaventure noted earlier – followed a similar pattern. The rate of acceptance and abandonment of a particular house style was affected by the actual rate of house construction in each settlement. The more rapid rate of replacing houses on the south side of the Bay facilitated the general dominance of a new style over older styles. On the north side of the Bay the rate of house construction was considerably lower; consequently it took longer for the effect of a new house style to be felt.

It is difficult to establish accurately the actual rate of house construction during this period. For the period 1857–1921 the number of "Houses now Building" were recorded in each census year. In the two communities on the south side of the Bay, Hant's Harbour and New Perlican, on the average, 12 houses were built per year in each community, as compared to 2.25 houses on the north side of the Bay. The more rapid population increase on the south side accounts, in part, for the higher annual rate of construction, but does not explain it entirely. For example, in 1884 Hant's Harbour had 134 houses and 23 "houses now building"; yet in 1891 the total number of houses had increased to only 136, indicating that at least 21 older homes had been replaced in this seven-year period. The lower rate of construction on the north side of the Bay suggests that individual houses may have persisted for a longer period of time before being replaced by new ones. The construction rate of 12 houses per year calculated for the south side of the Bay is very high. If this rate had been maintained all houses in the community would have been replaced in less than fifteen years. The meaning of the category "Houses now Building" is not defined and may include older homes under renovation. Certainly such a high rate of construction is not substantiated by actual field observation. Although new house styles appeared rapidly after 1870, there was considerable overlapping of styles between 1885 and 1905, particularly if one considers the actual building process (Fig. 3–4). During this period the first- and second-generation house styles declined in popularity, but it was not until 1900 that the number of third- and fourth-generation houses exceeded the number of houses built in the earlier styles. Field data suggest, however, that the area did experience a minor construction boom in the period 1880–1900. From 1884 to 1901, for example, the total number of houses in the four communities increased by only 31; yet 86 new housing starts were recorded in the field, indicating that the older houses were being quickly replaced by new and larger houses.

The process of innovation and replacement in Trinity Bay architecture is complex. Archival and field data are useful in reconstructing past housing practices but offer little insight into the many social and economic factors which influence individual decisions to build a new home. It appears, however, that social rather than economic factors were more dominant. A house was usually constructed by the owner with help from other members of his family, using timber which they cut and sawed themselves. The house represented a considerable investment in terms of labour, but the economic investment was not great. Certainly one could not explain variations in the second, third, and fourth-generation houses in economic terms, for all three houses were approximately the same size and required similar amounts of timber. Social pressure to conform to the latest style, as well as a desire for increased living space made new house types more attractive and played a critical role in their initial acceptance and subsequent popularity. Such social factors, however, are difficult to evaluate, especially for the earlier period of settlement, and their exact role in the design process is not clearly understood.

Summary and Conclusions

This investigation has focused on the development of the Trinity Bay house from the period of initial settlement until the decline of the folk architectural tradition in the early 20th century. Although a traditional style of architecture did develop in the region in the 19th century, it was not wholly of local origin. The major influx of settlers – West Country Englishmen from a variety of occupational backgrounds – arrived in the first quarter of the 19th century. English vernacular architecture of that period was characterized by a variety of forms. Cottages were common in the homeland, but comprised only one facet of the English vernacular architectural tradition. Yet, during the pioneer stage of settlement, the small, one- or two-room cottage was established as the almost exclusive house type in Trinity Bay. It is most likely that the early 19th century cottage favoured by immigrants was an imitation, not just of the West Country analogue, but of the style dominating Trinity Bay since the inception of permanent settlement a century and a half before.

Certainly the first-generation Trinity Bay house differed significantly from the first-generation Irish house of the Southern Avalon (Mannion, 1974:143–55). Similar cottages were constructed by English settlers in the American Southern Mountains in the 18th and 19th centuries (Glassie, 1968c:351) and Head notes that prefabricated house forms were being shipped from New England to Newfoundland in the 1770s (1976:116). Form and the construction technique varied in response to regional differences. The first settlers in Trinity Bay, like their American counterparts, immediately adopted native wood, which was the most readily available and environmentally suitable material, to construct their homes. In England, oak was the traditional material for heavy framing and this preference was retained in the American colonies

(Kelley, 1924:3). Oak was unavailable in Trinity Bay. The Newfoundland forest was predominantly small spruce and fir (with some pine) which were unsuitable for heavy framing but ideal for vertical stud construction, particularly for small one-storey cottages. This suitability may account for the re-introduction of this ancient construction technique in the Bay. Certainly, the stunted forest of eastern Newfoundland was less suited to horizontal log construction, but the absence of this tradition is perhaps as much the result of the isolation of eastern Newfoundland from mainland North America where horizontal log walls were popular during the frontier era.

As settlement developed beyond the frontier stage after c. 1850, new house forms were introduced. The small cottage developed into a one and a half storey saltbox and then into a full two-storey house. This sequence of development has strong parallels with the development of folk architecture in other parts of America settled by English people (Pillsbury, 1970:25) but occurred in Newfoundland at a much later date. The lean-to roof was a common feature of English vernacular architecture and was introduced into the American colonies in the 17th century. But this form was not adopted in Trinity Bay until after 1850, when improved economic and social conditions created a desire for more living space in larger homes. It is impossible to establish if the first saltbox houses in Trinity Bay were enlarged cottages or new houses or both. Certainly many small cottages were enlarged in the mid-19th century. The form of the saltbox, with its peaked roof and extended rear rafters, suggests a logical structural procedure for increasing living space in a cottage with a minimum outlay of capital and labour. Subsequent styles were equally utilitarian and could be adapted to pre-existing structures. In this way a regional style was maintained which reflected local environmental, social, and economic realities. The rapid changes in house morphology after 1860 were related more to major changes in communications and the economy as the frontier matured, than to variations in the material folk culture of the earlier settlers or to the diffusion of new ideas into the area. No style remained popular for more than two generations and longevity reflects the tenacity of individual structures rather than the continued popularity of a style. The traditional techniques of construction, however, showed an impressive continuity from the earliest period of settlement. The owner was the builder and he cut and prepared his own timber, selected the site and constructed the house with help from family and friends. The basic form was known to all and only minor decisions of site, orientation, or exact size remained to be resolved.

Trinity Bay was not entirely unaffected by development elsewhere in North America and England. Some innovations from both Canada and the United States were assimilated into local building practices with little local resistance. Balloon framing, for example, was used in Trinity Bay only twenty years after it became popular in the United States and at approximately the same time as it was introduced into other areas of eastern Canada. Iron stoves began to replace open fireplaces by 1865, only twenty years after this process became common in the Maritimes. Roofing felt largely replaced shingles as the dominant roofing material not long after it became popular on the mainland. Most of these innovations were introduced after 1865 with the development of communication and an improved economy. The geographical location of the Bay on the edge of North America reflects the time lag in the innovation-diffusion process.

From at least the mid-18th century, elements of the popular architectural tradition were evident in the more elaborate merchant houses at Trinity, constructed by professional carpenters employed by the various firms. By contrast, folk architecture in the Bay was starkly utilitarian. Harsh environmental and economic circumstances militated against many architectural embellishments. The folk house had deep roots in the English vernacular tradition which was equally utilitarian. Changing economic and social conditions, available materials, the tools and expertise of the builder, all combined to produce a distinct regional style. Strength and utility rather than stylistic appeal characterized this style. However, by 1900 elements of the popular architectural traditions were becoming increasingly evident in the field area. The mansard roof, which enjoyed great popularity in St. John's after 1850, became more and more common. Bay windows which extended the full height of the house, double windows, verandas, and off-set front doors were all incorporated into existing folk structures. The old emphasis on functionalism was replaced by a new emphasis on aesthetics and a desire to copy urban building practices, not always successfully.

The modern, urban-inspired bungalow has completely displaced the traditional Trinity Bay house. Municipal water lines are now a greater factor in site location than the direction of the prevailing winds, local topography, or a sight of the harbour. Modern work cycles have disrupted the traditional building process. Increasingly, outport homes are being constructed by professional carpenters, for the owners often lack both the time and skills required to construct their own dwellings. The traditional outport house was ideally suited to a particular way of life, being both aesthetically attractive, yet decidedly functional. Contemporary change is perhaps inevitable, but it is nevertheless unfortunate that traditional house forms and folk skills, which have evolved over a period of three hundred years will ultimately disappear.

Architectural research by cultural geographers has focused primarily on the use of folk structures as a diagnostic tool in delineating culturo-geographic regions or as an index of general patterns of diffusion in traditional rural America. Implicit in these studies is the idea that house types evolve over time, but little systematic research has been conducted so far to analyse the persistence/innovation process or to isolate the social, economic, and environmental factors which influence house designs. The macro-scale and superficial field methodology which place considerable emphasis on relic structures, but which generally neglect to investigate the many local factors influencing the production of the object, largely obscure significant regional variations. Although the detailed study of material objects and of traditional construction techniques is basic in establishing a typology of house forms, it is only the first step in understanding the complex relationship between the needs and desires of the builder and the environmental realities within which he must operate. There is a pressing need in future geographic research for a number of quantitatively-oriented micro-studies to establish the depth and longevity of traditional folk practices and to examine the process of architectural innovation before regional variations can be adequately explained.

In this study, one is struck not so much by the tenacity of traditional house forms as by the rapidity with which these traditional forms evolved and existing structures renovated to reflect changing social and economic conditions. On the basis of this evidence, it is suggested that future research concern itself with rates of architectural persistence and innovation, especially among settlers of differing cultural backgrounds, and with other factors such as family structure, the relationship between form and function, and the effects of internal migrations on the diffusion of local house

styles. Such basic research would provide a more complete understanding of traditional building practices and would throw new light on the general problem of persistence and innovation in folk architecture which may have wider application within the
broader field of folk cultural studies.

NOTES

1   D365 Dorset Record Office, Dorchester. Letter Book of the Lester and Garland Families, F.21,
1794–1815.
2   Faris estimated the average life of the outport house to be 25 to 30 years, or slightly more than one
generation. The average life span is difficult to calculate, but data on 47 English Harbour houses indicate an
average of 57 years.
3   *Census of Newfoundland*, 1836, 1845, 1857, 1869, 1874, 1884, 1891, 1901, 1911, 1921, 1935. Newfoundland, Department of Colonial Secretary, St. John's.
4   Floor area was calculated as $1^1/_2$ times the ground floor area for the first- and second-generation houses
and twice the ground floor area for the third- and fourth-generation houses.

REFERENCES: SECONDARY SOURCES

ALCOCK, N.
  1969 "11. Some Dartmoor Houses." *Transactions Devonshire Association*, 101:83–106.
ANSPACH, LEWIS
  1819 *A History of the Island of Newfoundland*. London, T. and J. Allman.
BARLEY, M.
  1961 *The English Farmhouse and Cottage*. London, Routledge and Kegan Paul.
BRUNSKILL, R.
  1970 *Illustrated Handbook of Vernacular Architecture*. New York, Universe Books.
EVANS, E. E.
  1969 "The Scotch Irish: Their Cultural Adaptation and Heritage in the American Old West." In E. R. R.
  Green (ed.), *Essays in Scotch-Irish History*. London, Routledge and Kegan Paul.
FARIS, J. C.
  1972 *Cat Harbour: A Newfoundland Fishing Settlement*. St. John's, Institute of Social and Economic
  Research, Memorial University of Newfoundland.
GLASSIE, H.
  1968a "A Central Chimney Continental Log House from Cumberland Country." *Pennsylvania Folklife*,
  18(1):33–9.
GLASSIE, H.
  1968b "The Types of the Southern Mountain Cabin." In Jan. H. Brunvand (ed.), *The Study of American
  Folklore*. New York, W. W. Norton.
GLASSIE, H.
  1968c *Pattern in the Material Folk Culture of the Eastern United States*. Philadelphia, University of
  Pennsylvania Press.
HEAD, C. G.
  1971 "The Changing Geography of Newfoundland in the Eighteenth Century." Unpublished Ph.D.
  thesis, Department of Geography, University of Wisconsin.
HEAD, C. G.
  1976 *Eighteenth Century Newfoundland: A Geographers Perspective*. Toronto, McClelland and Stewart.
HOSKINS, W.
  1954 *Devon*. London, Collins.
INNOCENT, C. F.
  1916 *The Development of English Building Construction*. Cambridge, Cambridge University Press.
JORDAN, T.
  1964 "German Houses in Texas." *Landscape*, 14(1):24–6.

JUKES, J. B.
 1842 *Excursions in and about Newfoundland during the Years 1839 and 1840.* London, John Murray.
KELLEY, F.
 1924 *The Early Domestic Architecture of Connecticut.* New York, Dover Publications.
KERR, B.
 1964 "Dorset Cottages." *Proceedings of the Dorset Natural History and Archaeological Society,* 86:184–199.
KIMBALL, F.
 1927 *Domestic Architecture of the American Colonies and of the Early Republic.* New York, C. Scribner and Sons.
KNIFFEN, F.
 1965 "Folk Housing: Key to Diffusion." *Annals American Association of Geographers,* 55(4):549–77.
KNIFFEN, F. and H. GLASSIE
 1966 "Building in Wood in the Eastern United States." *Geographical Review,* 56:40–66.
MANNION, J. J.
 1974 *Irish Settlements in Eastern Canada: A Study of Cultural Transfer and Adaptation.* Toronto, University of Toronto Press.
PILLSBURY, R. and A. KARDOS
 1970 *A Field Guide to the Folk Architecture of the Northeastern United States.* Geography Publications at Dartmouth, No. 8, Hanover, N.H.
REMPEL, J.
 1967 *Building with Wood.* Toronto, University of Toronto Press.
RYAN, S.
 1971 "The Newfoundland Cod Fishery in the Nineteenth Century." Unpublished M.A. thesis, Department of History, Memorial University of Newfoundland.
SHURTLEFF, H.
 1939 *The Log Cabin Myth,* edited by S. E. Morison. Gloucester, Mass., Peter Smith.
WACKER, P. and R. TRINDELL
 1969 "The Log House in New Jersey: Origins and Diffusion." *Keystone Folklore Quarterly,* 8(4):248–68.
WILHELM, H.
 1971 "German Settlement and Folk Building Practices in the Hill Country of Texas." *Pioneer America.* 3(2):15–24.
WILSON, E.
 1970 "The Single Pen Log House in the South." *Pioneer America,* 2(1):22–25.
WIX, E.
 1836 *Six Months of a Newfoundland Missionary's Journal.* London, Smith, Elder and Co.
WOOD, M.
 1965 *The English Mediaeval House.* London, Phoenix House.
WRIGHT, M.
 1958 "The Antecedents of the Double-Pen House Type." *Annals American Association of Geographers,* 48(2):109–17.
ZELINSKY, W.
 1953 "The Log House in Georgia." *Geographical Review,* 42(2):173–93.

A Modal Sequence in the Peopling of Central Bonavista Bay, 1676–1857

4

Alan G. Macpherson

Settlement and residence are recurring themes in the political history of Newfoundland and the records of the island are accordingly rich in demographic and economic statistics. The colonial Governors' annual returns on the fishery and inhabitants at Newfoundland, collected locally and collated by districts, run from 1675 to 1830 with few *lacunae* after 1723. They were followed by a century of enumeration and census-taking, beginning in 1836, which produced a wealth of information on the population and economy of each and every outport. In addition, many parishes kept registers of baptisms, marriages, and burials which are still extant from the end of the 18th century. Historians, however, have generally restricted their use of such material to a selection of aggregate figures to illustrate changes in population and economic activity in the colony. No comprehensive analysis of the official statistics has as yet been attempted to determine the regional pattern of population growth or social structure, and no parish register has been subjected to the standard techniques of the historical demographer. The present study attempts to remedy this with reference to the settlement and peopling of central Bonavista Bay between 1676 and 1857.

The area designated as central Bonavista Bay encompasses, for the purposes of this study, those settlements which first appeared in the Anglican registers kept at Trinity (1757–   ), Bonavista (1786–   ), Greenspond (1815–   ), and King's Cove (1834–   ), and in 1865 were incorporated into the new parish of Salvage (Fig. 4–1). The settlements of Gooseberry Islands, Flat Island, Bloody Bay, Barrow Harbour, Salvage, and Broom Close were the only inhabited places in the central part of Bonavista Bay to appear in the 1836 Census of Newfoundland. In the context of Newfoundland in the first half of the 19th century, they represent a group of secondary settlements, subordinate in both size and function to such places as Trinity, Bonavista, and Greenspond, and therefore are ideal for an inquiry into demographic aspects of the settlement process in Newfoundland as temporary occupancy gave way to permanent settlement.

TEMPORARY RESIDENCE, 1675–1806

The origin, modes, and growth of settlement in central Bonavista Bay are best understood against the history of the Bay as a whole, the data for which are provided by the Governor's annual returns on the fishery.

The first attempt to subject the demographic information in the annual returns to a regional time-series analysis was made by Head, who established an "index of residency" in which the total wintering population was expressed as a crude percentage of the population present in the ensuing summer (Head, 1971:138–9, Fig. 6.2; 1976:82, and Fig. 5.1). The total wintering population, measured by Head's index, seldom formed less than 60 percent of the summer population in the Bay after 1720, was often much higher, and never fell below 90 percent after 1800. However, in noting the seasonal presence of large numbers of migratory fishermen from southwestern

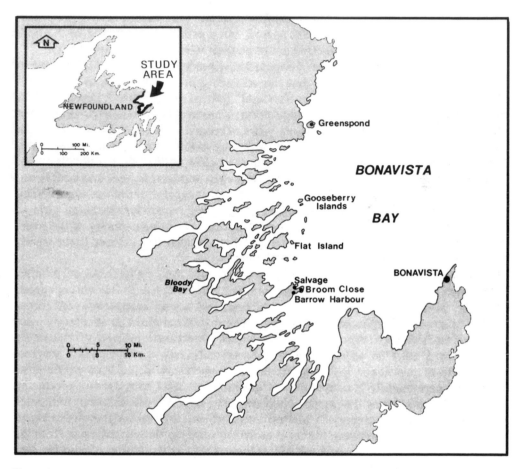

Figure 4–1   *Location*

England and southeastern Ireland, the index equates the over-wintering population with year-round residents, and fails to recognize the demographic significance of the "Men Servants" category which dominated the wintering population in Bonavista Bay and similar areas during the 18th century and later. Handcock's formula, presented elsewhere in this volume, assumes that numbers of women – "Mistresses" and "Women Servants" – in the wintering population are a better indication of permanent resident population; but it also assumes that the "Children" (under 15 years) belong to these women and includes normal age-distributions and sex ratios. These assumptions may well be true for much of Newfoundland, but a critical examination of the time series in Figure 2 throws considerable doubt on their validity for Bonavista Bay.

Figure 4–2 shows the categories of population wintering in Bonavista Bay between 1677 and 1828. The series show that the wintering population was so dominated throughout the entire period by "Men Servants" (joined after 1789 by "Dieters") as to maintain wide sex ratios in the adult population. A mode of one woman to five to seven men occurred in fourteen of the fifty-six years of record between 1723 and 1797. The ratios, moreover, fluctuated wildly from winter to winter, peaking at one woman to twenty-one men as late as 1795, and did not stay below one to three until after 1816. Woman:child ratios were equally erratic, subject to sudden changes and occasional peaks (1:15 in 1794; 1:20 in 1802) beyond the biological capabilities of the women. The "Women Servants," moreover, although never very numerous, included girls of fifteen years of age and tended to exaggerate the child-bearing capacity of the over-wintering women. Trends in the numbers of women were often opposed to the trends in numbers of "Children" over short runs of years.

All categories of wintering population, in fact, show striking fluctuations in numbers, which can be accounted for only by assuming that Bonavista Bay was occupied in winter, as in summer, by a rootless, shifting, and largely migratory work force, turning over with the speculative fortunes of the cod-fishery and its ancillary winter activities, and subject to the collective decisions of a mercantile oligarchy based in the British Isles. Until 1786, at least, the annual returns reveal no evidence of a progressive growth of population in Bonavista and its dependencies, such as would have resulted if permanently resident and settled families had been steadily producing marriageable girls during the previous half-century. That this did not occur until after 1800 suggests that the category "Children" was subject, throughout the 18th century, to the same disparities between the sexes as in the adult population and, apart from the few children born to the women each winter, consisted largely of boys of working age. The time-series, indeed, suggest that the "Children" might more logically be associated with the "Men Servants" – boys accompanying their fathers – rather than with the women; as a corollary to this, it must be assumed that most of the "Master" planters and "Mistresses" were equally as subject to replacement from the British Isles as the over-wintering categories of servants. The series demonstrate that the spectacular increase in "Children" which began in 1787 matched that of the "Men Servants," whereas "Women Servants" began to rise progressively only after 1800, and "Masters" and "Mistresses" after 1810.

The population which can be considered, therefore, as permanently based in Bonavista Bay in the 18th century fell considerably below the levels suggested by Head's index and Handcock's formula and was largely concentrated in Bonavista itself until 1787 and perhaps 1800. It appears that prior to 1800, a large proportion of the wintering population consisted of transatlantic migrants, only present in New-

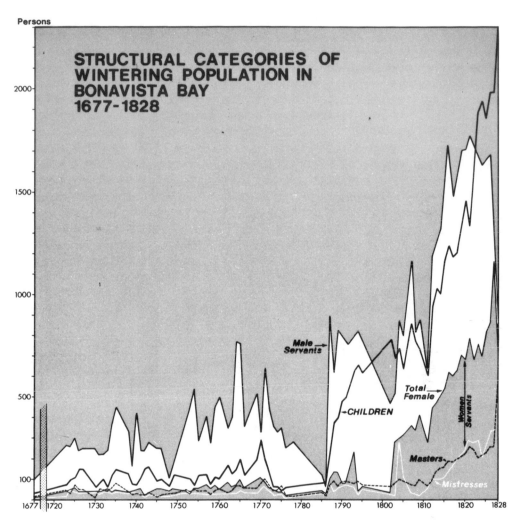

Persons

STRUCTURAL CATEGORIES OF
WINTERING POPULATION IN
BONAVISTA BAY
1677-1828

Male
Servants

Total
Female

CHILDREN

Women
Servants

Masters

Mistresses

Figure 4–2

TABLE 4–1

Population Structure in Central Bonavista Bay, 1676–1802

	1676		1681		1698		1702		1706		1802
	"Solvadge"	Barrow Hr.	Salvage	Barrow Hr.	"Salvoyags"	"Barry Hr."	Salvage	Barrow Hr.	Salvage	Barrow Hr.	Salvage & Gooseberry Is.
Planters (Masters)	6	2	7	2	2	1	2	3	1	1	4
Servants	48	35	44	25	11	5	10	16	3	6	—
Women	4	—	4	—	—	—	1	—	—	1	—
Children	8	—	12	—	—	—	2	—	—	4	8
Total:											
Winter	—	—	—	—	9	3*	—	—	—	—	12
Summer	66	37	67	27	13	6	15	19	4	12	—

*Given as 93 (*sic*).

foundland on a somewhat longer basis than the summer fishermen. This applies particularly to the summer fishing stations and wintering settlements in the central parts of Bonavista Bay, whenever the annual returns permit a glimpse of the population structure. Table 4–1 indicates that Salvage and Barrow Harbour were small year-round settlements in the period 1676–1706, lacking the demographic structure and continuity of true communities. A century later, in 1802, the population which had wintered at Salvage and the Gooseberry Islands was remarkably similar. Early references to the central Bonavista Bay settlements tend to corroborate this interpretation and to underline the temporary nature of occupance.

Gooseberry Islands does not appear in the "List of the Planters Names" for 1676, although it is mentioned with Port Bonavista, Keels, Salvage, Greenspond, and Cat Harbour as "settled on or before the year 1660 ... all which places the English have continued to fish at since first settled" (Capt. James Cook's Map of Newfoundland, 1763: marginal note, Lysaght, 1971). The Governors' Returns first mention them together with Salvage, as dependencies of Bonavista, contributing to the aggregated statistics for the Bay in 1765, prior to which they were probably subsumed under "Greenspond" or "Bonavista". Lester's of Poole (Dorset) and of Trinity, Newfoundland, had fishing servants in the Gooseberry Islands during the 1760s: Thomas Kedman, Thomas Harty, Jo. Kitts, and Mr. Black – none of them bearing surnames associated with the community as it emerges in the Greenspond register in 1830. Production consisted of fish, collected in July and August, and board and plank which were shipped to Trinity in May as a result of winter activities; salt ballast, bread, and other goods were supplied in return.[1] The baptismal register of St. Paul's Anglican parish at Trinity carries one or two early entries for Gooseberry Islands: a son to Patrick and Mary Ducey on the 26th October 1774 and a son and daughter to John and Eleanor Parker on the 18th June 1786 and the 12th September 1789; neither name recurs in the record.

The "Register of Fishing Rooms in Bonavista Bay" for 1806 records Black's Room, owned by Henry and Patrick Black by inheritance from ancestors, presumably the "Mr. Black" of 1767. But the aggregate picture for Salvage and Gooseberry Islands in the winter of 1801–2, as already noted, indicates the presence of a migratory group of which the Blacks probably formed part.

Flat Island first appears on record as an occupied place in the "Register of Fishing Rooms in Bonavista Bay" for 1806, in which year Grey & Collins built a stage and claimed the room "in right of building and possession." The registration was accompanied by the laconic note: "... no fishery within its neighbourhood," which may be interpreted as indicating that there were no independent fishermen residing in the locality in 1806. Grey & Collins' operation appears to have been a seasonal one, related perhaps to the migratory English fishery, but more probably based on older settlements in Newfoundland which were already becoming involved in an indigenous transhumant mode later associated with the summer stationer and floater fisheries.

Barrow Harbour, like Gooseberry Islands and Salvage, was an old centre of activity. Capt. Russell's "Accompt of the English Inhabitants in Newfoundland" for the summer of 1676 lists John Bayly and Christopher Cooke at Barrow Harbour. These men were operating as bye-boatmen rather than as true planters, for although Bayly had five boats and twenty-five fishing servants and Cooke two boats and ten servants, neither had wife or child with him and the place was apparently without women. Barrow Harbour was clearly a fishing station by 1676, but it was not yet a settled community. The general report accompanying the "Accompt" indicates that "about half the servants of these inhabitants [of Newfoundland] do go home every year [to England] and return to their masters the beginning of the fishing season." Perhaps this applied to all the men who were at Barrow Harbour in 1776, for Capt. James Story's list of planters "to ye northward of Bonavista" in the summer of 1681 shows a change of principal personnel: Ralph Trevers with two boats and twenty servants and William Danvers with one boat and five servants. Neither man was accompanied by his wife. Capt. Story noted that "These men in these north parts live mostly by furring in ye winter, being all togeather in the woods for the space of seven months;" his accompanying "Report" added that "The planters go a furring about the middle of September and take no provisions with them but bread and salt, finding beavers, otters and seals enough to feed them; they carry guns, and kill also a great deal of venison, which they salt down for the winter; they return about the 1st May." Neither Bayly nor Cooke appear elsewhere in Newfoundland in Sir William Pool's "Accompt of all the Inhabitants and Planters" present in the following summer of 1677 or in Capt. Story's nominal list for 1681, and neither their names nor those of Trevers and Danvers reappear in the later record of central Bonavista Bay.

When Lesters' of Poole expanded into Bonavista Bay from Trinity in the 1760s to enlarge their cod-fishing area and establish better winter bases for furring and sealing, and to catch salmon, they set up at Bonavista, Greenspond and Barrow Harbour. All references to Barrow Harbour in the initial phase of this expansion indicate that it was used primarily as a large-vessel harbour (Diary of Benjamin Lester, Trinity):

19 Aug. 1762:   "Sent ... for some of the provisions of Lemon's Brig ..."
14 May 1767:   "... the Barbell had a fine time bound to Barrow Harbour."
12 June 1767:   "... our shalloway from Barrow Harbour arrived with a load salt, discharged 30 hogsheads."
16 Oct. 1768:   "... the Rachel sail'd from Barrow Harbour with 4079 Q. fish and 16 tearces Salmon ... ."

In 1762, and again in the war against Napoleon, Barrow Harbour was used as a refuge and the best site for defence against French naval attack, but its primary function in Bonavista Bay was that of a depot to which fishermen and planters could bring their catches from as far away as Greenspond and, particularly, from King's Cove and its vicinity. Barrow Harbour was also a place where salt was stored and where temporary ship repairs and maintenance could be carried out. Ships loaded with cured fish were sailing direct to Poole and to the Mediterranean in increasing numbers by the 1790s.

The parish register for St. Paul's at Trinity records two baptisms at Barrow Harbour on June 3, 1804: the adult baptism of Sarah, daughter of George and Ann Stockley, born purportedly at Barrow Harbour in 1783, and the infant baptism of Maria, daughter of Thomas White and Ann Stockley, born in 1802. The "Register of Fishing Rooms in Bonavista Bay" for 1806 lists two "rooms" in Barrow Harbour: Stockly's and Lester's, both situated in Stockly's Cove. This placename, which never appears in the parish registers, seems to give primacy to Stockly at Barrow Harbour, and tends to confirm that his daughter was born there in 1783. Stockly's Room was claimed and occupied in 1806 by Jos[eph] Lane of Barrow Harbour by right of inheritance from the original proprietor, as from Lane's entry on August 6th, 1805; it seems a fair assumption that he was Stockly's son-in-law. Lester's Room was claimed and occupied by B. Lester & Co. of Poole "in right of building and possession" on the same day. The coincidence of dates of entry for both rooms seems to point to a legal or administrative link between them, perhaps related to Stockly's original enterprise in the cove. Lane had only a stage on Stockly's Room, but Lesters' had a stage and a capacious new storehouse "built [that year] to accommodate vessels sent hither to load," besides "Lester's Old Store" which had been built by the company and occupied and claimed in August 1805 "in right of building and possession."

The Trinity parish register recorded two marriages in 1806 involving women residing at Barrow Harbour, both occurring before the fishing season had opened: Robert King, of Old Perlican, to Ann French, of Barrow Harbour, Bonavista, on the 5th January; and Thomas Babstock, of Oborn, Dorset, to Sarah Stockley, of Barrow Harbour, Bonavista, on the 28th April. *King* and *Babstock* are the first surnames in the early history of Barrow Harbour that show any recorded connection with the community after 1830, although *Lane* occurs in nearby Salvage.

Salvage, like Gooseberry Islands, is mentioned by Cooke in 1763 as a centre of English activity in the Bay since 1660. Capt. Russell's "Acompt" for 1676 lists:

John Chambers	1 boat	5 servants	—
Richard Stocks	1 boat	5 servants	wife and one child
John Pritchard	1 boat	5 servants	wife and one child
John Pett	2 boats	11 servants	wife and two children
John Knight	2 boats	11 servants	wife and four children
John Warren	2 boats	11 servants	—

and at Little Harbour, which was part of Salvage:

| William Buckley | 2 boats | 10 servants | — |

Capt. Story's list for 1681 indicates an almost complete replacement of the principal personnel:

Arthur Planker	2 boats	20 servants	wife and one child
John Pencard	1 boat	5 servants	wife and four children
William Adlorn	1 boat	5 servants	—
William Warren	1 boat	5 servants	—
John Pett	2 boats	16 servants	wife and five children
Richard Succles	1 boat	5 servants	wife and two children
Thomas Bishop	1 boat	3 servants	—

As in the case of Barrow Harbour, the men present in 1676 but missing in 1681 fail to appear elsewhere in Newfoundland in the latter "Acompt," indicating that they returned to England or went to other colonies on the American seaboard. None of the surnames appear at Salvage in the registers of a century and a half later, and only *Warren* occurs in the vicinity with reference to a recent immigrant (see Appendix: Gooseberry Islands 24).

Like Barrow Harbour, Salvage was listed separately in the Returns for 1698, 1702, and 1706 and, like Gooseberry Islands, was subsumed thereafter under "Bonavista" until 1765 when it was listed among the dependencies of that place. From 1793 onwards returns were made for distinct parts of the district, and Salvage was subsumed or explicitly listed under "Greenspond," with the single exception of 1802 when it was listed separately (Table 4–1).

The "Register of Fishing Rooms" for 1806 lists three "one-stage" rooms in Salvage: Clinch's, claimed by John Clinch, Salvage, and adjacent to it, Haskell's, claimed by Haskell and Boon, Salvage; standing alone, Dick's, built by William Dick, Salvage, in 1806. All three were claimed "in right of building and possession." Of these, only Dick seems to have established a permanent connection with Salvage. In 1806, despite his designation, his connection with Salvage was still to some extent a seasonal one as he was based at Bonavista where a son, who appears later as a settler at Salvage, was born and baptised in June, 1809. On the other hand, if an inscription in the graveyard at Burton's Point, Salvage, has been transcribed correctly and can be associated with another recording the death of William Dyke in 1853, aged eighty (born 1773), then it would appear that one Henry Dyke (William's older brother?) died at Salvage on October 10th, 1811, at the age of fifty-six (born 1755). If burial can be taken to imply permanent residence, then this particular family of Dicks or Dykes must have moved finally to Salvage about 1810. However the case may be, Gaylor records William Dick as coming to Bonavista from Salvage in a skiff in mid-April, and again in late-May, 1828, suggesting 1827 as the latest possible year for his move. One Henry Brown, who also appears in the "Occurrences at Bonavista" in 1828, was almost certainly another resident at Salvage, as was George Oldford, whose tombstone indicates that he died there in 1825, aged sixty-two.

Gaylor also mentions a Mr. Sheldon arriving from Salvage in June, 1827, and as this man taught school there from 1823 (appendix: Salvage 22), the implication is that there was a considerable population of permanent residents by that time. The earliest official figure gives a population of 250 for Salvage and Barrow Harbour at the end of August, 1832, and the 1836 census indicates that there was a school already established. The most interesting of Gaylor's "Occurrences at Bonavista," however, was the arrival of "a boat from Salvage with a couple to get married" on the 7th October, 1827; the Bonavista Register confirms this with the marriage of Thomas Oldford and Maria Hunter, both of Salvage, the first entry of its kind on record (appendix: Salvage 1).

PERMANENT SETTLEMENT AND THE GROWTH OF COMMUNITIES

The basic information used in the second part of our inquiry consists of marriage and baptismal entries found mainly in the Greenspond register, but also in the Trinity and Bonavista registers, and, after 1841 for the Barrow Harbour/Salvage/Broom Close settlements, in the King's Cove register. Most of the entries refer to the period beginning in 1830, although projection back in time has been attempted where information exists. The method used to manipulate the information involved extraction, sorting, and compilation to reconstitute family profiles, which have been assembled in Figures 4–3, 4–4, 4–5, and 4–6 for each of the settlements, and numbered to correspond with the relevant notes in the appendix. Despite inevitable *lacunae* in the registers, the method is sufficient to permit a detailed examination of demographic processes involved in the permanent settlement of Central Bonavista Bay. Three census reports – 1836, 1845, and 1857 – have been used to provide evidence of development in the local economies and corroborative information on population. The enquiry terminates arbitrarily, but conveniently, in 1857.

Gooseberry Islands (Fig. 4–3)
The first reference to a settled population on Gooseberry Islands occurs in the journal entry of the Methodist preacher John Corlett for the 2nd July 1826: "... there are Protestants at the following places, which may be easily visited ... several times a year, as most of them are contiguous to Green's Pond, and all have intercourse with it;

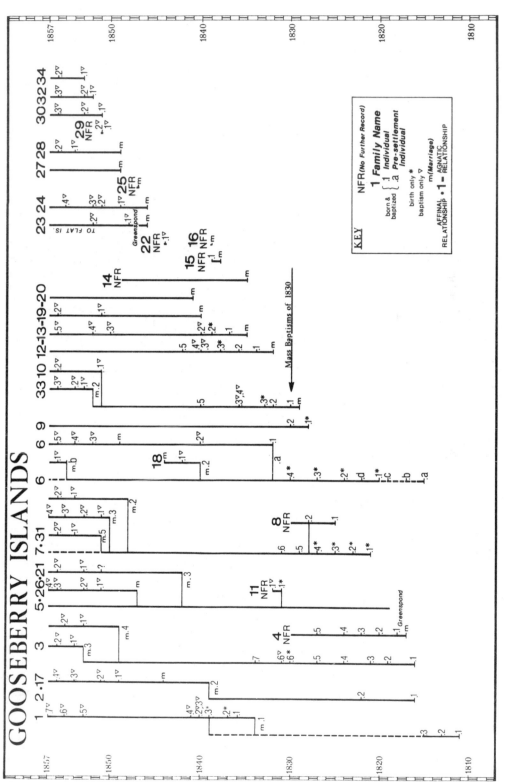

Figure 4-3

... Gooseberry Island ... on which families reside who seldom hear the Gospel"
(Lench, 1919:162, 163). Greenspond was evidently a central place for the Gooseberry
Islanders in 1826. The second reference appears in John Gaylor's diary of "Occurrences at Bonavista" (which covers the three sailing seasons of 1827–28–29) in a
solitary note for 31st May 1829: "Boat from Gooseberry Island, ... bound southward."

Although the Anglican parish registers for Trinity, Bonavista, and Greenspond
began in 1757, 1786, and 1815 respectively, no entries for Gooseberry Islanders appear
until 1829, when the Trinity register included an entry for the marriage of Francis
Wells and Elizabeth Saint, both of Gooseberry Islands, on the 15th of October. As the
marriage entry was unaccompanied by baptisms, it would appear that the couple was
present in Trinity for the occasion, and may well have drawn the resident clergy's
attention to the plight of the Gooseberry Islanders already noted by John Corlett.
Whatever the case, visits by the clergyman at Greenspond on the 9th of June and
5–11th of October, 1830, resulted in the baptism of thirty-five children ranging in age
from eighteen years to newborn, twenty-seven of them on the 5th of October in a mass
baptism. Thereafter annual baptisms took place: six in 1831, four in 1832, none in
1833, and two in 1834. Moreover, as the event was unaccompanied by the celebration
of marriages, it must be assured that the ten families involved were headed by couples
already married, in each case prior to the birth of the eldest child baptised in 1830. The
year of birth, therefore, gives an indication of the latest date of migration to and
settlement in Gooseberry Islands for each pioneer family. Thus, the Haywards or
Howards had arrived by 1811, the Rogers and Sweetapples by 1816, the Crosses by
1818, the Goulds by 1819, the Wells by 1820, the Taylors by 1821, the Bourns by 1825,
the Houses by 1828 (Fig. 4–3; 1–10); of these, only the Goulds, Wells, and House
families were accompanied by siblings or offspring who appear in the records after
1830 but were born and baptised elsewhere. The presence of unmarried siblings prior
to 1830, of course, implies that these families may have been accompanied by unrecorded members of the previous generation; the failure of older children, born and
baptised prior to settlement, to appear in the later record seems to indicate that
pioneer families usually consisted of newly married couples, and that settlement was
established by a process of aggregation, family by family, beginning about 1810. The
marriage of Thomas Cross and Mary Carter (4), both of Greenspond, late in 1817 – the
only one discovered so far for a pioneer family – and the birth of their firstborn in
Gooseberry Islands the following year, seem to confirm this.

Of the ten families present in the community in 1830, two (4, 8) immediately
disappear from the record, and one (2) finds its succession in the community through
daughters (13 and 17). The pioneer component in the later community was provided,
therefore, by seven families bearing six surnames. Two of the original families (Rogers
and Sweetapple) were already related before settlement, and this structural feature of
the community was reinforced by 1841 by the marriages of three House siblings with
women of the Hayward, Rogers, and Taylor families (12, 13, and 20). By 1857, in fact,
each of the surviving pioneer families was related by marriage to at least one other: and
in the cases of the House family to four others, of the Wells and Taylor families to
three others, with exchanges of women occurring between the Hayward and House
families, and between the Sweetapple and Taylor families. Furthermore, of the
sixteen new surnames which appear on record between 1831 and 1857, seven appear in
marriage entries involving women from pioneer families. Of the nineteen families

bearing these surnames, at least nine included wives from pioneer families, indicating an important part of the process which attached the in-coming men to the community.

The population reported for Gooseberry and Deer Islands on August 31, 1832 was 110, of which some 80 persons were on Gooseberry Islands (providing the ratios of the 1836 Census were valid four years earlier).[2] At least 60 of these persons can be identified in the parish registers, assuming survival to 1832.

Between 1831 and 1836 six new families were formed on the Islands, at least nine of the twelve spouses, including five husbands, stemming from the pioneer families of 1830. These raise the number of identifiable family units in the Anglican community to at least fourteen, consisting of some 71 known individuals (again assuming total survival from 1830), a figure identical with the 68 "Episcopalians" and 3 "Dissenters" recorded in the 1836 Census. What part the 26 Roman Catholics recorded on Gooseberry Islands for 1836 may have played in its original settlement cannot be determined from the nature of the information under consideration, and the presence of this non-Anglican component in the population (26.8 percent in 1836, 24.5 percent in 1845, and 21.5 percent in 1857) obviates any possibility of using census information to interpret or validate the picture derived from the Anglican registers. All that can be said is that the Anglican community's share of the eleven recorded dwelling houses must have included a number of two- or three-family households, implying that extended and joint family structures were common in the community. One of these probably included the widow Rogers, her two daughters, and her newly acquired son-in-law, William House (Fig. 3:2 and 13). Another probably included the Greenspond man (Pond, 14) who married a Wells in 1835.

From 1837 to 1845, ten families appear in the registers for the first time. Two of these seem to have arrived about 1836 and to have moved to Flat Island, probably together, about 1839 (Fig. 4–2; appendix, Flat Island: 23, 8), three made ephemeral appearances in 1838–39, 1839, and 1844 respectively (15, 16, and 22), and a sixth seems to have been terminated by death of the husband (18), and remarriage of the widow (17); none of these left any succession in the community. Thus, of the ten new families only four were significant to the future of the community: the Paynes (17) who began with a marriage with the remaining Rogers girl; two of the House siblings (19 and 20), and the Saunders family which began with the marriage of a Greenspond man to one of the Gould girls (21). By 1845 the Anglican part of the community consisted of at least sixteen families, eleven of whom were "Episcopalians," and occupied their share of the seventeen dwelling houses recorded in the census of that year.

During the intercensal period from 1846 to 1857 seventeen new families appeared in the registers, examination of which is instructive to our understanding of the process of aggregative growth. Six were headed by men of the pioneer families (3.3, 3.4, 7.2, 7.3, 6.b, and 10.3): four were headed by men married to women of pioneer families (3.5, 5.5, 6.4 and 7.3) and one to a Greenspond woman (3.3). Four were headed by new settlers from Greenspond, Indian Bay (two men), and Wimborne, Dorset (18, 26, 31 and 33) who were married to women of pioneer families (6a.1, 5.4, 7.4, and 10.2). Two more were headed by Dorset men (27 and 24) married to Greenspond women related to in-migrant men from Greenspond (18 and 28), and another was headed by a man who had been connected earlier with Salvage (34). This last and two others whose antecedents are unknown (30 and 32) appeared in Gooseberry Islands already married, their wives unidentifiable from the local registers. This is also true of a family (29) which appeared ephemerally in 1851. Finally, a family (23) which appeared first in 1848 with

Greenspond and Port de Grave (Conception Bay) antecedents, disappeared after 1852, to reappear in Flat Island with the remarriage of the wife (appendix, Flat Island:5a).

The period from 1839, and particularly from 1846 to 1857, therefore, was a time when much new blood, mostly from Greenspond and from Dorset *via* Greenspond, entered Gooseberry Islands to diversify its surname structure and at the same time integrate with the older pioneer component in the population. As the year 1857 moves the story of early settlement into the second generation, it is significant for both household structure and succession that some twenty families were in their reproductive cycles and were occupying the Anglican share, say twenty, of the twenty-four houses recorded for the community.

Flat Island (Fig. 4–4)
From the evidence of the surnames which appear in the parish registers between 1830 and 1857, Flat Island became a permanent settlement in the late 1820s. It was settled by families from Greenspond and King's Cove and developed further by an influx of settlers from Conception Bay – predominantly from the Port de Grave vicinity. By 1857 nine of the sixteen surnames in the community had originated in Conception Bay.

None of the Anglican registers from Bonavista Bay indicate the presence of a permanent population on Flat Island until 1830 when a Hallett family (1) presented two children for baptism, born in 1827 and 1829. The head of this family, which in the absence of other evidence must be taken as the pioneer family at Flat Island, was almost certainly a settler from Greenspond of Somerset origin. In 1832 a Dyer family headed by a woman (2) appeared ephemerally in the register to baptise a child born in 1827, and an eleven-year-old boy, with no family affiliation, was baptised James Cheater. The first family with this name appeared in 1853, headed by a man who might well have been James Cheater's older brother (3); it included older sons. No marriage record is in evidence within Bonavista Bay, and it may be surmised that the Cheaters had maintained an intermittent relationship with the incipient community at Flat Island until 1853, based perhaps on an earlier transhumant contact with the place as a fishing station. If so, in that sense they may have predated the Halletts. The Hallett family, in fact, preceded other settlers by some eight years, the next family appearing in the register in 1836 to baptise a child born in 1835.

The census of 1836 indicates a community at Flat Island in that year consisting of seven households, considerably smaller than the somewhat older community to the north at Gooseberry Islands. The population consisted of twenty-three individuals who were members of the community by family affiliation, and three male servants. As all were "Protestant Episcopalians" the census can be used to describe the economic basis for the incipient settlement at that time: the fishery was prosecuted from four small boats with a capacity of less than 15 quintals; 392 bushels of potatoes were harvested from the two-and-half acres of cultivated land; twelve hogs constituted the sole livestock. From the evidence in the parish registers it seems likely that the original Hallett pioneers, accompanied perhaps by the Dyer and Cheater families, had been joined by two Sanson or Samson families (4 and 5: first baptism in 1836 and 1838 respectively for children over a year old); by a Kelligrew family (6: first baptism in 1840 for a child nearly two years old); and by a Roff or Ralph family (7: first baptism 1840, again for a child over a year old). The arrival of the Ralph family by 1836 is dubious because of the fact that it was apparently accompanied by older children for

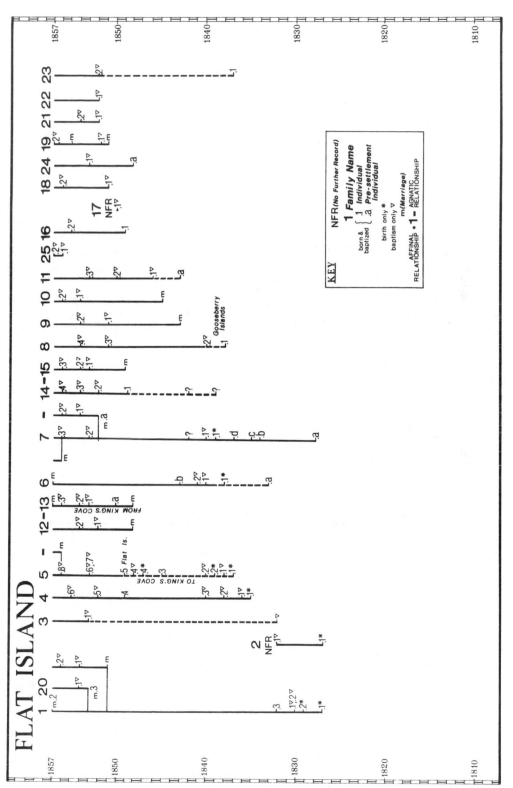

Figure 4-4

whom no baptismal record exists in Bonavista Bay and yet who were born after the census year. The explanation may lie in the fact that *Kelligrew* and *Ralph* are Conception Bay names: these were the families that began the influx from that quarter and some members of the family may have migrated later than others in the transition from "stationer" to "liveyer." The Sanson families originated in King's Cove, Bonavista Bay, where the name appears in the 1806 Register of Fishing Rooms, and to which one of the families (5) returned temporarily between 1840 and 1845, reappearing in Flat Island in 1849; again some ambivalence regarding the establishment of permanent residence seems to have prevailed for a few years. Indeed, it would not be carrying speculation too far to suggest that the decision to take up permanent residence at Flat Island from Conception Bay was signalled by the challenge from the Bonavista Bay settlements at Greenspond and King's Cove. What is certain is that the Sansons and Ralphs were accompanied or followed to Flat Island by siblings of both sexes who appear later in the marriage entries.

The Census of 1845 recorded eighteen households in the Flat Island community, an increase of eleven during the nine-year intercensal period – a figure difficult to reconcile with the family histories reconstituted from the parish registers. The original Hallett family was still there and still undivided, as were the more recent newcomers: the Ralph, Kelligrew, and remaining Sansom or Samson families; perhaps the Cheaters were also represented. They had been joined by the Hiscock and Hicks families from Gooseberry Islands in 1839, although the latter appeared on record in Flat Island only in 1852 (8 and 23). In the census year a Rogers family was established by the marriage of a widower with one of the Ralph siblings (10), and a Pike family which appears abruptly in the baptismal register in 1846 (11) was also probably present, accompanied by a pre-settlement son born in 1843. It is also possible that Edward Morgan (9) and his wife Frances Wills or Wells (Gooseberry Islands, 6.3), married within the Greenspond mission in 1843 but only appearing as baptising parents in Flat Island between 1851 and 1861, were also already present. Their marriage, in any case, is the first on record within the Bonavista Bay and Trinity registers representing any connection with Flat Island, a further indication of the more distant points of origin of the other families in the community and the recentness of settlement. This accounts for only ten resident families, and as the census population had grown from 26 individuals to 108 – only 2 of whom were Roman Catholic – one is forced to conclude that considerable numbers of seasonal fishing servants and transhumant "stationer" families were present when the census was taken. These latter probably included families who later appear on record as residents of Flat Island between 1845 and 1857.

Consonant with the increase in population associated with the settlement, the economy of Flat Island also exhibited growth by 1845. The cod fishery was being prosecuted from four small boats (4–15 quintals) and six larger boats (15–30 quintals), with the use of three cod seines; a seal fishery was also pursued with 36 sealing nets, indicating a winter, rather than a spring, operation. The landward resource was represented by 6 acres in cultivation and "in possession" on which 408 bushels of potatoes were grown; livestock consisted of 6 Newfoundland-raised "neat cattle" (cows), 11 sheep, 27 pigs, and 18 goats – in all, a substantial basis for the subsistence of the community.

The community continued to grow between 1845 and 1857: households increased from 18 to 24, and the population more dramatically from 108 to 210 individuals, indicating that much of the increase represented additions to existing households.

Baptised children, supposing that all survived until 1857, account for 53 individuals, while immigrant parents and in-migrating spouses account for a further 26 persons, or about 80 percent of the recorded increase. More specifically, second-generation and younger-sibling families of the first generation proliferated after 1845: a Cheater family, two Halletts, two Sansons or Samsons (5a and 12) – involving women from Lower Amherst Cove and Port de Grave (via Gooseberry Islands) – joined by a third Samson from King's Cove who arrived about 1851 (13), and four Ralph families, one of which appears abruptly in the baptismal record in 1849 (7, 14, 15): a total of ten. Hallett, Kelligrew, and Ralph women were responsible for attaching Philpott (20), Honnibon (26), and Petten (19) families to the community, the last joined by an in-migrating sibling family (24). A second Pike family, two Powers, two Butts, and a Crocker family also made their appearance (16–22, 24–26). The arrival of the Pettens, Pikes, Powers, Butts, and Crockers ensured that Flat Island thenceforward was dominated by the Conception Bay element in its population.

In 1857 the community on Flat Island was a homogeneous one, four of its 210 inhabitants born in England, the rest in Newfoundland, and all of them adherents of the Church of England. It was essentially a fishing community, based on 16 rooms, from which 16 boats of varying sizes caught 2370 quintals of codfish, using 45 nets and seines; four vessels were engaged in the seal fishery, catching 1147 seals with the aid of 17 seal-nets. The settlement itself consisted of 24 inhabited houses, containing 29 families – virtually the number identifiable in the parish registers (Fig. 4–2); and like Gooseberry Islands, it had an Anglican church and a school. In terms of a landward subsistence economy, the Flat Islanders were cultivating $12\frac{1}{2}$ acres of improved land, on which they raised half a ton of hay and 524 barrels of potatoes; stock consisted of 81 sheep and 39 swine and goats.

By 1857, therefore, Flat Island was equal in size to Gooseberry Islands, and had a well-developed and diversified fishing-and-farming economy. It had taken only thirty years (1827–57) to achieve a position which took Gooseberry Islands fifty years, largely because of family migration from Conception Bay.

Bloody Bay (Fig. 4–5)

Bloody Bay, the future site of Glovertown and future home of many of the Gooseberry and Flat Islanders when resettlement processes began in the 20th century, was a one-family settlement between 1834 and 1857. As such, it represents the beginning of that process which carried settlement into the inner recesses of Bonavista Bay.

Richard Elliott Stroud was an Englishman married to a woman reputed to be from Greenspond (1). Their eldest child was baptised at Greenspond in 1829, whereas their second was born and baptised at Bloody Bay in 1834, indicating settlement at the latter place some time between those years. Stroud seems to have been a true pioneer of the settlement frontier in that his interests included fur trapping and hunting, and this probably accounts for the presence of young unattached men at his establishment from time to time (see 2, 3, and 4).

The Census of 1836 bears out the solitary position of the Stroud family: it records one woman and four girls under fourteen years of age, but neither Stroud himself nor any other male belonging to the young family. Whatever the reason for his absence, he was not fishing, for he had no boat – unless a distant fishery accounted for the absence of both man and boat. He had no servants, yet a head of family who was a servant is listed, indicating perhaps that Stroud himself was an agent for a merchant elsewhere:

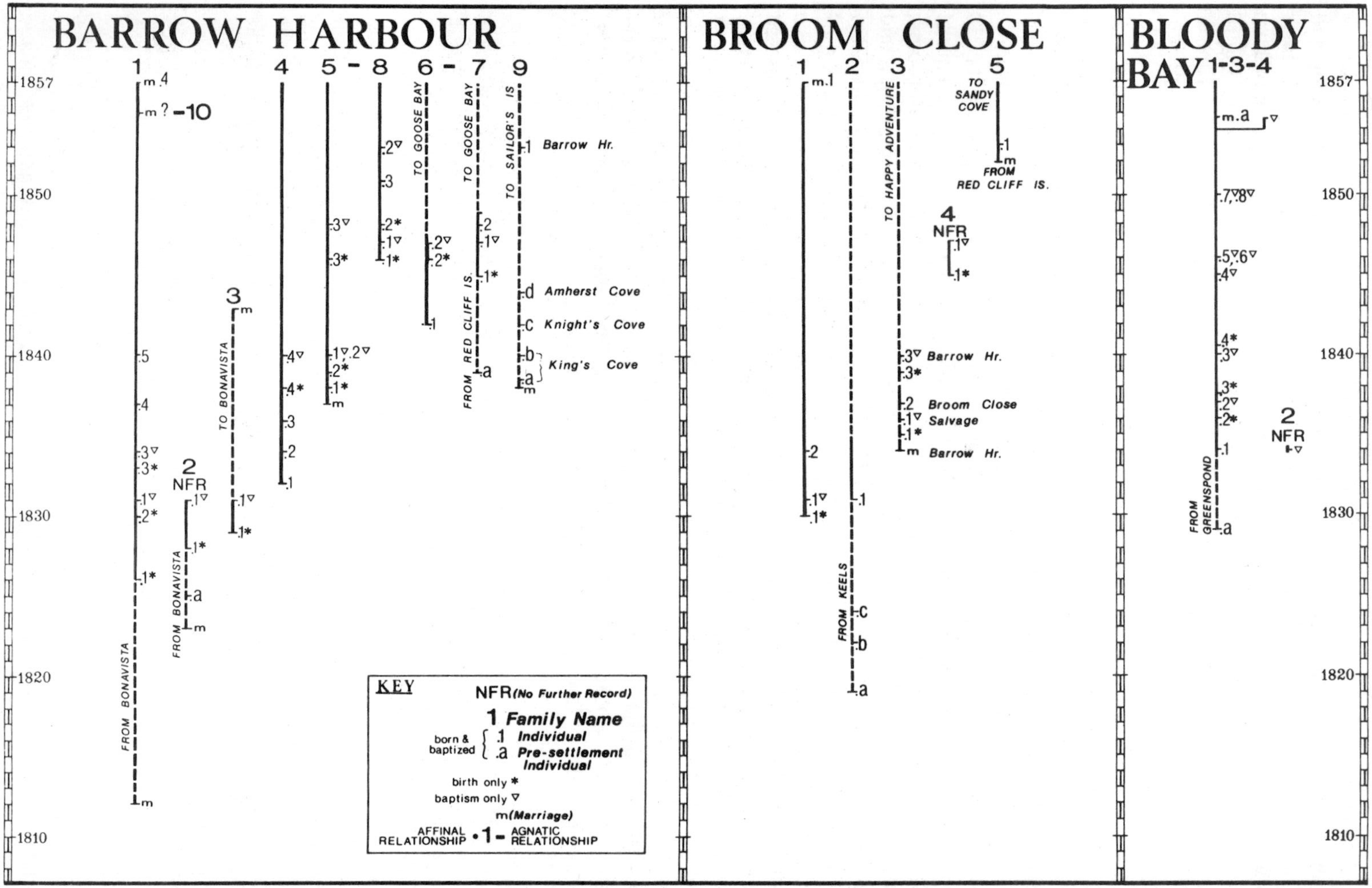
BARROW HARBOUR
BROOM CLOSE
BLOODY BAY
1857
1850
1840
1830
1820
1810
FROM BONAVISTA
TO BONAVISTA
TO GOOSE BAY
FROM RED CLIFF IS.
TO SAILOR'S IS
Barrow Hr.
Amherst Cove
Knight's Cove
King's Cove
FROM KEELS
TO HAPPY ADVENTURE
Broom Close
Salvage
TO SANDY COVE
FROM RED CLIFF IS.
FROM GREENSPOND
NFR
KEY
NFR (No Further Record)
1 Family Name
born & baptized
.1 Individual
.a Pre-settlement Individual
birth only *
baptism only ▽
m (Marriage)
AFFINAL RELATIONSHIP •1– AGNATIC RELATIONSHIP

Figure 4–5

there was only one household. The family had a quarter-acre of land under cultivation and was raising some seventy bushels of potatoes on it yearly. Livestock consisted of one solitary cow. The picture is one of recent and precarious settlement.

By 1845 the picture had changed and the household was firmly established. It now consisted of twelve souls: Stroud and two boys – probably servants – his wife, two girls over fourteen and six girls under fourteen, one or two of whom were probably servants: the parish register indicates a family of one older and four younger daughters. Stroud, at this time, had a small boat, but no cod seines or sealing nets, and all the evidence suggests that his main effort was directed towards developing a livelihood from landward resources. He held six acres "in possession" of which four were in cultivation, representing rather rapid reclamation of land as compared with the two island communities at that time. He was producing some fifty barrels of potatoes, but no other crops; his livestock then numbered four cows and five goats.

By 1857 the Strouds had had at least ten children, all but one, girls, the last of whom was baptised late in 1858. The eldest girl had married a man from St. Malo "in the Kingdom of France" in 1854, perhaps one of her father's servants, and had left the community for Greenspond where they were on record in 1862 (4). Bloody Bay had only eight inhabitants: Stroud himself, two boys (a son and a servant), two girls in their teens, and two little girls (one a baby). He was a widower, his wife having died within the year. The attenuated family was engaged in catching and curing fish from its solitary fishing room, on which stood three stores and barns, and two houses – one uninhabited, perhaps abandoned by the son-in-law. No boat is mentioned and no cod catch is recorded; but he was working thirty-one nets and seines, probably round the mouth of the Terra Nova River, to catch the nine tierces of salmon which constituted his sole recorded catch. His improved arable land had shrunk, more realistically, to one-and-a-half acres, producing half a ton of hay for his eleven sheep, and fifty barrels of potatoes for his family – the same amount as in 1845. Bloody Bay in 1857 demonstrated the fundamental difficulties of single-family settlements in maintaining momentum on Newfoundland's pioneer fringe.

Barrow Harbour (Fig. 4–5)
Thomas Gaylor, the agent for Bremner's of Trinity at Bonavista who made occasional reference to Barrow Harbour in his "Occurrences," mentions "John Wills [Wells] from Barrow Harbour" in April 1829.

Despite its history of early settlement and economic nodality within Bonavista Bay, Barrow Harbour makes its first appearance in the registers in 1831, when Wells, Powell, and Biddlecome families (1, 2 and 3) baptised children born in 1826, 1828, and 1829 respectively. Wells and Powell were almost certainly brothers-in-law, and it is significant for any attempt to establish the date and source of permanent settlement that both were married in Bonavista, Wells in 1812 and Powell in 1823; Powell also had a child baptised there late in 1825. This would indicate a move to Barrow Harbour in 1826. Biddlecome's antecedents are unknown, but with no succession at Barrow Harbour he was probably the widower resident in Bonavista who remarried there in 1843. A King family (4) was also present by 1831, probably coming from Old Perlican, but with earlier associations with Barrow Harbour.

The 1836 Census recorded seven households at Barrow Harbour, comprising thirty-seven souls, of whom eight were servants (seven of them males). The resident families included ten active males, but only five active women and girls. The community, which was largely Episcopalian (except for two Catholics, possibly servants), was therefore only slightly larger than Flat Island, and considerably smaller than Gooseberry Islands, suggesting that its origin as a permanent settlement was quite recent, and that Garland's comment of 1810 may have referred to "inhabitants" from elsewhere in Newfoundland who were beginning to frequent the place seasonally. Recency of settlement is also indicated by the facts that the economy was based on three small boats (capacity less than 15 quintals) and two somewhat larger ones (15–30 quintals), $2^3/_4$ acres of land in possession, of which but 2.5 acres were cultivated, producing $536^1/_2$ bushels of potatoes and $1^1/_2$ tons of hay annually. Livestock consisted of 1 horse, 6 "neat cattle," 1 hog, and 14 sheep.

Between 1836 and 1845 the Wells, Powell, and King families continued as nuclear units in the community. A marriage in 1837 added a Matchem family (5), the name originating in the Parish of East Orchard near Sturminster Newton in Dorset. Baptisms in 1847 of children born in 1845 or early 1846 suggest the in-migration of a second Matchem family (8) and two Holloway families (6 and 7) in the summer of 1845 or somewhat earlier, increasing the number of known families present to seven.

In 1845, however, the census again indicated a larger community than that suggested by the parish registers: a population of 80 (including Little Harbour), in 13 households, including 26 active males. All but seven were Episcopalian, suggesting Catholic servants or one Catholic family Access to marine resources was gained by four small boats (4–15 quintals), three larger boats (15–30 quintals) and two larger vessels (of over 30 quintals); there were 2 cod seines and 36 sealing nets in the community. An enlarged landward resource was represented by $8^1/_2$ acres in possession, of which $7^1/_2$ were cultivated, raising 262 barrels of potatoes and 6 tons of hay; livestock included 1 horse, 9 "neat cattle," 23 sheep, 15 pigs and 4 goats. The doubling of the population, in terms of individuals and nuclear families, since 1836 had been matched by considerable advances in both the fishery and supplementary agriculture.

Between 1845 and 1857 the community was joined by a Babstock family (9), which moved from King's Cove via Knight's Cove and Amherst Cove to Barrow Harbour sometime between 1844 and 1853, and by a family formed from the marriage of one of the Wells women to a Crocker (10), probably from Conception Bay (see Flat Islands, 17); the population now included nine identifiable families. The census taken at the end of this period shows that a slight increase in population had occurred: 85 persons, including 3 dissenters and 3 Catholics (probably servants). There were 12 households, 2 houses "building," and 2 abandoned (perhaps by the Holloways), and the fixed capital included 9 fishing rooms, each with a store, employing 30 people in catching and curing (15 of them fishermen). The marine side of the economy was represented by 12 fishing boats of 4–15 quintal capacity (one per family?), and 2 larger boats of 15–30 quintal capacity. From these they operated 39 nets or seines and had caught and cured 1157 quintals of cod, 9 tierces of salmon, and 203 barrels of herring, and had produced about 1157 gallons of cod oil. The seal fishery continued at about the same level, with 29 seal nets in use; but by this time the community at Barrow Harbour was also prosecuting the spring seal hunt in a single vessel with 25 crewmen – virtually the entire male population.

The landward aspect of the economy was equally impressive by 1857. Twelve acres of land had been improved to produce 8 tons of hay, 89 barrels of potatoes, and 2 barrels of turnips, and the obvious emphasis on fodder was reflected in the 11 milk cows, 4 horses, 41 sheep, and 57 swine and goats. Barrow Harbour, for all its

smallness and slowness of growth, was undoubtedly the most prosperous and successful settlement in central Bonavista Bay, its success perhaps in part a fulfilment of the
promise inherent in its long history, and in part a sign of adaptation and change in the
way of life of the people who lived there.

Salvage (Fig. 4–6)
When Salvage appeared in the parochial registers it was already the largest community
in central Bonavista Bay. Like Barrow Harbour it had a longer history than the rest of
the settlements.

Earlier evidence has already indicated that the names *Dick* or *Dyke, Sheldon,
Oldford, Hunter* and *Brown* were the first in Salvage, and their bearers the first
permanent settlers. This is confirmed by the Anglican registers, and since Salvage was
94 percent Anglican in 1836, these can be accepted as representative. Thus, baptismal
entries reveal the presence, by 1836, of three Oldford families (2, 4, and 10), three
Brown families (5, 6 and 7), and two Dyke families (9 and 11), while the marriage
entries show the formation of two Hunter families (16 and 18), a third Dyke family (24),
and a fourth Oldford family (10.1), involving wives from Babstock (Broom Close:3),
Oldford, Moss and Brown families respectively. Sisters of early settlers were responsible for the formation of Durdle/Hunter (14), Crisby/Dyke (20), and Troke/Hunter
(25) families, and a Samson family resulted from the remarriage of Sheldon, the school
teacher's widow (23). Besides these, the baptismal entries include two Lane families
(8 and 15), probably stemming from the man in Barrow Harbour in 1806, and Steed
(13), Bull (17), Trim (19) and White (26) families; the marriage entries include Garrett
(3), Fish (21), and Squire (12) families, the last involving a wife related to one of the
Oldford wives (10).

Thus, of the thirty-four nuclear families (twenty-three surnames) known to have
been in Salvage by 1857, twenty-seven were already there by 1836, indicating a
well-established community by that year at least. On the other hand, the recency of the
process is shown from marriages and baptisms elsewhere, and from the birth-years of
individuals who appear later in the registers: at least one of the Oldford families moved
from Bonavista after 1814, and possibly as late as 1822–24 (10); at least one of the
Brown families moved from King's Cove after 1825 (5), and possibly all of them about
1828; and at least one of the Dyke families moved from Bonavista as late as 1830 (11).

The 1836 Census corroborates the conclusions derived from the Anglican registers.
It shows Salvage as a settlement of some 30 households and a population of 181,*
including 27 male servants, and 4 female servants, or a resident population of 150. Of
these, over a hundred can be identified from the registers. There were 11 Catholics.
Thirty-seven active males from the resident families and 27 male servants (total 64)
fished from 11 small boats (4–15 quintals) and 8 larger boats (15–30 quintals). The
landward economy involved ownership of $6^1/_2$ acres, and actual cultivation of $11^1/_2$
acres on which $2756^1/_2$ bushels of potatoes and $5^1/_2$ tons of hay were grown. Livestock
consisted of 1 horse, 18 "neat cattle," 45 hogs and 13 sheep.

The period from 1836 to 1845 saw eight new families established by marriage in the
community: four of these were headed by men who were older sons or younger
siblings of earlier settlers (7a, 10a, 10c, and 27), the other four by men with new

---

* Indicating that the 1832 figure of 250 for Salvage and Barrow Harbour, if accurate, must have included
seasonal population.

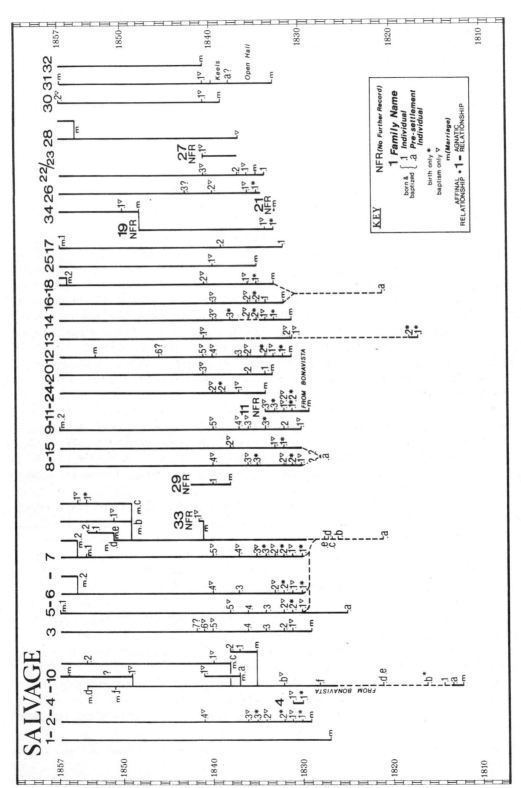

Figure 4–6

surnames who had married older daughters or younger sisters of early settlers: Bishop (29), two Burdens (30 and 32), and a Flinn (33). There is also some slight evidence of a Hapgood family, an offshoot of one at Broom Close (28). It was during this period, too, that a Moss family from King's Cove with connections by marriage with the Hapgoods of Broom Close (31), moved via Keels to Salvage, probably in 1839, and evidently began developing a farm at Salvage Bay (see Barrow Harbour:9). The total of identifiable families was thirty-six.

The period from 1845 to 1857 added only one new surname to the community: that of *Dunn*, introduced from Bonavista in 1848 by marriage to an earlier settler's daughter. But the same period saw the formation of at least fourteen new families among the Browns (eight), Oldfords (three), Dykes, Hunters, and Mosses (one each), the wives coming from established families (five), or from other settlements in Bonavista Bay (nine cases), bringing the total to about fifty by 1857. Thus it seems evident that by 1836, and to an even greater degree by 1845, Salvage was virtually closed to new settlers in terms of access to unclaimed foreshore. Virtually all growth stemmed from the families already established, and diversification of the local economy was already underway.

The rapid demographic advance of Salvage revealed in the registers is confirmed by the 1845 and 1857 censuses. These indicate that the number of households increased from 30 to 41 to 53, the population from 181 to 295 to 381, and the number of fishermen from 64 to 94 to 129. Its denominational composition had consolidated, the few Catholics, Presbyterians, and Wesleyans of 1845 having disappeared entirely by 1857. The Anglican school had 53 pupils in both 1845 and 1857.

Economic advance was equally dramatic, both at sea and on the land. Maritime activities were conducted from twenty-six fishing rooms in 1857, a reflection of the original tenure rights established by the original families before 1836. The size of the inshore fleets in the years 1836 and 1845 was approximately the same. In 1845 there were 11 small and 10 larger boats in the 4–15 and 15–30 quintal categories. But to this had been added seven boats over 30-quintals in capacity for the cod-fishery, and – even more impressive – two vessels, amounting to 100 tons, sailing to the seal fishery. By 1857 there were 31 of the small boats, 6 of the larger, and 5 boats of over 30-quintal capacity in the cod and salmon fishery; in addition there were 4 vessels, totalling 204 tons, in the seal fishery. Cultivated acreage increased from 11.25 to 19.5 to 27.5 acres in 1857, showing steady reclamation of land further up the peninsula. This increase, however, was not reflected in the harvested production: 5.5 tons of hay, the same as the 1836 figure after peaking at 17 tons in 1845; and 742 barrels of potatoes and 43 barrels of turnips, compared to 909 barrels in 1845. Livestock did increase: there were no horses in 1845 or 1857, but there were 19 "neat cattle" and five milk cows, 33 sheep, and 154 swine and goats in 1857. The swine/goats ratio was 2:1 in 1845.

Broom Close (Fig. 4–5)
Broom Close, unlike Barrow Harbour and Salvage, has no history of settlement prior to its appearance in the Greenspond Anglican register in 1831. In that year the Abgood (or Hapgood) and Knapper (or Napper) families had children baptised. The Knapper child had been born in 1830, presumably at Broom Close, and the family was probably accompanied by a daughter born elsewhere about 1822 (1). The Hapgood family had moved from Keels after 1822, and probably after 1824 (2). All indications, therefore, are that Broom Close was a new settlement when it appeared first in the record. The

1836 census confirms that it consisted of two families; it was, therefore, comparable in size to Bloody Bay among the central Bonavista Bay communities.

There are some indications in the register that a branch of the Babstock family at Barrow Harbour had some association with Broom Close (see Broom Close:3, Barrow Harbour:9, and Salvage:16, 21), and shared its tendency to migrate, being at Broom Close in 1832–34, at Salvage in 1836, at Broom Close in 1837, and at Barrow Harbour in 1840, eventually moving to Happy Adventure after 1857.

According to the 1836 Census, the community consisted of seven persons, including Knapper's widow with at least one child; they fished from one small boat, probably Hapgood's, and grew 117.5 bushels of potatoes from one-eighth of an acre; they had no livestock whatever. The 1845 Census indicates that this small Anglican community had been joined by sixteen Catholics who were responsible for raising the level of economic activity to two small and one larger fishing boat and an acre of land on which ninety-five barrels of potatoes were produced; livestock consisted of six pigs and three goats. By 1857, however, although the population numbered twenty-five persons living in three households, there was only one Catholic left. The passage of the Catholics, however, was marked in the Anglican registers by the ephemeral appearance of families of the names *Barron* and *Quinton* (4 and 5), the former in 1847, the latter arriving from Red Cliff Island in 1852. In economic terms, however, the community did not grow: from the two original fishing rooms (one store) two small boats and one net or seine were used to land the catch which was correspondingly small: 160 quintals of cod and 20 barrels of herring. Improved land diminished to a half-acre raising ten barrels of potatoes, and livestock consisted of one pig or goat. In 1857, therefore, despite recent marriages to establish successor families, Broom Close was a poor and stagnating community, and it is not surprising that at least two of the families associated with the settlement moved away to the new communities of Sandy Cove and Happy Adventure shortly after 1857.

CONCLUSIONS

Examination of the pattern and process of early settlement in Central Bonavista Bay by means of family reconstitution from parish registers reveals three characteristics which may have wider significance for any attempt to understand the settlement of coastal Newfoundland. These characteristics concern the initiation of permanent settlement, the surname structure of the community, and the processes of initial in-migration of settlers and later integration of newcomers.

Whatever may have been the story of earlier activities, permanent settlement of Central Bonavista Bay was a 19th century phenomenon, as suggested by the evidence in the parish registers for dates of initial settlement. These have been listed for each settlement (Table 4–2), with "theoretical" dates based on regression for the rate of growth in the landward economy – the essential component – as indicated by the "population" and "improved/cultivated acreage" parameters in the 1836 and 1845 censuses. This test appears to be justified, as growth in these parameters tended to continue at the same or a reduced rate in the next intercensal (1845–57). In every case the "theoretical" dates are later than the empirical ones, suggesting that the latter are, indeed, related realistically to the transition from seasonal to permanent settlement and all the decisional changes which this implied. Corroboration comes from the Governor's Returns which began to record acreage of improved land in 1802. The

TABLE 4–2

Empirical and Theoretical Dates of First Settlement (see Fig. 4–7)

| Settlement | Register | Census Regression | |
		"Population"	"Improved/Cultivated Acreage"
Gooseberry Islands	1810	1820	1827
Flat Island	1826	1833	1829
Bloody Bay	1830–34	—	1835
Barrow Harbour	1826	1827	1831
Salvage	1810	1822	1824
Broom Close	1825–29	—	1835

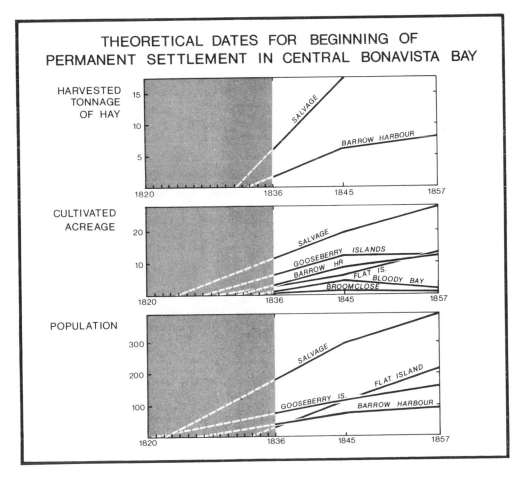

Figure 4–7

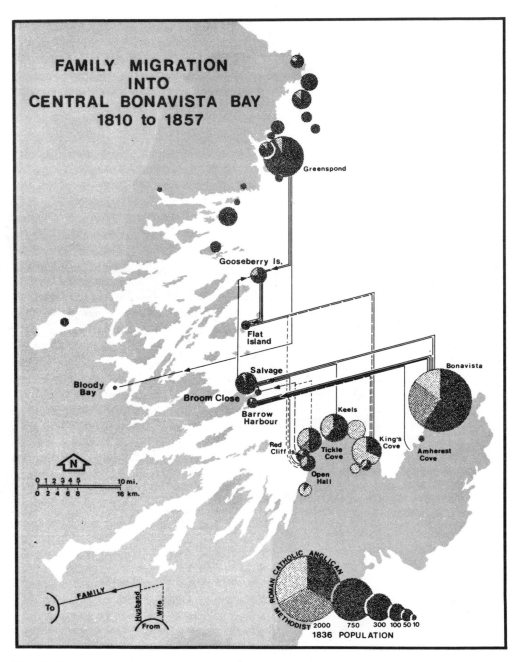

Figure 4–8

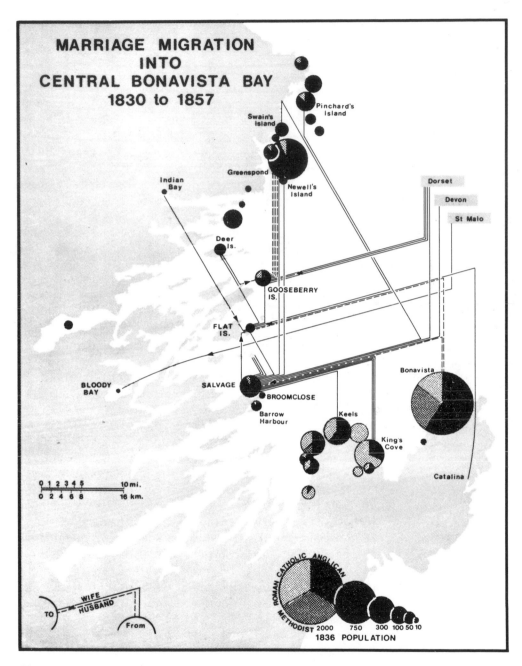

MARRIAGE MIGRATION
INTO
CENTRAL BONAVISTA BAY
1830 to 1857

Figure 4–9

Bonavista-King's Cove division of the Bay appears for the first time in 1812 with 80 acres, and records annual increments up to 850 acres in 1825, indicating a phase of rapid land reclamation along the south side of the Bay. In the same period the Greenspond-Salvage-Gooseberry Islands division of the Bay consistently records no measurable acreage, usually returned as "very little" or "only a little for gardens."

The Appendix demonstrates that each of the six early settlements had a distinctive assemblage of surnames. Only five of the seventy-five family surnames on record in the area between 1827 and 1857 appeared in more than one settlement: *Wells* (Gooseberry Islands and Barrow Harbour), *Samson* (Flat Island and Salvage), *Rogers* (Gooseberry Islands and Flat Island), *Babstock* and *Hapgood* (Salvage, Barrow Harbour and Broom Close). Only in the cases of *Babstock* and *Hapgood* is there any evidence of a close relationship between the families concerned. This characteristic, common in Newfoundland, can only be the result of peculiarities in the actual migration, land-taking, and integration involved.

Particular primary settlements played a dominant role in providing settlers for specific secondary settlements: Greenspond for Gooseberry Islands, Conception Bay (Port de Grave) for Flat Island, Bonavista for Salvage and Barrow Harbour. Figure 4–8, which is based upon evidence from the Bonavista Bay and Trinity registers exclusively and does not contain anything derived from Conception Bay registers, demonstrates this characteristic effectively, although it also shows the minor role of other settlements, including some within Central Bonavista Bay itself, in providing settlers for places chosen for permanent settlement. Secondly, family migration was often a group effort involving brothers, cousins, or brothers-in-law, and thus tended to concentrate resources in the new settlement in the hands of a few families from a single source area. Thirdly, once the settlement was established, the institution of marriage, endogamous to the community and sometimes involving exchange of women between settler families not already related, began to operate to strengthen social cohesion and consolidate the position of the earlier families. And fourthly, single men from elsewhere or already working in the community were able to secure a niche only by marrying into one of the original families. In addition later in-migrating families who were unrelated to the pioneer group were often obliged to move on. Thus, of thirty-four marriages in which the male spouses had come to work in the community first or migrated in at marriage, thirty-one involved wives who were sisters or daughters (or in one or two instances, widows) of original settlers. Small secondary communities tended, within one generation of initial settlement, to become tightly-knit structures restricting further access to local resources.

Migration of potential spouses, within and into Central Bonavista Bay (Fig. 4–9), bears a striking similarity to the pattern of family migration. Individuals of both sexes, seeking to bring a marriage partner into a settlement, tended to look towards the settlements from which earlier families had come; and since marriage migration is always preceded by social and economic contacts between the settlements involved, the implication is that the exclusive nature of the community which developed in secondary settlements was a reflection of their relationship with settlements from which each was derived and with which each continued to interact.

NOTES

1   Diary of Benjamin Lester, Trinity: 19/21/26 Aug. 1762, 18 May 1764, 25 May, 14 June, 28/29 July 1767.
2   C.S.0.2/11: Incoming Correspondence, Colonial Secretary's Office, September to December 1832: 53, 54.

REFERENCES: PRIMARY SOURCES

GAYLOR, THOMAS
Occurrences at Bonavista, 1829–29. Typescript, Gosling Library, St. John's.
GOVERNORS' RETURNS
These are to be found in the C.O. 1- and 194-series, P.R.O., London. A "Finding Aid" to these returns is appended to C. Grant Head's "Eighteenth Century Newfoundland," p. 281.
LESTER, BENJAMIN
1719–64 Diary of Benjamin Lester. Dorset County Record Office, Dorchester: D365.
POOL, SIR WILLIAM
An Accompt of all the Inhabitants and Planters from St. John's to Bonavista, 1677. C.O. 1:41, ff. 158–166.
REGISTER OF FISHING ROOMS
Bonavista Bay, 1806. Gosling Library, St. John's.
REGISTERS (ANGLICAN PARISH)
Trinity (1757–   ), Bonavista (1786–   ), Greenspond (1815–   ), and King's Cove (1834–   ). Vital Statistics, Confederation Building, St. John's.
RUSSELL, CAPT.
Accompt of ye English Inhabitants of Newfoundland, 1676. C.O. 1: 38, ff. 239– , P.R.O., London.
STORY, CAPT. JAMES
List of Planters, 1681. C.O. 1:47, f121r; and Report, 1681, Calendar of Colonial State Papers: Americas and West Indies, p. 106.

REFERENCES: SECONDARY SOURCES

HEAD, C. G.
1971 "The Changing Geography of Newfoundland in the Eighteenth Century." Doctoral dissertation, University of Wisconsin; now published as:
HEAD, C. G.
1976 Eighteenth Century Newfoundland: A Geographer's Perspective. Toronto, McClelland and Stewart.
LENCH, REV. CHARLES
1919 The Story of Methodism in Bonavista and of the Settlements Visited by the Early Preachers. St. John's, Robinson & Co., 2nd edition.
LYSAGHT, A. M.
1971 Joseph Banks in Newfoundland and Labrador 1766: His Diary, Manuscripts and Collections. London, Faber and Faber.

APPENDIX: Index to Figures 4–3 to 4–6

GOOSEBERRY ISLANDS (Fig. 4–3)

1 HAYWARD or HOWARD, Thomas. His son (.1) Joseph (c.1811–1890) married Anne HOUSE (c. 1815–1891), 28 Oct., 1834; his daughter (.3) Elizabeth married James BURRY of Greenspond, 9 Nov., 1835 (see 18).

2 ROGERS, ———. Catherine ROGERS (1793–1881) was probably his widow. Their daughters Frances (.1) and Anne (.2) married William HOUSE (13) and Robert PAYNE (17), respectively.

3 SWEETAPPLE, William and Sarah (ROGERS ?, probably a sister of 2). Their sons William (1816–1893) and Edward (1819–1889) died apparently unmarried and without succession, while Giles (.3) married Jane BURTON of Greenspond (1826–1880), 14 Nov., 1853, and John (.4) (1823–1907) married Jane TAYLOR (7.3). Their daughter Anne (.6) married William PETTEN, Flat Islands (Flat. Is. 19), in 1855; Sarah (.5) married John TAYLOR (7.3) 18 Nov., 1850.

4 CROSS, Thomas and Mary CARTER, married 27 Oct., 1817, both of Greenspond. No succession.

5 GOOLD, GOULD or GOLD, James (c. 1796–1879) and Elizabeth. Their son John (.1) died in 1892.

6 WELLS, Joseph and Elizabeth. Probable pre-migration sons were
  a WELLS, Simon (1815–1892) and (1) Mary, (2) Joanna HOUSE, married 22 Oct., 1838, (3) Elizabeth

POND of GOOSEBERRY IS., married 26 Oct., 1849, probably a sister of John POND of Greenspond who married Elizabeth WELLS, 4 Nov., 1835 and witnessed marriages 1838, 1839 and 1849.

b WELLS, Francis (1817–1888) and Elizabeth GOULD (5.5), married 31 May 1855;

c WELLS, Joseph (1819–1890).

d WELLS,Robert (1822–1881/2).

Of their daughters: Mary (.2) married Joseph BURRY (18), and perhaps Robert PAYNE (17) in 1840 and 1844 respectively; Fanny (.3) married Edward MORGAN (Flat Is. 9) and was in Flat Is. by 1851; and Jane (.4) married Thomas TAYLOR (7.2).

7 TAYLOR, Thomas and Bridget. Their sons John (.3) married Sarah SWEETAPPLE (3.5), 18 Nov., 1850; Thomas (.2, 1823–1892) married Jane WELLS (6.4), 8 Nov., 1848. Their daughters Mary (.1) married Joseph HOUSE (20), 22 Oct., 1841; Jane (.3) married John SWEETAPPLE (3.4), 24 Oct., 1849; Anne (.4) married Benjamin PARSONS (31), 19 Nov., 1851.

8 BOURN, John and Mary. No succession.

9 HOUSE, George and Jane (b. 1807/8). Their son John (.1) married Martha PERRY, probably a sister of Joseph PERRY (30), 21 May, 1859.

10 WELLS, Francis and Elizabeth SAINT (1809–1885), married 15 Oct., 1829, both of GOOSEBERRY IS. Their daughter Frances (.2) married William JACOBS (33), 17 July, 1852; their son James (.3) married (1) Elizabeth ――――, and (2) Bridget GOOLD (5.7), 10 Nov., 1858.

11 GOULD, John and Mary. No succession.

12 HOUSE, Charles and Susanna HAYWARD (1.2), married 2 Nov., 1832.

13 HOUSE, William (c. 1812–1880) and Frances (Fanny) ROGERS (2.1, c. 1817–1890), married 29 Oct., 1835.

14 POND, Edward, of Greenspond, and Elizabeth WELLS, married 4 Nov., 1835. No succession. He witnessed marriages in 1838, 1839 and 1849.

15 POND, John, of Greenspond, and Mary WELLS, married 21 May, 1838. No succession. See 10a, 14, and 25.

16 PAYNE, William and Ann Tiller of Swain's Is., married 20 Nov., 1839. No succession.

17 PAYNE or PAINE, Robert, and (1) Ann ROGERS (1.2), married 21 Nov., 1839, and (2) Mary BURRY, married 21 Oct., 1844. She was probably Mary Wells, widow of Joseph BURRY(18).
The Payne brothers were accompanied by a younger brother Edward, b. 1819 and ba. at GOOSEBERRY IS., 17 Dec., 1838.

18 BURRY, Joseph, of Greenspond, and Mary WELLS (c. 1824–   ), married 23 Oct., 1840. See 17. No succession.

19 HOUSE, James and Catherine FELTHAM, Deer Is., (1824–1891), married 22 Oct., 1840.

20 HOUSE, Joseph (1813–1882) and Mary TAYLOR (7.1, 1822–1900), married 22 Oct., 1841.

21 SAUNDERS, Andrew (1816–1895), of Greenspond, and Mary GO(U)LD (5.3, 1823–1897), married 4 Oct., 1842. Joseph SAUNDERS (1851–1920) was probably one of their sons, born and baptised elsewhere, but dying at the GOOSEBERRY IS. Andrew's brother, Benjamin SAUNDERS of Greenspond, married Sarah LANE of Open Hole, 20 May, 1855, but their first appearance in the GOOSEBERRY IS. was in Oct. 1861.

22 FAREWELL, Thomas and Caroline. No succession. He was, perhaps, the illegitimate son of Sarah FAREWELL, flaxdresser, of Bridport, Dorset, b. 1815, and related to Richard FAREWELL, Bridport, who married Sarah DIRHAM, Newell's Is., 30 Dec., 1856 (Greenspond C/E Register).

23 BLAKE, William, of Greenspond, and Mary CONOLY of Port de Grave, married 24 Oct., 1846. She later married Joseph SAMSON (FLAT IS. 5).

24 WARREN, Joseph (1815–1898), or Dorsetshire, and Elizabeth OSBORNE (1825–1879) of Greenspond, married 23 Oct., 1846. She was probably a sister of John OSBORNE (28).

25 HINDS, Edward, and Emma POND of Greenspond, married 21 Apr. 1847. See 6a, 14, 15. His sister Anne Hynes, married John MESH, 28 Aug., 1850 (King's Cove R.C. Register).

26 PARSONS, Robert (1821–1894), of Indian Bay, and Anne GOULD (5.4, 1824–1900), married 27 Oct., 1847.

27 VATER, Edward, of Belchalwell, Dorset, and Susannah BERRY (sic ? BURRY), married 3 June, 1849.

28 OSBORNE, John (1820–1899), of Greenspond, and Anne WELLS (6a.1), married 26 Oct., 1849.

29 WAREHAM, Stephen and Mary. No succession.

30 PERRY, Joseph and Mary.

31 PARSONS, Benjamin (1824–1912), and Anne TAYLOR (7.4, 1829–1812), married 19 Nov., 1851.

32 DALEY or DEALY, Timothy (c. 1797–1880, d. Road to Salvage Bay) and Anne (c. 1815–1889, d. at Dark Cove. No succession.

33 JACOBS, William (1826–1909), of Wimborne, Dorset, and Frances (Fanny) WELLS (10.2, 1832–1900), married 17 July, 1852.

34 DAINTY or DENTY, Abraham and Amy (or Emma, 1820–1891). He witnessed a marriage at Salvage, 1837; see also SALVAGE 3. She may be 5.2.

FLAT ISLAND (Fig. 4-4)

1 HALLETT, Jonas (1801–1883) and Sarah. A pre-migration son Reuben married Susanna RALPH (1833–1900), 23 Oct., 1851; she was probably a pre-migration daughter of Stephen RALPH (7). Another son John (.2, 1829–1914) married Hannah HICKS (probably a daughter of Bernard HICKS (23)), 5 Nov., 1857. Reuben HALLETT, Somerset England, who married Jane BARFIT, Fool's Is., at Greenspond, 22 Aug., 1834, was probably a brother.
2 DYER, Fanny. No succession.
3 CHATER, CHEATER or CHEATOR, William (1813–1891) and Anne. James CHEATER (1843–1891) and John CHEATER (1846–1918) were probably sons of this couple, born and baptised elsewhere. James CHATER, b. c. 1821, ba. in Flat Is. 5 Oct., 1832 was probably William's brother.
4 SANSOM, SANSON, SAMSON or SAMPSON, Thomas (1804–1887) and Jane (1813–1891).
5 SANSON or SAMSON, Joseph Sr. and Elizabeth. He witnessed the marriages of two pre-migration sons:
   a SAMSON Jr., Joseph (1811 or 1822–1890 or 1898), widower, married Mary CONOLY (1822–1896), formerly of Port de Grave and widow of William BLAKE (GOOSEBERRY IS. 23), 9 Oct., 1856.
   b SAMSON, James and Susannah BUTT, married 30 Nov., 1858. She was probably the widow of Samuel BUTT (22).
6 KELLIGREW, William (1802–1881) and Rachel (1805–1881). William KELLIGREW (.a, 1833–1915) was probably a pre-migration son, and Henry KELLIGREW (.b, 1843–1918) an unregistered son.
7 RALPH or ROFF, Stephen (1801–1884) and (1) Jane. Probable pre-migration sons were: Thomas RALPH (1834–1910), married Hannah SAMSON (5.2), 27 Oct., 1859; Noah RALPH (1835–1908); John RALPH (1837–1914); Eli RALPH (.a, 1828–1903), married Caroline FELTHAM of Deer Is., 19 Oct., 1852; William RALPH married Mary Ann HAYWARD of Salvage, 28 Nov., 1856.
   —— and (2) Elizabeth BRIGHT of Catalina, married 8 Nov., 1852; she was probably related to Charles RALPH's wife (15).
8 HISCOCK, William (1811–1883) and Mary. They were in the Gooseberry Is. in 1838, and probably arrived with one son Edward (1836–1916) b. and ba. elsewhere. He witnessed William RALPH's marriage in 1856, and was possibly related to Robert HISCOCK of Trinity who married Mary Dwyer of Trinity, 30 Nov., 1837.
9 MORGAN, Edward (1816–1886) and Frances Wills (WELLS) (1827–1906), married 24 Oct., 1843. She was probably a daughter of Joseph WELLS (GOOSEBERRY IS. 6.3). He witnessed Eli RALPH's marriage in 1852.
10 ROGERS, Timothy, widower, and Amy ROFF (RALPH), both of Flat Is., married 12 Sept., 1845. No succession. He witnessed marriages in 1849, 1861, 1852.
11 PIKE, James Joseph and Elizabeth. James PIKE (.a, 1843–1901) was probably a pre-migration son. See 25.
12 SAMSON, William, Jr. and Maria BENGER of Lower Amherst Cove, married 6 Nov., 1848.
13 SAMSON, John, of King's, and (1) Hannah GOULD of Open Hall, married 2 Nov., 1848; their son Richard was b. 16 Jan., and ba. 21 July, 1850 at King's Cove, whence they migrated to Flat Is. 1851–2; and (2) Adelaide or Adeline KEATES, married late 1856 or 1857.
14 RALPH, James and Annabella Eliza (Beliza: 1817–1905). Thomas (1839–1916) and James John RALPH (1842–1905) were probably older sons of this couple.
15 RALPH, Charles (1828/30-1903/05) and Mary Anne BRIGHT, married 3 Nov., 1849.
16 POWER, Edward and Mary Anne.
17 CROCKER, Edward and Ann. See BARROW HR. 10.
18 POWER, John and Elizabeth.
19 PETTEN or PETTON, William and (1) Mary RALPH, married 21 May, 1851, and (2) Ann SWEETAPPLE (GOOSEBERRY IS. 3.6), married 14 Dec., 1855.
20 PHILPOTT, James, of Bonavista, and Hannah HALLETT (1.3), married 12 Oct., 1853. No succession. He was a witness of marriages in 1851, 1852, 1857.
21 BUTT, Edward and Anne.
22 BUTT, Samuel and Susanna. No succession. She remarried with James SAMSON (5), 1858.
23 HICKS, Bernard and Mary. Were in Gooseberry Is. in 1837. No succession.

24 PETTON, Abraham and Emma. John PETTEN (1848–1892) was probably a pre-migration son.
25 PIKE, Charles and Elizabeth. See 11. The PIKE brothers may also have used the surname ASH. A third brother, Henry Thomas PIKE, married Mary Anne RALPH (7.1), 14 Dec., 1859.
26 HONNIBON or HONNIBURN or HONEYBUN, Robert (1823–1906), and Mary Ann KILLIGREW (6 ?), both of Flat Is., married 7 May, 1857.

BARROW HARBOUR (Fig. 4–5)

1 WELLS, Thomas and Mary WELLS, both of Bonavista, married 13 Oct., 1812 (same date as the OLDFORD-CLOUTER marriage (SALVAGE). Their daughter Selina (.4) married Thomas OSBORNE, Ship Is., 23 Oct., 1857. No succession.
2 POWELL, William and Sarah WELLS, married 30 Nov., 1823, both of Bonavista where a daughter Mary was born and baptised, 25 Oct., 1825. Sarah was probably a sister of Thomas or Mary WELLS (1).
3 BIDDLECOME, Thomas and Sarah. No succession. If he is to be identified with Thomas, son of William and Jane BEDLECOME, Bonavista, ba. 30 Dec., 1814, he must have been at least six years old at baptism. He was probably Thomas BIDDLECOMBE, widower, of Bonavista, who married Sarah HUMPHREYS of Ragged Harbour, 5 Dec., 1843 (Bonavista C/E P.R.).
4 KING, Thomas and Mary. He was probably a son of Robert KING of Old Perlican and Anne FRENCH, Barrow Harbour, married 5 Jan., 1806 (Trinity C/E P.R.). Their daughter Hannah (.1) married George BLACKMORE, Pinchard's Is., 11 Nov., 1857.
5 MATCHEM or MATCHAM, William and Jane BROWN (1814–1899), married 26 Oct., 1837.
6 HOLLOWAY, William and Mary. In Barrow Harbour by 1842; no succession, although Samuel HOLLOWAY whose twin sons were born in Goose Bay in 1865, and who was possibly the father of Mary Ann HOLLOWAY (b.c. 1867) of White Rock, Goose Bay, who married William SIMMONDS, Canning's Cove, Goose Bay, 18 Dec., 1890, was designated in 1865 as "of Barrow Harbour," he was probably a pre-migration son who retained property there.
7 HOLLOWAY, Thomas and Ann. No succession. They were in Red Cliff Island in 1839 and in Barrow Harbour by 1847 (Bonavista and King's Cove C/E P.Rs.).
8 MATCHEM or MATCHAM, Henry and Mary.
9 BABSTOCK, George, of King's Cove, and Amelia Moss of Open Hall, married 14 May, 1838. He was probably a son of Sarah STOCKLEY of Barrow Harbour and Thomas BABSTOCK, married 5 Jan., 1806 (Trinity C/E P.R.), and related to William BABSTOCK (BROOM CLOSE 3); she was probably a sister of William Moss (SALVAGE 31). They were a restless couple, in King's Cove till 1840, in Knight's Cove in 1842, in Amherst Cove in 1844, and in Barrow Harbour in 1853. In the interval an unregistered son Thomas was born who was the subject of an Apprentice Indenture between George BABSTOCK and William Moss, planter probably in Salvage, 28 Nov., 1857, to serve as "servant, fisherman, or any other work," and who in consequence later received a Deed of Gift of Land "within MOSSE's farm at Salvage Bay."
10 CROCKER, Alexander and Elizabeth WELLS, married 3 Dec., 1855. See FLAT IS. 17. She was probably a pre-migration daughter of 1.

SALVAGE (Fig. 4–6)

1 OLDFORD, Thomas and Maria HUNTER (1807–1891), both of Salvage but married at Bonavista, 7 Oct., 1827. No succession.
2 OLDFORD, William and Joanna or Joan. Their son James (.4) died at Salvage in 1907.
3 GARRETT, William, of Dorset, and Dinah DENTY of Salvage (see GOOSEBERRY IS. 34), married 25 Sept., 1829.
4 OLDFORD, William and Grace.
5 BROWN, Henry and Hannah, Anne or Susannah. Their daughter Charlotte (.a) was born at King's Cove, 7 Aug., 1825; their sons John (.1, 1830–1903, d. at Bishop's Hr.) married Mary Anne SQUIRES (12.2), married 15 Oct., 1857; and William (.4, 1836–1906), d. at Bishop's Hr.).
6 BROWN, Joseph (1803–1879) and Jane. Of their sons: Joseph (.1) had a son Joseph Henry, b. 1858; Robert (.2, 1832–1908), married Emma OLDFORD, 22 Oct., 1855, and d. at Bishop's Hr., as did Henry (.4, 1840–1910). Their daughter Mary (.3) married William BOUND, Red Cliff, 6 Nov., 1857. Joseph BROWN d. at Bishop's Hr.

7 BROWN, William and Margaret. Of their sons: George (.1, 1830–1907), married Ellen PAYNE, Newell's
  Is., 23 Nov., 1854; James (.2) married Mary Anne BRINE, widow, Ship Is., 7 Nov., 1855; and Edward
  (.3), d. at Salvage, 1893.
  Pre-settlement sons of the BROWNS:
  a BROWN, Joseph (1821–1903) and Mary Ann CURTIS of King's Cove, married 20 Oct., 1844.
  b BROWN, William (1826–1908, d. at Dark Cove) and Susanna HOBBS, married 12 June, 1849, both at
    Salvage.
  c BROWN(E), Thomas (1827–1901) and Caroline GREEN of Ship Is., married 28 Nov., 1849.
  d BROWN, Richard (1827–1911, d. at Bishop's Hr.) and Jane Amelia CARTER (1825–1901) of Ship Is.,
    married 4 June, 1851.
  e BROWN, Henry and Louisa CURTIS (1827–1883) of King's Cove, married 19 Nov., 1851. She was
    probably a sister of Mary Ann CURTIS (7a).
8 LANE, John and Elizabeth (? 1799–1883). See 15.
9 DYKE or DICK, John and Elizabeth. He was a son of Mary Dick of Bonavista, ba. 11 Dec., 1797. Their
  son John (.2) married Mary TULK of Pinchard's Is., 23 May, 1857.
10 OLDFORD, James and Martha CLOUTER, both of Bonavista, married 13 Oct., 1812. She was probably
   related to George SQUIRE(S)' first wife (12). He and 1, and 2 or 4, were probably sons of George OLDFORD
   who died and was buried at Salvage in 1825, aged 62 (b. 1763). Their son William (.1) was b. and ba. at
   Bonavista, 2 Jan., 1814, and married Elizabeth BROWN, Salvage, 21 Oct., 1835.
   Other pre-settlement offspring of the OLDFORDS: 1, 2, 4, 10:
   a OLDFORD, James (1813–1891, d. at Squid Tickle), married Ann CAINS of Greenspond, 24 Oct., 1837.
   b OLDFORD, Elizabeth, ba. at Salvage, 15 July, 1832, aged 16 (b. 1816).
   c OLDFORD, James and Mary YETMAN, both of Salvage, married 7 Nov., 1838.
   d OLDFORD, Andrew and Anne BROWN(E), married 28 Nov., 1854. He was one of two Andrew
     OLDFORDS, both born c.1821, who died 6 Sept., 1904, and 7 Oct., 1908, respectively.
   e OLDFORD, William and Maria HANCOCK of King's Cove, married 23 Oct., 1856. He was probably the
     youth ba. 18 June, 1937, aged 16 years (b. 1821).
   f OLDFORD, John and (1) Mary, (2) Rebecca HOBBS of Keels (1828–1879), married 18 Oct., 1851. But
     see 12.
   g OLDFORD, Mary, married Thomas CARTER of Greenspond, 19 Dec., 1848.
   h OLDFORD, William and Ann (1831–1906).
11 DYKE or DICK, Richard and Susan or Hannah ABBOTT (Trinity C/E P.R.), or HIBBERT (Bonavista C/E
   P.R.), of Bonavista, married 17 Dec., 1829. He was a son of Richard and Elizabeth DYKE of Bonavista,
   ba. 1 Jan., 1807.
12 SQUIRE(S), George (1801–1883) and (1) Mary CLOUTER, both of Salvage, married 5 Sept., 1831. He was
   born in Winterborne Zelstone, Dorset, to John Squier and Mary Rolles, married there 6 Feb., 1798; John
   Squier was born in Newfoundland in 1775–6 (Census, Winterborne Zelstone, 1851); George broke a
   butcher's apprenticeship to run away to Catalina, later to Salvage, ca. 1815 (SQUIRE, H. Newfoundland
   Outport in the Making, 1974). She was probably related to Martha CLOUTER (10). Of their sons: John (.1)
   died at Salvage in 1901; George (.5) and William (.6) in 1890, both at Salvage Bay (Eastport).
   ———(2) Rebecca OLDFORD, widow of John OLDFORD (10f), married 21 May, 1853: curiously, her child
   by OLDFORD was born 9 Mar., 1854 and she was bu. in 1879 as Rebecca OLDFORD.
13 STEED(S), William (1818–   ) and Temperance BROWN ? (1816–1891) d. at Bishop's Hr. He was ba. at
   Salvage, aged 12 years, with a sister Mary aged 13, in 1831. His son John (.1) d. at Salvage in 1911.
14 DUROLE or DURDLE, James and Anne (Hannah) HUNTER (1809–1896), married 3 June, 1831. She was
   probably a sister of the HUNTERS (16 and 18).
15 LANE, Joseph and Elizabeth (? 1799–1883). John LANE (1828–1887) was probably a pre-settlement son
   of this couple or 8 (q.v.).
16 HUNTER, James (1804–1888), and Elizabeth BATSTOCK (BABSTOCK?) of Broom Close (1814–1891; see
   BROOM CLOSE 3) married 9 Nov., 1832. Elizabeth HUNTER (1783–1882) was probably his mother,
   Mary HUNTER, ba. 18 June, 1838 aged 16 years (b. 1821), his sister.
17 BULL, John and Jane. He emigrated from Christchurch, Hampshire, ca. 1800. Their son Henry (.1)
   married Anne GARRETT (3.3), 5 Oct., 1857. Susanna BULL, who married William HUNTER (18.2) 3 Nov.,
   1856, was probably a pre-settlement daughter.
18 HUNTER, John (1808–1884), and Elizabeth OLDFORD (1816–1889), married 21 Oct., 1833. Their son
   William (.2) (1841–1902) d. at Salvage, and may have been the man married to Susanna BULL (see 17), 3
   Nov., 1856 (witness: John HUNTER).
19 TRIM, Joseph and Mary (d. 1859). No succession.

20 CRISBY or MARTIN, John, of Torbay, England (1806–1889, d. at Bishop's Hr.), and Anne DYKE
   (1813–1879, d. at Bishop's Hr.), married 17 Nov., 1833 at Greenspond. He used the surname MARTIN
   when baptising their third child. He was born at Penn Inn, Combeinteignhead, Devon, son of a
   Dartmouth shipwright; ran away from a bastardy charge in Dartmouth; original name was Crispin;
   mother's maiden name Sampson.
21 FISH, Thomas, of Salvage, and Hannah BATSTOCK (BABSTOCK ?) of Broom Close (see BROOM
   CLOSE 3), married 30 Apr., 1832. No succession.
22 SHELDON, Jane. Widow of Mr. SHELDON, a school teacher at Salvage in 1823 (Squire, H.: Eastport
   Peninsula Newsletter, March 1970, p. 6), mentioned by Gaylor as sailing between Salvage and Bonavista, 1827. No succession.
23 SAM(P)SON, SANSON, or SAMSON, John and Jane SHELDON (1802–1879) widow (see 22), married 15 July,
   1835.
24 DYKE or DICK, Edward and Mary Moss (1814–1884), both of Salvage, married 30 Oct., 1834. He was a
   son of William and Mary DICK of Bonavista, ba. there, 18 June, 1809. She was probably a sister of
   William Moss (31).
   Martha DYKE (ba. at Salvage, 2 June, 1831, aged 14; b. 1816/17), who married Charles QUINTON of Red
   Cliff Is., 21 Nov., 1839, was probably a sister of Edward or John DYKE (9).
25 TROKE or CROCK, George, and Jane HUNTER (see 16 and 18) married 28 Oct., 1835 (witnesses: James
   FLINN (33) and John HUNTER (18)).
26 WHITE, John (1797–1883, d. at Salvage Bay), and Grace. William WHITE (1843–1881) was probably an
   unregistered son, and Charlotte WHITE who married John Richard WHITE of Kingstone, Dorset, 22
   May, 1847, was probably a pre-migration daughter.
27 SANSON or SAMSON, James and Mary LANE (see 8 and 15), married 1 June, 1837. No succession.
28 ABGOOD, HABGOOD or HAPGOOD, James, ba. 18 June, 1837, aged 19 years (b. 1818). No succession is
   apparent, but he was probably a son of Jacob HAPGOOD, Broom Close (BROOM CLOSE 2), as was John
   HAPGOOD (2.1) who married Anne OLDFORD (2.3), 29 Oct., 1855. George (1845–1908), and Jacob
   (1845–1884) were unregistered children of unknown parentage who died in Salvage.
29 BISHOP, William and Hannah DENTY (see 3 and GOOSEBERRY IS. 34), both of Salvage, married 7
   Nov., 1838. No succession.
30 BURDEN, James (1817–1894) and Elizabeth BROWN, married 18 Nov., 1839. See 32.
31 Moss, William (1805–1888) of Open Hole, and Sarah HAPGOOD (1813–1899) of Brown (sic. Broom)
   Close, married 24 May, 1833. She was probably a daughter of Jacob HAPGOOD (BROOM CLOSE 2).
   They were probably the parents of John Moss who married Emma HUNTER (18.1), 5 Nov., 1857, and the
   William and Ann Moss of Keels whose son Thomas was ba. there, 12 May, 1838.
32 BURDEN, William (1818–1900) and Mary HUNTER, married 30 Oct., 1841. He was probably a brother of
   James BURDEN (30); she a sister of James and John HUNTER (16 and 18).
33 FLINN or FLING, James, and Mary BROWN, both of Salvage, married 1 May, 1841. He witnessed George
   TROKE's marriage in 1835 (25). No succession.
34 DUNN, Joseph (1823–1909), of Bonavista, and Sarah TRIM of Salvage, married 30 Nov., 1848. She was
   probably a pre-settlement daughter of Joseph TRIM (19).

BROOM CLOSE (Fig. 4–5)

 1 KNAPPER, Joseph (d. 1834) and Susanna. Their son Samuel (.1) married Jane POWER, Flat Is. (see FLAT
   IS. 16 and 18), 15 Nov., 1856 at Greenspond. Mary NAPPER, Salvage, who married Henry STRICKLAND,
   Lymington, Hampshire, 19 Oct., 1842 at King's Cove, was probably a pre-settlement daughter.
 2 ABGOOD or HABGOOD or HAPGOOD, Jacob and Joanna. A son William b. at Keels, ba. 21 Nov., 1822
   (Bonavista C/E P.R.); d. at Salvage, 12 Jan., 1908. Other probably pre-migration sons: James HABGOOD,
   b.c. 1818, ba. 18 June, 1837, aged 19, at Salvage, and perhaps the James HAPGOOD of Barrow Harbour
   involved in a probate court case, 29 July, 1826 (L. 237: Administration Bonds, 1826–1827); Richard
   (1824–1911); and daughter: Hannah, married John Young, Greenspond, 19 Nov., 1835. "Jake" YOUNG
   witnessed the marriage of their son John HAPGOOD, Salvage, to Anne OLDFORD, Salvage, 29 Oct., 1855
   (SALVAGE ?).
 3 BABSTOCK, William and Anne PRICE of Barrow Hr., (c.1809–1889), married 13 July, 1834. He was
   almost certainly a son of Thomas BABSTOCK of Oborn, Dorset, who married Sarah STOCKLEY of Barrow
   Harbour, 28 Apr., 1806 (Trinity C/E P.R.); see BARROW HR. 9. They were somewhat migratory, in
   Salvage in 1836, Broom Close 1837, and Barrow 1840; she died at Happy Adventure.

4 BARRON, Robert and Ann. No succession.
5 QUINTON, John, of Red Cliff Island, and Ann OLDFORD (1803–1896), widow, of Keels, married 25 May, 1852. She died at Sandy Cove.

BLOODY BAY (Fig. 4–5)

1 STROUD, Richard Elliott and Deborah Viney. He was born in England, probably in Pimperne, Dorset, near Ringwood, Hampshire; probably Richard Stroud, master of the *Friends* for G. & J. Kemp & Co., sailing between Poole, Harve de Grace, Brigus and Carbonear, (Poole Port Books: 16 Aug. 1816 and 6 June 1817). They had a pre-settlement daughter Susanna (3 and 4), ba. 1 Nov., 1829, at Greenspond.
2 DICK (DYKE), George. Ba. 16 Nov., 1834, aged 15 years; no succession. Probably from Bonavista or Salvage.
3 BARNES, John and Susanna Elliott STROUD (1.a.). No marriage record; he died or disappeared before the baptism of their son Philip, 8 Aug., 1854; see 4.
4 BREFET, Augustus John, of St. Malo, Kingdom of France, and Susan Elliott STROUD, married 8 Aug., 1854; see 3. He witnessed the marriage of Thomas WELLS, Gooseberry Is., and Dorcas STROUD, Bloody Bay (1.4), at Greenspond, 5 Nov., 1862.

The Evolution of Sealing and the Spread of Permanent Settlement in Northeastern Newfoundland

5

Chesley Sanger

In those areas where exploitable resources are marginal or uncertain, are spatially segregated, and are accessible only seasonally, settlers develop strategies and distinctive settlement patterns geared to the exploitation of these resources throughout the year. To such areas belong the coastal margins of Newfoundland which include a land environment with scattered resources of limited potential, yet front a bounteous sea. Faced with these geographical conditions, the early settlers of Newfoundland developed an economy and settlement pattern focused on the commercial exploitation of the fisheries and the cultivation, at a subsistence level, of small areas of land. These were supplemented both directly and indirectly by other subsistence activities such as berry-picking, the hunting of wild game and fowl, and the procurement of timber for purposes of building, repairs, and firewood. Marginal lands surrounding the settlements were also used widely for the grazing of livestock.

The utilization of these different resources was woven into an annual round according to their seasonal availability (Fig. 5–1). Ideally, each exploited resource complemented the others throughout the year, and if two or more resources became available concurrently, labour specialization within the family units was necessary. There was usually a period of relative inactivity between the decline in the forest-based occupations of winter and the first appearance of the cod stocks in the late spring and early summer.

For settlers moving into the isolated harbours and coves in Bonavista and Notre Dame Bays (Fig. 5–2) during the 19th century, however, this period often became a time of intensive and commercially rewarding activity. By late winter and early spring the northeastern coast of the island, in most years, was blockaded by extensive fields of local and arctic ice (Fig. 5–3). The advance and retreat of these ice-fields facilitated the seasonal appearance of large numbers of harp seals (Fig. 5–4), first for a brief period of one to two weeks in late December and early January, as the herds migrated southwards from the Arctic along the coast of Labrador and northern Newfoundland, and then again in late February and early March as they swam northwards to give birth on the southward-drifting ice floes. Because the harp is naturally gregarious and whelps at approximately the same time each year, the young are usually born in close proximity to one another, forming large whelping 'patches.'

The early inhabitants in the more northerly parts of island Newfoundland quickly realized that the migrating seals could be ensnared with relative ease in nets attached to shore as they swam south. This was known as the landsman prosecution of the seal fishery. Later, towards the end of the 18th century, the "patches" of newly whelped "whitecoats" became the foci of a large-vessel, spring seal hunt close to shore. Seals, therefore, constituted an additional resource during a commercially quiet period in the traditional annual round.

Consequently, the seal fishery became a major factor influencing the spread of permanent settlement along the northeastern coast of the island throughout the 19th century. Together with the availability of fur-bearing animals and salmon, it encour-

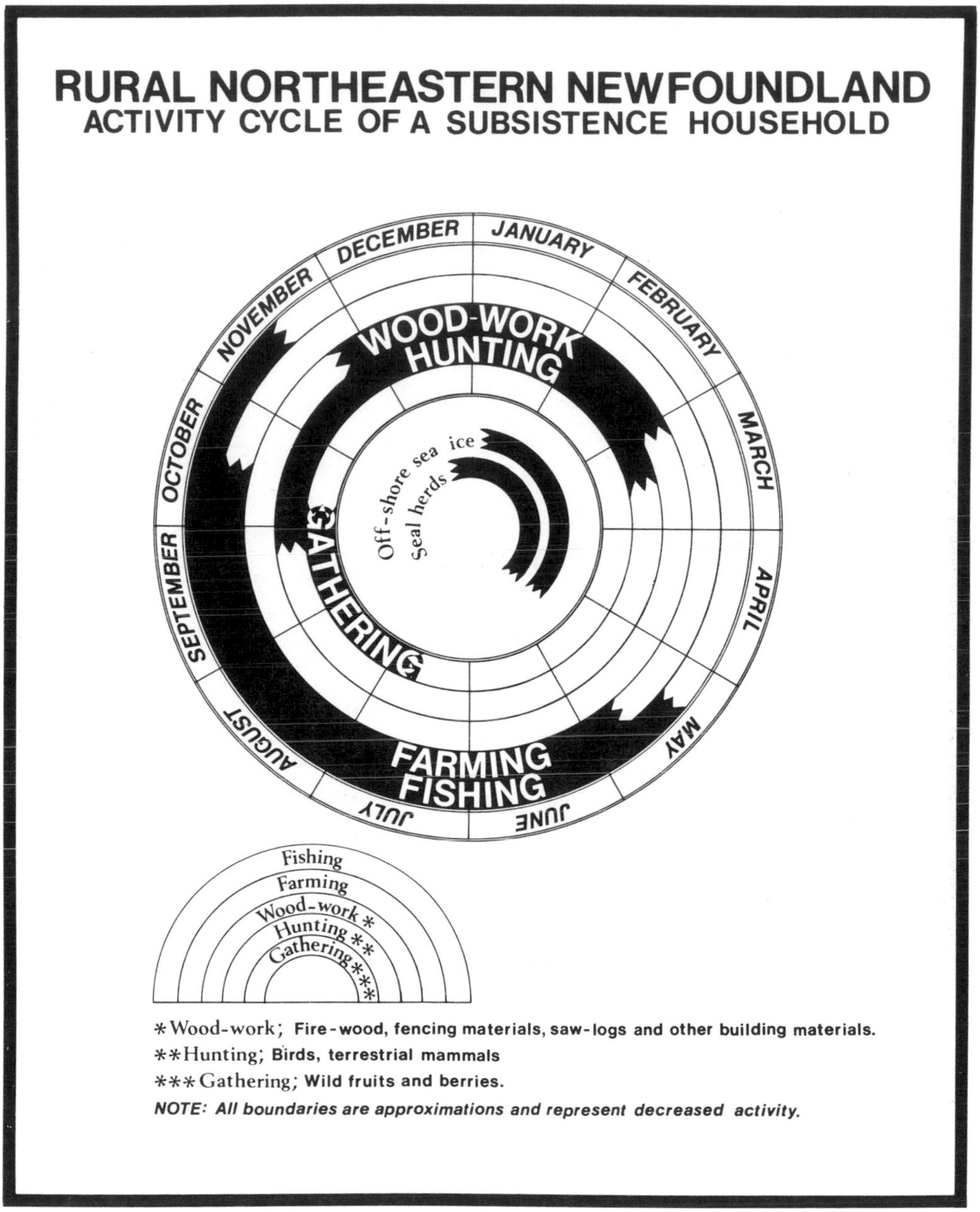

RURAL NORTHEASTERN NEWFOUNDLAND
ACTIVITY CYCLE OF A SUBSISTENCE HOUSEHOLD

NOVEMBER DECEMBER JANUARY FEBRUARY MARCH APRIL MAY JUNE JULY AUGUST SEPTEMBER OCTOBER

WOOD-WORK
HUNTING

Off-shore sea ice
Seal herds

GATHERING

FARMING
FISHING

Fishing
Farming
Wood-work *
Hunting **
Gathering ***

*Wood-work; Fire-wood, fencing materials, saw-logs and other building materials.
**Hunting; Birds, terrestrial mammals
***Gathering; Wild fruits and berries.
NOTE: All boundaries are approximations and represent decreased activity.

Figure 5–1

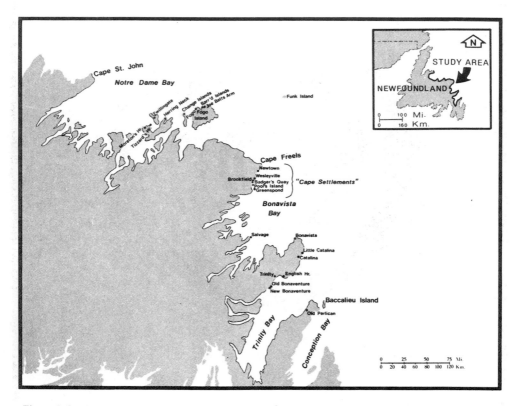

Figure 5–2   *Location*

Figure 5–3

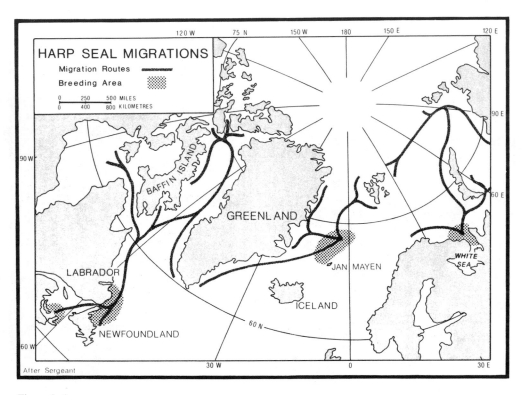

Figure 5–4

aged individuals to winter in the more northerly portions of the island, in southern Labrador, and along the Lower North Shore of the Gulf of St. Lawrence (see Remiggi, and Thornton, this vol.). In the early 18th century Bishop Raynal reported that "Canadians go to this frozen and almost uninhabitable coast [Labrador] towards the middle of October, and remain there till the beginning of June" in order to obtain seals (1969:252); and Joseph Banks, who visited Newfoundland in 1766, noted in his diary that many of the summer fishing crews were left to winter in the more northerly regions for the express purpose of hunting fur-bearing animals during the fall and winter, and to catch seals when they appeared off the coast in early spring (Lysaght, 1971:144–46). Further south, the residents of Fogo and Twillingate Island were able to export seal oil valued at £12,550 as early as 1742 (Chafe, 1924:18), but it was generally considerably lower in value and fluctuated greatly (Head, 1976:176). By 1770, Fogo, Greenspond, Bonavista, and Trinity had become major centres for the processing of seals. However, the fact that large segments of the northeast coast had been placed under limited French jurisdiction proscribed permanent settlement during most of the 18th and 19th centuries. Nevertheless, the French frequently complained that upon their arrival in the spring they found their fishing stages "foul with the stinking refuse" of the seals taken during the winter months by fishermen from the English communities to the south (Head, 1976:77).

Other factors which contributed to the increase in population on the northeast coast were: (1) increased pressure on resources in the Avalon Peninsula occasioned by the rapid increase in the number of permanent settlers there during the early part of the 19th century; and (2) the growing awareness that the income earned by participants in the recently launched large-vessel seal fishery could also be supplemented by a landsman operation on the northeast coast. These factors acted as a fresh incentive for people to move and settle in areas close to the migratory route of the harp seal.

The Landsman Operation
In order to capture seals from the shore, the early inhabitants of northeastern Newfoundland and southern Labrador developed two principal techniques – the use of seal (or shoal) nets and seal traps (or frames). The latter were more common north of Cape St. John where the seal herds characteristically "trimmed" close to shore as they migrated southwards. As early as 1818, Chappell, patrolling the Labrador summer fishery, wrote a detailed account of the modification of the single seal net and the development of the seal trap, or frame, which consisted of a fixed outer net running parallel to the shore. Smaller nets which could be raised or lowered individually from the shore by the use of capstans were perpendicularly attached to this net. The men then used small open boats to direct the migrating seals into the frame, and the women, children, and older men on shore would ensure their capture by raising the smaller "stop" nets. In their attempt to escape by swimming under the nets, the animals became enmeshed and thus drowned as "they have not the sagacity or courage enough to leap boldly over the top" (1818:199).

Although the seals did not follow the shore line with the same intensity and regularity as they approached the more southerly regions of the island, the inhabitants of Notre Dame and Bonavista Bays, were still able to ensnare the migrating herds in specially constructed seal nets. John Bland of Bonavista described them in 1802: "about fifty pounds weight of strong twine ... [and] ... the half worn small hausers, which the boats have used in the summer fishery, serve for foot ropes; new ratline is necessary for head ropes, and each net is required to be about forty fathoms in length, and nearly three in depth'' (Prowse, 1896:419). This practice was continued until quite recently. Eighty-one-year-old Captain A. Greenham of Twillingate recalled, in 1971, how the residents of that community used nets to capture seals in late December before the local and arctic ice had blockaded the coast: ''We'd use the nets – seal nets. They were pretty common, most everyone had them. We'd use them up in the bight in anywhere from 20 to 60 to 70 fathom of water. They were right on the bottom. Two nets (a fleet) and they would be shot out from shore straight'' (personal communication).

Seals could be captured from land with relatively little capital investment in a fashion that neither required the participants to leave home for extensive periods nor forced them to face the risks associated with the large-vessel seal fishery. This landsman prosecution compensated for the obvious disadvantages of increased isolation and a shorter summer cod fishery due to the frequent presence of arctic ice along the northeast coast in spring. In a letter to vice-admiral Seymour, in 1853, for example, the captain of the H.M.S. *Sappho* reported that the prosecution of the seal fishery ''never fails to reward those who systematically pursue it. The outlay is small, and the profits, in the fortunate years, very great; ...''[1]

Records on the seal fishery are sparse for the early 19th century. Notre Dame Bay was not reported in the census until 1845, and the areas north of Cape St. John were not included until later. The 1845 census was the first to provide statistics specifically relating to the seal fishery, the four subsequent censuses (1857, 1869, 1874, and 1884) also incorporate information on sealing, such as the number of seals caught by community (without differentiating between vessel and landsmen catches); one census (1874) records the total value of seal oil rendered in each settlement. The only ''landsman'' information contained in all of the 19th century censuses, however, is the number of sealing nets used by the residents of each community. By dividing the number of seal nets per community by the total adult male population (15–60 years) it is possible to arrive at a crude index of the relative importance of the operation for each settlement in Notre Dame, Bonavista, and Trinity Bays during the 19th century (see Figs. 5–5, 5–6, 5–7, and 5–8). In 1845, for example, Twillingate had an index of 1.35 (797 sealing nets divided by 686 adult males) while Little Catalina, in the same year, had an index of .32, representing 18 sealing nets and 56 potential sealers (Fig. 5–5). It is obvious that the landsman seal fishery, although important in Little Catalina, was far more so in Twillingate in 1845. Figure 5–5 also reveals that 82 percent of the 6,744 inhabitants of Notre Dame Bay were living in 18 larger communities optimumly located for the capture of seals on the outermost islands and headlands; an index of .5 was calculated for 14 of them. All eighteen settlements were also favourably situated for the prosecution of the cod fishery. There were numerous smaller communities (of less than fifty people) located further in the bay and on the landward sides of the many islands away from the extended resource base represented by the migrating seal herds. The strategic importance of headland locations in the outermost reaches of bays is also evident in Bonavista Bay, but to a lesser extent in Trinity Bay. In Bonavista Bay the larger settlements were located only in areas accessible to the migrating seal herds; in Trinity Bay, although settlement did develop in the inner reaches of the bay where logging was important, the only large settlements on the northern shore were located northeast of English Harbour, the southernmost extension of 'onshore' harp seal migrations.

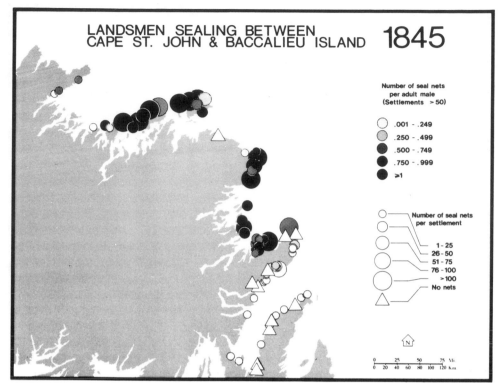

Figure 5-5

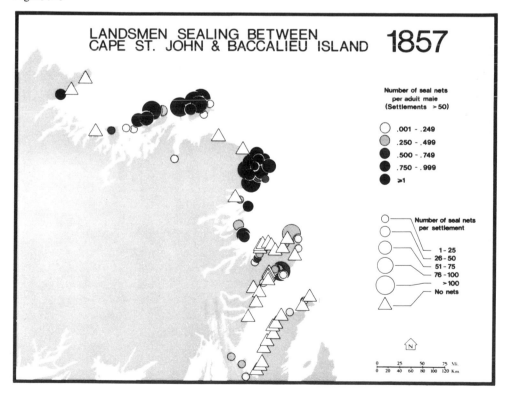

Figure 5-6

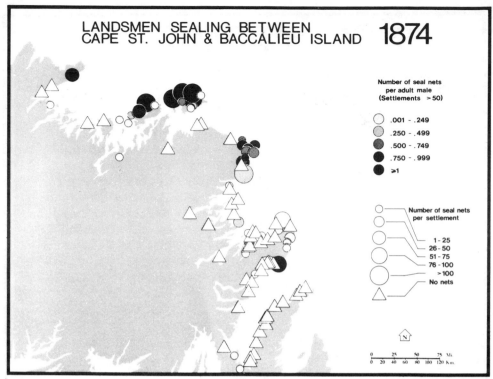

Figure 5-7

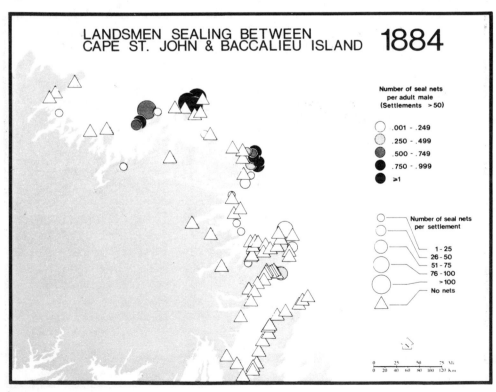

Figure 5-8

Although there was a slight drop in the total number of sealing nets recorded in Notre Dame Bay during the interval 1845–1857 (Fig. 5–6), the total population increased by 28 percent. Sealing was still important, however, in the overall economy of the majority of settlements in the Bay, and in some of the larger settlements the number of nets actually increased. On the other hand there was further dispersion of sealing activity along the coast and a concomitant proliferation of communities in the northwestern areas of Bonavista Bay between Cape Freels and Greenspond which resulted in a rearrangement of the existing population. Between 1845 and 1857 the population of Greenspond declined by 40 percent, from 1076 to 643, whereas the total population in the northern Bonavista Bay area increased by 111 percent – from 867 to 1829. Interestingly enough, the total number of seal nets in Greenspond declined from 430 to 150 during this period while the number of nets in the Northern Bonavista Bay area increased from 428 to 751. It appears that selective migration was occurring in that the inhabitants moving from Greenspond northwards to the Cape area were "sealing" families wishing to re-locate in an area where seals were more plentiful and where sealers were better disposed to take advantage of the larger sealing vessels sailing from the Bonavista Bay North communities each spring.

Unfortunately, the 1869 returns do not appear to contain reliable sealing information. Twillingate and New World Island, for example, are listed as having no seal nets, but this quite clearly was not the case. Nevertheless, this census and that of 1874 (Fig. 5–7) do show that the landsman sealing operation continued to contract. By 1874, three areas, all situated along the principal migration route of the harp seal, emerged as the foci of the winter seal fishery: Twillingate and Change Islands, the northern or seaward communities on Fogo Island, and the 'Cape settlements' in the Bonavista Bay North area. But by 1884, even these settlements were less dependent on the landsmen seal fishery (Fig. 5–8), although Twillingate still maintained 602 nets, and Fogo and Joe Batts Arm reported a combined total of 247 nets.

Sealing on the 'New' French Shore
Partly as a result of advancing British settlement along the northeast coast, the French Shore was redefined in 1783 and extended north from Cape St. John. During the Revolutionary and Napoleonic Wars, however, British settlers moved into the area beyond Cape St. John for a brief period. "... from the year 1792, to that of 1814, with the short interruption of the Peace of Amiens, British subjects occupied that part of the coast called the French Shore, and had erected stores, stages and flakes at a great expense ..."[2] Immediately after the war, the French destroyed some of the British fishing stations and drove the settlers or summer visitors from the Treaty Shore. A letter from a Mr. W. Taylor of Carbonear, addressed to the special committee established by the Newfoundland House of Assembly in 1857 to investigate the possible implications contained in proposals being made to have French rights on the Treaty Shore increased, expressed the frustration experienced by British settlers at that time. It reads, in part: "I know, by sad experience, what French concurrent rights of fisheries mean. During the period of 1815 I repaired to the French Shore to occupy my fishing premises and to prosecute my usual business, when to my great annoyance and loss, I found that all I possessed was totally destroyed; and worst of all, I was forced from the shore altogether, by swarms of Frenchmen who threatened to do me further injury."[3]

On the other hand, the French, in a sense, contributed towards the year-round settlement of the British by retaining British fishermen as caretakers in French harbours over winter. A combination of winter furring and sealing, subsistence farming, and a salmon and cod fishery supported a scattered British population on this shore. In 1855 fear was expressed that if the French were given the additional rights they were seeking, it would "take from the British settlers, of whom there are about 2,000 between Cape St. John and the Bay of Islands alone, a valuable seal and salmon fishery, by which they now support themselves in comfort and independence."[4] It is also clear from the returns that the sealing operation represented the mainstay of their economy. Captain Charles Power, for example, reported in 1857, that "From Cape John to Cape Norman is the best fishing ground on the coast of Newfoundland for seals. The British residents between these points prosecute the salmon and seal fishery exclusively, and the cod fishery to a very small extent."[5]

The British resident population on the Treaty Shore, which numbered 1,019 between Quirpon in the north and Cape John in the south,[6] were enjoying, according to the 1866 report of the General Superintendent of Fisheries, a relatively high standard of living: "The English residents on this coast are nearly all well off, and latterly have been turning their attention more to agricultural pursuits – one person having ten cows, and another fifty sheep, so that they are enabled to make the better part of their clothing. The seals they catch in winter, with their catch of cod fish and salmon in summer, add considerably to their means of living."[7]

The Vessel Operation

While a thriving landsman sealing operation was being carried out in the more northerly areas of the colony by the end of the 18th century, the inhabitants of St. John's, and the larger centers primarily located in Conception Bay, began to make sealing voyages to northern regions in sailing vessels each spring in search of the newly formed whelping patches. It is reported that, "The boats that used to be employed in the hazardous voyage were open fishing-boats; but, in 1793, two small schooners, of about forty-five tons each, were fitted out for the ice, and sailed from St. John's on the first week in April" (Wilson, 1866:287).

Further indication of the nature of these vessels, which were the predecessors of the large commercial sealing fleets of the late 19th and early 20th centuries, is given in a report written to Governor Waldegrave from Harbour Grace in 1795:

The account of the decked vessels and open boats employed in the seal fishery, I conceive will attract your excellency's attention, when you consider not only the great advantage of the seal fishery, and the adventurous undertaking in their boats of about thirty or forty tons burthen; manned with from eight to ten hands, who encounter the storms in the months of March and April, thirty or forty leagues from land, which I am convinced makes more and better seamen in one season than the cod fishery does in seven; ... (Pedley, 1863:194).

By the year 1800 this large-scale commercial seal fishery was well established. In reply to Governor Gambier's request for information regarding the seal fishery on the coast north of Bonavista, John Bland, for example, was able to report, in 1802, that "This adventurous and perilous pursuit is prosecuted in two different ways – during the winter months by nets, and from March to June in ice-skiffs and decked boats, or schooners" (Prowse, 1896:419). Bland further noted that the sealing adventure by large vessels, which sailed about the middle of March, had been prosecuted for approximately nine years.

The vessel fishery had a far greater economic impact than did the landsmen operation. Fleets of well-equipped sealing vessels represented not only significant amounts of capital investment, but also involved large numbers of local inhabitants. Coincident with the growth of the resident cod fishery in the more populous southeastern areas of the island, traditionally visited by the migratory English fishing fleet, the Newfoundland seal fishery experienced a substantial change in character and began to play a more important role in the overall economy of the island. The first sealing vessels were simple fishing schooners designed for the northern, or Labrador, cod fishery. Anspach, for example, noted in 1819 (p. 415) that: "This plan of a winter fishery appears to have been generally pursued there [Labrador and Northern Newfoundland] until the latter end of the century, when the enterprising and industrious spirit of the inhabitants of Conception Bay contrived a method to consolidate the interests of both the seal and cod fisheries without any prejudice to the latter."

The success of these two complementary activities appears to have been rapid, for by 1825 the number of vessels annually outfitted for the Labrador cod fishery was reported to be between sixty and seventy from the port of St. John's alone, with a further two hundred schooners sailing from the various Conception Bay communities (Black, 1960:268). The increasing importance of the spring sealing venture to the owner/outfitters of these schooners is demonstrated by the increase in the number of skins reported: from less than 5,000 in 1793 to 81,000 in 1805, 281,000 in 1819 and 687,000 in 1831, the highest total ever recorded (Fig. 5–9).

The growing importance of the seal fishery and its impact on the colony in the second half of the century is verified in the writings of the Rev. W. Wilson. He noted that the sealing vessels averaged from "... fifty to one hundred and fifty tons, and were manned with crews of from twenty-five to forty men; while the interest of every individual to the north of St. John's, from the richest to the poorest, was to be so interwoven with it, that its prosecution and results should cause more speculation, more anxiety, more excitement and solicitude, than perhaps does any single branch of business in any part of the world" (Wilson, 1866:276). During the period 1820–1860, more men participated, more vessels sailed, and a greater number of seals were killed than at any other time.

The large-scale sealing venture was restricted initially to the coastal settlements from Cape Race in the south to Bonavista Bay in the north. The social and economic effects on settlement in this sealing region brought about by the rapid growth of the industry were significant. Bonnycastle recorded in 1841, for example, that "... all is bustle during the latter part of February, and the stone-ballast which had been collected in the fall of the year and during the winter, is now put on board the sealing vessels, with the requisite supplies of water and provisions; ..." (Bonnycastle, 1842:128). Prowse, also, noted that "The wonderful growth of the spring seal fishery just about this period [about 1840] completely changed the social habits of the people; the work required for outfitting the vessels, building parts, repairing and strengthening the sealing schooners, kept masters and crews at work all through the winter; what had formerly been a carnival of drinking and dancing now became a season of hard, laborious toil" (1896:450).

When steamers were introduced to replace the traditional sailing vessels in 1863, the socio-economic distance between owner/operators and ordinary sealers became greater. Higher capital investments were required and the lesser entrepreneurs were

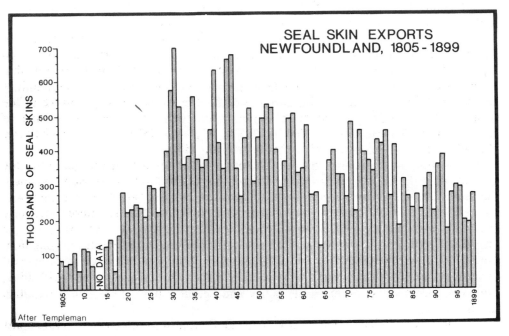

Figure 5-9

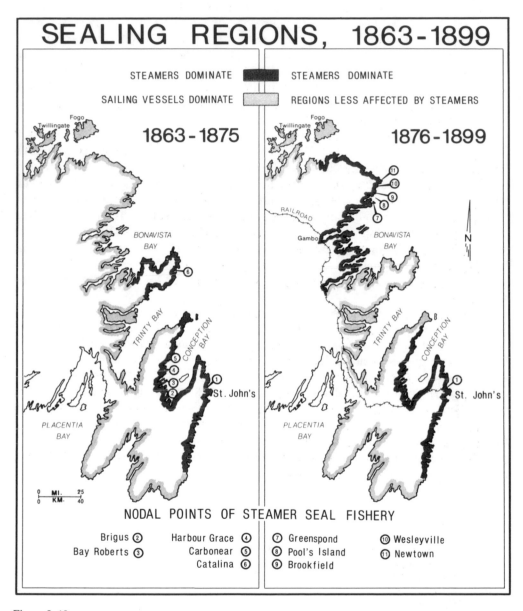

Figure 5–10

gradually displaced. As the industry began to consolidate in terms of investment capital, St. John's emerged as the major residential centre for vessel owners (Fig. 5–10). There were fewer men and vessels participating, and this also initiated rapid changes in the areal pattern of crew recruitment (Sanger, 1973:204–19). Because of the decline in the number of vessels and the growing practice for sealing steamers to sail from St. John's during the first few years of the steam-vessel period, the northern boundary of the sealing region shifted southwards, excluding the traditional sealing areas along the northeast coast. The ordinary sealers came from the Southern Shore communities, from settlements in Conception Bay, and areas of Trinity Bay which were fairly accessible to St. John's.

By the late 1800s, new forces were at work within the industry. There was a preference on the part of the steam-vessel owners to hire experienced sealing captains from the more northerly communities to command their vessels; there was an attempt to have older steamers clear for the ice-fields from the northern areas, closer to the resource; and a more efficient transportation system was developed, enabling the sealers from Bonavista and Trinity Bay communities to obtain berths on the St. John's steamers. These developments resulted in the sealing region spreading northwards again to the growing Bonavista Bay North communities of Greenspond, Pool's Island, Brookfield, Badgers Quay, Wesleyville, and Newtown. By the end of the 19th century, there existed a dichotomous sealing region polarized on Bonavista Bay North and St. John's.

In the days of the sealing vessel, every major community in the sealing region had produced seal oil and prepared the hides. These domestic industries declined with the introduction of steamers. Now profits were controlled by a few St. John's firms with home offices in the United Kingdom. Furthermore, as the number of sealers declined late in the 19th century and the total population of the northeast coast continued to increase, the seal fishery, which had made such a significant contribution to the overall growth of the economy throughout the 19th century, diminished greatly in importance. In mid-19th century, seal products amounted to roughly one-quarter of the island's exports: by the end of the century seal exports had dropped to less than 10 percent (Ryan, 1971). Even on the northeast coast, sealing had become a minor activity in the traditional annual round.

NOTES

1 Journal, House of Assembly, Newfoundland (1853):129.
2 Ibid. (1837):541.
3 Ibid. (1857):327.
4 Ibid. (1857):49.
5 Ibid. (1857):294.
6 Ibid. (1865):624.
7 Ibid. (1866):715.

REFERENCE: PRIMARY SOURCE

Census of Newfoundland, 1845, 1857, 1869, 1974, 1884. Newfoundland, Department of Colonial Secretary, St. John's.

REFERENCES: SECONDARY SOURCES

ANSPACH, L. A.
1819 *A History of the Island of Newfoundland: Containing a Description of the Island, the Banks, the Fisheries, and Trade of Newfoundland and the Coast of Labrador*. London, T. and J. Allman.

BLACK, W. A.
1960 "The Labrador Floater Fishery." *Annals, Association of American Geographers*, 50(3):267–93.

BONNYCASTLE, R. H.
1842 *Newfoundland in 1842: A Sequel to "The Canadas in 1841,"* Vol. II. London. Henry Colburn.

CHAFE, L.
1924 *Chafe's Sealing Book: A History of the Newfoundland Sealfishery from the Earliest Available Records Down to and Including the Voyage of 1923*, third edition. St. John's, Trade Printers and Publishers Limited.

CHAPPELL, E., LT.
1818 *Voyage of H.M.S. "Rosamond" to Newfoundland and the Southern Coast of Labrador*. London, J. Mawman.

HEAD, C. G.
1976 *Eighteenth Century Newfoundland: A Geographer's Perspective*. Toronto, McClelland and Stewart.

LYSAGHT, A. M.
1971 *Joseph Banks in Newfoundland and Labrador, 1766: His Diary, Manuscripts and Collections*. London, Faber and Faber Limited.

PEDLEY, C.
1863 *The History of Newfoundland: From the Earliest Times to the Year 1860*. London, Longman, Green, Roberts and Green.

PROWSE, D. W.
1896 *History of Newfoundland from the English, Colonial and Foreign Records*, second edition. London, Eyre and Spottiswoode.

RAYNAL, G. T. F.
1969 *A Philosophical and Political History of the Settlements and Trade of the Europeans in the East and West Indies*, second edition, trans. J. O. Justamond. New York, Negro University Press.

RYAN, S.
1971 "The Newfoundland Cod Fishery in the Nineteenth Century." Unpublished M.A. Thesis, Department of History, Memorial University of Newfoundland.

SANGER, C.
1973 "Technological and Spatial Adaptation in the Newfoundland Seal Fishery during the Nineteenth Century." Unpublished M.A. Thesis, Department of Geography, Memorial University of Newfoundland.

TEMPLEMAN, W.
1966 *Marine Resources of Newfoundland*. Fisheries Resource Board of Canada, Bulletin 154.

WILSON, REV. W.
1866 *Newfoundland and Its Missionaries*. Halifax, Dakin and Metcalf.

1964 *Ice Summary and Analysis, Eastern Canadian Seaboard*. Meteorological Board, Department of Transport, 1964–69.

The Demographic and Mercantile Bases of Initial Permanent Settlement in the Strait of Belle Isle

6

Patricia A. Thornton

The frontier thesis represents one of the most exciting attempts by historians to explain the social and political growth of America, at the same time serving as an important tool of historical interpretation in this century. In 1893, Turner systematized for Americans their frontier ideology: "The existence of an area of free land, ... its continuous recession, and the advance of American settlement westward explain American development" (1894:201). Thus, he isolated the frontier as a place: the initial toe-hold of European colonization on the eastern seaboard and subsequently its westward-moving cutting edge. More importantly, Turner identified the frontier as a process during which the European was stripped down to his vital human essences; these basic elements then combined together to form a new and better being. It was an evolutionary process, a series of reconstructions of social character in which the European background was uprooted and in its place, a rugged individualist and a democrat developed.

As with all broad generalizations Turner's frontier thesis has been widely impugned. Critics assert that Turner and his disciples overemphasized the uniqueness of American development and thus oversimplified it. The main error may not be in the frontier hypothesis itself, but in the scale of its conception and its application. Turner, like other historians of the day (Bancroft, 1864), conducted his work on a continental scale, identifying specific aspects of community life which lend support to a broad theory. Such theory must be tested empirically by a series of case studies in different localities and different conditions, for the demographic, social and economic characteristics of the frontier vary greatly.

Despite a good deal of scholarly writing on frontier North America, this task has barely begun. The complex process of population migration to the frontier and the demographic, social and economic conditions there, remain largely unexplained. There has been much romanticizing about the lonely frontier farm, the self-sufficient farmer, his ingenuity and versatility – the typical Turnerian picture – but such reconstructions of backwoods life have often been developed from sparse and dubious evidence (Cross, 1970:59). We require more penetrating analyses of the origins and destinations of the frontiersmen and their economic, demographic, and social characteristics. One historian has recently advocated that in order to bridge the gulf existing between such generalized overviews and the intimate detail of local frontier life, one must study a single community "from its inception ... through the first century of its existence" until it becomes possible to sense the unity of a multi-faceted local life, "and to understand the slow evolution of the whole ... . Only from such knowledge, geographically confined but comprehensive in terms of human activity, can there emerge truely sophisticated hypotheses ... ." (Lockridge, 1970:xiv).

Unfortunately, all recent micro-studies of this type by historians have been confined to New England (Demos, 1970; Greven, 1970; Lockridge, 1970; Norton, 1971), from which it is impossible to make any generalizations about colonial frontier settlement, since New England is not typical. Among the New England, the middle and the southern colonies, there were substantial demographic differences resulting, at least in part, from different patterns of immigration. The southern and middle colonies of the 17th and 18th centuries were settled predominantly by single males, whilst New England was settled predominantly by families (Potter, 1965). More significantly, economic and social conditions under which people settled differed between regions. The New England immigrants consisted of groups of people, often entire congregations or communities who came out to escape economic and ideological pressures at home. The Virginian settlers, on the other hand, came out as individual servants or planters working on large plantations, and only later gained their independence. It may be that the economic and demographic structure of early Newfoundland had more in common with that of Virginia than New England, although Virginia's plantations were land-based whereas Newfoundland's looked to the sea.

The macro-historical approach has not only over-generalized and simplified the development of the American frontier, it has also been responsible for prolonging the myth that the great English trading companies which sponsored North American colonial ventures retarded successful settlement. From this point of view both the Virginia Company and the Massachusetts Bay Company were legal and economic obstacles to colonial initiative in creating permanent communities in the New World. The historical sociologist, Sigmund Diamond, however, argues that the idea of an independent American society was the consequence, if unintentional, of the Virginia Company policy (1971:3–31). It is suggested in this paper that similar contradictions between short and long-term objectives of the southwest English and Jersey merchants eventually, albeit unwittingly, encouraged the growth of permanent settlement in Newfoundland.

The importance of trade in the initial settling of colonial North America is often not appreciated and its lack of consideration in the original Turnerian frontier thesis is a major shortcoming. Vance, for example, insists that wholesaling and towns "were as much tools of pioneering as the axe and hoe" and has argued that the colonies were initially trading economies rather than producing economies in the narrow sense of local self-sufficient systems (1970:10). Settlement takes place and population expands in fairly direct proportion to the avenues of trade open to the colonists. In Newfoundland, perhaps more than in any other part of North America, it was the commercial, or more specifically, the mercantile organization that created and fashioned initial settlement. The continuous dependence on fishing meant that settlement expanded linearly along the coast so that the frontier remained a marine one. Even today almost all settlement clings to the coast.

The concept of "the frontier" is probably as relevant to the understanding of the historical geography of Newfoundland as of any part of North America, for the frontier condition has been a real phenomenon in Newfoundland's development.

For a century and a half settlement in Newfoundland was confined to "the English shore" (see Handcock, this vol.), one of the earliest and most enduring North American frontiers of Europe. Gradually population developed on the fringes of this area, in Placentia Bay to the south, and in Bonavista Bay and outer Notre Dame Bay to the north. The English shore, in the meantime, developed a more mature commercial and demographic structure so that it, in turn, became the main source for the flow of people, institutions, and commercial support to these newly settled bays (see Staveley, this vol.). As yet, however, very little knowledge of this process exists. Much basic research must be conducted at the micro-level, especially in the more

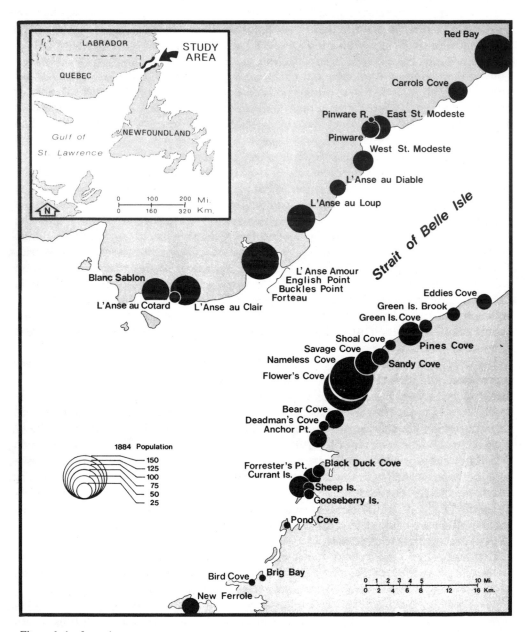

Figure 6–1 *Location*

recent areas of settlement where parish records, census data, other documentary sources, and oral evidence are more readily accessible.

One such area is the shores of the Strait of Belle Isle (Fig. 6–1). Initial settlement here is still within folk memory. Many of the oldest inhabitants represent only the third generation of settlers. Furthermore, since this area was the object of political dispute between the French and the English for a large part of its early history, documentary sources are more plentiful. The political and economic circumstances surrounding the peopling of the Strait are in many ways similar to those which existed on the English shore a century or more earlier. In both areas there was a combination of *ship* and *shore* fisheries, and ostensibly clandestine settlement. This paper, then, should shed light on the processes of early transatlantic settlement, not only in the area under investigation, but also, along the old English shore. It will also illuminate a common New World pattern of frontier development involving the movement of people from demographically and commercially more mature areas of North America to the frontier. It will examine the area ethnocentrically, in terms of the dynamics of the relationships of the people in the area with the area and with the external core. Two particular dimensions of these relationships will be focused upon – the economic and demographic – and through them the stages of development of the frontier will be identified.

The Exploitation Phase of the Frontier
The Strait of Belle Isle forms the northeastern entrance to the Gulf of St. Lawrence; at its narrowest point, it separates by nine miles the northern tip of island Newfoundland from the southern coast of the Labrador Peninsula. For almost five hundred years these waters have been acknowledged as being among the richest fishing grounds on the east coast of North America. It is generally believed that Basque cod and whale fishermen came here as early as 1470, and Breton fishermen were also interested in the cod fishery of the area at this early period (Gosling, 1910; Chambers, 1912; Innis, 1931; Biggar, 1924).[1] By the early 1700s, the seas of this area were fished regularly and most of the later foci of settlement on the north side of the Strait of Belle Isle had already been identified and their major potential recognized.[2] Brouague's annual list of vessels name such places as Isle à Bois, Blanc-Sablon, Carcoteaux (Lance au Cotard), Forteau, L'Anse au Loup, St. Modeste, and Red Bay as bases for the French fishery between 1717 and 1743[3] (Innis, 1954:23) (see Fig. 6–1). No places were ever mentioned on the southern shore of the Strait, probably because it lacked sheltered harbours, making it less suitable as a base for a ship fishery.

In 1702 Augustin LeGardeur de Courtemanche, born at Bayonne, obtained a concession from the Governor of New France for ten years to trade with the natives and to fish for whales, seals, and cod all along the south coast of Labrador, between Kegaska and what is now called Hamilton Inlet.[4] Subsequent division of the area into a series of concessions occurred, in which the economic emphasis was increasingly upon the seal fishery. These concessions were occupied almost continuously by a succession of different personnel, initially French but latterly Canadiens, from 1712 until the end of the French Regime in 1763.[5] The geographical pattern of these concessions is shown in Figure 6–2. It was within the context of a sealing economy that the potential of the Newfoundland shore of the Strait of Belle Isle was first recognized. During this early period, two contrasting forms of occupancy and exploitation developed and operated independently. One was the migratory French cod

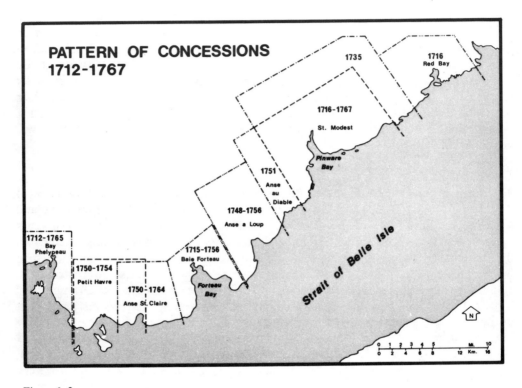

Figure 6–2

fishery centred in Brittany, which was a ship-based operation restricted to a three-month summer season. The other, the Canadien seal fishery, was sedentary, requiring exclusive rights to a certain amount of waterfront and a considerable capital expenditure in terms of gear and buildings. Both operations, however, were conceived and conducted for the economic gain of another country or colony by individuals whose economic and demographic roots were firmly established in the mother country.

Although seal and cod, the two resources influencing later permanent settlement, were being exploited by the early 18th century, permanent settlement (that is, year-round internally regenerative occupancy) was not established for over one hundred years. In the context of a frontier, any assessment of this phenomenon must be made with respect to conditions in the area itself, and to the stage of development of the external core and its relation to the frontier. By the 1760s the British northern frontier of settlement in Newfoundland had not expanded beyond outer Bonavista Bay and a few sites in Notre Dame Bay such as Fogo Island and Twillingate. Even if the Strait had been 'ready' for settlement, so were many other areas closer to the core along the south coast and in Notre Dame Bay after 1783 when that area was ceded to the English. Within the Strait, factors other than the potential of the natural resources were important in determining permanent settlement.

It has been postulated that marauding Eskimos were responsible for inhibiting settlement in the Strait. When Labrador was ceded to the British in 1763, it was said the "Esquimaux so infested the Strait of Belle Isle that it was not safe for a fishing vessel to go there alone"[6] (Chambers, 1912:96). Courtemanche reports that the Eskimos forced the French to abandon their productive cod fishery in the Strait "... parce que quand ils [the French] revenaient [at the beginning of each season] ils trouvaient leurs Chaloupes et échaufants bruisée et brulée que même ils étaient toujours en risque de perdre la vie s'ils se laissaient surprendre."[7] Such interference may have been a contributory element, but other more important factors precluded permanent settlement. One necessary internal prerequisite was the adaptation of the existing seasonal exploitative patterns into integrated year-round occupations which could attract and support a resident population.

In order to comprehend the combination of circumstances which ultimately facilitated the development of such an economy in the Strait, it is necessary to review briefly those policies that were to become the unwitting agencies of integration and concomitant permanent settlement.

Policies Pertaining to Settlement in the Strait of Belle Isle
In 1713 the Treaty of Utrecht granted France fishing rights to a specific section of the Newfoundland coast, which included the southern shore of the Strait. In 1763 and 1783 the precise limits of the so-called "French Shore" were altered, but still included this part of the Strait (Fig. 6–3). The original terms of the Treaty gave France the right to dry fish on this shore, and to cut wood for the erection of fishing premises and the repair of vessels; the reciprocal arrangements were made quite explicit in the Treaty of Versailles (1783). "... the French fishermen building only their scaffolds [drying platforms], confining themselves to the repair of their fishing vessels, and not wintering there; the Subjects of His Britannic Majesty on their part not molesting in any manner the French fishermen during their fishing nor injuring their scaffolds during their absence" (Prowse, 1896:259).

After 1763 when Labrador was ceded to the British, the whole coast was completely

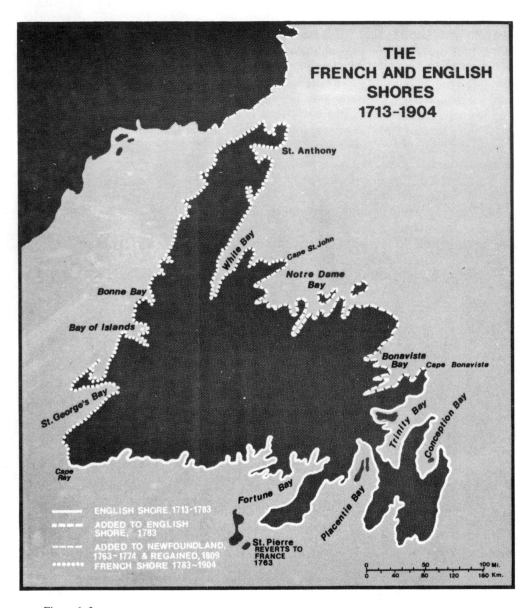

Figure 6–3

reorganized in terms of the British fish trade. The official Newfoundland viewpoint on settlement and the exploitation of the fisheries was contained within the "Regulations for the coast of Labrador" proposed by Palliser, the Governor of Newfoundland, in 1765:

1 That no inhabitant of Newfoundland, no By Boat Keeper nor any person from any of the colonies shall on any pretence whatever go to the Coast of Labradore (except whale fishers within the Gulf of St. Lawrence from the colonies ...).
2 That no person whatever shall resort to Labradore to fish or trade but fishers annually arriving from His Majesty's Dominions in Europe lawfully cleared out as ship fishers, carrying at least 21 men all engaged to return after the season is over ... .[8]

These and earlier regulations were designed primarily to safeguard the fisheries from deterioration both as a result of the growth of settlement within the colony, and the control of France from without. As such they represent British policy for the non-resident exploitation of Newfoundland from the 16th to the 19th century.

The desired effect of these various regulations in the Strait of Belle Isle did not transpire, although they did retard permanent settlement until it was deemed necessary by those exploiting the area, and then they governed the settlement pattern.

For three hundred years, then, the Strait was exploited by outside agencies, either by European vessels annually fishing its shores and returning home with highly prized green fish to feed its own and foreign markets, or by small winter crews supported and directed from Quebec. This was an exploitative frontier where the economic and demographic initiative remained entirely in the control of people and interests from outside the Strait.

The Transition Phase
Palliser's "Regulations," in fact, paradoxically established the prerequisites for permanent settlement:

... as further encouragement to British Ship Fishers the First arriving Ship in any Harbour on the Coast ... shall have the privilege of leaving in that Harbour one small vessel ... with a gang of twelve men and no more for the next winter seal and whale fishery and no other people whatever shall stay the winter in that Harbour ... . The Master of the 2nd arriving British Fishing Ship in any Harbour ... shall ... have the exclusive right to all the salmon fishery in that Harbour during that season. The Master of the 3rd arriving British Fishing Ship ... shall enjoy in common with the 1st and 2nd Ships the exclusive privilege of trafficking with the savages ... .[9]

These privileges were offered as bonuses to encourage the development of the new British ship fishery in Labrador. Ultimately, however, they came to be seen by both the participants and the authorities as *necessary* complementary activities if the summer fishery were to be economically viable. Specifically, the Governor recognized the importance of the subsidiary income provided by spring and winter employment. '... the business of sealing is certainly very advantageous winter employment. There are a great many good posts unoccupied which are situated contiguous to harbours very proper for the carrying on of the Cod Fishery ... ." Moreover, even though the salmon was not generally good enough to start a business, "... when annexed to the cod fishery, some of the rivers are worth attending to."[10]

In 1773 the trader, George Cartwright, who had been at St. Charles Bay, Labrador since 1770, wrote to the Secretary of State stressing the importance of the seal fishery in his total operation in Labrador, and the necessity of granting permanent exclusive rights to specific stretches of the coast, to ensure its proper prosecution. Furthermore, the nature of the seal, salmon, and furring operations was such that it was not economical to exploit these resources sporadically, or at different places each year. The seal fishery demanded that nets and frames be designed for the particular physical dimensions of a site or "berth," and that the "shore apparatus be likewise constructed differently for different posts." Similarly, the salmon fishery required "dwelling houses ... and other erections" to be built on each river. The furring business was also dependent upon a thorough knowledge of an area, as well as the construction of huts at strategic points in the interior trapping grounds. Cartwright went on to stress that sealing and furring, in particular, were winter and spring employments, and must be prosecuted by residents, and not by men transported annually from Europe as in the cod fishery. Finally, he suggested that in Labrador, where these associated activities were important for the viable conduct of a British ship-fishery, "it will in general be found most beneficial that the cod fishery be made subservient to the other more certain and important objects."[11]

This evolution in thinking implied recognition of the principle that in a marginal economy, it was not the major source of income, which in the Strait was the summer cod-fishery, but the remaining potential income that determined whether an enterprise would be economically viable from year to year. Hence, in a decade, the concept of a viable form of resource utilization had changed from a three-month, ship-based operation as intended by Palliser, to a year-round, diversified, sedentary form of exploitation in which furring and sealing became the crucial resources in determining the viability of an otherwise marginal cod-fishing economy.

In the last quarter of the 18th century, business enterprises similar to the one operated by Cartwright began to develop on the Labrador side of the Strait. This area represented the zone of overlapping spheres of influence of three distinct waves of mercantile expansion. The first, of which Cartwright's own venture was a part, was a movement by Devon merchants, especially from Bristol and Dartmouth, up the northeast coast of Newfoundland to eastern Labrador. Each merchant possessed several cod fishing stations at various locations throughout this area, as well as adjacent seal and salmon posts. In the Strait this process was epitomized by the firm of Noble and Pinson (1774–1806), and subsequently by Pinson and Hine (1806–1830), Dartmouth merchants whose crews and agents appear to have been recruited from south Devon.[12] Possibly as early as 1774 this firm had a cod fishing station at L'Anse au Loup, a sealing post at L'Anse Amour and West St. Modeste, and a salmon post at Pinware; by 1784 it had several other establishments on the Labrador coast[13] (Chappell, 1818; Gosling, 1910:385).

A second wave of expansion came from Jersey, whose merchants had long been involved in trading in Newfoundland and in the Gaspé after 1763. They were among the first British concerns to become established in the Strait. Precise dates cannot be verified, but one source postulates that the firm of DeQuetteville was established at Forteau in 1774, and a branch opened at Blanc-Sablon in 1779[14] (Browne, 1909:52). If not the first Jersey firm to exploit the area, it was undoubtedly the most important[15] (Hubert, 1926:III). DeQuetteville maintained direct contacts with Jersey Island and their Blanc-Sablon establishment became their headquarters. Almost all other Jersey merchants who came later had headquarters in Bay de Chaleur or elsewhere in Gaspé, their Labrador establishments functioning as branches only. From the outset, the Jersey firms concentrated on cod and most of their personnel returned to Jersey each fall.

A third sphere of mercantile interest later reached the Strait. About 1800 an English firm, Joseph Bird and Thomas Street, based in Poole and Sturminster Newton in Dorset, established a base. At this time Poole served as an *entrepôt* for the Jersey trade, and it is interesting that in the Strait, Bird's domain reflected an amalgamation of both Jersey and Devon spheres of mercantile influence with stations at Harbour Breton on the south coast of Newfoundland, Bonne Bay on the west coast, and Seal Islands and Tub Harbour on the east coast of Labrador, and with headquarters centrally located in the Strait of Belle Isle at Forteau. Like the Labrador firms, Bird emphasized winter resources, especially furs and seal oil.

By 1830, a pattern of merchant establishments was in existence which remained essentially unchanged until the 1870s. In Figure 6–4, the location of these firms shows clearly that they are the same locales which the Basques and Bretons used as bases for their ship fisheries for several centuries. Figure 6–4 also shows that the Jersey firms predominated, centering their operations on the western end of the Strait on the islands and mainland around Blanc-Sablon and the west side of Forteau Bay, while English firms were located east of Forteau, at English Point and Schooner Cove. By 1830, all the major merchant firms on the coast were firmly established. The Strait can be seen as the point of contact for two major commercial spheres of influence: the first based in England, controlled northeast Newfoundland and Labrador entering the Strait from the east; the other, composed of Jersey merchants, was based in the Gulf entering the Strait from the west. The watershed occurred in Forteau Bay.

Initial permanent settlement in the Strait of Belle Isle began contemporaneously with the establishment of merchant houses. Prior to, and following the Napoleonic Wars, the English and Jersey firms brought out annually fishing crews and shoremen for their fishery, and these men then formed a large pool of potential settlers. The earliest comprehensive report (1848) estimated that at the four Jersey houses in Blanc-Sablon, "the principal fishing station on the Labrador ... there were upwards of 300 inhabitants during the season," whilst at the five fishing establishments at Forteau "upwards of 400 people were employed."[16] The numbers of summer fishermen employed at L'Anse au Loup about the same time was 140. From this and subsequent reports, it can be seen that, on the average, between 700 and 1,000 persons were brought out to this part of Labrador each year as summer employees.

At the close of the season, it was the practice to leave behind a few men as caretakers of the fishing premises, or as winter crews to carry on the seal fishery and fur trapping. In 1848, for example, four people remained at Blanc-Sablon, and winter crews were normally much larger at the British establishment. This practice ultimately undermined the British mercantilist philosophy of exploitation in the Strait, since these "winter men" became the first year-round residents, constituting an embryonic pioneer population.

The Strait was also the exploitative frontier of the Quebec seal merchants. Since about 1780, the Labrador Company monopolized the seal fishery on the north shore of the St. Lawrence and the Strait of Belle Isle, outside the British merchant domain. A decline in the supply of seals, however, meant that sealing became inadequate as the sole basis of a merchant enterprise and the company closed shop in 1821 (Chambers, 1912:103). It is doubtful if the individual seal fishermen who chose to remain and settle permanently could have done so if it had not been for the trading organization of the British and, in particular, of Jersey merchants in the area to whom they could trade their seal-oil and skins for provisions and gear. A combination of factors now emerged

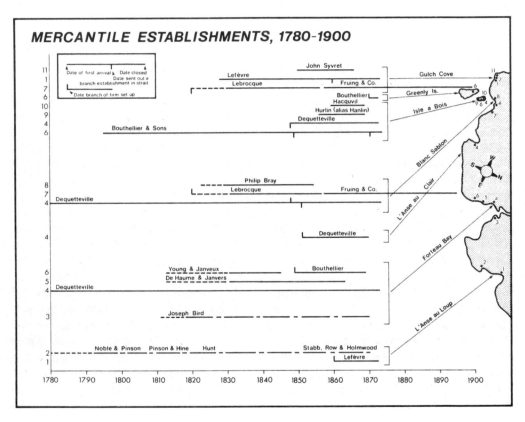

Figure 6–4

which allowed the occupants to remain in the area and evolve the commercial initiative required for subsequent internal development.

It is possible for an area to continue to be undeveloped and unsettled as an extension of the resource base of another country for an indefinite length of time. However, once it is transformed into a settlement frontier, the seeds of self-perpetuation (not synonymous with self-sufficiency) are planted and it is only a matter of time before the economic and demographic *raison d'être* of the area is controlled from within. In the Strait of Belle Isle the transition phase witnessed the development of a pattern of resource utilization which could effectively maintain a permanent population, and the appearance of the embryo of a pioneer population. The necessary internal preconditions for permanent settlement had been established; however, these were not sufficient to effect such settlement unless an outside (core) area acted as an agent, either deliberately or unwittingly.

The Settlement Frontier: The Pioneer Phase 1830–1850

The ethnocentric focus of this paper on the changing economic and demographic relationships of individuals in the Strait of Belle Isle with the area and frontier institutions and agencies outside the area makes it necessary to identify that generation of settlers who first decided to make the Strait their permanent home. These settlers, the true pioneers, prepared the way for a subsequent large influx of other permanent settlers and should be distinguished from the latter, who, in the literature, have frequently been called pioneers. In particular the economic and demographic aspects of the commitment of these pioneers to the area will be examined. The precise dates of the pioneer period, 1830–50, are defined more specifically from an interpolation of the characteristics of migration illustrated in Figure 6–5. Of the 38 pioneer settlers, 80 percent were British and the remaining 20 percent Newfoundlanders. In Figure 6–5, the immigrants are divided according to sex and place of origin. A single man is equated with a family, and a single female who arrived without family is not independently counted, since her future husband has been counted under the category of bachelor. In this respect the difference between single males and females is one of potential versus actual. Figure 6–5 shows that not all the British settlers arrived within the arbitrarily defined temporal limits of the pioneer phase: fourteen came between 1850 and 1870, the majority of whom were from Jersey. It would, however, be spurious not to consider the British settlers as a unit in terms of their origins, even though those who arrived after 1850 do not conform precisely to the definition of "pioneer."

Of the 57 British settlers who came to the Strait, 75 percent were English and 25 percent from Jersey. In the light of the relative importance of the Jersey Island merchants in this area, it is perhaps surprising that more settlers did not come from there. An explanation might lie in the recruitment patterns of these firms. Of the English settlers, it is possible to locate over 80 percent by county of origin. (Fig. 6–6 and Table 6–1.) Dorset, Somerset, and Devon contributed almost equal numbers. A comparison with Handcock's findings for the whole of Newfoundland (this volume) brings out the relative importance in the Strait of Jersey and Somerset source areas, and the relative insignificance of Devon. The Strait's source areas resemble those of the south coast of Newfoundland which was an important area for Jersey immigrants, but their relative significance there is less than in the Strait. There was also an unusually high proportion of settlers from Devon, a factor which can be attributed to

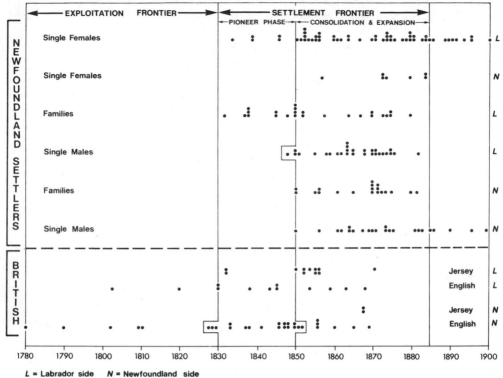

Figure 6–5

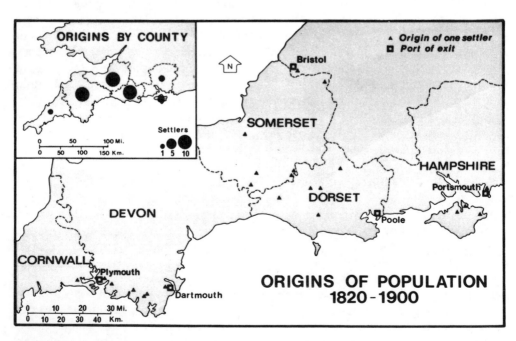

Figure 6–6

TABLE 6–1

Source Areas of English Settlers in the Strait of Belle Isle[17]

County	Number	Percentage
Dorset	10	23
Somerset	9	21
Devon	9	21
Hampshire	5	12
Cornwall	1	2
Gloucestershire	1	2
Others	8	19
Total	43	100

the existence of a Devon-based firm. The total number, compared with Handcock's findings is small, and it is probable that the idiosyncrasies can be explained in terms of the recruitment patterns of individual employers.

An arbitrary breakdown by county in some ways obscures our understanding of the geographical origins of the first settlers. Most of the English settlers came from localized areas often straggling county boundaries, the most important of which runs along the border of Dorset and Somerset (Fig. 6–6). A second important source area was centred on the villages around Plymouth, and a third and lesser one around Portsmouth and the Isle of Wight. There is little correlation between date of arrival and source area of these immigrants, with the possible exception of Portsmouth from whence later settlers came. The same villages in central Dorset and Somerset were also source areas for immigrants on the south coast of Newfoundland, who arrived at the same time as the Strait settlers via a similar mixture of Poole and Jersey merchants. Bird's ships with crew and supplies regularly called in at Harbour Breton, Bay of Islands, and Bonne Bay on their way to Forteau in the Strait of Belle Isle.

The geographical pattern of recruitment was largely dependent upon the location of merchants, supply agents, and sea captains. For example, the Plymouth source area, anomalous in the general context of English emigration to Newfoundland (see Handcock, this vol.), can probably be attributed to the influence of one or two such individuals. Certainly the residential location of the merchant Joseph Bird at Sturminster Newton, a small town in inland Dorset, was crucial in determining the significance of the Dorset-Somerset border country as a source area. After Bird's death in 1841 this firm recruited its labour through one of the Jersey firms, DeQuetteville, which in turn recruited much of its labour from Dorset through supply agents there.[18]

A striking characteristic of Figure 6–6 is that almost all the British migrants to the Strait came from inland areas. This implies that most of the settlers did not come from a fishing background. Why these people entered the Newfoundland cod fishery is explicable only in the context of the social and economic conditions of these inland areas. One of the most persistent folk traditions in the Strait surrounding these original settlers was that almost every man "had a trade" in the homeland. Among those mentioned and sometimes recorded in early death registers and on gravestones are farmers, butchers, carpenters, coopers, blacksmiths, tinsmiths, locksmiths, masons, and tailors. It may be that in some cases these were the trades of the fathers of these settlers, since most of the latter were recruited as boys, or that merchants apprenticed these youngsters to teach them some of these trades. In any case, the majority of first settlers were rural artisans, and not farmers, as has been asserted. It is probable that rural artisans were more likely to become redundant through industrialization or general economic depression than were farmers. Furthermore, most of the initial immigrants worked as shoremen in the Strait, rather than as members of fishing crews, especially those from Dorset and Somerset. This practice of recruiting shoremen from Britain continued until 1870, whereas prior to this date fishing crews were often recruited from St. John's and elsewhere in Newfoundland, Gaspé, and the Magdalen Islands.[19] None of these fishermen, nor, indeed, New England or Nova Scotian migratory fishermen ever settled in the Strait. It is likely that the added skills of the shoremen, with possible artisan antecedents, made them more suitable wintermen and permanent settlers.

The eight Newfoundland settlers who arrived before 1850 can be clearly distinguished from those who arrived after this date (unlike their British counterparts) in terms of both their origins and their marital status. All migrated from Carbonear, Conception Bay; all were married and had families on arrival; and all settled in one of three locations at the eastern end of the Strait – East St. Modeste, Carrols Cove, or Red Bay.

The Demographic Basis of Initial Permanent Settlement

An examination of the dates of arrival of the first permanent settlers on the coast (see Fig. 6–5) shows that infiltration began about the 1770s, and averaged only one settler every ten years until about 1830. All were Englishmen. From about 1830 to 1850, British immigrants to the Labrador side were joined by eight Newfoundland families and five Newfoundland girls. On the Newfoundland side, the English continued to be the sole settlers until approximately 1850. The rate of immigration on both sides of the Strait increased between 1830 and 1850, when twenty-two British (almost exclusively English) men settled, compared with seven over the preceding fifty years.

Without exception, the personnel brought out by the merchants were single males, either bachelors or widowers. Yet women were a necessary prerequisite for the initiation of permanent pioneer settlement. This vital role of women has been largely ignored in the literature on the history of Newfoundland settlement. As shown in Figure 6–5 large numbers of single females migrated to the Labrador side of the Strait from a relatively early date; conversely, the Newfoundland side remained for a long time the recipient only of single males. Until the 1850s the only female spouses were the progeny of a daughter of a nearby settler. This daughter married an English bachelor who settled on the Newfoundland side and had fourteen daughters (Richards, 1953:18).[20] Nine of them married English bachelors who had settled on this side of the Strait.

The phasing of British permanent settlement, as shown in Figure 6–5, reflects the availability of spouses as the critical element. The first five settlers on the Newfoundland side were bachelors who maintained a continuous residency by means of a chain migration to the area of kin. There was a break from roughly 1810 to 1825 in the flow of permanent settlers to the area. From then through to the 1840s the stream started once again and its rate increased rapidly, coinciding with the coming of marriageable age of the only eligible females (mentioned above) in the area. No indigenous source of wives was available on the Labrador side which depended upon the immigration of single females, arriving alone, or as unmarried daughters *en famille*, from east-coast New-

TABLE 6–2

Estimated Age at First Marriage of First Generation English-born Male Settlers
and their Spouses on the Newfoundland side of the Strait of Belle Isle, 1830–1850s

Year of Marriage (Birth 1st Child)	Male			Female		
	stat	gen	Age	stat	gen	Age
(1829)	b	(1)	41.44	s	(2)	19.44
1834	w	(1)	27.00	s	(2)	18.37
(1833)	b	(1)	33.33	s	(2)	17.51
(1835)	b	(1)	27.28	s	(2)	17.21
(1840)	b	(1)	30.71	s	(2)	17.28
(1843)	b	(1)	31.78	s	(2)	14.00
(1843)	b	(2)*	23.92	s	(2)	18.73
(1849)	b	(1)	25.99	s	(2)	18.55
(1850)	b	(1)	27.10	s	(2)	n.d.
Sub. average			29.84			17.63
Amended sub. av.			(30.47)			(18.15)
(1848)	b	(1)	27.93	s	(2)	21.92
(1850)	b	(1)	45.06	s	(1½)	20.31
1852	b	(1)	30.91	s	(1½)	17.57
1855	b	(1)	n.d.	s	(2)	20.00
1858	b	(1)	27.67	s	(1½)	22.13
1853	b	(1)	30.65	s	(2)	20.35
Sub. average			32.44			19.08
Average			(31.29)			
1862	w	(1)	—	s	(1½)	23.82
1858	w	(1)	—	s	(1½)	22.00
1852	w	(1)	—	s	(1½)	23.32
Sub. average						23.04
Average						19.87

Legend: b = bachelor, s = spinster, w = widower. *not included in average.
stat = marital status. gen = generation. (1½) represents a female who had come to
the area earlier as a member of a family.
Source: Parish Registers.

foundland. The rate of increase in permanent settlement in this area, consequently,
was much slower and peaked later. It is also worth noting that an early peak in the
arrival of single Newfoundland females is reflected in a corresponding peak in the
arrival of British male settlers in the early 1850s.

The significance of the general lack of potential wives is reflected in the marriage
ages of the first English settlers to the Newfoundland shore and their spouses (see
Table 6–2). The average age at first marriage of the nine sisters, who were the spouses
of the first nine English male settlers to the Strait, was 17.6 years, or 18.2 years if the
dubious figure of 14 years for one spouse is ignored. Excepting two cases, the date of
birth of the first child was used in place of the date of marriage, since the latter was
unrecorded. Consequently, the average age so derived is slightly elevated, possibly by
about nine months if the average period on this shore between marriage and the birth
of the first child for the period 1850 to 1880 is used. Thus it can be assumed that the
actual age at first marriage of these first pioneer women was, in fact, nearer 17.5 years.
The average age of the remaining spouses, whose husbands were likewise first

generation English males (mainly after 1850) was 20.4 years, and the overall age for all spouses, 19.1 years. By contrast the average age at first marriage of the English male permanent settlers on this coast was 31.3 years. This figure does not include second marriages, that is, marriages of widowers. By both the British standards of the time, and post-1850 figures for first marriages for the Strait, these ages were much higher for men, and much lower for women[21] (Wrigley, 1969:45, 87). These figures clearly suggest a severe imbalance between the sexes, sufficient to retard the growth of a pioneer population.

The high mean age at first marriage among male immigrants is particularly significant when oral and documentary evidence concerning their average age at time of first contact with the area is taken into consideration. The men brought out by the firms were youngsters, often chosen at fourteen and apprenticed for two summers and a winter to merchants' agents (Richards, 1953:18; Ferland, 1917). This suggests that many of the young men either came out to Labrador for a series of eighteen month periods over fifteen years or so, returning to Britain between contracts, or they remained in the area as servants of local planters. Oral evidence would tend to support the latter. In both cases, these men ultimately settled at the time of marriage.

Eight English- or Jersey-born single men whose deaths, at fifty or over, are recorded on gravestones in the cemetery at Anchor Point are described as either planters or servants. Four of their names appear in the Account Books of J. S. Bird in 1840, on the average of twenty years prior to their date of death. This fact and their advanced age at death suggest a continuous residency in the Strait for at least this period. Furthermore, the death register for the Labrador side of the Strait over the period 1850–1866 contains the names of three planters, a carpenter and seaman, a cooper, and a blacksmith, and six fishermen, all of whom appear to have died unmarried at an average age of forty-one, suggesting that they would have become pioneers had spouses been available.

The Economic Basis of Initial Permanent Settlement

The first settlers were originally employed as caretakers, as winter crews attached to British merchant establishments, or as sealers for the Labrador Company. Until approximately 1830, most of the winter crews were attached to merchant establishments whose labour requirements were fixed. Settlement was strictly controlled to meet the needs of the merchants, and thus the increase in the number of permanent residents was very small in a period which stretched over half a century. After 1830, these wintermen – sealers, furriers and salmon fishermen – started to settle permanently. Summer employment was assured in the fishery; the essential economic problem which they faced, and one which has largely continued to the present time, was that of generating sufficient additional income to support year-round settlement. The winter income derived from seals and fur was the critical element in setting up "on their own account" – that is, becoming pioneers.

It appears that Bird and Company controlled the fur economy in the Strait in the pioneer phase, since the account books show that all the first "liveyeres" on both sides of the Strait and the Jersey merchants sold their furs to this firm. They also show that in the 1820s, furring was an important element in the economy, and was probably the dominant commercial winter activity on the Newfoundland side. Between 1824 and 1828, Bird and the major local "planter" on the Newfoundland side, Genge, appear as partners, albeit unequal, in the furring venture; but from 1828 onwards they operated independently. Genge became a petty trader and controlled trapping along the entire shore from River of Ponds to Boat Harbour (Richards, 1953:18). Initially, these were the only names which figured in the books, but in 1834, Buckle (the earliest resident planter at Forteau) appeared for the first time, and likewise each liveyere thereafter made the transition to individual enterprise by taking out his own furring account with the company instead of having his catch automatically recorded as part of the winter catch of the establishment itself.

The salmon fishery was also commercially important in the early period. Richards, for example, noted that "it was the river that had the value, not so much the land on its bank, and the rivers were bought and sold as any other property" (1953:18). One of the earliest settlers, according to folk tradition, was a Frenchman who lived at Buckles Point at the mouth of an important salmon river, and who was reported as selling the river to Buckle, the earliest English planter. Furthermore all the initial English merchant establishments held salmon posts. Good salmon rivers, however, were restricted in the Straits and their overall economic importance, therefore, was small.

In the 1830s the seal industry revived. A description of conditions on the coast of Labrador has been left by Samuel Robertson (1856:35), a contemporary resident of Canadian Labrador. "... for the last ten years, there has been a considerable increase both in produce [seals] and settlers. There is now [c. 1840] in the first one hundred and fifty miles from the Province Line, [between Lower Canada and Newfoundland] about 50 establishments, more or less extensive, chiefly sedentary seal fisheries; of these, nearly half are in the neighbourhood of Bradore ..." In 1839 Bird disposed of an important salmon post at L'Anse Amour and a seal post at L'Anse au Diable to local planters. This is the first reference to the changeover in ownership in this area of seal and salmon posts fished by servants to those fished by individual planters.

The merchant establishments were quick to recognize that seal, salmon, and fur industries executed by independent liveyeres were more flexible and efficient than those prosecuted by hired employees. The firms consequently supplied these liveyeres with provisions in return for their produce. A letter from Joseph Bird to his agent at Forteau as early as 1836 stated, "I think if you were to calculate on fitting out 6 boats next year ... employing about 26–28 hands it would do .... The extra provisions could then be sold to produce fish, oil, fur or salmon." In a subsequent letter, Bird writes: "What I wish is to have a few fixed planters ... who look to us for supplies."[22]

As owners/operators of posts, the planters worked independently and sold their produce to the merchant in return for provisions. This transformed the relationship between traders and settlers from one of owner to supplier, creating a leak in the mercantilist system which ultimately brought about its demise. The local planters began to employ men on their own account. Fishermen were brought out in the usual fashion by the British Ship merchants, and in the fall were shipped to various local planters, who established them in certain locations along the coast to prosecute the seal fishery and/or to trap. "Gradually, English 'youngsters' coming out to Labrador were attracted to the long low strand across the Strait, and employed by Genge [a local planter]. He alloted to each the section of coast he wished him to hunt"[23] (Richards, 1953:18). In the summer these youngsters would either fish for the same planter, fish on their own account, or work for one of the British firms. Local planters soon started hiring men directly from Britain through the merchants. "If any of the planters order youngsters this season they must send home the amount in the Fall for their outfit and passage or they will not be sent out."[24] Ultimately both planters and youngsters obtained their supplies from the British merchants who took their catches in return. The economic interdependence of merchant and liveyere became well established, and has continued to the present.

The extensive ship fishery, with seal oil and fur adjuncts, was now transformed into a small supply business, better conducted from the North American side of the Atlantic. Mercantilism, with its nationalistic, monopolistic, and exploitative philosophy, an institution adapted to the exploitation frontier, had given way to the *laissez-faire* policy based on local Newfoundland agents of British-based firms, a practice which was better adapted to the pioneer phase of frontier development.

Responsible Government was established in Newfoundland in 1832, reflecting a turning point in the development of St. John's and the traditional "English Shore." Among the opponents of Responsible Government were West Country merchants, especially those based in Poole, because they saw it as the ultimate expression of an economically and demographically mature colony, implying the end of English exploitation. St. John's and eastern Newfoundland now became the core, with the Strait as part of its frontier until 1880; but it was both an exploitation and settlement frontier.

The "stationer" fishery, a shore-based summer fishery in Labrador, was prosecuted by east coast Newfoundlanders throughout the 19th century. It began with fishermen sailing to Labrador each year as crews for Newfoundland merchants.[25] In Red Bay, the centre of the Stationer fishery within the Strait, Carbonear fishermen first came out as employees of a Carbonear merchant, but gradually they began to operate independently. In 1848 Captain Loch reported the existence of thirteen rooms "operated by separate planters" who were still being carried down as "freighters" in the schooner of this same merchant.[26] From about one hundred Stationers, forty returned to Carbonear that fall while the remainder stayed in Red Bay for the winter seal fishery. Those who stayed each winter constituted a pioneer population in the same way as did the British liveyeres.

It has been a central theme of this paper that pioneer settlement occurs only when a personal commitment is made to an area. Economically, this implies individual enterprise, meaning that a settler invests his own capital in the area at considerable financial risk. For the first time in its long commercial history, settlers were tied to the area by virtue of their own interests and not by virtue of a large-scale, transatlantic-based, mercantile organization. The exploitation frontier was replaced by the settlement frontier. Demographically speaking, this implies a 'familial' commitment: a pioneer settler ties himself to an area *in toto*, obeying the dictates of Genesis 1 to "be fruitful and multiply and replenish the earth and subdue it ... ."

The English firms continued to adapt to evolving local conditions until they were eventually absorbed. They gradually reduced the size of their transatlantic operations and by 1872, less than one hundred men were employed by English firms in the Strait.[27] Early in the 1820s the English merchants had begun to re-export their fish via St. John's. When traders from the capital expanded their operations in Labrador, especially in the 1840s, it was logical that the English merchants would exploit these links. From then on, the English firms were gradually absorbed into the mercantile sphere of St. John's. By 1830 the English firm at L'Anse au Loup, for example, had changed hands from Noble and Pinson of Dartmouth, to Hunt, and Stabb of Torquay. After Stabb took over, the headquarters were transferred from Britain to St. John's. At this time Stabb was joined by two partners, Row of St. John's, and Holmwood of London.[28] Through the gradual devolution of more and more power to their Newfoundland agents, this firm transferred its entire base from Britain to St. John's by 1855.

One of the biggest problems faced by English firms in the Strait was lack of control over local agents who often acted to the detriment of their firms by adopting short-term profit policies. For example, because of the decision-making of local agents, the Bird firm, originally a large, vertically integrated enterprise controlling all operations – from the catching of fish and seals to the building of vessels and the carrying of cargo to market – was gradually reduced to a supply business supporting an indigenous population. The power was transferred to the resident agent, who was himself dependent upon the more economically efficient and comprehensive infrastructure provided by major St. John's merchants and Halifax trading vessels.

The Geographical Expression of Pioneer Settlement
The first permanent settlers in the Strait focused on a winter economy. Proximity to winter resources influenced both the location and spacing of settlements (Fig. 6–7): salmon rivers were normally considered the property of one person; fur trapping required control over large areas; the seal fishery was even more demanding territorially. Robertson (1856:35) described the technological basis of the seal fishery in the Strait in the following way:

Seals are migratory animals, issuing out of the north in the month of December, to winter in the Gulf of St. Lawrence, and returning in June. While on their voyage, they generally congregate in shoals of thirty to one hundred, and commonly touch on several parts of the coast in passing. When a seal fishery is to be established, houses and stores are built, fixtures erected, crafts, with nets, hawsers, leads, anchors, etc., to be procured ... costing several hundred pounds, sometimes thousands. A solid frame of nets is fixed in a convenient place, into which the seals enter – get entangled among the nets – drown, and are taken ashore in boats ... .

... if a very trifling net is placed before the aforesaid frame of nets, it will effectively bar it off as a stone wall: if another frame is placed too near, it will, either partially or wholly do the same. By this it will be seen that all seal fisheries require a berth of limit.

The French Government, in the late 17th century, decided that sealing berths should be approximately twelve miles apart, and although this distance was generally regarded as excessive by 1830, older settlers argued that the distance should be greater than that proposed by newer settlers. As late as 1906, a lawsuit was filed and fought on this issue. Obviously, the use of the seal frame which Richards claims was invented locally had a major impact on the distribution of settlements: "the first settlers had peculiar ideas ... with the seal frame each crew monopolized a large portion of the coast west of his frame" (Richards, 1953:16, 23). This spatially-extensive nature of winter resource exploitation is highlighted by the story of how a prospective Newfoundland settler coming into Savage Cove was summarily ejected by the only inhabitant there, a fur trapper, because there was no room, though the cove was a mile long!

The change in status from servant to self-employed fisherman was reflected by a move away from the headlands and islands where cod-fishing establishments were located, to the river-banks and to the heads of bays. The cod-fishing locations of the merchant firms such as those at Isle à Bois, Greenly Island, and Schooner Cove, to this day, have remained devoid of settlement; others, such as the west side of Forteau Bay remained unoccupied as long as the merchant firms were there. Several factors may account for this relocation, such as the physical crowding around merchant premises,

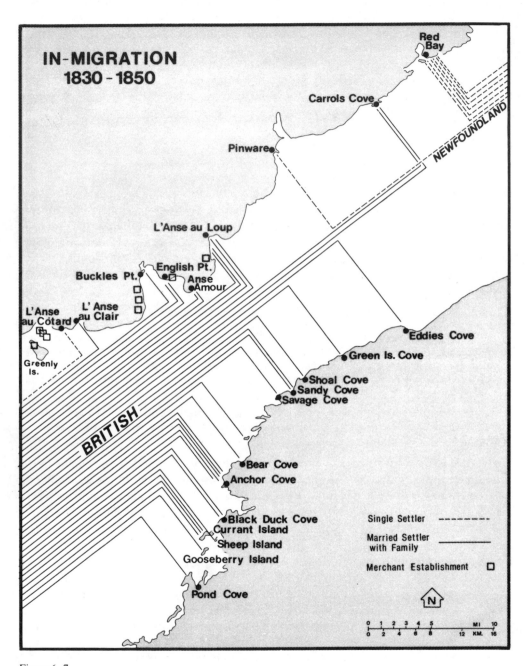

IN-MIGRATION
1830-1850

Red
Bay

Carrols Cove

Pinware

NEWFOUNDLAND

L'Anse au Loup

English Pt.

Buckles Pt.   Anse
                  Amour

L'Anse   L' Anse
au Cotard   au Clair

Greenly
Is.

BRITISH

Eddies Cove

Green Is. Cove

Shoal Cove
Sandy Cove
Savage Cove

Bear Cove

Anchor Cove

Black Duck Cove
Currant Island
Sheep Island
Gooseberry Island

Pond Cove

Single Settler   - - - - - - - -

Married Settler   _____
with Family

Merchant Establishment   ☐

N

0 1 2 3 4 5   MI 10
0   2   4   6   8   12 KM. 16

Figure 6-7

but the most important were shelter and easier access to wood, fur, salmon, and seals at sites by rivers or at the heads of bays. Figure 6–7 shows the dichotomous loci of the cod-fishing mercantile establishments and the pioneer settlements in approximately 1850. By this time winter bases of settlement, or at least those from which the winter resources could be readily exploited, had become the permanent loci.

The Settlement Frontier: Expansion and Consolidation

The relatively small number of pioneers who entered the Strait between 1830 and 1850 paved the way for a larger influx of about three times the size between 1850 and 1880 (see Figure 6–5). The latter wave of immigration stemmed almost entirely from east-coast Newfoundland. This influx had been adumbrated, on the mainland side, by a small number of families who had come during the pioneer phase from Carbonear to Red Bay. The major influx of settlers, which was made up of single males on the mainland side and both single males and families on the island side, did not occur, however, until around 1850. The coincident timing of the initial arrival of immigrants within these three categories is very marked, though the numbers are small, and many of the dates are approximations. Where direct evidence was lacking, dates of the arrival of permanent settlers were calculated as one year prior to date of marriage. The rationale for such an assumption was based on the evidence that, although men and women often visited the Strait every summer for years, it was marriage which precipitated their settling permanently on the coast. About 1880 this immigration came to an abrupt end. Thereafter, only two groups of immigrants are recorded: a few young men came to the island side from Bonne Bay on the west coast of Newfoundland and a constant stream of young women came to the mainland side. These women can hardly be said to contribute to initial settlement at this stage, since they did not establish households by themselves. The peak of the Newfoundland-derived settlement on the Strait was between 1860 and 1875.

Between 1850 and 1870 twenty-one British immigrants, mainly from Jersey, and seven Frenchmen settled in the area. However, 80 percent of the immigrants in this period were Newfoundlanders, numbering eighty-six single males or families. Tables 6–3 and 6–4 provide a summary of the origins of the Newfoundland settlers to both sides of the Strait. Approximately 70 percent came from Conception Bay, and this proportion is approximately the same for both sides. The subsidiary sources of population, however, diverge markedly. On the island side the only other source area of significance is Trinity Bay (16 percent), and one centre, in particular, Catalina. Oral evidence suggests that there may well be some connection between Catalina and the Conception Bay ports. It was common for Brigus "stationers" in particular to call in at Catalina on their way to the Strait, and several families were known to have come out together from these two centres and settle next to one another. On the Labrador side, St. John's was the major secondary source area (24 percent) and Trinity Bay was the third (6 percent); the communities of Trinity Bay were different from those involved with the island side. Furthermore, the Labrador side received a large influx of Newfoundland females who came from the same communities as the male settlers.

From the 1850s onwards the backflow of settlers from the Labrador to the New-foundland side of the Strait ended. The two sides maintained completely different links with the east coast of Newfoundland. On the Labrador shore precise patterns are discernible when the specific source areas of migrants are associated with their timing of arrival, specific destination, and their sex and marital status. For example, the most

TABLE 6-3

(a) The Origins of Newfoundland Male Settlers in the Strait of Belle Isle, by Source Area, 1850–1880

Source Area	Newfoundland Side		Labrador Side	
Conception Bay	26	70%	35	69%
Brigus	4		2	
Carbonear	n.d.		28	
Bell Island	n.d.		4	
Portugal Cove	n.d.		2	
Trinity Bay	6	16%	3	6%
Catalina	6		0	
New Chelsea	0		1	
New Perlican	0		2	
Saint John's	0	0%	11	24%
South Coast	3	8%	0	0%
Notre Dame Bay	2	5%	0	0%
Others	0	0%	1	1%

(b) The Origins of Female Newfoundland Settlers to the Labrador Side of the Strait of Belle Isle, by Source Area, 1850–1880

Source Area	Number	Percentage
Conception Bay	28	60%
Spaniard's Bay	4	
Brigus	4	
Carbonear	8	
Portugal Cove	4	
Trinity Bay	8	17%
New Chelsea	4	
New Perlican	1	
Hants Harbour	3	
Saint John's	8	17%
Others	3	6%

Source: Parish Registers, gravestones and oral tradition.

striking feature of these patterns (see Tables 6–3 and 6–4) is the large number of settlers who came from Carbonear and immediate environs, which, in fact, constituted the initial source area (in Conception Bay) of Newfoundland migrants to this part of Labrador. Most of the other source areas, with the exception of St. John's which started to send settlers to this area in the 1850s, did not become important until after 1860 – Trinity Bay not until the 1870s. It would seem, therefore, that the phasing of settlement reflected, first of all, a definite evolution in the areal relationships of the various Newfoundland source areas with Labrador, and the shifting geographical emphasis of the whole east-coast Newfoundland-based Labrador fishery. It also reflected different processes in bringing out settlers to the coast. No such phasing is evident on the island side of the Strait. It is also evident that specific source areas were associated with specific destinations, thus suggesting the existence of definite links

TABLE 6–4

Origins of Newfoundland Settlers to the Labrador side of the Strait of Belle Isle, by Source Area, Destination, Date of Arrival, Sex and Marital Status

Each settler entry is given as three stacked values: marital status / date of arrival / destination code.

Source Area		Settler entries (status · year · destination)
Carbonear:	males	m·1832·P, m·1837·RB, m·1838·RB, m·1838·RB, m·1838·RB, m·1845·RB, m·1845·RB, m·1848·RB, s·1848·EM, m·1850·CC, s·1850·LD, m·1850·WM, m·1850·EM, m·1852·EM, m·1852·EM, s·1864·CC, s·1864·P, s·1865·RB, m·1867·RB, m·1869·RB, m·1870·RB, s·1870·RB, s·1875·LL, m·1875·RB, m·1877·LL, m·1880·RB, s·1880·EM
	females	s·1856·EM, s·1856·EM, s·1857·EM, s·1857·EM, s·1859·EM, s·1861·EM, s·1879·CC, s·1886·EM
St. John's:	males	m·1850·F, s·1850·F, s·1850·F, s·1851·LD, m·1858·WM, s·1859·LL, s·1861·WM, s·1861·WM, s·1864·WM, s·1865·WM, s·1868·WM, m·1873·LL, m·1875·RB
	females	s·1852·LL, s·1853·LL, s·1855·WM, s·1860·LL, s·1861·P, s·1862·LL, s·1868·WM, s·1880·LL
Bell Island:	males	s·1865·LD, s·1868·LL, s·1875·LD, s·1875·LD, w·1852·LL, s·1855·LL, s·1880·LL, s·1884·LL
Portugal Cove:	males	s·1860·P, s·1864·WM, s·1859·WM, s·1861·WM, s·1868·WM, s·1871·WM
	females	
Brigus:	males	m·1867·F, m·1870·F, s·1862·F, s·1870·F, s·1870·?, s·1884·F
	females	
New Chelsea:	males	s·1876·WM, s·1889·WM, s·1894·WM, w·1900·LD, w·1901·WM
	females	
New Perlican:	males	s·1871, s·1872, s·1878·WM
	females	
Spaniard's Bay:	females	s·1871·WM, s·1884·F, s·1870·?, s·1901·WM
Hants Hb.:	females	s·1862·F, s·1880·F, s·1896·F, s·1855·LL, s·1880·LL, s·1884·LL

Legend: m = married, s = single, F = Forteau; LL = L'Anse au Loup; LD = L'Anse au Diable; WM = West St. Modeste; CC = Carrols Cove; RB = Red Bay; P = Pinware; EM = East St. Modeste

Source: Parish Registers, gravestones and oral tradition.

between particular settlements in Labrador and particular Newfoundland communities. Immigrants from Carbonear settled almost exclusively in the three communities at the east end of the Strait of Belle Isle: East St. Modeste, Carrols Cove, and Red Bay, and two of those who lived initially at L'Anse au Loup moved to East St. Modeste within a few years; on the other hand, migrants from St. John's settled at Forteau and L'Anse au Loup. Four men from St. John's also came to West St. Modeste, but all subsequently left. All the Trinity Bay settlers were centred on West St. Modeste, those from Brigus on Forteau, those from Bell Island on L'Anse au Loup and adjacent L'Anse au Diable, and those from Portugal Cove on Pinware and contiguous West St. Modeste.

The pattern of immigration of young girls mirrors that of the men, but Carbonear is of less importance in this respect. Within the consolidation phase, two new source areas, Spaniard's Bay and Hants Harbour, emerge. Girls from the former settled in L'Anse au Loup and those from the latter in Forteau. Otherwise the connections between places and timing of settlement by females from various source areas correspond to those found among the men. One significant point which is not readily apparent from the tables is the frequent occurrence of precise connections between the settlement of single girls and families. It is possible that a large number of Newfoundland families would not have settled in Labrador if it were not for daughters or sisters of these same families marrying men from the coast and settling there; at least ten Newfoundlanders were known to have come to Labrador for the summer fishery every year for as many as twenty years before they eventually settled. Contacts and channels were originally established by families, but the actual decision to take up permanent residence was often precipitated by the earlier establishment, through marriage, of a daughter in the area.

If the stages in the life cycle of the migrants are taken into consideration, two groups can be identified: (i) single males and females of marriageable age, and (ii) families in the "expanding phase." An examination of the ages of children reveals that the oldest child of most of the families whose size could be ascertained at the time of immigration was in his late teens or early twenties. This is consonant with the existing migration theory which states that single people and families in the "expanding phase" of family formation have a greater propensity to migrate (Jansen, 1969:71; Leslie and Richardson, 1961:984–902). Within the geographical context, this evidence also supports the prevalent view that the east coast of Newfoundland was overpopulated, thereby encouraging emigration to Labrador and other parts of the island at this time. If overpopulation was a major reason for out-migration to Labrador, it is to be expected that the age (at first marriage) of spouses who were married before emigrating to Labrador would be greater than the age of either those who were born in east-coast Newfoundland but migrated to Labrador as young people, or those indigenous spouses who were born and married in Labrador. The actual mean age (at first marriage) of Newfoundland male migrants who were married before emigrating to Labrador was 35.4 years, the mean age of single male Newfoundland migrants was 26.8 years, and the mean age at first marriage of indigenous-born second-generation Labrador males was 25.5.

A comparison of these three groups of data reveals that there was a significant difference at the 99.9 percent level between the age at first marriage of married Newfoundland migrants and each of the other two groups.[29] East coast Newfoundlanders deliberately delayed marriage, probably because of pressure on the existing resource base. More significant from a demographic viewpoint is the age at first marriage of women, since it is the female who ultimately determines the fertility of a marriage. The earlier she marries, the greater is the likelihood of her producing more children. The mean age at first marriage of women who married in Newfoundland before migrating to Labrador was 26.1 years, whereas single Newfoundland female migrants to Labrador married, on the average, at 23.2 years, and indigenous girls at 21.2 years. There was a significant difference between the first group of women and each of the other two groups at the 98 percent and 99 percent level, and a somewhat less significant (88.5 percent) difference between the ages at first marriage of single Newfoundland women and indigenous women.[30] These differences in ages at first marriage are considerable, since demographers consider that an age differential of almost five years between the two most extreme groups would reduce the fertility of a marriage in the western world by two to three children (Wrigley, 1969:87). In Labrador where fertility rates at this period were significantly higher than the average, its impact was even greater.

Between 1850 and 1880, the economy in the Strait shifted from being based on winter resources to the summer fishery. This may have been both a cause and a consequence of the influx of transient east coast Newfoundland fishermen which peaked between 1860 and 1875, and which was paralleled by an influx of resident Newfoundland cod fishermen. In order to understand this influx it is necessary to examine the area's commercial infrastructure.

The Evolution of the Merchant Organization in the Strait 1850–1870
British merchant firms continued to operate in the Strait until 1870 (Fig. 6–4). The Jersey merchants remained inflexible in their operations, conducting a transient summer fishery until the 1873 crash of the Banque Union in Jersey itself, and maintaining their headquarters either in Jersey or Jersey-controlled locations in Newfoundland and the Gulf of St. Lawrence.[31] A number of these Jersey firms continued to recruit some of their personnel in Jersey and in southwest England until the 1870s. However, from the 1840s some of them did engage part of their crews from areas bordering the Gulf. The majority of the latter were fishermen; shoremen were still recruited in Jersey, and a few settled.

Commercial establishments existed only on the Labrador side of the Strait and were of three different types. The English merchant firms in the area were run by local agents with headquarters in St. John's. From 1870 these and the Jersey houses were taken over by Job Brothers, whose headquarters were in St. John's and Hant's Harbour. Job Brothers monopolized the Newfoundland-based mercantile Shore Fishery in the Strait until well into the 20th century with establishments at Longue Point, Isle à Bois, Greenly Island, Blanc-Sablon, L'Anse au Clair, Forteau, and L'Anse au Loup. This firm brought out married men with families, along with single men and single girls, the men as fishing crews and wintermen, the girls as servants or cooks. The locations of the merchant firms were generally towards the western end of the Strait (Fig. 6–4).

The second type of enterprise, the stationer fishery, focused more on the eastern end, between East St. Modeste and Red Bay. Emanating out of Carbonear, Conception Bay, the stationer fishery had been in operation in the area throughout the pioneer phase and continued after 1880, when it ceased to be a means of bringing settlers, usually whole families, to the coast. In the later stages of the consolidation phase, the

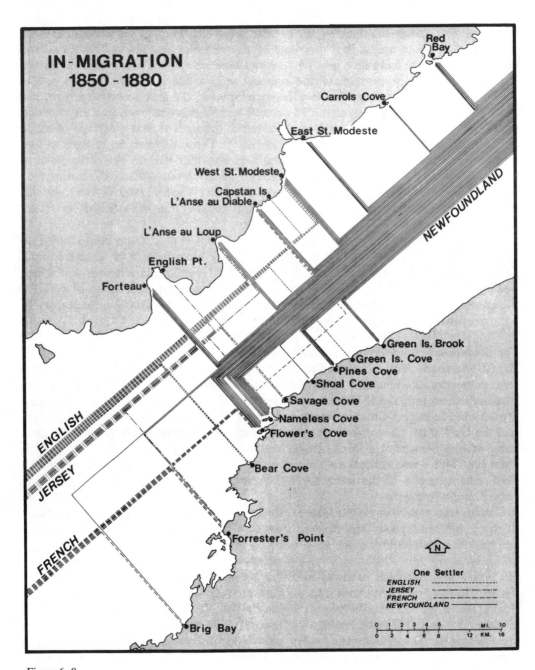

Figure 6–8

fishery became a channel by which *sharemen* were brought down to these locations for the local residents.

Finally, at Forteau, L'Anse au Loup, and West St. Modeste, between the locations of the merchant firms and those of the Stationers, Newfoundland 'planters' operated rooms from bases in Brigus, Bell Island, and New Chelsea, Trinity Bay. Many of these planters never settled, but continued a transient operation throughout. They were, however, channels for others who came down as passengers, and who ultimately settled. Like the single males and females who came out to the merchant firms, they were sharemen and cooks. Servants, passengers, and sharemen were much more likely to take up residence in the area than planters. It is probable that Labrador offered to the former a means of establishing themselves in their own right, a situation less readily attainable in the Avalon Peninsula.

In the pioneer phase, commercial enterprises were concentrated at the western end of the Strait, at Blanc-Sablon, Forteau, and L'Anse au Loup, whence settlers dispersed. In the consolidation/expansion phase, individual Newfoundland planters had rooms in all the bays. In this respect, specific locations in Labrador maintained links with specific Newfoundland centres. The whole process of initial settlement on the Newfoundland side operated via Labrador in the pioneer phase. Subsequently, the two sides of the Strait developed completely independently. Figure 6–8 points to the different pattern of distribution of Newfoundland immigrants on the two sides of the Strait. On the Labrador side, the geographical pattern was one of continuity from the pioneer locations, whereas on the Newfoundland side, the immigrants were interspersed between settlements established by the pioneers. This geographical pattern can be explained by the different economic orientation of the two groups. The English pioneers concentrated exclusively on the winter economy on the island side, whereas the Newfoundlanders were essentially cod fishermen. The resultant choice of different sites was a product of the spatial separation within this area of winter and summer resources, a situation which was not as evident on the Labrador side.

Summary and Conclusions
The unique character and distinctive personality of the Strait of Belle Isle stems from the changing nature and intensity of its areal relationships with the outside world. For three centuries before 1763 it was on the extreme frontier of several commercial empires. As such it was manipulated according to the economic and political motivations, needs and whims of these nations. After the conquest of New France in 1763, the Strait was drawn increasingly into the economic sphere of Britain and in particular of West Country and Jersey merchants. This commercial link tied the Strait into a network which extended as far afield as the markets of southern Europe and West Indies; the homes of West Country artisans and Jersey islanders, the fishing villages of Gaspé and the Magdalen Islands; and the ports of New England, Nova Scotia, Newfoundland and Quebec. In the Strait, the whole area became integrated into one commercial operation, although the heart of the British merchant emporium centred around Blanc-Sablon and Forteau. From here people, provisions and ideas circulated throughout the area, and settlers spread out to other locations on both sides of the Strait. By 1850 Britain was firmly established in a *laissez-faire* policy, which precipitated the death of the West Country ship fishery. In its place a ship and shore fishery had grown up on the Avalon, developed by local merchant elites. The commercial basis of the Strait contracted as a consequence of this both in terms of its organization and the

geographical extent of its operation, and this contraction produced an increasingly inward looking community in the Strait. The two sides of the Strait of Belle Isle operated completely independently. The southern shore, isolated from the transient fisheries of east coast Newfoundland merchants, turned in on itself and maintained only incidental contacts with the outside world. Meanwhile the Labrador shore became more individualistic and more narrowly confined geographically in its external contacts. By 1880 the frontier stage had effectively come to an end. Politically the coast came increasingly under local government control: the Church was established in 1848, schools in the 1860s; the first census was conducted in 1857. More important-ly, however, the area gained economic independence with the establishment of a postal and transportation service in the 1870s which was non-mercantile. Traders increasingly replaced fish merchant establishments as the supply mechanism.

The concept of the 'frontier' is highly relevant to the understanding of the initial economic and demographic development of the Strait of Belle Isle. Its application has permitted the demonstration and further refinement of the essential features of the frontier as suggested by Wyman and Kroeber (1959) from a series of recent compara-tive studies of frontiers in different countries at different times. Firstly, the frontier passed through several phases but with the pioneer characteristics fading fast. Sec-ondly, it is related to a core or cores, whose national government or other institutions were of fundamental importance in its direction; and finally the distance and isolation of the frontier from these core areas are of fundamental importance in the history of frontiers.

The first of these features has been the particular organizational focus of this paper. The first phase in the development of the Strait as a frontier extended over three centuries and was characterized by the arrival of the first frontiersmen who were maintained through a symbiotic relationship with the external mercantilist structure. During the transition phase the merchants developed an economic and demographic base of self-perpetuation, by evolving a year-round pattern of exploitation, and leaving men to 'winter' on the coast. The pioneer phase occurred finally when these men set up on their own account, married and set up their own households. Mercan-tilism and exploitation had given way to pioneer settlement. These pioneers were still entirely dependent upon the merchant infrastructure but they were self-employed. Following these pioneers there was a flow of settlers largely from east coast New-foundland. However, by 1880 immigration had ended and the Strait had ceased to be a frontier although the merchants and stationers from outside continued to exploit the fishery. The permanent settlers or "liveyeres" on the Strait lived separately and independently with an identity of their own. What had once been a base from which to prosecute the British ship fishery now supported a sedentary society with an initiative of its own.

All in all, it becomes possible to clarify what has in the past been a vague and indefinite use of the term 'frontier' in the literature. The frontier is an area on the edge of the ecumene, exploited and developed by agencies who have their economic and demographic roots outside the area. The exploitative phase can, although it need not, last for a considerable length of time. It can be accompanied by settlement or not. However, as soon as a pioneer population develops it is only a matter of time before the frontier must move on. The pioneer phase is that period of settlement when economic and demographic initiative first emanates from *within* the area, and can, therefore, last only one generation. This is usually followed by a phase of consolidation and expansion during which massive immigration occurs. It too can only be short-lived, since inevitably, within a generation or two, the indigenous population, which is demographically and economically self-perpetuating, will dominate.

NOTES

1   Canada, *Journaux de L'Assemblee Legislative*. Session 1858, xvi, Appendix 31.
When Cartier was commissioned in 1532 to make his voyage to the New World, he applied (among the Bretons) for pilots since they were known to have executed the Baccalos Fishery at the entrance to the Gulf for some time. Gosling reported how Courtemanche found extensive remains of whaling establishments and whale bones at Bradore, Forteau, and Red Bay in the Strait of Belle Isle in 1705.
2   Public Archives of Canada, Ottawa, 1705. "Mémoire du voyage qu'a fait le sieur de Courtemanche à la côté des Esquimaux depuis Kegaska jusqu'au havre Saint Nicholas." In P. Magnix Collection, December, 1883:211–12.
3   Archives de la Province de Québec, Québec, 1717–1743. "Lettres de Francois Martel de Brouague, Commandant au Labrador, au Conseil de Marine, France." *Rapport de L'Archiviste de la Province de Québec*, 1922–23:356–406.
4   Great Britain, Privy Council, 1923. "In the matter of the Boundary between the Dominion of Canada and the Colony of Newfoundland in the Labrador Peninsula" (hereafter referred to as the *Boundary Documents*) VII:3679.
5   *The Boundary Documents*, VII:3175–87.
6   He also maintained that the Eskimos traded with the Europeans.
7   P.A.C., "Memoire de Courtemanche ..." *op. cit.*:212. Yet Courtemanche established friendly relations with both Indian and Eskimo.
8   C.O. 194/16, 1765.
9   *Ibid.*
10   *Ibid.*, 31:168–9.
11   *The Boundary Documents*, III:1060–62.
12   Richards, Canon J. T., unpublished diaries, 1904–19 (privately held) gives Dorchester as the place of residence of George Davis, agent for this firm in 1820. According to gravestone evidence Thomas Crockwell, agent, L'Anse au Loup, was born in Torquay.
13   P.A.C, "List of Fishing Posts, December 12, 1774."
There were cod fishing stations at Temple Bay, and seal fisheries at Temple Bay, Seal Islands, Cape Charles and Spear Islands where they employed 48 men in 1784 and caught 4,300 seals. Salmon fisheries were at Mary Harbour, St. Francis River, Black Deer Bay, Sandwich Cove, and Sandwich Bay, where they employed 32 men and caught 676 tierces of salmon.
14   Since no reference is given to the source of this information this date must be regarded as somewhat speculative.
15   "De Quetteville faisait annuellement pour plus de cent mille piastres d'affaires, de chaque côté du détroit de Belle Isle, depuis Mécatine sur la Côte Nord, jusqu'a la Baie des iles, Terre-Neuve."
16   *J.H.A.*, 1848:198, 1849:197–8, 1851:148.
17   Parish Registers, gravestone inscriptions, and family bibles. See especially: Church of England Mission, Strait of Belle Isle, 1848–; Wesleyan Mission, Carbonear, 1850–, Red Bay, 1878–; Roman Catholic Mission, Blanc Sablon, 1849–, Harbour Grace, 1875–.
18   Nicolle to Balston and Son, Poole, Feb. 6, 1844. In possession of Dr. Matthews, Poole.
19   *J.H.A.*, 1864:24, 49; Hubert, Madeleine, :112; P.R.O., London, "Bird Papers, 1824–44," Chancery 108, Masters Exhibits 69, 1956, April 7, 1837, April 20, 1838, July 10, 1837, August 1, 1838, April 10, 1839, April, 1840, July, 1841.
20   The paper is a recording of the folk tradition of the Strait some seventy years earlier.
21   Age at first marriage in Colyton, Devon (near the source area of Newfoundland settlers) between 1770–1837 was 27 years for men and 25 for women. The average age at first marriage of marriages occurring after 1850 in the Strait was 27.1 for men and 23 for women.
22   Bird Papers, B. 1460, July 6, 1836, April, July, 1939, April, 1841. P.A.C. Reel B-1460.
23   Genge had a fishing "Room" at Forteau beside Bird's premises and it seems likely that such contact with the firms on the Labrador was the mechanism by which Genge employed these youngsters.

24 Bird Papers, B. 1460, July 1841.
25 Black, W., "Report of the Development of the use of Resources of the Labrador and White Bay Districts" unpublished, Reel M-704, P.A.C. (1971:65.
26 *J.H.A.*, 1849:193.
27 *J.H.A.*, 1866:509.
28 Registry of Deeds, June 9, 1830.
29 F Ratio = 15.5; $p < 0.001\%$: analysis of total variance
      t test   Group I : Group II $t = 3.9$ $p < 0.001\%$
                   Group I : Group III $t = 4.6$ $p < 0.001\%$
30 F Ratio = 4.6; $p < 0.025\%$: analysis of total variance
      t test   Group I : Group II $t = 2.07$ $p < 0.025\%$
                   Group I : Group III $t = 2.77$ $p < 0.01\%$
                   Group II : Group III $t = 1.3$ $p < 0.125\%$
31 In 1872 more than 500 fishmen were still employed each summer on the Jersey rooms.

REFERENCES: SECONDARY SOURCES

BANCROFT, GEORGE
   1864 *History of the United States.* Boston, Little, Brown & Co.
BIGGAR, H. P.
   1924 *The Voyages of Jacques Cartier.* Public Archives of Canada, No. 11, Ottawa, F. A. Acland.
BROWNE, REV. P. W.
   1909 *Where the Fishers Go: The Story of Labrador.* Toronto, Mission Book Co.
CHAMBERS, E. T. D.
   1912 *The Fisheries of the Province of Quebec.* Quebec, Department of Colonization, Mines and Fisheries.
CHAPPELL, LT. E.
   1818 *Voyage of H.M.S. 'Rosamund" to Newfoundland and the Southern Coast of Labrador.* London, J. Mawman.
CROSS, MICHAEL S. (ed.)
   1970 *The Frontier Thesis and the Canadas: The Debate on the Impact of the Canadian Environment.* Toronto, Copp Clark Co.
DEMOS, JOHN
   1970 *A Little Commonwealth: Family Life in Plymouth Colony.* New York, Oxford University Press.
DIAMOND, SIGMUND
   1971 "From Organization to Society: Virginia in the Seventeenth Century." In Stanley Katz (ed.), *Colonial America.* Boston, Little, Brown & Co.
FERLAND, ABBE J. B. A.
   1917 *Le Labrador, Notes et Recits de Voyage.* Montreal, Librairie Beauchemin.
GOSLING, W.
   1910 *Labrador: Its Discovery, Exploitation and Development.* Toronto, Mission Book Co.
GREVEN, PHILIP J. JR.
   1970 *Four Generations: Population, Land and Family in Colonial Andover, Massachusetts.* Ithaca, Cornell University Press.
HUBERT, PAUL
   1926 *Les Isles de la Madeleine et les Madelinots.* Rimouski, Imp. Generale de Rimouski.
INNIS, H. A.
   1931 "The Rise and Fall of the Spanish Fishery in Newfoundland." *Transactions of the Royal Society of Canada*, Section 2:51–70.
INNIS, H. A.
   1954 *The Cod Fisheries: The History of an International Economy.* Toronto, University of Toronto Press.
JANSEN, C.
   1969 "Some Sociological Aspects of Migration." In J. A. Jackson (ed.), *Migration.* Sociological Studies No. 2, Cambridge, Cambridge University Press.

LESLIE, G. R. and A. H. RICHARDSON
    1961 "Life-Cycle, Career Pattern and Decision to Move." *American Sociological Review*, 26(4):894–902.
LOCKRIDGE, KENNETH A.
    1970 *A New England Town: The First One Hundred Years, Dedham, Massachusetts, 1636–1736*. New York, Norton and Co.
NORTON, SUSAN
    1971 "Population Growth in Colonial America: A Study of Ipswich, Massachusetts." *Population Studies*, 25(3):433–52.
POTTER, J.
    1965 "Growth of Population in America 1700–1860." In D. V. Glass and D. E. C. Eversley (eds.), *Population in History: Essays in Historical Demography*. London, Edward Arnold Ltd.
PROWSE, D. W.
    1896 *A History of Newfoundland from the English Colonial and Foreign Records*. London, Eyre and Spottiswoode.
RICHARDS, CANON J. T.
    1953 "The First Settlers on the French Shore." *Newfoundland Quarterly*, 52(3):17–19, 44; (4):15–16, 23.
ROBERTSON, SAMUEL
    1856 "Notes on the Coast of Labrador." *Transactions of the Literary and Historical Society of Quebec*, 4:27–53.
TURNER, FREDERICK J.
    1893 "The Significance of the Frontier in American History." *Annual Report of American Historical Association*, 1893. Washington, 199–227.
VANCE, JAMES E. JR.
    1970 *The Merchant's World: The Geography of Wholesaling*. Englewood Cliffs, N.J., Prentice-Hall.
WRIGLEY, A. E.
    1969 *Population and History*. New York, McGraw-Hill.
WYMAN, WALKER D. and CLIFTON R. KROEBER (eds.)
    1959 *The Frontier in Perspective*. Madison, University of Wisconsin Press.

Ethnic Diversity and Settler Location on the Eastern Lower North Shore of Quebec

7

Frank W. Remiggi

Concept of Ethnicity

Although the literature on ethnicity and ethnic groups is generally extensive, including works by anthropologists, sociologists, geographers, historians, linguists, and others, research on this topic remains relatively unsophisticated and simplistic. In a recent paper, Kolm (1973:59) points out that the most important questions related to the field of ethnicity have not yet been answered or treated adequately. Essentially, the two major weaknesses of most of the existing literature are (i) the lack of a clear, theoretical framework and (ii) an over-emphasis on what may be termed "negative attitudes" towards ethnic groups, implying their acculturation, assimilation or loss of identity. Also emphasized are prejudice, discrimination, stereotyping, social distance, and intergroup conflict, all of which are dysfunctional rather than functional aspects of ethnicity in society (*op. cit.*:60).

Traditional definitions have usually cast ethnic groups as minorities surrounded by a numerically dominant group whose culture and way of life are different, and consequently, with whom the ethnic groups *must* be in constant conflict in order to survive (see for example, Morris, 1968:167; Narroll, 1964:286 ff.). Barth argues that the traditional definition of ethnicity hinders our understanding of the very nature of ethnic groups and their place in human society and culture:

... because it begs all the critical questions: while purporting to give an ideal type model of a recurring empirical form, it implies a preconceived view of what are the significant factors in the genesis, structure, and function of such groups.

Most critically, it allows us to assume that boundary maintenance is unproblematical and follows from the isolation which the itemized characteristics imply: racial difference, cultural difference, social separation and language barriers, spontaneous and organized enmity (1969:11).

Such concepts as the American "melting pot" have emphasized the immigrant status and, hence, the minority position of ethnic groups with their voluntary or forced integration and ultimate assimilation into the dominant culture. Even in countries such as Canada where the concept of the "ethnic mosaic" has long been popular, the anthropological and sociological literature has frequently demonstrated the eventual disappearance of this mosaic (Dawson, 1936; Breton, 1968:190 ff.).

Research on ethnicity in European North America has, until recently, been neglected by social scientists (Spiro, 1955:1240 ff.; Dégh, 1968:101). According to Kolm (*op. cit.*) this same neglect was true of North American historians and folklorists. Cultural geographers, on the other hand, have shown greater interest in ethnicity, both in Canada and the United States, concentrating more on the development of distinctive cultural landscapes than on the inner characteristics of the ethnic groups and their problem of group survival *per se*. According to Jakle and Wheeler (1969:442), the geographical literature has dealt mostly with the distribution of ethnic groups and with distributional changes through time, as manifested on the landscape, while proceeding largely incognizant of important anthropological and sociological concepts such as acculturation, assimilation, and persistence.

Since the late 1960s a new trend in research shows a more positive outlook on ethnic groups and attempts to develop a more realistic and useful definition of ethnicity. Ethnic groups are no longer seen as temporary societies, destined to disappear in the 'melting pot' unless they remain in continual conflict with neighbouring groups; but rather, they are seen as viable social organizations whose structures, cultures, and boundaries (both social and spatial) are constantly undergoing change. The Mosaic persists. A milestone in this new trend is Barth's study, previously mentioned, in which he defines ethnic identity as one's basic identity, presumptively determined by origin and background.

Barth argues that all ethnic groups erect social boundaries by which they are able to reveal and emphasize their identity and by which they are also able to differentiate themselves clearly from others – essentially by a we-they distinction. "Self-ascription" is the recognition of a group's own identity, whereas ascription is the recognition by others of that identity. He emphasizes that all ethnic groups can interact constantly with other groups and that this interaction – which may be social, political, economic, and/or ecological in nature – does not necessarily lead to a breakdown of ethnic boundaries. On the contrary, ethnic boundaries persist despite a flow of personnel across them; furthermore, stable social relations are maintained across such boundaries and are frequently based on dichotomized ethnic statuses. Consequently, it is not that ethnic distinctions depend on an absence of mobility, contact, or interaction, but rather, that they entail processes of *exclusion* and *incorporation* by which discrete categories are maintained. Given this point of view, Barth concludes that the critical focus of investigation in the field of ethnicity "becomes the ethnic *boundary* (Barth's emphasis) that defines the group, not the cultural stuff that it encloses. The boundaries to which we must give our attention are of course social boundaries, though they may have territorial counterparts."

Barth's approach to ethnicity does not suggest that processes of acculturation and assimilation between ethnic groups are non-existent or that they should not be studied. He recognizes that the cultural features signalling the boundary between groups may change. Indeed, even the organizational form of the group may change. However, Barth also argues that the persistent dichotomization between the members of an ethnic group and outsiders allows us to specify the nature of continuity, and to investigate the changing cultural form and content. This type of approach has recently been exemplified by Cole and Wolf (1974).

For geographers, the new trend has meant a more inter-disciplinary approach to the study of ethnic groups, together with a greater reliance on concepts developed by anthropologists and sociologists. Jakle and Wheeler (1969), Bjorklund (1964), Doeppers (1967), and Meinig (1971) are especially noteworthy in that they emphasize the need for geographers to incorporate social and cultural processes with geographical research. (See also Brookfield, 1964; Mikesell, 1967; Sopher, 1973; Sunderland, 1974). Bjorklund realizes the value of examining spatial contexts and the relatedness of cultural forms, features, and other expressions of people reflecting distinctive ways of life. Similarly, Doeppers suggests that the study of ethnicity provides a ready set of geographical questions such as the spatial expression of an ethnic community and how spatial patterns might reinforce the identity of a social group.

Although a step in the right direction, the new approach to ethnicity has yet to answer important questions. Kolm delineates eight areas that require careful examination, including the demography and ecology of ethnic groups, their size, composition, and distribution, all areas of direct relevance to geography. But more significantly, there is as yet no general agreement on the definition of ethnicity. Barth's definition may be intuitively sound, but it has not gained universal acceptance by social scientists. Before a consensus can be reached, Barth's and other models must be retested empirically.

Modern geographical research on ethnicity is likewise faced with certain lacunae. Until the present, most geographical research has been concerned with modern urban centres, rather than rural areas, and the ethnic ghettos and neighbourhoods they contain. This is true of the studies done in North America, especially for the modern period. Those that concentrate on rural areas have been approached largely at the macro-level.[1] Although ethnic studies on this scale are empirically valid, work conducted at a micro-level would better facilitate the task of establishing criteria useful in defining ethnic groups and in delineating local ethnic boundaries and shifts. Such data would be more appropriate for cross-cultural comparison.

Among the objectives of this chapter is to demonstrate the relevance to geography of Barth's thesis and the new approach to ethnicity through an examination of the evolution of an ethnically diverse population in an isolated area of Quebec from the early 19th to the early 20th century. The Lower North Shore is situated in the northeastern corner of the Gulf of St. Lawrence, between the villages of Kégashka and Blanc-Sablon, the eastern-most settlement in Quebec (Fig. 7–1). The area has a present-day population of over 5,000 which is grouped in fifteen discrete coastal settlements scattered over 224 miles of rugged shoreline. Its multi-ethnic background, its present bilingual (English/French) character, its religious diversity, together with its continuing social and economic links with both mainland and island Newfoundland make it a unique area of study within Quebec. Only 20 percent of its population is Francophone compared to 80 percent for the whole province, where the majority of the non-French population is concentrated mostly in the urban area of Montreal and the Eastern Townships. The long history of close, continuous interaction between the French- and English-speaking residents on the isolated Lower North Shore and their common involvement in the political and economic evolution of the region provides a laboratory for analysing ethnic relations. There have been few attempts by geographers or other researchers to examine, at the local folk level, the historical development of French-English relations in Canada, despite the obvious importance of this theme in contemporary Canadian society.

Fieldwork for the present study was restricted to the five eastern-most settlements on the Shore near the Newfoundland-Labrador boundary: Blanc-Sablon, Lourdes-du-Blanc-Sablon (commonly known as Long Point), Bradore, Middle Bay, and St. Paul's River (Fig. 7–1).[2] These are the only five contiguous settlements on the Lower Shore connected by a road. Each settlement includes not only its specific location, but also the surrounding *posts* whose populations eventually merged with them. Hence, Blanc-Sablon includes the posts of Pointe-au-Pot, Ile-à-Bois, and Greenly Island; Lourdes of Gulch Point and l'Anse-aux-Dunes; Bradore of Bradore Plain, Bassin Island, and Bradore Bay; Middle Bay includes Belles-Amours; and St. Paul's River encompasses all the islands in the Archipelago as well as the mainland posts of Five Leagues, Little Fishery, and Salmon Bay. Three religio-linguistic groups are represented on the Lower North Shore today: Francophone Catholics, Anglophone Catholics and Anglophone Anglicans. These three groups are an amalgam of a more culturally diverse population originally occupying this short strip of shore, and thus

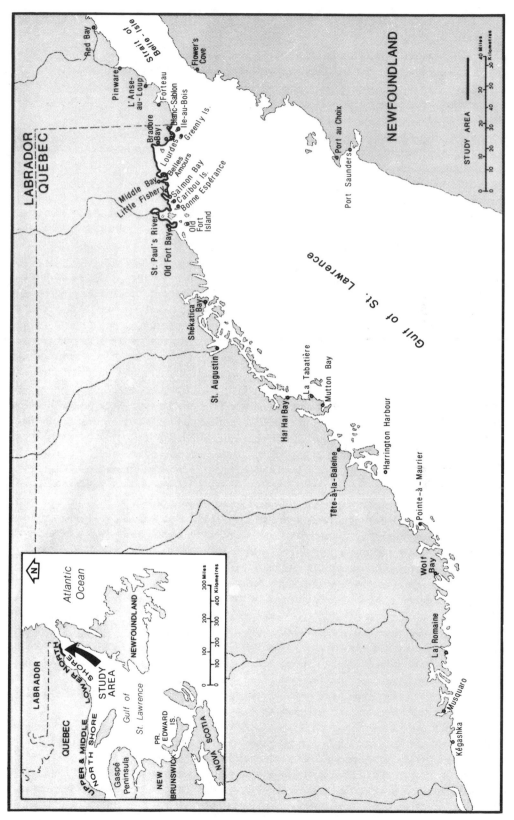

Figure 7-1 Location

form an apposite background for a micro-level examination of the geography of ethnic-group interaction. The following section describes the peopling of the area.

In-Migration: 1820–1890
Although the Lower North Shore was known to European explorers at least as early as the 15th century, it was not until 1820 that the area was truly opened up to free permanent settlement.[3] Prior to that date, seigneurs, concession-holders, and companies such as the Lymburner Brothers of Quebec City, effectively curtailed permanent settlement by means of a monopoly of fishing and hunting rights at all posts along the Middle and Lower North Shores of the Gulf of St. Lawrence. For example, by 1784 the Lymburner Brothers held a monopoly of all sealing posts from Petit-Mécatina to Black Bay in Newfoundland-Labrador; and when they formed the Labrador Company in 1807, the same fishing rights were retained in all the posts of the present lower North Shore, with the exception of St. Paul's River and Bradore which were privately owned by the Lloyd brothers and the Jones family, respectively (Chambers, 1912:103). This monopolistic control of the Lower Shore ended in 1820 when the Labrador Company went bankrupt and relinquished all its posts to its former employees or to squatters. The move paved the way for permanent settlement and for approximately the next seventy years the area saw a continual influx of population.

Between 1820 and 1890 a total of 52 young unmarried adult males, 13 unmarried females, and 7 families trickled into the study area. Single females frequently came to the Lower Shore as employees of mercantile firms that operated an extensive summer fishery on the eastern Labrador coast from the St. Paul's River Archipelago to Red Bay, whereas the individual men and nuclear families usually arrived independently, attracted by the reputed wealth of the Lower North Shore's marine resources, particularly seals and salmon (Lavoie, 1873:41; 1875:35). The period of in-migration to the eastern Lower North Shore can be divided into two distinct phases (see Thornton, this vol.). The first forty years (1820–1860) saw a compound stream of West Country English, Scots, and Jerseymen, as well as French-Canadians mainly from the rural counties of Berthier-en-bas, Montmagny and L'Islet; the next thirty years witnessed a weaker influx of immigrants, most of whom were English-speaking Newfoundlanders[4] (Lavoie, 1875:84–5; Charest, 1970:59–90).

The permanent population in the St. Paul's-Blanc-Sablon region included members of 6 ethnic groups: 44 English and Scots from Britain, some coming *via* Newfoundland; 14 French-Canadians from Quebec; 7 Irish from Newfoundland; 5 Jerseymen; and 2 Acadiens from the Magdalen Islands. More importantly, the permanent settlers also constituted two distinct linguistic and two religious categories: the French-Canadians, Jerseymen, and Acadiens were French-speaking whereas the English, Scots, and Irish spoke English; the French-Canadians, Irish, and Acadiens were Roman Catholic whereas the Jerseymen, and most of the English and Scots were members of the Church of England. There were a few Presbyterians, Methodists, and Congregationalists in the early period who either left the area or were absorbed by the Anglican Church. From the earliest period of permanent settlement, then, the eastern Lower North Shore was a meeting place for members of diverse ethnic stocks who could be identified as sharing either a common language or a common religion.

The members of virtually all of these six groups were too few to be biologically self-perpetuating, and so in a rapid process of integration, the immigrants aligned themselves either along linguistic or religious lines, resulting in the present-day

TABLE 7-1

Ethnic Origins of Resident Population in
'Bonne-Esperance'

	1871	1881
English	176	241
Scots	15	1
Irish	12	11
French	61	86
Others	2	2
Totals	266	341

Sources: Census of Canada: 1870–1871,
Volume I, Table 3, 306–307, Table 4, 309–
391; *Census of Canada: 1880–1881,*
Volume I, Table 3, 248–249, Table 4, 346–
347; Field Work.

composition of French-speaking Catholics, English-speaking Catholics, and English-speaking Anglicans. The few Jersey settlers were French-speaking and Anglican (Feild, 1849:65), but since there were no Jersey women on the Shore, all Jerseymen had to marry either outside their linguistic community to an Anglican or outside their religious community to a Francophone. The former practice led to their Anglicization, the latter implied their conversion to Catholicism. For example, the Fequets and Robins of Old Ford Island retained the Anglican religion but became English-speaking, as did most of the Jersey settlers on the Newfoundland side of the border; whereas the Legresleys and Letempliers of Lourdes and Blanc-Sablon, respectively, converted to Catholicism after their marriages to French-Canadian women.

Language and religion were important criteria in determining residential segregation on the Lower North Shore. In this study, language is defined as the mother or hearth tongue in which the children were reared. The abbé Ferland, in a report for 1858, writes that the posts around Blanc-Sablon and Lourdes were French-speaking whilst those to the west, between Bradore and St. Paul's River, were all English-speaking by the end of the first phase of in-migration (Ferland, 1917:41). This form of voluntary segregation continued to be a determining characteristic of the settlement pattern in the St. Paul's-Blanc-Sablon region throughout the second phase of in-migration (Fig. 7–2). Only two of the English-speaking families (from Newfoundland-Labrador) were known to have elected residence in the French-speaking enclave of Lourdes-Blanc-Sablon and the only two known Francophone immigrants of this period settled in Lourdes.

Residential segregation along religious lines was also apparent throughout the entire period of in-migration (Fig. 7–3). Despite incursions by both Catholic and Protestant settlers, Blanc-Sablon, Lourdes, and Middle Bay emerged at the end of this long period with a basically Catholic population. Only 8 Protestants moved to the 3 settlements in the 70-year period, and 3 of these married Catholics, eventually converting to Catholicism. On the other hand, Bradore and St. Paul's River were characterized by largely Anglican populations with a Catholic minority in both settlements. In Bradore, this minority consisted of only one French-speaking family of nine persons whose descendants today form the total Catholic population in that settle-

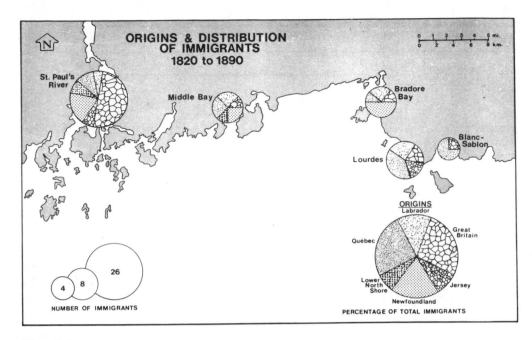

Figure 7–2

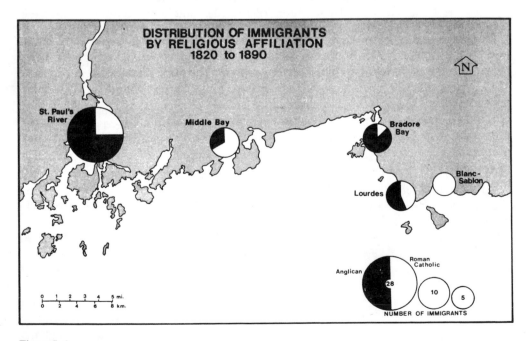

Figure 7–3

ment. The Catholic population in St. Paul's River represented a larger, more readily identifiable group, constituting at least 10 of the 29 families (34.5 percent) who resided permanently in the St. Paul's Archipelago about 1890.

The high Protestant:Catholic ratio in the St. Paul's Archipelago provides a good example of the spatial, as well as the social boundaries which separated the two religious factions. Oral evidence suggests that from the time of initial settlement, the Catholics were concentrated on the eastern posts of the Archipelago whereas the Anglicans usually resided on the central and western islands and mainland posts (Fig. 7–4). The only exception was the post of Salmon Bay where a mixed population was always present. Breton notes that Catholic fishing sites bordered the Middle Bay area, whereas Anglican posts were in closer proximity to Old Fort Bay, a totally Protestant settlement just west of St. Paul's River (Breton, 1970:125). In subsequent years, these two neighbouring settlements played a vital role in the survival of both the Catholic and Anglican populations of St. Paul's River since they each provided an important source of marriage partners of the same denominations.

Integration and Consolidation: 1890–1920
In the three decades (1890–1920) following the end of in-migration, the importance of the two languages and religions as the diagnostic criteria by which the resident population aligned itself became increasingly apparent. The social and spatial boundaries already established, persisted. During this period marriage became the principal channel through which the integration and assimilation of the different ethnic stocks took place. In Barthian terms, marriage was the most important vehicle through which the members of the six ethnic components could effectively control the flow of personnel amongst them by invoking the processes of exclusion and incorporation of marriageable partners on the basis of their linguistic and religious affiliations.

Patterns of Marriage
An examination of the marriage patterns in the St. Paul's-Blanc-Sablon region from the 1840s to 1920 reveals that there was a tendency towards endogamous marriage throughout this period; that is, marriage in which both partners were either from the same linguistic or religious community (Table 7–2).[5] Only 37 unions involved partners of both linguistic groups compared to 169 marriages which were endogamous and there were only 32 mixed religious marriages compared to 170 endogamous unions.

This preferential selection of marriage partners, illustrated in Table 7–3, was exercised by both men and women of each linguistic and religious community. The figures include only those marriage partners who were resident in the St. Paul's-Blanc-Sablon region; in other words if a marriage involved a partner from outside, only the resident's choice was recorded. When both marriage partners were from the St. Paul's-Blanc-Sablon region, both choices were recorded. This measure is adopted in order to give a more accurate reflection of the preference of the population under study. In Table 7–3 the number of individuals "at risk" in each category for each period are calculated and converted into percentages. Thus, of 74 men who were married prior to 1890, 46 percent (34 individuals) were Catholic and 54 percent (40 individuals) were Protestant. These percentages were then used as measures to indicate the expected patterns of marriage if the men and women were to exercise a non-prejudiced choice in their selection of spouses, providing, of course, that there was a balanced sex ratio in the population. Consequently, if 46 percent of all the men

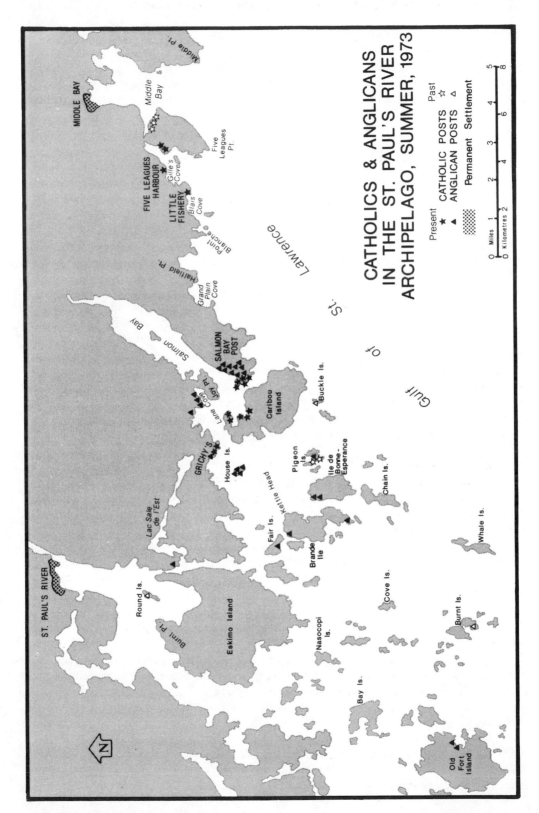

CATHOLICS & ANGLICANS
IN THE ST. PAUL'S RIVER
ARCHIPELAGO, SUMMER, 1973

Past
CATHOLIC POSTS ☆
ANGLICAN POSTS △

Present
★
▲

Permanent Settlement ▦

Miles
0   1   2   3   4   5
Kilometres
0   2   4   6   8

Figure 7–4

TABLE 7–2

Patterns of Marriage: 1840–1920

Language		Religion	
Endogamous marriages			
Francophone	40 (19.2%)	Catholic	91 (43.7%)
Anglophone	129 (62.0%)	Anglican	79 (38.0%)
Total	169 (81.2%)	Total	170 (81.7%)
Exogamous marriages	37 (17.8%)		32 (15.4%)
Unknown	2 (1.0%)		6 (2.9%)
Total	208 (100.0%)		208 (100.0%)

who married before 1890 were Catholic, then approximately half of them (or 23 percent of the total male population that was married) would be expected to marry Catholic women and the other half to marry Protestant women. Similarly, half the Anglican men (27 percent of the total married male population) would be expected to marry Protestants, and half to marry Catholics. However, in comparing the expected with the observed patterns of marriage, it is evident that with the exception of one important anomaly (to be discussed later) the resident population of the eastern Lower North Shore exercised a preference with regard to both the language and the religion of their marriage partners. Although the figures presented above do not reveal any substantial differences in the preferences between linguistic homogeneity and religious homogeneity, religion provided the more important criterion in the exclusion of marriageable partners. Most informants, in fact, avoided questions related to interdenominational marriages and those who did discuss the matter were unequivocal about mixed marriages being generally unacceptable to both Catholics and Anglicans.

In examining the occurrence and nature of these exogamous unions, two further points become apparent. Firstly, mixed marriages tended to occur only in certain settlements and posts, particularly in the St. Paul's River Archipelago where both religious groups were present in fairly large numbers and where 22 mixed marriages were recorded prior to 1920. This figure, as well as all subsequent figures on marriage in the individual settlements, include all marriages involving at least one partner (either male or female) from that particular settlement. Thus, if a husband resided in St. Paul's River and his wife came from Middle Bay, the marriage is recorded twice: once in the husband's settlement and a second time in the wife's. If a marriage involved two individuals from the same settlement, it is recorded only once, except in Table 7–3. This approach is adopted in order to ascertain the differences (if any) in the choice of marriage partners of the population of each of the five settlements. On the other hand, in discussing the St. Paul's-Blanc-Sablon region as a whole, all marriages are recorded only once.

St. Paul's River Archipelago apart, in the four other settlements on the Shore where one of the two religious groups dominated, the number of exogamous marriages was limited. This is especially evident in Blanc-Sablon and Lourdes where the few mixed unions are probably attributable as much to the overwhelming Catholic majorities in both settlements as to the presence of a resident priest in Lourdes and the establishment of a permanent chapel after 1879 (Carrière, 1958:243). In Bradore and Middle

TABLE 7-3

Expected vs. Observed Patterns of Marriage, 1840–1920

MALES

Categories of Marriage	1840–1890			1890–1920			1840–1920		
	N	E	O	N	E	O	N	E	O
RC × RC	32	23.0%	43.2%	46	31.4%	53.5%	78	27.5%	48.8%
RC × C of E	2	23.0	2.7	8	31.4	9.3	10	27.5	6.3
C of E × C of E	27	27.0	36.5	27	18.6	31.4	54	22.5	33.8
C of E × RC	13	27.0	17.6	5	18.6	5.8	18	22.5	11.3
Totals:	74	100.0%	100.0%	86	100.0%	100.0%	160	100.0%	100.0%
FR × FR	25	17.1%	32.9%	12	21.6%	13.6%	37	19.5%	22.6%
FR × ENG	1	17.1	1.3	26	21.6	29.6	27	19.5	16.5
ENG × ENG	48	32.9	63.2	49	28.4	55.7	97	30.5	59.2
ENG × FR	2	32.9	2.6	1	28.4	1.1	3	30.5	1.8
Totals:	76	100.0%	100.0%	88	100.0%	100.0%	164	100.0%	100.1%

(N) Actual number of marriages
(E) Expected percentage of marriages
(O) Observed percentage of marriages

(RC) Roman Catholic; (C of E) Church of England
(FR) French speaking; (ENG) English speaking

FEMALES

Categories of Marriage	1840–1890			1890–1920			1840–1920		
	N	E	O	N	E	O	N	E	O
RC × RC	24	26.8%	42.9%	31	24.0%	42.5%	55	25.2%	42.6%
C of E × RC	6	26.8	10.7	4	24.0	5.5	10	25.2	7.8
C of E × C of E	22	23.2	39.3	33	26.0	45.2	55	24.8	42.6
RC × C of E	4	23.2	7.1	5	26.0	6.9	9	24.8	7.0
Totals:	56	100.0%	100.0%	73	100.0%	100.1%	129	100.0%	100.0%
FR × FR	17	18.1%	29.3%	11	9.6%	15.1%	28	13.4%	21.4%
ENG × FR	4	18.1	6.9	3	9.6	4.1	7	13.4	5.3
ENG × ENG	34	31.9	58.6	49	40.4	67.1	83	36.6	63.4
FR × ENG	3	31.9	5.2	10	40.4	13.7	13	36.6	9.9
Totals:	58	100.0%	100.0%	73	100.0%	100.0%	131	100.0%	100.0%

TABLE 7-4

Distribution of Mixed Religious Marriages By Settlement: 1840–1920

Decades	Blanc-Sablon	Lourdes	Bradore	Middle Bay	St. Paul's River
1840–1850	—	—	—	2	1
1850–1860	—	—	1	—	—
1860–1870	—	—	1	—	2
1870–1880	—	1	3	1	2
1880–1890	1	1	—	—	6
1890–1900	2	—	1	—	5
1900–1910	1	—	—	1	4
1910–1920	—	—	—	1	2
Totals	4	2	6	5	22

Bay, there were more exogamous marriages in each village, but as shown in Table 7–4, they occurred on a more or less sporadic basis. Secondly, of the 32 exogamous marriages recorded prior to 1920, 19 involved at least one partner in whose family a mixed marriage had already been contracted; and 4 other marriages involved partners with a history of at least one previous exogamous union. In all cases, these individuals were either themselves the progeny of mixed marriages, or else they had been preceded by a brother or sister who had married across the religious barrier. In terms of the number of individuals "at risk" in the 32 marriages, 48 were resident in the St. Paul's-Blanc-Sablon region; of these, 73 percent (35 individuals) came from 10 extended or nuclear families in which at least 2 mixed marriages were recorded, whereas only 27 percent belonged to families in which theirs was the sole exogamous marriage.

The data presented above suggest that the mixed religious marriages were not as widespread as their total number would indicate. Although there were approximately as many mixed religious unions as exogamous linguistic marriages, the former were concentrated mostly in one area where the two religious groups were in close contact. Moreover, these marriages, although endorsed by the immediate families, were not necessarily given general assent by the population of the eastern Lower North Shore (Breton, 1968:139).

Language was not as significant a deterrent in the choice of marriage partners. All the informants, particularly in Lourdes and Blanc-Sablon, stated quite explicitly that there was never any stigma attached to mixed linguistic unions. This is substantiated in Table 3 by the smaller, but significant, differences between the expected and observed patterns of marriage using language, rather than religion, as the defining criterion. Similarly, the only critical anomaly in this table appears in the linguistic category for men in the 1890–1920 period, when a much smaller percentage of Francophone men than expected married within their own linguistic community. This fact merits deeper examination since it does not indicate a sudden change of attitude on the part of the French-speaking men to marry freely without exercising a linguistic preference; rather, it is a reflection of the general lack of Francophone women from about 1890 to 1920.

There had always been an imbalance in the sexual distribution of the population on the Lower North Shore, especially during the frontier phase or period of in-migration which lasted until about 1885 (see Thornton, this vol.). Throughout this period, and particularly in the early decades of in-migration, the resident population was made up mostly of either single men or male settlers who had married prior to their arrival on the Lower Shore. Ferland gives evidence of this for the French-Canadian community in his report of 1858 (p. 26):

Les six ou sept postes du Labrador ne renfermaient que des hommes, presque tous originaires de Berthier. Ceux-ci étaient célibataires ou avaient laissé leurs femmes dans leurs paroisses natales. Plusieurs, après avoir réussi à faire des épargnes et à découvrir quelques lieux avantageux pour la chasse et la pêche, s'y bâtirent des demeures et commencèrent à travailler pour leur propre compte; la femme et les enfants venaient bientôt après occuper la maison et prendre part aux travaux du chef de famille.

Similarly, all of the pre-1890 censuses of the Lower Shore reveal a greater proportion of male residents than females. In the 1871 and 1881 censuses, the only two censuses prior to 1890 containing a breakdown of the sexes, the number of males in the enumerative district of Bonne-Espérance totalled 151 and 182 compared to 115 and 159 females, respectively. Of the unmarried residents for those years, there were 111 males to 78 females in 1871, and 128 males to 103 females in 1881, yielding respective male ratios of 142 and 124 to 100.[6]

After 1890, in-migration diminished and the frontier phase was replaced by a period of stabilization and consolidation of the resident population. Any increase in population now occurred solely through natural growth, with a resultant evening out of the male to female ratio. This levelling process began about 1870 when several single male settlers found spouses either on the Lower Shore or elsewhere and started families. There was a sudden increase in the number of marriages and a resultant decrease in the ratio of males to females in the decade between the 1871 and 1881 censuses.

Only two Francophone immigrants arrived on the eastern Lower North Shore after 1860, both settling in Lourdes, but the imbalance in the sex ratio of the Francophone community persisted as a result of the overwhelming number of male births in the period 1860–1890. Figure 7–5 shows that during these three decades, more than twice as many males were born to French-speaking Catholic parents as females. Although the actual figures are not large (60 male to 27 female births), the sexual imbalance that was thus created later led to a larger number of mixed marriages between Francophone males and Anglophone females.

Similarly, in the two English-speaking communities, more males than females were born prior to 1890, but as can be seen in Figure 7–6, these sexual imbalances were not as great as in the French community, nor were they as decisive in influencing the subsequent patterns of marriage. Indeed, there were only 103 English-speaking Catholic males and 108 English-speaking Anglican males born for every 100 females in each category, respectively, compared to the male-female birth ratio of 180:100 in the French-speaking community.

The difficulty of finding Francophone wives was further compounded by the growing isolation of the eastern Lower North Shore from other French-speaking areas in the Gulf. The Francophone men in the St. Paul's-Blanc-Sablon region had already been separated from the home-parishes of their forefathers by more than a generation. With the exception of three Halifax and three Quebec traders who came to the study area three times each year (Huard, 1972:474), the major links with the outside world by this time were those with island-Newfoundland, and with the Newfoundland-based firms such as Job's and Whiteley's (then established in Blanc-Sablon and St. Paul's River, respectively), all of which were English-speaking.

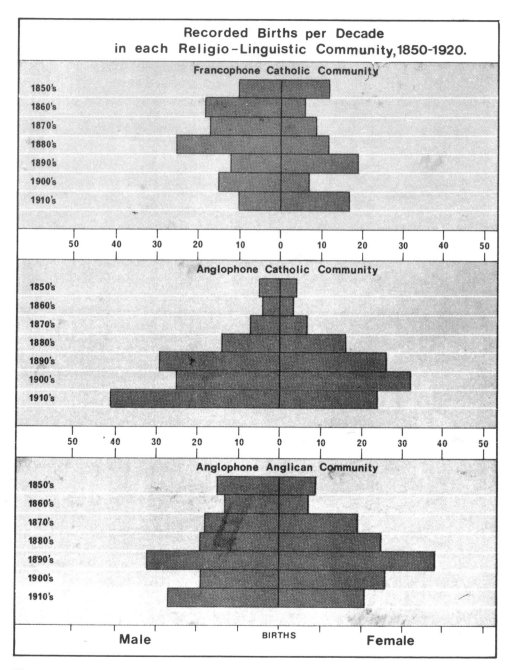

Figure 7–5

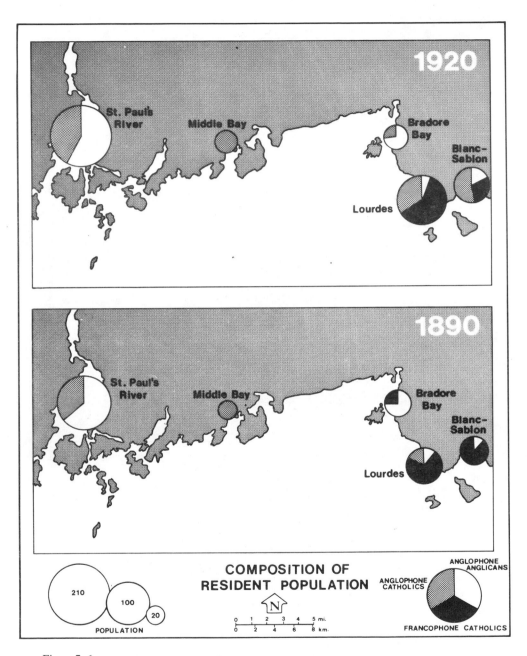

Figure 7–6

TABLE 7–5

Average Age at Marriage: 1840–1970

| | Francophones | | Anglophones | |
	Male	Female	Male	Female
1840–1890:	26.0	22.0	29.8	23.5
1890–1920:	30.6	21.9	27.2	21.2
1920–1970:	25.8	21.0	26.4	20.8

Given the sexual imbalance in the Francophone community and its geographical isolation in the Gulf, it is obvious that the Francophone men had only two choices: they could either marry outside their own ethnic group, or remain single. Consequently, it would be misleading to argue that the large percentage of exogamous linguistic marriages in the 1890–1920 period was the result of an altogether non-prejudiced choice of marriage partners. Similarly, it would be as misleading to argue that the criterion of language in the selection of spouses was losing its importance by the end of the 19th century. Two additional factors point to this: (1) the marriage patterns of the Francophone and Anglophone women; and (2) the difference in the average ages of marriage of the French-speaking men and women on the one hand, and those of their English-speaking counterparts on the other.

Of the fourteen Francophone women who married between 1890 and 1920, only three married outside their own linguistic community. Since this figure is even lower than that of exogamous marriages prior to 1890, it is clear that these women, who were in a better position than Francophone men to marry freely, continued to exercise a linguistic preference in the choice of their marriage partners. Likewise, there were only ten of a total of forty-nine Anglophone women of the St. Paul's-Blanc-Sablon region who married across the linguistic barrier. Thus the Francophone men were also forced to seek wives outside the study area, and did so mostly on the Newfoundland-side of the border.

An examinination of the computed ages at marriage of both the French- and English-speaking populations reveals that during the 1890–1920 period, the men in the former group were usually much older than in the latter when they married (see Table 7–5). This condition was a total reversal of the pre-1890 pattern when the Anglophone men married at an average age of 29.8 years compared to 26.0 years for the Francophones. This reflects the changing numerical strength of both groups of men within their own communities from one period to the other, and their relative ease in finding spouses of the same linguistic affiliation. Thus the English-speaking males, who faced a frontier situation until about 1890, found themselves with a shortage of eligible Anglophone spouses until that time. Consequently, they tended to marry later in life. On the other hand, since the French-speaking community had already entered a more stable phase of development by the 1860s, they were not faced with a comparable shortage and could therefore marry much earlier. As mentioned above, this latter situation changed noticeably after 1890, and although many of the French-speaking males married Anglophones thereafter, their preference to marry within their own community is evidenced by the considerable increase (4.6 years) in their average age at marriage. This increase is highlighted by the fact that the 1890–1920 period saw a decrease in the average age of marriage in the three other categories, as well as by the

anomaly which it presents in the general downward pattern of the age of marriage from
the 1840s to the 1960s.

Re-Organization of Ethnic Boundaries

The patterns of marriage described in the preceding section are related directly to the
changing ethnic composition and concomitant spatial distribution of the population in
the St. Paul's-Blanc-Sablon region throughout the first century of permanent European occupancy. The tendency to marry endogamously influenced the survival of the
three religio-linguistic groups, but the limited number of exogamous marriages was
paramount in changing the relative numerical strength of these groups.

The Francophone Catholics. Throughout the period of in-migration the French-
speaking settlers tended to congregate on the eastern posts within the study area, so
that by 1890 all but one of these families resided either in Lourdes or in Blanc-Sablon
(Fig. 7–6). However, in the three decades after 1890, Blanc-Sablon experienced a
rapid process of Anglicization, mostly as a result of the high incidence of intermarriage
between Francophone men and Anglophone women (Fig. 7–6).

Prior to 1890, the majority (74 percent) of the marriages in Blanc-Sablon were
between French-speaking persons; but after this date, only three such marriages were
recorded, two of which involved female residents of Blanc-Sablon who married men
from Lourdes, where they resided after their marriages (Fig. 7–7). The marriages
recorded in the five histograms constituting Figure 7–7 include all marriages involving
at least one partner from that village. For example, if a marriage involved one partner
from Lourdes and one from Blanc-Sablon, that marriage was recorded twice in the
histograms for each settlement. The rationale for this approach is to give a more
accurate account of the marital behaviour of all the residents, both male and female, in
each of the five villages. If a marriage united partners from the same settlement, it was
recorded only once. The number of mixed linguistic marriages rose from two before
1890 to twelve over the next thirty years. Of the twelve families residing in Blanc-
Sablon in 1920, only one was headed by a French-speaking couple, compared to six in
1890. There were eight households headed by Francophone men and Anglophone
women, and only one in which the wife was Francophone and the husband
Anglophone. This larger number of mixed households ultimately led to the integration
of many of the Blanc-Sablon Francophones into the Anglophone community, since
the nine English-speaking partners were all unilingual, and their spouses bilingual.
The latter learned English through their dealings with the English- and later
Newfoundland-controlled firms around Blanc-Sablon, and after 1927, with the Hudson's Bay Company. Junek (1937:105) writes: "The *habitant* fisherman, whose language at one time was essentially French, with the admission of an occasional English
word or phrase, realized that by acculturation to a binguality he could more effectively control his own economic situation – at least as regards the Hudson's Bay
Company, whose personnel is composed of English-speaking Canadians, and with
which he is forced to do business."

More importantly, because tradition kept women housebound, they usually assumed the role of raising the children – especially during the summer fishing season
when the men were absent for most of the day. Women were the major transmitters of
language; and since the majority in Blanc-Sablon was English-speaking, the hearth
language in the mixed households was English, rendering the children unilingual. In

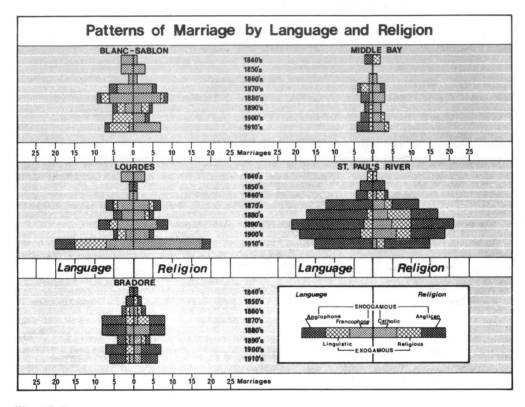

Figure 7–7

their explanation of the adoption of the English language, all informants in Blanc-Sablon maintained that the mixed marriages of the fathers, and particularly being raised by Anglophone mothers, were instrumental. Junek adds that the proximity to Newfoundland had some bearing on the change to English, but he too points to the importance of the Anglophone women: "The proximity of Newfoundland is no doubt also responsible for this mixture of the two languages. Again ... several of the Blanc-Sablonite men have married women from Newfoundland who brought into Blanc-Sablon with them their own culture, determining, to a certain extent, the language usages of their husbands" (*op. cit.*:106).

Finally, although the Francophones still constituted 29 percent of the total Blanc-Sablon population in 1920, they were mostly married men whose wives and children were English-speaking. In fact, of the nineteen Francophones recorded during that year, only two were women, one of whom came from Lourdes and is reported to have been totally ignorant of English. According to some informants a few children also had a knowledge of French at this time. But this was mostly a passive kind of bilingualism, being restricted to those boys who were admitted to the social gatherings of the Blanc-Sablon men. French continued to be spoken in Blanc-Sablon at least until the early 1930s, but as the Francophone men died, so did the usage of the language. When the field work for this study was completed in 1974, there remained only seven men professing to have a knowledge of French, only one of whom was able (and willing) to converse in that language. The other six either refused to speak in French, claiming that their French had deteriorated to the point where they no longer felt at ease with it, or else they professed to have only a passive knowledge of the language.

Lourdes, on the other hand, was able to maintain its identity as a French-speaking community, even though the general pattern of marriages in that settlement was not altogether different from that of its eastern neighbour. As in Blanc-Sablon, the percentage of endogamous Francophone marriages decreased from 65 percent in the 1820–1890 period to 38 percent in the 1890–1920 period, while the percentage of exogamous linguistic marriages rose from 6 percent in the earlier phase of settlement to 35.5 percent in the subsequent phase. Unlike Blanc-Sablon, however, the actual number of endogamous Francophone marriages in Lourdes increased slightly from eleven in the pre-1890 period to thirteen subsequently, one more than the total number of mixed linguistic marriages between 1890 and 1920. This meant that less than half the spouses marrying into Lourdes during these three decades were English-speaking, and more significantly, that well over half the new families in the settlement continued to be headed by French-speaking couples. Of the 27 families resident in Lourdes in 1920, 18 (66.7 percent) could be identified as entirely French-speaking, and approximately 80 individuals (61.5 percent of the total population) were Francophone. The survival of French in Lourdes was further reinforced by (i) the concentration – through secondary migrations to Lourdes – of several Francophone families and individuals; (ii) the institution and continuous presence of a French school; and (iii) the permanent residence of the parish priest and the establishment of the Catholic Church in Lourdes.

Between 1872 and the early 1900s there were at least twelve cases of secondary (intra-Shore) migration to Lourdes. Half of these were families, three of which were Francophone, while the other half were unmarried males, four of whom were French-speaking. These settlers came from Bradore (4 families and 2 men), Blanc-Sablon (1 family and 1 man), and Middle Bay (2 men). There was also one family from Havre St.

Pierre on the Middle North Shore, and one English-speaking male from West St. Modest, on the Newfoundland-Labrador coast. The motives for these moves were apparently twofold: according to several informants, Lourdes was a better fishing site than either Bradore or Blanc-Sablon because it was located closer to its fishing grounds. Although the catches were not more plentiful off the shores of Lourdes, it was possible for the fishermen to haul in their fish with the help of special "bags" and trawl lines. Since there were few motorboats on the Lower Shore before 1920, the technique used in Lourdes eliminated the more difficult and time-consuming task of rowing back and forth between the cod-traps and the stages where the fish were cleaned and processed.

Marriage prospects may have been the second motive for some settlers moving to Lourdes; the six single male settlers married women from Lourdes. The dominant pattern of post-marital residence in the whole of the St. Paul's-Blanc-Sablon region was virilocal, but there were also cases of uxorilocality (Table 7–6). It is difficult to ascertain whether the unmarried settlers moved to Lourdes before or after the marriages. Local informants were inconsistent in their reports, although more tended to agree that the men married after they had already been established in Lourdes. What is certain, however, is that these marriages reinforced the choice of place of settlement and discouraged the possibility of further moves out of Lourdes.

This slow trickle of settlers into Lourdes influenced the composition of the Francophone Catholic community in the study area. Firstly, it reduced the size of the French-speaking populations of Blanc-Sablon, Bradore, and Middle Bay. This was particularly evident in Bradore and Middle Bay where the Francophone population was never large and where the out-migration of a few individuals stunted the potential growth of the settlement. The corollary was an immediate and long-term increase in the size of the Francophone population of Lourdes by the addition of the new settlers themselves, by the retention in Lourdes of the women they married, and eventually by the birth of their offspring. There were 37 new residents, 22 of whom were Francophones. Moreover, given the role of women as transmitters of language and the fact that all the single male settlers married Francophones, the offspring of these 6 couples constituted 36 additional Francophone residents, since it is assumed that they would have been born and raised elsewhere along the Shore had their parents followed the general pattern of virilocality. Consequently, the 12 intra-Shore migrations to Lourdes contributed a total of 73 new residents to that settlement, 58 of whom were Francophones. Twenty-seven of the offspring of the migrants, only 3 of whom were Anglophones, ultimately contributed to the future growth of Lourdes by marrying and residing there permanently.

The French language in Lourdes was further bolstered by the school system. Evidence exists of a French-Canadian teacher from Quebec City near Lourdes before 1860. All the children in Lourdes, including those of mixed backgrounds whose mother tongue was English, as well as those whose backgrounds were totally English, learned to speak French. On the other hand, because Blanc-Sablon was under the legal jurisdiction of Newfoundland until 1927, at which time the decision of the British Privy Council placed it under Canadian (Quebec) jurisdiction, the Catholic Bishop of Harbour Grace controlled the administration of the early school there. As a result, the teachers usually came from either island-Newfoundland or Labrador and were always English-speaking Catholics. In Blanc-Sablon the English language was emphasized both in the home, where most of the mothers spoke only English, and in the school.

TABLE 7–6

Pattern of Post-Marital Residence: 1840–1920

	Virilocal	Uxorilocal	Partner from same Village	Unknown or Other*
1840–1890	45	15	26	8
1890–1920	64	15	27	8
Totals	109	30	53	16

*Includes the out-migration of couples from the Lower North Shore, or a move to another settlement where neither partner had previously resided.

Informants were unequivocal in assessing the importance of the French school in Lourdes: "What keeps the French up in Lourdes [is that] they always had French schools."

Several informants cited the presence of a resident priest as an advantage in the maintenance of the French language in Lourdes. A priest was stationed in Lourdes on a permanent basis from about 1879, although both secular priests and missionaries had made regular annual visits to the Lower North Shore since the middle of the century. They usually came from lower Quebec, and in some instances from France. Between 1903 and 1946, the Eudist missionaries of France were given charge of the Catholic posts of the Lower North Shore. All were French-speaking, but a knowledge of English was also required (see Carrière, 1958:243).

Because of his ecclesiastical position and the importance of religion in the daily life of the inhabitants, the priest in Lourdes was the most influential member of the local community, as indeed were priests in other parts of Catholic rural Quebec and outport Newfoundland. The role of the priest in Lourdes included the protection and survival of the French language, as it did elsewhere in Quebec. For example, it is reported that through his persistent use of French, he was able to foster the practice of speaking French in the home, even when the mothers were initially English-speaking unilinguals. The priest was also influential in running the school. Ultimately, the school was the more important mechanism in the retention of French in Lourdes, and the role of the priest in enforcing school attendance was paramount in preserving the language among the young.

Certain conclusions can be made regarding changes in the composition and structure of the Francophone Catholic community between 1890 and 1920. The most obvious is the decrease in the numerical strength of the community in proportion to the total population of the eastern Lower North Shore. Although there was an increase, albeit marginal, in the absolute numbers of Francophone Catholics from 1890 to 1920, the community represented only 22 percent of the total population in 1920 compared to 29 percent thirty years earlier. Similarly, the territory occupied by this community was reduced to basically one settlement.

Marriage with members of the Anglophone communities was the most important factor leading to the reduction in the Francophone Catholic community. The secondary migrations to Lourdes were also influential in reducing the size of the Francophone population in neighbouring settlements, but at the same time, they were significant in the survival of French in Lourdes and in the maintenance of an overt linguistic and ethnic boundary between the inhabitants of Lourdes and those of the other settlements in the St. Paul's-Blanc-Sablon region. Similarly, the establishment of a parish church and of a French school in Lourdes reinforced the residential boundary between the Francophone Catholic and the two Anglophone communities.

The Anglophone Anglicans. By 1890 the Anglophone Anglican community constituted 44 percent of the total population in the study area, the largest of the three religio-linguistic groups. However, like the Francophone Catholic community, it too declined proportionately and by 1920 made up only 35 percent of the total population. This decrease is attributed to two basic phenomena: integration into the Anglophone Catholic community and out-migration from the St. Paul's-Blanc-Sablon region.

Despite the fact that there were only 32 exogamous religious marriages recorded prior to 1920, marriage was the catalyst in the integration of the Anglophone Anglicans into the Anglophone Catholic community. In the first instance, the majority of these marriages led to the conversion of the non-Catholic male and female spouses, whereas very few marriages resulted in conversion to the Anglican faith. Between 1840 and 1920 only 2 adult Catholics became Anglicans compared to 20 Anglicans who became Catholic through marriage. Although these gains were small, they ultimately led to a more substantial increase because of the birth of offspring. Conversion of Anglican spouses brought the Catholic community 74 new members (12 of whom were French-speaking) compared to 10 new members in the Anglican community. Similarly, the Anglophone Catholic community experienced an increase since the offspring were raised as Catholics in half the marriages in which neither spouse converted; there was only one family in which the children were Anglican and another family in which some of the children were raised as Catholics and some as Anglicans. The Anglophone Catholic community gained 69 percent of all the offspring of the mixed unions, compared to only 19 percent for the Anglophone Anglican community, and 11 percent for the Francophone Catholic community. The effects of marriage on the size of the Anglophone Anglican community – like those of the exogamous linguistic marriages on the Francophone population – were therefore felt more deeply in terms of the loss of future or potential personnel rather than in the actual loss of members through conversions to Catholicism.

According to some informants, including both the Anglican and Catholic priests who were serving the study area at the time of fieldwork, the tendency of mixed partners to raise their children as Catholics is attributable to the more 'unyielding' and formal position of the Roman Catholic Church vis-à-vis mixed marriages. Although the dogma of the Church has altered considerably since the Vatican II Council, in the period before 1920, Roman Catholics were taught that theirs was the only "true faith" and that abandonment of that religion led inexorably to eternal damnation. Similarly, anyone not baptized in the Catholic Church was not considered a true Christian and was condemned to the same fate. For most Catholic spouses, therefore, the long process of indoctrination by successive local priests, teachers, and by the parents and extended families, was such that he/she eventually demanded that the Anglican spouse agree to convert and to have the children raised as Catholics. Failing attempts to convert, the Roman Catholic Church demanded that the non-Catholic spouse formally swear to have the children baptized in that Church. Only the more audacious Anglicans, or those whose families had high local status in the settlement and Anglican community, refused to follow this practice.

A second factor contributing to the decrease in the size of the Anglophone Anglican

TABLE 7–7

Out-migration by Settlement and Community: 1890–1925

Settlements	Francophone Catholics		Anglophone Catholics		Anglophone Anglicans	
	Moves	People	Moves	People	Moves	People
Blanc-Sablon	8	8	—	—	1	6
Lourdes	8	20	—	—	—	—
Bradore	—	—	—	—	7	14
Middle Bay	—	—	1	1	—	—
St. Paul's River	—	—	14	70	23	64
Totals	16	28	15	71	31	84

community was the out-migration of eighty-four Anglicans between 1890 and 1925, all but six of them from St. Paul's River and Bradore. As shown in Table 7–7, out-migration during this period was not restricted to the Anglican community, but the effects were greatest on it since (i) there was a larger number of Anglican out-migrants, and since (ii) the Anglophone Anglican community was also losing a considerable number of members through intermarriage with Catholic settlers.

With the exception of the families that migrated from St. Paul's River to the west coast of Newfoundland, in particular to Corner Brook and the Bay of Islands, it is difficult to establish the motives for out-migration. Three explanations posited by the older informants included (1) the fluctuating and uncertain nature of the fishery; (2) the wish to better one's economic position by moving to urban centres such as Montreal and Quebec City where steady employment could be found; and (3) the familial or kin ties which acted as a pull factor to such places as island-Newfoundland and other settlements along the Lower and Middle North Shores. For example, several Anglicans moved from St. Paul's River to the neighbouring settlement of Old Fort Bay which was totally Anglican and closely related by marriage with St. Paul's River. Similarly, many of the Francophone Catholic moves to Quebec City and the rural counties of Berthier and Montmagny were prompted by the presence there of relatives upon whom the North Shore migrants could depend for help in settling down.

Movement from St. Paul's River to the west coast of Newfoundland was the culmination of a pattern of seasonal migration to the winter herring fishery from about 1880 to 1925; the opening of the Bowater mill in Corner Brook enticed most of the seasonal migrants to settle permanently there. The annual migrations were limited largely to Catholic families in St. Paul's River. Seasonal migration also took place from the summer settlements on the coast to inland settlements in winter. Most of the families in St. Paul's River were involved in one of the two migrations. The only notable exception was the Chevalier family whose ancestors had once owned the entire St. Paul's Archipelago and whose only activity involved the exploitation of the salmon fishery at the site of the winter settlement.

Unlike their French-speaking Catholic counterparts, whose declining population was reflected in a contraction of the residential boundaries, the Anglophone Anglicans persisted as the main occupants of both Bradore and St. Paul's River. In Bradore this was a consequence of the secondary migrations to Lourdes of most of its Catholic population, and in St. Paul's River, of the out-migration of Catholics to Corner Brook.

The process of centralization from the islands to the winter settlement in St. Paul's River also contributed to the maintenance of a strong Anglican majority in that settlement, since the concentration of the entire population in one location – even if for only part of the year – helped to reinforce their identity through the establishment of both a church and a school.

These factors, in turn, slowed down the process of integration with the Catholic community by giving the Anglican partners in mixed marriages a stronger voice in the upbringing of the children. Anglican community pressure could be brought to bear more readily than when the population was dispersed over an extensive and often inaccessible territory. The year-round presence of an Anglican priest in St. Paul's River was another important factor in altering the pattern of conversion to Catholicism described previously, to one of the wife's conversion – regardless of her religious affiliation – to that of her husband's religion. This is seen more clearly in the modern period of settlement (1920–1970) when the number of Catholic conversions to the Church of England increased substantially. Another effect of this change was a more balanced exchange of personnel between the Anglican and Catholic communities of St. Paul's River and a more even rate of growth, factors which eventually led to a less antagonistic relationship between the two groups.

The Anglophone Catholics. Because the pattern was one of integration into the Anglophone, rather than the Francophone milieu, and towards Catholicism rather than Anglicanism, the English-speaking Catholics emerged at the end of the first century of European settlement as the largest of the three religio-linguistic groups on the eastern Lower North Shore. By 1920, the Anglophone Catholics constituted 43.5 percent of the total population in the study area. Subsequently, the larger number of births, compared to those in the Anglophone Anglican and Francophone Catholic communities, ensured the numerical supremacy of the Anglophone Catholics. This increase in population was accompanied by an expansion of residential boundaries, so that by 1920, both Middle Bay and Blanc-Sablon could be identified as basically English-speaking Catholic settlements. Moreover, unlike the other two communities, the Anglophone Catholics were present – albeit as minorities – in the three remaining settlements of St. Paul's River, Bradore, and Lourdes.

Concept of Ethnicity on the Lower North Shore

From a purely biological perspective, it may be argued that because of the miscegenation of the resident population, the three religio-linguistic groups that had emerged on the Lower North Shore by the end of the first century of settlement did not constitute real ethnic groups. However, since these three groups retained the most explicit ethnic trait(s) (language and/or religion) of those characterizing the six original groups, the members of all three groups could describe themselves and could be described by other groups as being different and distinct. Distinctions are still made today between the "French" and the "English" and between the "R.Cs" and the "Protestants" – terms commonly used by the North Shore inhabitants either to describe themselves or others. The Anglicans refer to Catholics as "R.Cs" even though the latter prefer to call themselves "Catholics." Similarly, although the Anglican population always specifies its affiliation to the Church of England, it is referred to as "Protestant" by both the Francophone and Anglophone Catholics. As in the past, little or no reference is made to the genetic purity of the individual members of any ethnic community. For example, the Jones of Lourdes, although of English paternity, are considered French-Canadians by themselves as well as by their neighbours because they are French-speaking and Catholic, and they behave in a manner identifiable with that of the French-Canadians in Lourdes.

During the period of in-migration the identity of the three ethnic groups was further distinguished by their residential segregation into five fairly homogeneous settlements on the Lower North Shore. Through marriage and secondary intra-Shore migrations, these spatial boundaries were slightly re-organized, becoming stabilized after 1890. These boundaries greatly affected the three ethnic groups, particularly the Francophone Catholics and the Anglophone Anglicans. The concentration of the French-speaking population in Lourdes initiated a series of events (for example, the establishment of a French school) which were paramount in the survival of the French language in that settlement. Similarly, the aggregation of Anglophone Anglicans in the winter settlement of St. Paul's River created a new awareness within that community and a reinforcement of their ethnic identity which affected subsequent patterns of marriage and conversion.

Viewed together, the emergence and consolidation of the three ethnic identities and their spatial expression in the settlement pattern on the eastern Lower North Shore point to the importance of Barth's concept of social boundaries and its role in defining and maintaining ethnic groups. For more than a century marriage was the principal mechanism regulating the nature of these social boundaries, and is an index of the flexible and inflexible nature (using the criteria of language and religion, respectively) of the social boundaries that existed between the three ethnic groups. Marriage regulated the flow of personnel from one group to another and became the means through which integration and assimilation occurred. Although members of the six original ethnic groups present on the eastern Lower Shore became integrated, they maintained through marriage social boundaries that reflected those ethnic traits they valued most. Other phenomena, including, for example, visiting patterns and the level of social and economic interaction, were also significant in defining the social boundaries on the Shore.

These ethnic boundaries have persisted to the present and have been re-emphasized by such factors as the introduction of a telephone service which is operated from Lourdes, and the building of a road. These innovations have permitted a greater degree of communication and interaction between the five settlements, intensifying the awareness of ethnic identity. Recent attempts to obtain special grants from the Provincial Government for infrastructural facilities have also reinforced social and spatial boundaries, and indeed, have generated new competition and antagonism between the three groups. The Francophones of Lourdes have been the major recipients of this aid and both the Anglophone Catholics and the Anglophone Anglicans resent this. Growing French nationalism in Quebec has also contributed to the antagonism between the Anglophones and Francophones. The Francophones of Lourdes have become more aware of their ''Frenchness'' because of the in-migration of other French-Canadians from Lower Quebec who have found jobs such as teaching on the Lower Shore, and because of the increased mobility of the ''Nord-Côtiers,'' themselves, particularly the younger generation of Francophones who have gone to school in areas such as the Gaspé Peninsula, Sept-Iles, and Quebec City. This contact with other French Canadians has made them aware that, although a minority on the

Lower North Shore, they are members of a majority on the provincial level. On the other hand, the new official liaison between the Church of England and its Roman Catholic counterpart, the gradual abandonment of active participation in organized religion among the young, and the forced integration of Protestant and Catholic schools in heterogeneous settlements such as St. Paul's River, have resulted in a noticeable improvement in the relationships between Anglophone Catholics and Anglophone Anglicans.

Marriage patterns in the first century of settlement reflect the increasingly favour-able relationship between Francophone and Anglophone Catholics, and the increas-ingly negative relationship between Catholics and Anglicans. Similarly, continuing residential segregation, despite modifications in the 'actual' pattern of settlement (for example, the expanding territory of Anglophone Catholics early in this century), reflects the determination of the three ethnic communities to retain their own distinct identity, and hence their traditional language and religion. The changing character of the spatial boundaries of these groups is indicative of their evolution and of the geography of inter-ethnic relations on the Lower Shore. Ethnic group solidarity was sustained, in part, through the spatial segregation of its members.

Future work on ethnicity must attempt to close the gap between geography and the other social sciences, especially anthropology and sociology which would improve the geographer's understanding of cultural processes and of ethnic boundaries. Given the importance and complexity of establishing what exactly constitutes an ethnic group and ethnic identity, such research is best prosecuted at the micro-level. Finally, the long history of fluctuating amicable and inimical relations between the three groups of the Lower North Shore illustrates the need for refocusing ethnic studies on a more objective perspective that would not be unduly or solely concerned with negative, problematic, or dysfunctional aspects of ethnicity.

In a purely Canadian context, there is, perhaps, also a need to re-examine past French-English relations elsewhere in Canada, including other areas in Quebec, to determine at the folk level rather than at the official political level, whether these two ethnic groups were as hostile to one another as popular belief would indicate.

NOTES

1   For bibliographies on the geography of ethnic group settlement in North America see: John A. Jakle and Cynthia Jakle, 1973; John J. Mannion, 1974.
2   Air travel is the only year-round means of transportation. Water-based transport is available in the summer months, and snowmobiles in winter. The availability of all forms of transportation is dependent on the weather. During the two-month period of freeze-up and break-up of ice, usually there is no available means of transport.
3   For a detailed historical account of the pre-1820 period, see Paul Charest, 1972:29–38.
4   According to Charest, whose study involves settlement on the entire Lower North Shore, there were three phases in the period of in-migration: 1820–1840 – the pioneer phase; 1840–1860 – the French-Canadian phase; and 1860–1900 – the Newfoundland phase. All maps and tables are based on a combination of documentary records and information collected in interviews.
5   The earliest parish records for the eastern Lower North Shore are the Roman Catholic records of "Labrador" for the years 1847 and 1848 in the Archives of the Catholic Diocese of Quebec City. The Catholic records of the Lower North Shore proper (Lourdes) were begun in 1849, and the Anglican (Harrington Harbour) in 1873. Marriages which were not recorded in the parish registers are included here if children resulted from these unions. The date of marriage was set arbitrarily as the year prior to birth

(baptism) of the first child. Gravestone evidence, family bibles, and family tradition yielded further information.

6 *Census of Canada: 1870–1871* (Ottawa: I. B. Taylor), 1973, 1, Table 1:56–57; *Census of Canada: 1880–1881* (Ottawa, Maclean, Roger and Co.), 1882, I, Table 1:44–45.

REFERENCES: SECONDARY SOURCES

BARTH, FREDERIK
1969 *Ethnic Groups and Boundaries.* Boston, Little, Brown and Co.
BJORKLUND, ELAINE M.
1964 "Ideology and Culture Exemplified in Southwestern Michigan." *Annals Association of American Geographers*, 54:227–41.
BRETON, RAYMOND
1968 "Institutional Completeness of Ethnic Communities and the Personal Relations of Immigrants." In W. E. Man (ed.), *Canada: A Sociological Profile.* Toronto, Clark.
BRETON, YVAN
1968 "St. Paul's River: Etude monographique." Quebec, Université Laval (unpublished).
BRETON, YVAN
1970 "Morphologie sociale et mariage à Saint Paul River." *Recherches Sociographiques*, XI:125.
BROOKFIELD, H. C.
1964 "Questions on the Human Frontiers of Geography." *Economic Geography*, 40:283–303.
CARRIÈRE, GASTON
1959 *Les Oblats de M.I. dans le Vicariat Apostolique du Labrador, 1844–1956.* Ottawa, Editions des Etudes Oblates.
CHAMBERS, E. T. D.
1912 *The Fisheries of the Province of Quebec.* Quebec, Department of Colonization, Mines and Fisheries of the Province of Quebec.
CHAREST, PAUL
1970 "Le peuplement permanent de la Basse-Côte-Nord du Saint-Laurent." *Recherches Sociographiques*, XI:59–90.
CHAREST, PAUL
1972 *Ecologie culturelle de la Côte-Nord du Golfe Saint-Laurent.* Québec, Université Laval.
COLE, JOHN W. and ERIC R. WOLF
1974 *The Hidden Frontier: Ecology and Ethnicity in an Alpine Valley.* New York, Academic Press.
DAWSON, C. A.
1936 *Group Settlement: Ethnic Communities in Western Canada.* Toronto, MacMillan.
DÉGH, LINDA
1968 "Survival and Revival of European Folk Cultures in America." *Ethnologia Europaea*, 2:97–107.
DOEPPERS, DANIEL F.
1967 "The Globeville Neighborhood in Denver." *The Geographical Review*, 57:506–22.
FEILD, EDWARD
1849 *Voyage of a Visitation on the Coast of Labrador and Round Newfoundland in 1849.* London, Society for the Propagation of the Gospel.
FERLAND, ABBÉ J.-B.-A.
1917 *Le Labrador: notes et récits de voyage.* Montréal, Librarie Beauchemin.
HUARD, ABBÉ V.-A.
1897 & 1972 *Labrador et Anticosti.* Montréal, Beauchemin.
JAKLE, JOHN A. and CYNTHIA JAKLE
1973 *Ethnic and Racial Minorities in North America: A Selected Bibliography of the Geographical Literature.* Monticello, Ill., Council of Planning Librarians.
JAKLE, JOHN A. and JAMES O. WHEELER
1969 "The Changing Residential Structures of the Dutch Population in Kalamazoo, Michigan." *Annals Association of American Geographers*, 59:441–60.
JUNEK, OSCAR
1937 *Isolated Communities: A Study of a Labrador Fishing Village.* New York, American Book Company.

KOLM, RICHARD
    1973 "Ethnicity and Ethnic Groups: Research Needs." *The International Migration Review*, 7:59.
LAVOIE, N.
    1873 "Rapport annuel sur les pêcheries canadiennes dans le Golfe Saint-Laurent." *Documents de la première session du second Parlement du Canada*, 4:41.
LAVOIE, N.
    1875 "Rapport annuel sur les pêcheries canadiennes dans le Golfe Saint-Laurent." *Documents de la seconde session du troisieme Parlement du Canada*, 5:35.
MANNION, JOHN J.
    1974 *Irish Settlements in Eastern Canada: A Study of Cultural Transfer and Adaptation*. Toronto, University of Toronto Press.
MEINIG, D. W.
    1971 *Southwest: Three Peoples in Geographical Change, 1600–1970*. New York, Oxford University Press.
MIKESELL, M. V.
    1967 "Geographic Perspectives in Anthropology." *Annals Association of American Geographers*, 57:617–23.
MORRIS, H. S.
    1968 "Ethnic Groups." *International Encyclopedia of the Social Sciences*, 5:167.
NARROLL, RAOUL
    1964 "On Ethnic Unit Classification." *Current Anthropology*, 5:286–91.
SOPHER, DAVID E.
    1973 "Place and Location: Notes on the Spatial Patterning of Culture." In Louis Schneider and Charles M. Bonjean (eds.), *The Idea of Culture in the Social Sciences*. New York, Cambridge University Press.
SPIRO, MELFORD E.
    1955 "The Acculturation of American Ethnic Groups." *American Anthropologist*, 57:1240–52.
SUNDERLAND, ERIC
    1974 *Elements of Human and Social Geography: Some Anthropological Perspectives*. Oxford, Pergamon Press.

Highlands Scots Migration to Southwestern Newfoundland: A Study of Kinship

8

Rosemary E. Ommer

Writers on the Highland Scots in Canada frequently hint at some kind of spatial ordering of the immigrant population and their descendants. Accents, customs, and folklore in Canadian areas of Highland Scottish settlement, such as Cape Breton, suggest that there still exist today local groups whose antecedents are rooted in particular Scottish source areas. Dunn (1968:141), for example, comments: "The Highland emigrants from each particular district of Scotland settled in groups together when they came to Cape Breton ... . Today more than 100 years later, the offspring of these settlers still speak Gaelic with a Lewis or a Barra or a North Uist or a South Uist accent, depending on the locality [i.e. in Cape Breton] in which they were reared." Yet, kinship as a rationale for the manner in which original Scots immigrants located themselves in the New World has not been examined.

Generally, the conclusions of most studies of trans-Atlantic migrations have been that mobility, with few exceptions, strains and weakens kinship ties. Handlin (1951), for example, emphasized the isolation and disorientation of the individual immigrants torn loose from all the familial ties of the homeland. Recently, studies of Canadian immigrants reveal that unrelated individuals or the nuclear family dominated the social structure of the immigrant stream across the Atlantic (see, for example, Mannion, 1974).

Since it would appear that the Highland Scots emigrations to Canada do not fit this model, it becomes essential to examine the mechanisms that operated to influence this seemingly atypical migration. Johnston (1971) has established the importance of kinship in the retention of population within an area; it is suggested that the importance of kin must be considered as a cohesive factor among social groups under conditions of mobility also. Despite the evidence offered by anthropologists, sociologists, and historians, the study of kinship has yet to achieve prominence in geographical research on migration. Even Mikesell, in a cogent argument for links between geographers and anthropologists, does not recognize the value of studies of complex kinship structure for geographers: "... with the possible exception of some highly technical work on kinship ... virtually the entire range of anthropological research is both intelligible to geographers and relevant to geography" (1967:617–34). However, it is precisely this unwillingness to grasp what Wagner and Mikesell have called the "inner workings of culture" that has weakened and obscured the findings of those few geographical studies which do concern themselves with kinship. Johnston (*op. cit.*) in Britain, and Brunger (1973) and Bohland (1970) in North America reflect a general unawareness of the intricacies inherent in anthropological concepts concerning kinship: the first two confine themselves to same-surname (only agnatic) ties, while Bohland is constrained by simplistic definitions of kinship structure, specifically the conjugal/extended family.

A notable exception is Macpherson's historical study of kinship and land tenure in the Scottish Highlands (1969; see also 1966, 1967, and 1968). He has uncovered an intricate and delicate balance in the functioning of familial relationships which operated locally in the peasant society of the Scottish Highlands under primarily, but not exclusively, male inheritance patterns. It was on these complex relationships that land tenure patterns were based, and Macpherson has demonstrated that kinship was a critical element in the social, economic, and territorial organization of this society as it operated until the mid-19th century. Whereas Macpherson studied a group of Highland Scots who had a fixed territorial base, this study will examine Highland Scots at the beginning of the 19th century when they began to emigrate. More specifically, it will examine the effects of kinship on the migration and subsequent settlement of Highland Scots from the west coast of Scotland to Cape Breton and thence to southwestern Newfoundland in the 19th century.

The investigation proceeded retrospectively, identifying first the Cape Breton source areas for the Newfoundland immigrants and then the Scottish source areas for the Cape Breton immigrants. This was done in order that the reasons for spatial selectivity in these successive migrations could be determined. In so doing, it became necessary to refer back to the social structure of the Highland society at its original source, particularly the *clan* system, regarded as the frame of reference without which the migrations could not be fully understood.

The clan comprised three nested groupings: the *clan* itself, the *sliochd*, and the minor *clann*, the inter-relationships of which must be understood both diachronically and synchronically (Fig. 8–1). Diachronically, the *clan* was an agnatic descent group, consisting of a number of major lineages (*sliochdan*) each composed of a number of minor lineages (*cloinne*) of lesser generational depth.[1] Synchronically, every living member of a *clan* was also a member of one of its *sliochdan* and of one of the localized *cloinne* comprising his or her *sliochd*. In a contemporary sense the Highland *clan* was a patrilineal structure of extended families. Territorially, men of the minor *clann* – brothers and close cousins – tended to possess conjoint rights to usufruct in a single farm, often in community with others. Under threat, or in any kind of transaction involving such rights, the principle of "ancient possession" was invoked, and support could be expected from the leading men of the *sliochd* to which the minor kin-group belonged; if the threat came from outside the larger *clan*, the chief could be expected to intervene on behalf of his clansmen; within the *clan* he would arbitrate disputes.

Marriage patterns developed over time between the various *cloinne*, and therefore *sliochdan*, as they grew sufficiently distant; marriage was usually confined to persons who were separated by more than two degrees of cousinship. A pattern of both *clan* endogamous and *clan* exogamous marriages developed, and both preserved existing rights (*clan* endogamous) and acquired rights (*clan* exogamous). 'Follower' clans were sometimes acquired in this manner, although they were also acquired as the result of political decisions.

The categories of *clan, sliochd*, and *clann* were also important as an identification system. A clansman could be referred to generically as, for example, "a Macdonald," or more precisely, "of the Slioch-an-Taighe branch of the Keppoch Macdonalds," or familiarly, as "Domhnuill MacAonghais 'ic Neil' ic Eoghain" (that is, by his father, grandfather, and great-grandfather). This system of patronymics served to identify clansmen, both to outsiders and to themselves, according to varying levels of familiarity.

For the purposes of this paper, what is important is that these categories defined the social and economic position of Highland clansmen regardless of where they might find themselves. Therefore, if facets of the clan system had been preserved during the

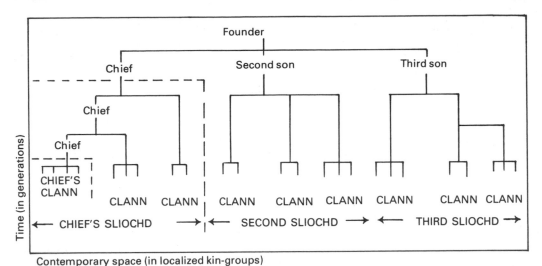

Figure 8–1   *Structural composition of the Scottish clan in time and place*

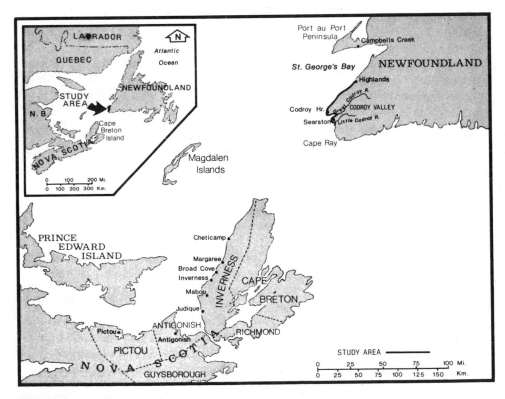

Figure 8–2   *Location*

trans-Atlantic migrations, one could expect that Highland Scots migrants would be found in groups of families related to one another and aware of the precise nature of the relationship. Immigrant Scots in Codroy Valley, Newfoundland, were examined in this respect.

The Scots in Codroy Valley

Codroy Valley lies in the southwestern corner of Newfoundland, facing the Gulf of St. Lawrence (Fig. 8–2). An investigation of oral evidence consistently dates the Scots immigration as having commenced in the year 1841. Census data after this date are not helpful, in that all emigrants from Nova Scotia are classed as "British colonial" and are not distinguished by ethnic origin or religion – all being Roman Catholic. Parish registers become continuous only after 1867; prior to that date entries are intermittent. Oral evidence, parish registers, and government documents, taken together, combine to give a history of the immigration which indicates its continuation over a twenty-year period, ceasing about 1860. The source of the emigration, in all but a few cases, was Inverness County, Cape Breton, and the migrants were not only Highland Scots in ethnic origin, but also Irish and Acadian. Although precise figures of each ethnic group cannot be calculated because of incomplete census data, ethnic backgrounds have been generally identified from parish records and oral evidence. Surname data had to be treated with caution: for example, a name such as O'Quinn, which appears to be Irish in origin, was in fact an anglicization of Aucoin, an Acadian name; likewise the repeated occurrence of Scottish surnames did not necessarily indicate that people of the same surname were related. Different surnames, therefore, were used to indicate, not the correct number of original nuclear families involved in the migration, but its proportionate ethnic components. Of the 37 surnames in the study area, 15 were French or Acadian, 9 were Irish, and 13 were Scots.

Table 8–1 shows the distribution of ethnic groups in the study area twenty or more years after the migration. The Scots dominated Little River and Highlands, but almost all settlements had an intermingling of Scots and others.

Table 8–2 shows that from a total of 51 verifiable Scottish 'moves' into southwest Newfoundland, 19 had originated in Broad Cove (Inverness County), 11 in Margaree, 5 each in Mabou and Judique, 5 in other parts of Inverness County, while the remaining 6 were from other areas in the Gulf of St. Lawrence. A 'move' consisted of at least one nuclear family; some extended families also moved, but since their exact number could not be determined, the number of moves represents an underestimate of the total number of nuclear families involved in the migration. A breakdown of origins by settlement shows the highly restricted nature of the source areas over a twenty-year migration interval, in which Broad Cove and Margaree were dominant. This suggests that a selective process was operating among the Scots. Broad Cove and Margaree were, therefore, examined in order to establish motivations for the movement to Newfoundland, and the social composition of the migrant stream.

The Scots in Cape Breton

MacDonald (1939:470) comments of the Scots migrants into Cape Breton: "They sent home such favourable accounts of the country that many of their friends and relatives were persuaded to join them ..." By 1836, the population of Cape Breton was over 30,000, most of which resulted from an extended wave of Scottish immigration. This movement, which started in the late 1700s and continued to about 1850, included the

TABLE 8–1

Ethnic Components of Codroy Valley and Highlands c. 1880*

	English	Irish	French	Scots	Others	Total	% Scots
Codroy Harbour	18	7	4	3	—	32	8.8
Highlands	4	2	—	12	—	18	66.6
N. Bank ⎱ Grand Codroy	12	13	3	4	1	33	12.1
S. Bank ⎰ River	8	12	25	23	1	69	33.3
Little River	—	1	1	37	—	39	94.8
	42	35	33	79	2	191	40.9

Sources: Searston Parish Mission Register, oral evidence, and cadastral map of Highlands.
*Numbers designate heads of household for all but Highlands, where they refer to pioneer males owning land.

majority of the initial settlers of Broad Cove and Margaree. It differed from an earlier wave of Scottish immigration into Canada in that it represented an exodus of poor people of lower social status than those involved in the 1770 migration (Adam, 1919:280–93; 1920:73–89). Writers on this immigration have concluded that actual numbers will never become obtainable, since many immigrants did not enter Canada through the normal ports of entry. Flewwelling (1949:75) states that "If they were landed in Halifax, Pictou or Sydney, their arrival was usually recorded by customs officials or in the newspapers; if, however, they were set down in a lonely harbour or on uninhabited shores … no one knew how many began their struggle with the wilderness alone, or in pioneer settlements where their arrival was unrecorded."

However, for certain individual areas of immigration, an account of the personnel involved in the process of initial settlement may be, at least partially, obtained. MacDougall's *History of Inverness County* (1922) offers valuable insights into the pioneer history of the area, and similar books exist for other areas settled by Highland Scots. These throw light on such matters as pioneer population, the internal mobility of this population after initial settlement, the marriage patterns of the early generations, economy and land use, and inter-ethnic and kin relations of the pioneers and their descendants. Such valuable documentary evidence has been under-utilized by researchers, perhaps because of the awkwardness of the material (which is essentially a collection of genealogies with commentaries by the author), and because an appreciation of the diagnostic features of the clan system is needed before it becomes possible to analyse the information contained in such books.

Macpherson (1969) has used the joint criteria of surname, residential location, and juxtaposition with other surnames in a given area to identify *clan* affiliation in Scotland. The application of his criteria to the information presented in such a genealogical account as MacDougall's *History*, corroborated and supplemented by census data, oral evidence, and parish records, provides a methodology for the assessment of a pioneer Highland Scots population in terms of *clan* structure. Religious affiliation has been found to be a useful adjunct to Macpherson's original criteria. MacDougall's genealogies reveal that the main Scottish source areas of the Broad Cove/Margaree immigrants were Morar, Moidart, and the Isle of Canna in Scotland. Other source areas were Arisaig, South Uist, Barra, Skye, and Lochaber. All immigrants came from territory historically under the domination of Clan Donald (Fig. 8–3); the major source

TABLE 8–2

Cape Breton and Gulf Source Areas for Scottish Settlements in Southwestern Newfoundland

	Margaree	Broad Cove	Judique	Mabou	Other Inverness County	Sub Total	Antigonish and	Pictou	Other Gulf	Total
Little River	3	7	—	5	4	19	—	—	—	19
Grand River	8	4	—	—	—	12	2	—	1	15
Highlands	—	—	5	—	—	5	—	—	2	7
St. George's Bay	—	8	—	—	1	9	—	1	—	10
Total for S.W. Nfld.	11	19	5	5	5	45	2	1	3	51

Sources: Oral evidence; parish register for Searston Mission (Codroy Valley).

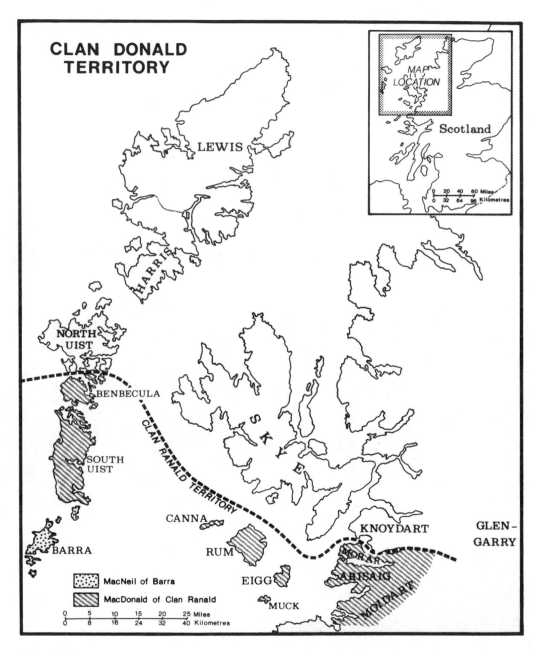

Figure 8–3

areas were within the territory of the Clanranald branch of Clan Donald, while the other areas had, in Scotland, links with the Clanranald family through marriage.

The MacDougall genealogies and the National Census for Cape Breton (1861)[2] also permitted the identification of the group of surnames found juxtaposed in Broad Cove and Margaree, as well as the particular Scottish location of many of the immigrants. For example, the genealogies show that MacLellans, MacIsaacs, MacDonalds, and Gillises, all from Morar (Scotland), were pioneers in Board Cove/Margaree, as were MacIsaacs from Canna and MacLeods from Eigg. All were Roman Catholic. It is this evidence of surname, Scottish location, religious affiliation, and juxtaposition of surnames within the Broad Cove/Margaree district, jointly considered, that permitted the allocation of the pioneers of Broad Cove to Clanranald. For example, whereas the surname MacDonald alone could not define *clan* affiliation beyond the broad classification Clan Donald, MacDonald of Morar – Roman Catholic and living in the same location as Gillises and MacLellans – allowed specific identification with Clanranald. The pioneers of Margaree could not be identified with any one *clan*, but it will be shown later that the Newfoundland migrants from both Broad Cove and Margaree were clearly of Clan Donald origin, and most were specifically of Clanranald affiliation.

From the genealogical details found in MacDougall, however, these Broad Cove immigrants were linked not only by *clan* ties, but also by ties of close kinship. Some of the kin links were specifically recorded, as in the following excerpt taken from seven pages of genealogy devoted to the Gillises of Margaree: "Other Morar Gillises who settled at South West Margaree were Archy Gillis (Ban) Egypt, John Gillis (Mac Raonuill ruaith 'ic Alistair) an uncle and cousin, respectively, of Alexander Gillis (mac Ian ic Alistair) and Allan Gillis Ban (Mac Alistair ic Ian ic Dhugail) ..." (MacDougall, *op. cit.*:401).

The excerpt is important, not only because it supplies a clear example of the migration of kin from a specific Scottish source area to a specific locale in Cape Breton, but also because it exemplifies the continued usage of Scottish patronymics in the Cape Breton context. That these patronymic designations were preserved over four generations following the migration – Mac Dougall wrote in the early 1920s – emphasizes the continuing awareness of Cape Breton Highlanders of their kin connections. It also provides the researcher with an invaluable tool for the identification of kin who have not been grouped together in MacDougall's genealogies, in particular for the identification of affinal kin, who might otherwise be 'lost.' For example, the following excerpt, from a six-page genealogy of McLellans (*op. cit.*:393) shows how the patronymic provides precise identification of affinal kin links: "In 1826 James McLellan, his wife and his son Angus, and two daughters, ... came here from Morar ... . This James MacLellan was also the paternal uncle of the wife of John McLellan, big, (Iain macAoghnais ic Neil) who lived at Rear Broad Cove ... . He was also the maternal uncle of Alexander Gillis (mac Iain ic Alistair) ... ." That is, James was the maternal uncle of the Alexander Gillis whose patronymic was given in the previous excerpt. The affinal kin links shown in MacDougall's genealogies of Cape Breton Highlanders allows a more detailed analysis of Scottish kin networks than merely agnatic relationships would have permitted. This awareness of affinal links in Cape Breton was also found among the later migrants to southwestern Newfoundland and their descendants, and raises a question of one facet of Scottish kinship which has so far remained unresearched. Macpherson (1968), however, has noted that clan-exogamous marriage in Scotland was functional, in that it provided "new blood" for the local *clann*, whereas clan endogamy reinforced the cohesion of the whole *clan*. It may be that such a mechanism operated in Cape Breton as indicated by the specific awareness of affinal kin links shown above, and repeatedly, in MacDougall's genealogies.

Clearly, the system of patronymics was transferred from Scotland to Cape Breton, and it was there adapted so that a newly-developing Cape Breton-based set of patronymics could serve to identify later generations in their Cape Breton context. One such example is that of the McLellan family of Broad Cove Marsh, of whom Mac-Dougall comments. "There is that branch of the McLellan family locally identified as [Cloinn Fhearchair] branching out from five brothers, namely: Archibald, Donald, Alexander, John and Ronald ... of B[road] C[ove] Marsh" (p. 369). It is significant that this identification system was transferred to Cape Breton Island, both in usage and motivation, reinforcing the traditional Highland awareness of kin ties in a situation that might have been expected to sunder them. Quantification of information in MacDougall's genealogies, based on the analysis of patronymics, reveals that the number of pioneer adult males who were already related to adults other than their wives on arrival in the Broad Cove/Margaree district was 134 persons out of a total adult male pioneer population of 188 persons. That is, 71 percent of the pioneer population of the district were related kin before they left Scotland. When the number of other adults in the Gulf of St. Lawrence to whom these 134 persons were related was calculated, the number of those with kin ties rose by a mere 4 percent, and these other relatives were spread throughout Inverness County, Pictou, and Antigonish. In other words, the pioneer population of Broad Cove/Margaree may be said to represent a core of related kin.

It is suggested that if a different district were examined, and identical calculations made, similar results would be obtained. In this respect, however, it is important to note that such selectivity cannot have been a product of all migrations direct from the Scottish source areas. The mechanics of the Highland emigrations involved too many different methods of recruitment and passage: people left from Glasgow, Aberdeen, Edinburgh and from small bays in the Highlands such as Tobermory, singly and in groups, and it cannot be concluded that they were all organized by kin at source. Indeed, a feature of the pioneer settlement of Inverness County is the considerable mobility demonstrated by some families for whom the initial migration process had resulted in their being scattered all around the Gulf of St. Lawrence. One example is that of a shipload of early settlers who arrived in Pictou about the year 1791, some of whom went to Parrsboro, in Cumberland County. MacDougall and oral evidence record the subsequent move of families from Parrsboro to Broad Cove Marsh and its vicinity, settling near families of the same Scottish source area and the same immigration: two Kennedy brothers from Canna and a MacLeod and MacDonald from Eigg. In the following generation, intermarriage took place between the MacLeod and Kennedy families, and branches of the Kennedy and MacDonald families later migrated to southwestern Newfoundland. There, intermarriage again took place in the following generation, between the offspring of the (Newfoundland) marriage of a Kennedy daughter to a Campbell (who had himself originally come from Strathlorne, near Broad Cove, Cape Breton), and the offspring of the main Kennedy line; thus it was a second-cousin marriage, although it was not recorded as such in the parish register for Codroy Valley. Such marriages served to reaffirm kinship ties in a migration context, just as the clan-endogamous marriages in Scotland had served to reaffirm *clan* cohesion in a territorial sense.

The evidence for the Scotland to Broad Cove/Margaree migration indicates that the transfer of the *clann* had occurred. The concepts of lineage connection and the larger *clan* were also transferred in the migration, and operated in terms of social interaction and settlement in the early years, although the political, territorial, and economic complex of which they were an intrinsic part did not exist in the New World. However, the basic local kin structure of the *clan* system was not destroyed by migration.

Figures 8–4 and 8–5 show the Broad Cove/Margaree bias towards particular Scottish source areas and particular surnames. They further show that the emigration from these places to southwestern Newfoundland was not in any way a random selection of the pioneer population of Broad Cove and Margaree. In both cases, a large percentage of the migrants were of the surname 'MacIsaac'; in the case of Broad Cove, the Scottish source areas for the Newfoundland migrants were predominantly Moidart and Canna, whereas in the case of Margaree, Moidart and Morar were the predominant Scottish source areas. In post-emigration Broad Cove and Margaree, the relative number of MacIsaacs decreased considerably, whereas the percentage of Gillises increased. After the Scots emigrated to Newfoundland, Margaree's population was completely rearranged: the Irish were almost totally absent, according to the Census of 1861 and oral evidence. The brevity of Irish settlement can be accounted for by the fact that many of these settlers arrived late in the Cape Breton immigration period, occupied marginal land temporarily, and moved on within a generation, claiming that the best land had been taken up. The reasons for the selective Scottish emigration are more problematic. Much of the Scottish in-migration to the Cape Breton shore was completed between 1800 and 1840, while the out-migration from this shore (not only to Newfoundland, but also to Upper Canada, New England, Australia and New Zealand) appears to have gained impetus as in-migration decreased (1840–1860). This time sequence may be indicative of land pressure; oral evidence, both in Cape Breton and the Codroy Valley, strongly supports this explanation.[3]

Reasons for the selection of southwestern Newfoundland as a destination are also difficult to establish firmly. However, Margaree and Broad Cove are similar in their physical features to Codroy Valley: both have wide flood plains and extensive intervale land. Furthermore, Margaree represented the 'boundary' of British settlement on the west coast of Cape Breton. The shores to the north were settled by Acadians, and the next available area was across the Cabot Strait in Codroy Valley, where the quality of the land and a good salmon fishery were already known to the Margaree Scots by the year 1842. A Scots visitor from Margaree to Codroy Valley in the same year noted that he had heard, "the land on both sides of the river is of excellent quality and would admit of extensive settlement," and that the "Codroy was a very fine river for salmon."[4]

Although it seems likely that good land, a perceived need for an expanding frontier, and a similar physical environment were important factors in the migration to southwestern Newfoundland, oral evidence from the descendants of the migrants themselves provides further insight into their motivation. The prospect of confederation with Canada seems to have been important, threatening to impose financial penalties on all land not in production. Since the Scots held relatively large lots compared to other ethnic groups in the area – two to three hundred acres was common – much of it

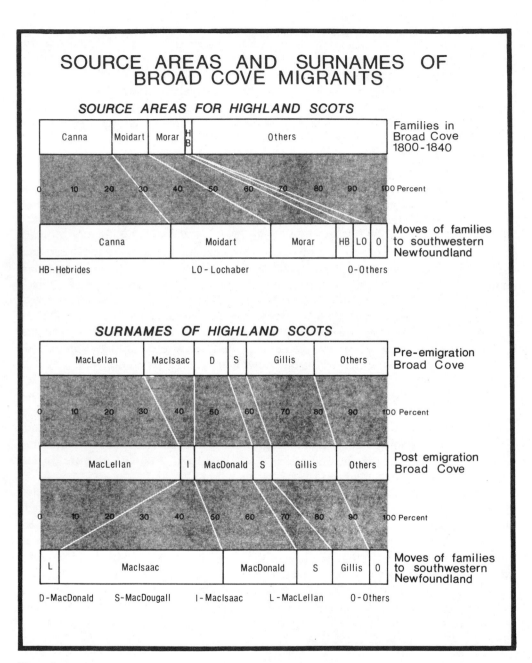

Figure 8–4

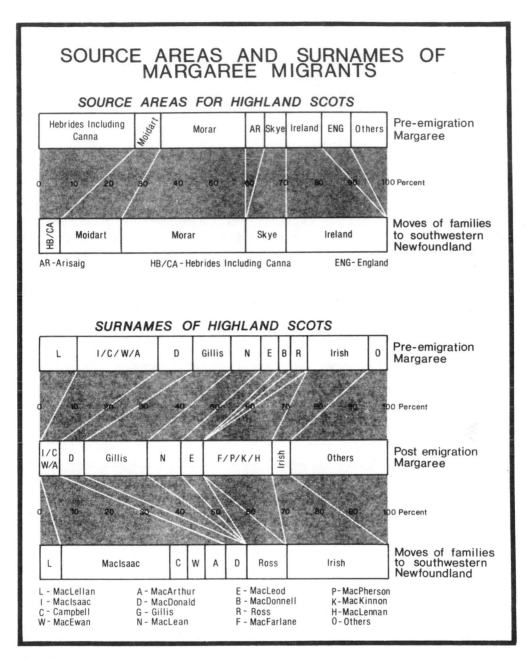

SOURCE AREAS AND SURNAMES OF MARGAREE MIGRANTS

Figure 8–5

kept in timber rather than farmed – confederation would have restricted their methods of land holding.[5] Insecurity of tenure in Cape Breton, as a result of absentee land-lordism, was also widely cited as an important 'push' factor in the move to Codroy. When land pressure is considered in conjunction with tenurial difficulties, the situation must have seemed reminiscent of those conditions which helped to promote the original Scottish migrations. It is not too surprising that the emigrants were a land-hungry people – a possible explanation for the large acreage of their New World lots – determined to prevent past deprivations from repeating themselves, as these emigrants seem to have thought they were threatening to do.

Yet, although these factors may comprise the general rationale for the migration, they are inadequate as an explanation for its selectivity. If such economic 'push' factors were the sole reason for the emigration it would be expected that late settlers, if forced to occupy marginal lands, would be amongst the first who would want to leave; and this was the case with the Margaree Irish. Likewise, the earliest settlers might find that their expanding families had insufficient land. Such factors did not affect all Newfoundland Scots immigrants: some were affected by one, some by another, and those who might have been expected to move first did not necessarily do so. In fact the opposite occurred: not all MacIsaacs owned poor or insufficient land, and one family was known to have owned as much as six hundred acres on the banks of Broad Cove; yet they sold out and were among the very first to come to Codroy, Newfoundland, in 1841 (MacDougall, *op. cit.*:326).

It appears that some social factor or factors operated to encourage an emigration of MacIsaacs. Within the context of an operative *clan*/kin system in Broad Cove and Margaree, rooted in a localized combination of Scottish source areas, it is likely that social pressures, derived ultimately from Scotland, were functioning to promote this bias. The MacIsaacs were socially unimportant in Scotland in the dying years of the Scottish *clan* system, and the immigration into Broad Cove and Margaree of more prominent Clan Donald/Clanranald surnames might have threatened their social status. It is clear from MacDougall's genealogies that the Gillis surname, in particular, had been important in Morar and Moidart: many of the Gillis genealogies mention people of military rank, as well as some who were probably principal tenants or "tacksmen" in Scotland. MacDougall mentions two surnames in particular in his genealogies of whom this was true: Gillis and MacDonald, each of which also appears to have married preferentially with the other rather than to other surnames in the Broad Cove/Margaree district, although precise numbers have not been calculated. Genealogies include such persons as Captain Donald Gillis of Stole, North Morar; Catherine Gillis, nighean [=daughter] Eoghain an Obain [in Scotland the preposition "an" often denoted land-holding]; Colonel Gillis of Kenloch Morar; Captain Allan MacDonald; Alasdair Mhor MacDonald, whose son James married Margaret Gillis, daughter of Captain Alexander Gillis of the Fraser Regiment of Highlanders, and whom MacDougall specifically mentions as being "MacDonalds of the Kinloch-moidart family in Scotland, and ... descended from John, son of Allan, eighth Chief of Clan Ranald (*op. cit.*:370).

The likelihood of kinship factors being important in the selectivity of the migration is strengthened by evidence from southwestern Newfoundland, in the form of both oral tradition and parish records, of local prejudice against marriages between Gillis and MacIsaac families. It is said of the only Gillis-MacIsaac marriage in southwestern Newfoundland up to the present day that it resulted in a forced change of residence for the couple concerned in order to escape local censure. Reasons for this marriage 'block' were stated by the families concerned as being part of a long-standing tradition of antipathy between the Gillis and MacIsaac clans. Macpherson (1968:91) also notes a custom of avoiding marriage between certain families in the Scottish setting; and further weight is added to the argument when it is considered that, at least until the time of the 1955 electoral roll in Newfoundland, no Gillis and MacIsaac families settled in the same area, despite the fact that they are among the more numerous of the Scottish families in southwestern Newfoundland, and despite the fact that although other Scottish surnames are spread evenly throughout the district, Gillis and MacIsaac families remain discrete. It is therefore possible that the exodus of MacIsaacs from Broad Cove and Margaree resulted from the influx of Gillis families into the area shown on Figure 8–5. In a frontier situation, the MacIsaacs could remedy such a social threat by the simple expedient of removing to a new area where they and their kin would be numerically dominant.

Figures 8–6, 8–7, 8–8, and 8–9, represent an aggregate picture of data and material derived from three sources: MacDougall's *History*, from which genealogies were constructed for some of the pioneer Codroy Valley families; oral evidence from Cape Breton and Codroy Valley; and the Searston parish register, in which sporadic references to degrees of consanguinity are found. Figure 8–6 shows surnames and families by generation. Figure 8–7 shows the location of pioneer families of the same surname, who are known to have been related agnatically, for the years 1845–1870. The purpose is to express spatially the most basic kin relationships of the pioneer era. The family centred on Cb1 (grandparent's residence) is the dominant kin group of the pioneer era of Codroy Valley; not surprisingly, these are MacIsaacs of Broad Cove and Margaree. All Codroy Valley MacIsaacs, except those centred on Db2, are agnatically related, and are included in this kin group. They are reported by present-day inhabitants of the area as being amongst the first to arrive, and as having deliberately spread out all over the Valley on arrival in order to acquire the best land. This is borne out by their non-contiguous locations despite early immigration and simultaneous arrival. In Figure 8–7, three main areal groupings can be discerned: (1) Db2 (MacIsaac); (2) Cb1 (MacIsaac); and (3) Aa3 and Ab1 (Gillis and MacLean). These are territorially discrete, and reflect three separate locations in the area: the coast with an economy emphasizing fishing, and the two rivers with their agriculturally-focused economies based on fertile intervale land. Figure 8–8 shows the known cognatic and affinal links of the pioneer generation, drawn to one member of an extended group only, to avoid visual confusion. The three main areal groupings remain generally discrete, but all MacIsaacs are now seen to have been related, and indeed only families Ec1 and Dc3 remain apparently unattached. Figure 8–9 shows the post-immigration marriages up to 1870. They reinforce extant relationships, and perhaps the most interesting feature is the continued aloofness of the coastal (Gillis and MacLean) group, especially in the light of earlier comments. The preponderance of Scots:Scots marriage is clear. The figures are:

Scots/Scots	12
Scots/English	3
Scots/French	1
Scots/Irish	1
Total number of marriages	17

Figures 8–6 to 8–9, therefore, show the Scots in Codroy Valley to have been an extension of the Broad Cove/Margaree concentration of kin from the same general

CODROY VALLEY: SURNAMES AND ETHNIC ORIGINS

Gillis
Murphy
Hynes
MacIsaac
MacLean
Gillis
MacLean
Broussard

Hall
Gale
Collins
AuCoin
Campbell
Campbell
MacNeil
MacDonald
Campbell

Gillis
Delaney
MacIsaac
MacArthur
MacNeil
MacLellan

Downey
Jennings
MacDonald
MacIsaac
Cormier
MacEwan
MacIsaac
Benoit
MacDonald

Ryan
MacIsaac

MacKinnon
Doucette
St. Martin
Doyle
Kennedy

MacIsaac

MacIsaac

Farrell
MacNeil
MacIsaac
MacIsaac
MacDonald
MacDougall
MacDonald

MacNeil
MacIsaac
MacDonald
MacNeil
MacIsaac
Campbell
MacQuarrie
Wall
MacIsaac
MacDougall
MacDonald

MacQuarrie
MacIsaac
Chaisson
Campbell
MacIsaac

SCOTS
IRISH
ENGLISH
FRENCH

Numbers (e.g. 1) denote individual families within a grid square (e.g. Aa).

approx. 0 miles

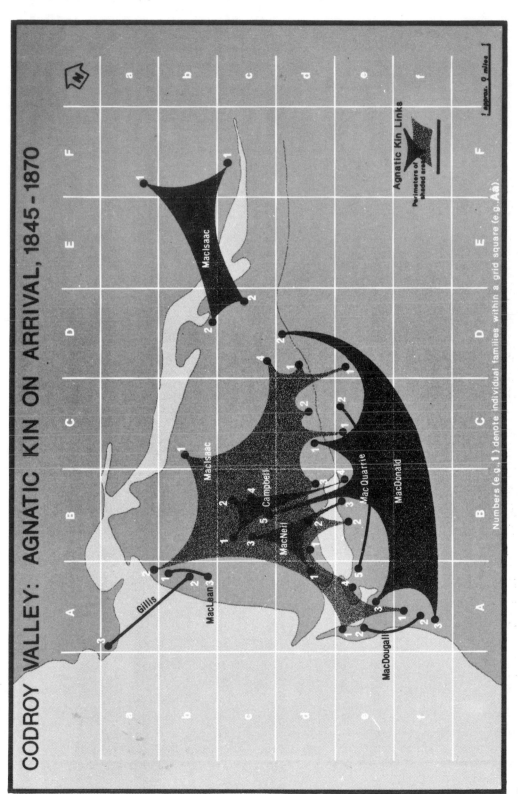

CODROY VALLEY: AGNATIC KIN ON ARRIVAL, 1845–1870

Agnatic Kin Links

Perimeters of shaded areas

Numbers (e.g. 1) denote individual families within a grid square (e.g. Aa).

approx. 0 miles

Figure 8–7

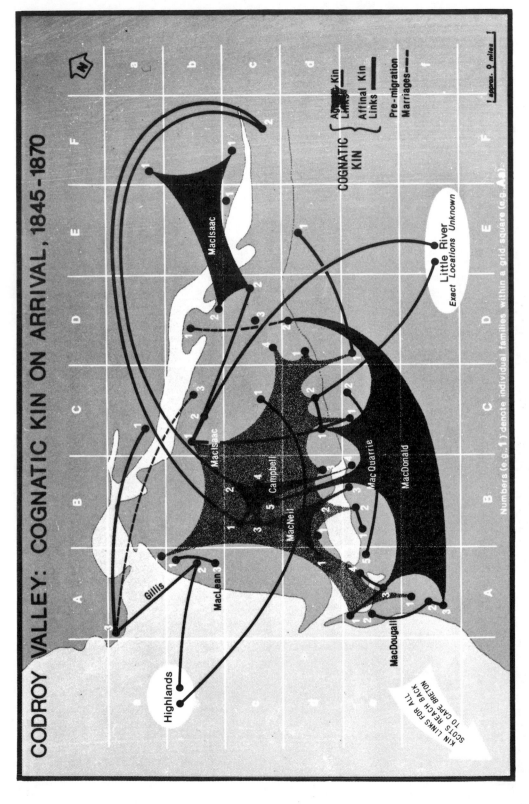

CODROY VALLEY: COGNATIC KIN ON ARRIVAL, 1845-1870

COGNATIC KIN { Agnatic Kin Links / Affinal Kin Links }

Pre-migration Marriages———

Numbers (e.g. 1) denote individual families within a grid square (e.g. Aa)

1 approx. 9 miles

Gillis

MacLean

MacIsaac

MacIsaac

Campbell

MacNeil

MacQuarrie

MacDonald

MacDougall

Little River
Exact Locations Unknown

Highlands

KIN LINKS FOR ALL SCOTS REACH BACK TO CAPE BRETON

Figure 8-8

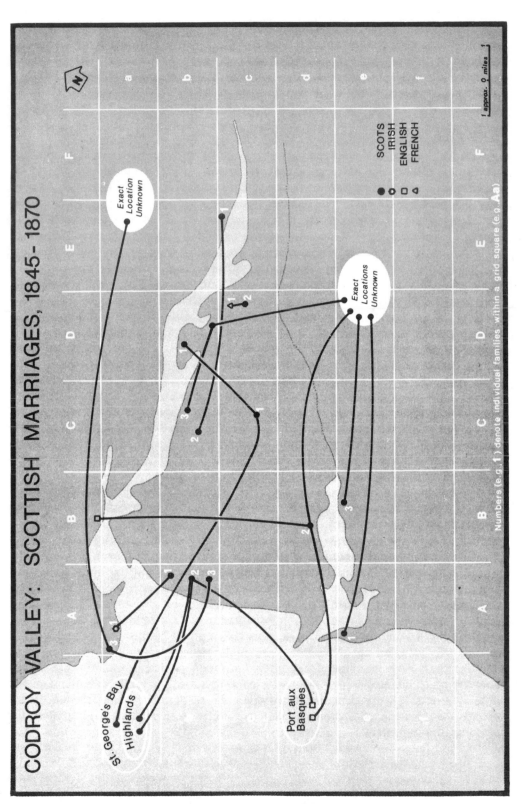

CODROY VALLEY: SCOTTISH MARRIAGES, 1845 - 1870

Exact Location Unknown

Exact Locations Unknown

St. George's Bay
Highlands

Port aux Basques

SCOTS
IRISH
ENGLISH
FRENCH

Numbers (e.g. 1) denote individual families within a grid square (e.g. Aa)

1 approx. 0 miles 1

Figure 8-9

Cape Breton source area, who were themselves a concentration of kin from the same general source area of Clanranald territory in the western Highlands and islands of Scotland. Settlement in the pioneer stage took place in such a manner that the spatial pattern of kin networks reflected the three different settlement locations of the area; kinship patterns at the time of immigration were already those of a well-established network.

Conclusions

As stated at the outset of this paper, almost all the literature concerning the impact of mobility on kinship ties has argued that traditional bonds of kinship are frayed or sundered as a result of migration. In the history of the Atlantic migrations, by and large, it is held that the social composition of the migrant stream was one of unrelated individuals or nuclear families: the familiar supportive network of kinship was believed to have been unravelled by the upheavals of the Atlantic crossing. However, this study, examining one small fragment of the great migrations, has shown that the Highlanders of Codroy Valley crossed the Atlantic usually neither alone, nor as unrelated nuclear families, but in large extended kin groups. The social cohesion of these groups was generally maintained, despite geographical mobility, and despite the hardships of settling in an alien land. Indeed, on occasion, further mobility was the means by which strained kin links were reinforced. To quote Samuel Johnson on the emigration of mainland Scots to the islands (1773:323), "Whole neighbourhoods formed parties for removal, so that their departure from their native country is no longer exile ... He sits down in a better climate surrounded by his kindred and his friends ... they change nothing but the place of their abode ... This is the real effect of emigration, if those that go away together settle on the same spot and preserve their ancient union." It was the Scottish *clan* in the homeland which suffered disruption and dissolution. MacKenzie (1946:186) commented on the Highland evictions that promulgated so many of the emigrations: "There is now scarcely one of the name MacDonald in the wide district once inhabited by thousands."

The persistence of kinship ties amongst the migrating Scots, although often intuitively recognized, has been difficult to establish for the following reasons: (1) analysing a kinship network requires a detailed knowledge of that network; (2) kinship can be established only when it is examined at the individual, rather than group, level; and (3) following kinship ties over periods of migration requires that they be traced, not only through time, but sometimes across considerable distances. Further difficulties arise from the unlikelihood of being able to trace affinal linkages, or even to establish that such links need to be traced. Finally, the establishment of *clan* affiliation among emigrant Scots was impossible until some diagnostic criteria for this became available, and until the necessarily detailed data were discovered. To this end, MacDougall's *History* proved to be an invaluable document, providing detailed genealogies of emigrant Scots from the time of their arrival in the New World, recording, not only their surnames, but also their patronymics, and their location both in Scotland and in the New World. It is this complex of individual-specific information that made possible the identification of Scottish kinship networks over such a wide spatial and temporal migration span.

The importance of marriage with affines among the Highland Scots in the New World becomes apparent through an analysis of MacDougall's genealogies. Whether this type of linkage, or marriage with cognatic kin, was important in the Scottish *clan* system in the homeland is unknown, perhaps because it tends to remain undetected among the exogamous marriages of the agnatic kin-group. One explanation that must be considered is that the changed social and economic conditions of emigrants in the New World endowed affinal ties with a new importance. More generally, this pattern of affinal links may also exist in other New World kinship systems, either as an adaptation, common to all pioneer ethnic groups or societies in their life on an expanding frontier, or as a traditional kinship system carried from the homeland. Cognatic kin marriage would maintain the social cohesion of any isolated group, while its availability would prevent in-breeding; such a control might well be a natural device of any pioneer group operating within a genetically-restricted community.

Reasons for the persistence of kinship ties among the emigrant Scots are hard to establish. They may have clung together, not only because these ties had been traditionally cherished, but also because they believed that group movement would be economically and psychologically beneficial in the New World. The old blood ties of the Scottish Highlands were not merely, or even primarily, emotional, but rather functional. The *clan* system was no longer operating in its entirety by the time emigration to Canada was fully under way. As a political unit, the *clan* was no longer effective; the *sliochd* remained only as a symbol of the clansman's awareness of his own particular ancestry; only the local *clann* can be said to have survived as an operating unit and transferred to the New World. It is, therefore, the functions of this local kin group which must be considered in explaining its persistence and survival.

The *clann* in Scotland was a functioning economic and social unit. From the point of view of transfer to the New World, it should be seen as the kin base from which joint farming operated; it was a compact unit, providing social and economic cohesion and security. During the "tacksman" emigrations of the 1770s, local kin-groups (*cloinne*) of "tacksmen" and their sub-tenants are known to have emigrated together, in an effort to preserve the ancient Highland social order; later, when the poorer people of lower status left their homeland *en masse*, the persistent solidarity of kin groups was considerable. In addition, the mechanism of chain migration functioned efficiently through kin; immigrants already established in North America provided promise of shelter and economic support for kin wishing to follow. Such *clann* ties channeled migration flow from specific source areas to specific destinations in the New World. The migrations to Cape Breton occurred in this way and kin ties were a potent force even in the secondary chain migration of Cape Breton Scots into southwestern Newfoundland. In this series of small migrations, no single element was discernible as being in control of decision-making in the migration process: women moved to marry and their kin followed later; families moved because of insecurity of tenure and their kin followed later; families also moved concurrently in large extended kin groups.

Gould (1965:24) has suggested that "nuclear families almost invariably appear to be merely phases in the developmental cycle," and such research as has been done on immigrating European peasantry to North America appears to support him. Future research may or may not show that most eastern Canadian pioneer families were nuclear at the time of initial settlement, and that over succeeding generations, if left undisturbed, they slowly evolved into extended kin groups; this was the case with the Cape Shore Irish of Placentia Bay, Newfoundland (Mannion, *op. cit.* and 1976).

The Highland Scots, however, did not experience this disruption of kinship. This study has discerned no break in the operating extended family network which was the basis of the ancestral society in the Old World. They retained a structurally complex and functionally sophisticated network of kin links through two separate migrations and subsequent settlement in an area which was ethnically diverse.

This experience of the Highland Scots may, or may not, be eccentric in the overall pattern of the great migrations. Greven (1970:72–3), for example, notes of Colonial Andover: "... kinship often served as an influential factor in bringing additional settlers to Andover ... . From the outset there were several embryonic kinship groups settled together in Andover." Almost all studies, to date, of the social structure of migrating groups are overgeneralized and simplistic. Examination of the fine detail of actual kinship links for a small group of Highlanders has demonstrated the survival of a traditional kinship pattern over an extended time period, despite, or in some cases because of, considerable mobility of the migrants concerned. The demonstration of one exception to the generally-accepted pattern of social disruption among immigrants to the New World would suggest that careful examination, at the micro-level, of other ethnic groups which were involved in the European exodus is needed. Such studies, especially if they consider social conditions both before and after immigration, may well bring to light further examples of hitherto unsuspected social cohesion among the supposedly "uprooted" pioneers of North America.

NOTES

1 *Clan* is the name given to the complete kin group at its widest extent; *sliochd* is the Gaelic for 'lineage' or 'descent' and is formal; *clann* (plural *cloinne*) is the Gaelic for 'children' and is more familiar. The terms are in common usage in Gaelic and are not a specialist terminology (see MacAlpine and MacKenzie, 1973).
2 Census of Nova Scotia, 1861. Halifax, E. M. MacDonald.
3 Land pressure, however, although referred to by various writers in Cape Breton, has not as yet been proven. What is important in this respect is the feeling of land pressure, real or imagined.
4 Newfoundland, Department of Colonial Secretary, Incoming Correspondence 43 (1842) p. 34. Letter of Norman Campbell, dated September 10th and written from Margaree, Cape Breton.
5 Census of Nova Scotia, 1861. Halifax, E. M. MacDonald.

REFERENCES: SECONDARY SOURCES

ADAM, M. I.
    1919 "The Highland Emigration of 1770." *Scottish Historical Review*, 16:280–93.
ADAM, M. I.
    1920 "The Cause of the Highland Migrations of 1783–1803." *Scottish Historical Review*, 17:73–89.
BOHLAND, J.
    1970 "The Influence of Kinship Ties on the Settlement Pattern of North East Georgia." *Professional Geographer*, 22(5):267–69.
BRUNGER, A. G.
    1973 "Settler Location in the Talbot Settlement, Upper Canada." Paper presented to the Canadian Association of Geographers.
DUNN, C. W.
    1968 *Highland Settler: A Portrait of the Scottish Gael in Nova Scotia*. Toronto, University of Toronto Press.
FLEWWELLING, R. J.
    1949 "Immigration to and Emigration from Nova Scotia 1839–1851." *Nova Scotia Historical Society Collections*, 28:75.
GOULD, HAROLD A.
    1965 "Lucknow Rickshawallas: The Social Organisation of an Occupational Category." In R. Piddington (ed.), *Kinship and Geographical Mobility*. Leiden, E. J. Brill.

GREVEN, P. J. JR.
1970 *Four Generations, Population, Land and Family in Colonial Andover*. Massachusetts, Cornell University Press.

HANDLIN, O.
1951 *The Uprooted*. New York, Grosset and Dunlap.

JOHNSON, SAMUEL
1773 "Journey to the Western Islands of Scotland." In Arthur Murphy (ed.), *The Works of Samuel Johnson LLD*, 12 vols., 8:323. London, T. Longman, 1796.

JOHNSTON, R. J.
1971 "Resistance to Migration and the Mover/Stayer Dichotomy: Aspects of Kinship and Population Stability in an English Rural Area." *Geografiska Annaler*, 53B:16–27.

MACALPINE, N. and J. MACKENZIE
1973 *Gaelic-English and English-Gaelic Dictionary*. Glasgow, Gairm Publications.

MACDONALD, N.
1939 *Canada, 1763–1841 Immigration and Settlement, the Administration of Imperial Land Regulations*. London, Longmans, Green and Co.

MACDOUGALL, J. L.
1922 *History of Inverness County, Nova Scotia*. Truro, Nova Scotia, News Publishing Co. Ltd.

MACKENZIE, ALEXANDER
1946 *The History of the Highland Clearances*. Second Edition. Glasgow, Alexander MacLaren & Sons.

MACPHERSON, A. G.
1966 "An Old Highland Genealogy and the Evolution of a Scottish Clan." *Scottish Studies*, 10:1–43.

MACPHERSON, A. G.
1967 "An Old Highland Parish Register." *Scottish Studies*, 1(12):149–92.

MACPHERSON, A. G.
1968 "An Old Highland Parish Register." *Scottish Studies*, II(12):81–111.

MACPHERSON, A. G.
1969 "Land Tenure, Social Structure and Resource Use in the Scottish Highlands, 1747–1784." Unpublished Ph.D. dissertation, Department of Geography, McGill University.

MANNION, J. J.
1974 *Irish Settlements in Eastern Canada: A Study of Cultural Transfer and Adaptation*. Toronto, University of Toronto Press.

MANNION, J. J.
1976 *Point Lance in Transition: The Transformation of a Newfoundland Outport*. Toronto, McClelland & Stewart.

MIKESELL, M.
1967 "Geographic Perspectives in Anthropology." *Annals Association American Geographers*, 57(3):617–34.

Settlers and Traders in Western Newfoundland

John J. Mannion

9

One of the fundamental themes in the historical geography of Newfoundland is the relationship between the origins and growth of settlement and the development of overseas trade. Unlike so many parts of frontier North America, established trading patterns preceded permanent settlement under the old migratory cod fishery, and the merchants and traders who organized and controlled the flow of commodities to and from the island ultimately played an important part in its peopling. Rarely did the settlers or primary producers have direct links with their market areas or with their source areas of supply. In isolated rural Newfoundland the marketing of surplus produce and the distribution of imported goods were almost entirely conducted by merchants or small traders through a primitive system of exchange frequently involving the extension of credit and the use of barter.

This essay seeks to examine the commercial relationships between settlers and traders in a section of western Newfoundland during the 19th century, and especially the extent to which traders influenced the distribution and development of rural settlement there, and their role in the formation of central places. This is done in three steps: first there is a description of the patterns of migration to the area, with emphasis on the source areas of the immigrants, then of the evolving patterns of resource utilization, and finally of the ways in which mercantile involvement influenced the patterns of immigration and settlement and diversified the exploitation of local resources.

I. THE PATTERNS OF IN-MIGRATION

The area examined extends from St. George's Bay to Bonne Bay and includes the Bay of Islands and the Port au Port Peninsula (Fig. 9–1). Along with the Codroy Valley, these pockets of settlement were the most populous on the west coast throughout the 19th century, accounting for at least 60 percent of the total population. St. George's Bay was the first to receive a substantial number of settlers in the late 18th century when a small group of southwestern English and French-speaking Jersey Protestants moved in to exploit commercially the local resources of salmon and fur. It remained the most populous part of the coast (Fig. 9–2).[1] The trickle of Old World migration continued during the early decades of the 19th century and the Protestant settlements were augmented by some Newfoundland-English from the south coast. Inter-marriage was common but the permanent population expanded slowly: 4 or 5 families in 1801, 11 in 1808, 13 in 1813, 28 in 1822, and 32 by 1828. After 1820 Catholic Acadians from the west coast of Cape Breton, interested initially in the cod and herring fishery, began to occupy the inner bay: Wix (1836:189) reported 54 new settlers in 1830 and 25 Acadian families were recorded in 1838. The migration intensified in the 1840s and by 1850 they outnumbered the Protestants, a pattern that persisted to the end of the century. These Acadians were joined by settlers from St. Pierre and by single adult males mainly from Normandy and Brittany, the latter being deserters from French

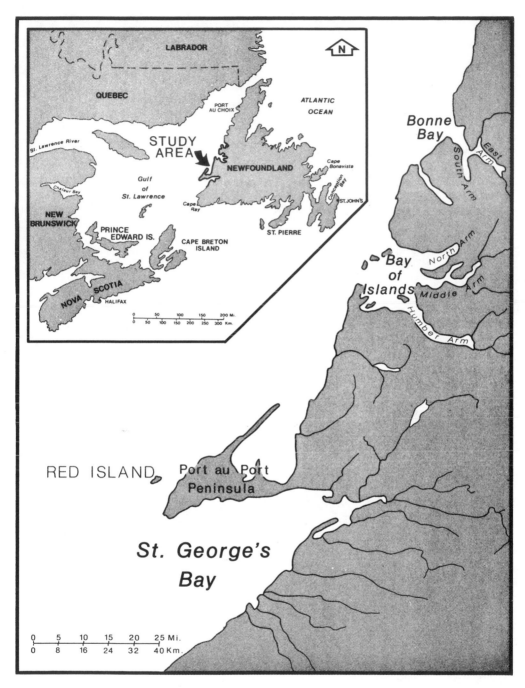

Figure 9–1 *Location*

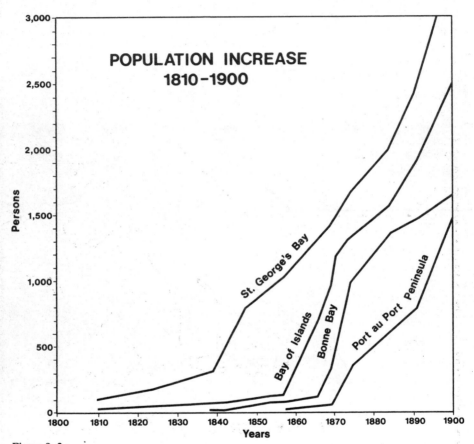

Figure 9–2

men o' war or from the fishing ships, who later married Acadian girls. A few Catholic Irish and Scots coming usually via Cape Breton also settled, but in 1850 the Catholic population of the bay was overwhelmingly French-speaking and was served by a French-speaking priest appointed that year.

Figure 9–3 shows the distribution of the two major groups: the Catholics were concentrated mainly in the inner bay and the Port au Port, while the Protestants inhabited the three Barrisways – Crabbes, Middle Brook, and Robinsons – as they did at the beginning of the century. In Sandy Point, the only harbour and the commercial hub of St. George's Bay, there was a mixed population with Protestants predominating. Opposite Sandy Point was a band of Micmacs from Cape Breton whose contacts with St. George's Bay extended back to the early 18th century when they came over seasonally to catch fur for the French. Apparently they were encouraged to settle in the bay by the British during and after the American War of Independence. Mainly French-speaking and Catholic, some intermarried with the local Acadians and French and were called "Jack A' Tars." Because they were primarily trappers of beaver and other fur-bearing animals far inland, their numbers in St. George's Bay fluctuated: 30 families were recorded in 1788, 150 persons in 1794, 100 in 1797, 30 in 1801, 70–80 in 1810, 97 in 1813, and 66 in 1830.[2] Besides trapping, the Indians also caught seals and caribou, made baskets and moccasins, and in winter caught eels, an important item in their diet.

North of St. George's Bay, settlement was sparse until the 1860s (Figs. 9–2 and 9–3). Seven heads of household were recorded in Humber Sound, Bay of Islands at the beginning of the 19th century; four of these came from southwest England, and three from the Burin Peninsula.[3] All were Protestant. A few other immigrants trickled in from the same source areas in subsequent decades with the population increasing from 36 persons in 1808 to only 86 three decades later; of the 19 householders then listed, 8 came from southwestern England (mainly Dorset) 4 from the Burin, 1 each from Burgeo and France and 5 were natives of the Sound. There was virtually no further in-migration until the 1860s; in 1857 only 3 of the 143 persons (22 families) settled in the area were born outside Newfoundland.

The pattern of immigration in Humber Sound was replicated in Bonne Bay, but settlement there was established later and was even less substantial. It is extremely unlikely that there was permanent settlement in Bonne Bay in the 18th century; in 1808 only one family was recorded. There were 5 families of southwest English origins in the bay in 1838 and another family of similar provenance in Trout River. The population (12 families: 90 persons) in 1857 was almost entirely derived from these early settlers.

After 1860 Bonne Bay, Bay of Islands, and Port au Port attracted a considerable number of immigrants from various source areas. St. George's Bay, however, grew largely through natural increase at a somewhat less precipitous pace. The most significant influx to these areas were the Catholic Gaelic-speaking settlers from Cape Breton of Highland Scottish provenance who occupied Highlands (Newfoundland) about the middle of the century and then Campbells Creek on the Port au Port Peninsula (mainly via Codroy) two to three decades later. The Acadian population of the inner bay multiplied rapidly and the number of French-speaking settlers was increased by a trickle of movement from Cape Breton and northwestern France (Appendix 9–1). Of the 750 Catholic children born in St. George's Bay and the peninsula between 1850–68, 68 percent were of Acadian paternity, 12 percent French,

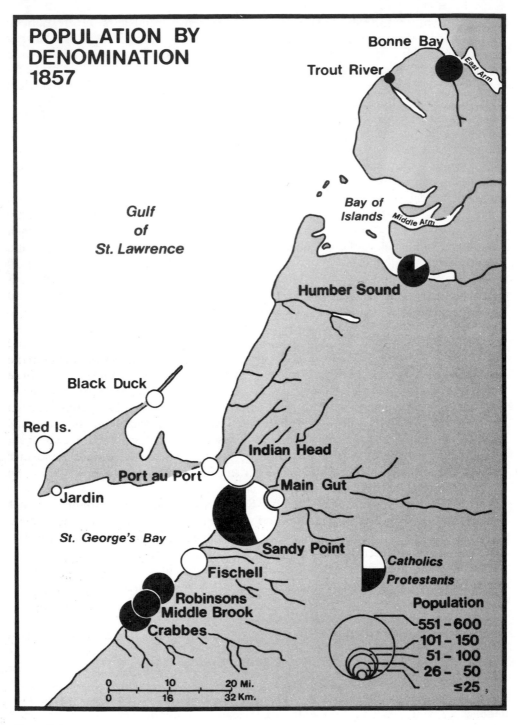

POPULATION BY
DENOMINATION
1857

Bonne Bay

Trout River

East Arm

Gulf
of
St. Lawrence

Bay of
Islands

Middle Arm

Humber Sound

Black Duck

Red Is.

Indian Head

Port au Port

Main Gut

Jardin

St. George's Bay

Sandy Point

Catholics
Protestants

Fischell

Population

Robinsons
Middle Brook

551 – 600

Crabbes

101 – 150
51 – 100
26 – 50
≤ 25

0   10   20 Mi.
0   16   32 Km.

Figure 9–3

9 percent Irish, 6 percent Scottish, 3 percent Micmac and 2 percent English.[4] Figures 9–3, 9–4, and 9–5 reveal the stability of the ethno-religious character of the outports in all areas during the second half of the 19th century, a spatial pattern that had its roots in the early part of the century. Overall, the Protestant proportion in St. George's Bay declined slightly after 1850, partly because of the in-migration of some Catholic Scots, Irish, French, and Acadians, and partly because of the departure of some Protestant families for the rapidly developing areas of the north.

The Port au Port Peninsula was sparsely inhabited until the 1870s (Figs. 9–2, 9–5). Six families were recorded there in 1857, 15 in 1866, 10 in 1869 and 20 in 1871.[5] According to the censuses the population trebled over the next few years, totalling 1600 persons by the end of the century (Appendix 9–2). This increase was largely a result of an influx of Acadians from Cape Breton and of French fishermen stationed on Red Island and Long Point who married local Acadian girls and settled. Apart from the inhabitants at Boswarlos and a few families around the isthmus, the population of the peninsula was almost entirely Catholic and mainly French-speaking.

Bay of Islands witnessed the most dramatic population increase after 1860 (Fig. 9–2), the total number growing from about 200 to 1000 by 1870 and to 1500 five years later. The Labrador stationer fishery provided most of the new settlers. Families from Conception Bay, especially Carbonear and Harbour Grace, and from other parts of the Avalon and east coast began to winter in Bonne Bay and Humber Sound after the summer fishery in Labrador. There was plenty of fuel in the shelter of the bays and the prospect of alternative winter employment in the commercial herring and logging operations. Similarly, fishermen from England who came to Labrador for the cod fishery began to winter on the west coast instead of re-crossing the Atlantic (Appendix 9–1). Even Labrador families, offshoots of the Conception Bay/southwest English fishery, joined the migrations down the Gulf and established permanent homes on the western shore. Other settlers came from Newfoundland's south coast, from St. George's Bay, and from Cape Breton and elsewhere in Nova Scotia, a natural extension of the earlier movement to St. George's Bay. The opening of a large sawmill in Corner Brook in 1865 brought loggers from the south shore of Nova Scotia and from the Restigouche Valley in northern New Brunswick. French fishermen, some of whom were winter caretakers for the French fleet, married local women and became residents. There were also some immigrants from Ireland, Wales, and Jersey.

Despite the diversity of source areas and the polyethnic character of the migrant stream, the proportion of Catholics to Protestants remained consistent throughout (Appendix 9–2). Irish from Ireland or from Conception Bay and other parts of the east coast, and French fishermen comprised the major Catholic element. There were few Acadians and Catholic Scots, in contrast to St. George's Bay. Most of the settlers from Nova Scotia and New Brunswick were of Scottish-Presbyterian background. Unlike many of the settlements in St. George's Bay, there was considerable interdigitation of families of varied background in the typical Bay of Islands outport and intermarriage was not uncommon. This initially heterogeneous character of the pioneer settlements reflects the rapidity of the colonization process and its essentially individualistic and uncoordinated nature.

Bonne Bay lay directly in the path of the south-flowing current of migration from Labrador to the Bay of Islands and some of this flow was siphoned into it. The periodicity of inflow and the growth of population in Bonne Bay mirrors that of the Bay of Islands (Fig. 9–2). Always the least populous of the western bays, it had only about

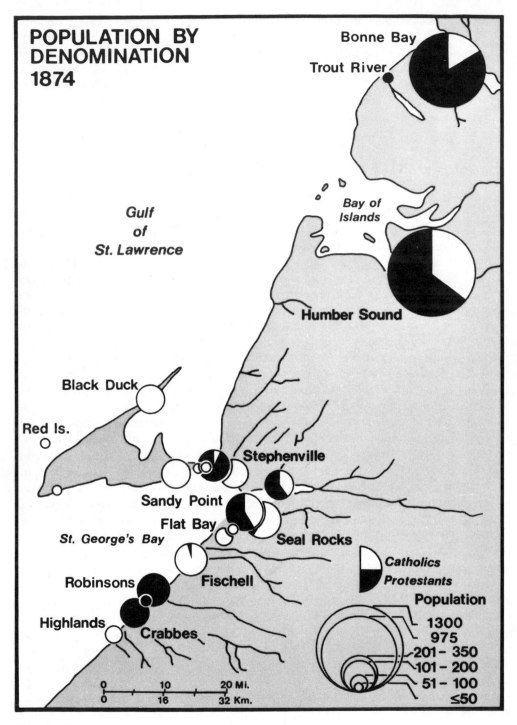

Figure 9–4

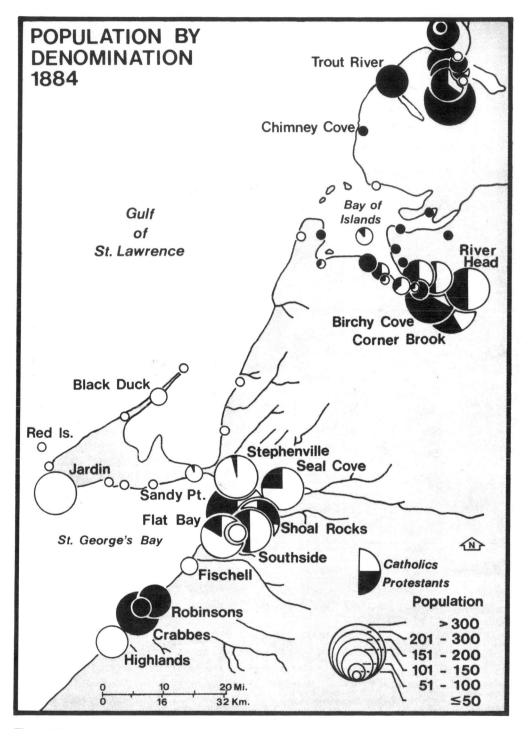

POPULATION BY
DENOMINATION
1884

Trout River

Chimney Cove

Gulf
of
St. Lawrence

Bay of
Islands

River
Head

Birchy Cove
Corner Brook

Black Duck

Red Is.

Jardin

Sandy Pt.

Stephenville
Seal Cove

Flat Bay

St. George's Bay

Shoal Rocks

Southside

Fischell

Catholics
Protestants

Population

Robinsons

Crabbes

Highlands

> 300
201 - 300
151 - 200
101 - 150
51 - 100
≤ 50

0   10   20 Mi.
0   16   32 Km.

Figure 9–5

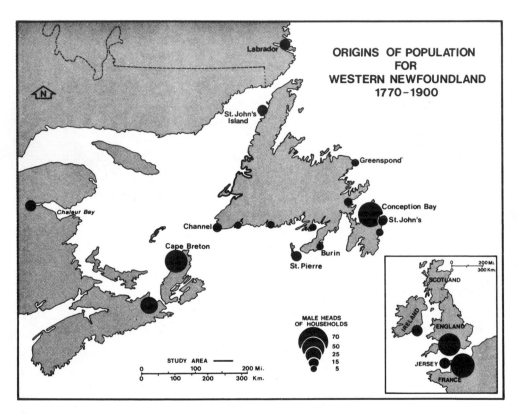

Figure 9–6

100 persons in 1860, and 350 a decade later, but with increased in-migration in the early 1870s, mainly as a result of a boom in the herring fishery, the total population rose to 1000 by 1875. By the end of the century there were over 1600 persons in the bay. Ethnically, these were more homogeneous than in the Bay of Islands. A considerable proportion of settlers came from the South Coast (Appendix 9–1), almost all of them being of Protestant English derivation and thereby reinforcing the pre-existing ethnic stock in the bay. Indeed the only major Catholic settlement, St. Joseph's, established mainly by Conception Bay Irish, was abandoned early in the present century.

Figure 9–6 summarizes evidence drawn from various sources (see Appendix 9–1) on the homelands of the people moving to the western shore. To some extent the Bay of Islands was the terminus or meeting point of two currents of migration along the coast. On the one hand Protestants from England and Conception Bay moved via Labrador south to Bonne Bay and the Bay of Islands, whilst Catholic French and Acadians and some Catholic Scots and Irish moved north to occupy St. George's Bay and the Port au Port. St. George's Bay attracted more Jerseymen and the Bay of Islands more Presbyterian Scots; all three bays were settled early by English emigrants. In the final analysis the most salient feature of the colonization of the west coast was the diversity of cultures; it was a migration low in volume by 19th century standards, but of high complexity. Strewn along this isolated littoral were immigrants from England (mainly from Dorset and Devon), Jersey, Normandy, Brittany, and elsewhere in northwestern France, and from southeastern Ireland; Micmacs and Acadians came from Cape Breton, Scots and Irish Catholics from Cape Breton, and Scots of Presbyterian background from peninsular Nova Scotia, Cape Breton, and northern New Brunswick; St. Pierrais; and lastly there were Newfoundlanders of English and sometimes Irish ancestry from a great variety of source areas and from Labrador. The next section seeks to explain the complexity of purpose underlying these various migrations.

II. THE PATTERNS OF RESOURCE UTILIZATION

Because of the diversity of source areas it is impossible to present clearly the factors influencing movement from the homelands. However, it can be assumed that in all these maritime areas (Fig. 9–6), economic pressure of some form was the major motivation. Furthermore, during the 19th century certain combinations of opportunity developed on the western shore which attracted these people. Different groups or individuals came to occupy the west coast sometimes for different reasons and, as we have seen, at different points in time. What follows is an account in rough chronological order of the emerging commercial opportunities (or activities) that attracted settlers initially to the coast.

Salmon and Fur

One of the first marine species to be caught commercially and to help initiate permanent settlement in all three bays was salmon. Early in the second half of the 18th century, fishermen from southwest England and Jersey joined the French in prosecuting the summer fishery along the western shore, and by at least the 1770s a handful of British fishermen began to winter in St. George's Bay, basing their economy primarily on winter trapping and the summer salmon fishery.[6] This tiny group operated mainly as winter caretakers for British mercantile concerns and only a few remained permanently in the bay. The search for salmon and fur extended the pattern of settlement and brought British settlers to the northern coast into White Bay, to coastal Labrador and along the south coast of the island.

The Treaty of Versailles redefined the French Shore in 1783 to include the area from Point Riche, north of Bonne Bay, to Cape Ray. Considerable friction arose between the British residents – now illegal to French eyes at least – and the migratory French fishermen over rights to catch salmon. In 1785 the French destroyed at least two salmon posts in St. George's Bay and ordered the settlers off the coast. Prior to British settlement the French had prosecuted the salmon fishery on the western shore and intensified their efforts after Versailles.[7] This attempt was interrupted by the Napoleonic Wars and the British quickly resumed control of the salmon fishery in the bay, moving north to establish similar enterprises in the Bay of Islands and after 1800 in Bonne Bay.

Although early estimates are crude and fragmentary, it appears that salmon catches per fisherman were initially high. In 1787, for example, a Dorset settler on the Humber River – probably the most prolific source of salmon on the west coast – salted 76 tierces in a season (Innis, 1954:215). Consistently through the first half of the 19th century, sources indicate that salmon was the chief commercial commodity in the three bays, but according to the records, yields fluctuated widely.[8] Close to 800 tierces were recorded in 1808, over half of which came from St. George's Bay; yet three years later the total catch recorded was only 370 tierces. Cormack (1822:92) reported about thirty salmon crews of two-three men scattered around St. George's Bay in 1822 and estimated the catch at roughly 300 tierces; subsequent estimates for the bay range from 500 tierces in the early 1840s to 200 tierces in 1848 and 1851. The average summer catch by the Bird mercantile enterprise at Bonne Bay in the early 1820s was about 160 tierces and less than half that amount two decades later. Despite the decline, salmon was still the most valuable commodity collected by Bird. Six settlers delivered £100 worth of salmon to the company in 1840, less than 1/5 the traditional amount, but still exceeding the combined value of oil and cod delivered by 14 dealers.[9]

The salmon fishery required less inputs of labour and capital than did cod and it was its distinct commercial appeal that induced British migratory fishermen to settle in so remote an area as the western shore in the late 18th and early 19th centuries. The mouths of brooks and rivers where salmon gathered became the foci for early permanent settlement, especially in St. George's Bay (Fig. 9–3). Nets were strewn at right angles from the shore in the coves beside the river mouths, or they were sometimes placed directly across the river. The season usually extended from late May to late July and was in direct competition with the cod fishery.

The continuing commercial importance of salmon is underlined by the renewed efforts of the French to oust the British residents after the Napoleonic Wars. The Birds, for example, expressed concern for the security of their salmon posts in 1816 and contemplated moving them from Bonne Bay to the Lower North Shore of Quebec where some of their salmon fishermen had been employed.[10] In 1821 the French did appropriate Birds' Bonne Bay station but the British government supported an appeal and confirmed the company's rights to the salmon fishery, a situation which the French did not subsequently contest.[11] Actually the French naval authorities encouraged the resident fishermen by granting them exclusive rights to salmon rivers on the French shore and sanctioning the transmission of those rights to heirs.[12]

There is little evidence of French interference in the salmon fishery after 1840.

There was, however, increasing internal competition for prime river sites even between potential heirs, and growing demands from residents for official recognition of their tenure from Britain.[13] Whether officially sanctioned or not, rights to rivers were often transmitted to descendants, effectively excluding later settlers from exploiting prime sites. Indeed, one of the notable features of the salmon fishery through the 19th century was the extent of tenurial control by descendants of early English and Jersey immigrants.[14]

After 1840 salmon yields declined, primarily because of over-fishing or lack of conservation. The practice of placing nets, weirs, or wooden racks across river mouths, or building dams with traps at both ends, became common in all three bays and often prevented salmon from spawning.[15] With the rise of the commercial herring fishery, the importance of salmon diminished further, but it was still caught in considerable quantities. Detailed censuses in 1874, 1884, 1891, and 1901, together with other occasional estimates give an idea of the total yields and spatial distribution of the catch (Appendix 9-3).[16] St. George's Bay remained the principal source for salmon, producing an average of 200–250 tierces per season. Settlements near the mouths of the longer rivers flowing into St. George's Bay were the most productive, although yields fluctuated through time. Only a few settlements (or families) on the Port au Port Peninsula were involved since the brooks there were small and unsuitable for spawning. Apart from the Humber River the most fertile locations in the Bay of Islands were on the river mouths in Middle and North Arm and the bulk of the salmon caught in Bonne Bay was at the mouth of the bay and up the East Arm.

The other important local commodity was fur. Indeed, long before the settlers came, commercial exploitation of the fur resources of the west coast was taking place. Early in the 18th century, Montagnais Indians from the Lower North Shore were enlisted by the French for winter furring. Armed with provisions and gear, a band of about seventy of them would cross the Strait of Belle Isle in shallops each September and range as far south as St. George's Bay, returning with their furs in April.[17] This French-Canadian-style fur trade did not last too long, however. The most productive furriers in the 18th and early 19th centuries were the Micmacs from Cape Breton, who were recruited by the French at Louisbourg, by the migratory French fishermen, and occasionally by New Englanders. They were taken across Cabot Strait each fall to Cape Ray or elsewhere in southwestern Newfoundland from whence they ranged over the vast inland waterways, sometimes as far north as White Bay or Notre Dame Bay and then back to the south coast.[18]

The British authorities maintained that the French-Indian fur trade on the island was illegal, politically dangerous, and a loss of potential revenue; they proposed proscribing Indian participation. As early as 1763, they maintained that their own winter men were superior trappers and produced a better pelt than the Micmacs who, moreover, were exterminating the beaver, the principal source of fur. Indian control of trapping areas, at least close to the shore, was gradually appropriated by the settlers, some of whom found furring as lucrative as fishing in the pioneer phase. Frequent reference is made to the trapping of beaver, red fox, patch, black and silver fox, lynx, otter, marten, and muskrat in Bird's Bonne Bay ledger.[19] It is unlikely, however, that fur remained a significant staple for more than a brief period for the majority of settlers. Prices for fur declined after 1840 and in 1843 Bird, for example, advised his agent in Bonne Bay to discontinue supplying furriers there because of the trappers' rising credit.

Trapping persisted as a winter activity, however, and like the salmon fishery, was prosecuted mainly by a few descendants of the early English settlers who had established proprietary rights to locally recognized trapping areas.[20] Trapping was usually conducted several miles inland, the early settlers sometimes having two homes, one on the coast to prosecute the summer fishery and farm the land, and a winter house in the woods where fuel, fur, and game were available. Seals were an important source of fur and oil in the settlements fringing the northeastern corner of the Gulf of St. Lawrence and winter sealing was of vital importance in promoting year-round settlement there. Bonne Bay and the bays to the south lay beyond the zone of commercial sealing. Although late in the 19th century a few sealing vessels were sent to the ice, sealing never became a tradition along this section of the western shore.

Cod

Little is known of the extent of the French involvement in the summer cod fishery along this coast prior to the advent of the British there early in the second half of the 18th century. However, it is certain that by that time the French had accumulated generations of experience in the area. Following the explorations and detailed descriptions of the coast by Captain Cook, British fishing fleets began regularly to pass round Cape Ray into the Gulf,[21] provoking conflict with the French that endured through the 19th century. Sedentary settlement grew out of these seasonal voyages when local resources such as salmon and fur made year-round residence feasible. Most of these first settlers continued to fish for cod. For example, all but 3 of the 20 heads of household resident in the study area were reported involved in the cod fishery in 1808, but when one considers that over 60 fishermen were employed, the total yield of 640 quintals for the three bays is very low.

There is widespread evidence that in St. George's Bay, at least, the cod fishery was only a minor commercial adjunct throughout the period under review.[22] The paucity of cod production in St. George's Bay contrasts sharply with the high yields on the Port au Port Peninsula after 1850. In 1857, for example, the only catch reported in the bay was at Sandy Point, where 800 quintals, an average of 5 quintals per fisherman was dried as compared to an average of over 50 quintals per fisherman on the peninsula.

By this time the herring fishery was the major commercial activity in the inner bay, but was rarely prosecuted on Port au Port. However, partly as a reaction to the uncertainty of the herring migrations in the bay, the settlers began to emphasize the cod fishery in the late 1860s, and even launched a small Labrador fishery.[23] Although the average catch per fisherman still remained less than one-quarter the average on the Port au Port, total production increased steadily from about 2,000 quintals in the mid-sixties to 3,000 a decade later and to a peak exceeding 10,000 by 1884 (see Appendix 9–3). Subsequently the rise of the lobster fishery affected cod production and the average household catch dropped back to 6 or 7 quintals in the bay and Port au Port isthmus area.

Apart from competition from other local species, the underdevelopment of the cod fishery in the inner bay may be explained by the distance between the settlements and the fertile fishing grounds off the headlands and at the mouth of the bay, the absence of harbours, and competition from schooners from Newfoundland's south coast, Nova Scotia, New England, and especially northwestern France.

Some of the same problems beset the cod fishery in the Bay of Islands. Settlement was strategically located in Humber Arm for the exploitation of salmon, herring, fur and timber, but was poorly placed in relation to the rich cod grounds around the islands and headlands at the mouth of the bay. Throughout the 19th century this distance was the principal factor in the sluggish growth rate of the cod fishery. Only fifty quintals were cured in 1808 and three decades later, ten of the eighteen fishermen recorded caught cod.

Herring and salmon were far more important. As settlement expanded the fishermen began to exploit the more distant grounds at the mouth of the bay. There is considerable evidence, both archival and according to local oral tradition, of fishermen, sometimes with their families, moving to the various coves near the mouth of the bay to fish for cod each summer.[24] Fishermen exploiting the nearer grounds were centralized on Woods Island and returned each week-end to their farms and families in the Sound, but fishermen prosecuting the "outside" areas usually migrated to the coves and harbours from Serpentine River to Cape St. Gregory each summer. Eventually, sedentary settlements were established in some of these places, such as Lark Harbour. After 1865 settlers went further afield in their quest for cod. The coast of Labrador had, by this time, become a major focus for fishermen from eastern Newfoundland and other areas, with the Humber Sound fishermen gradually joining the seasonal flow.[25] Only a few schooners left for Labrador during the early period, but by the end of the century close to half the total cod catch came from there. Moreover, the seasonal migration helped initiate a movement of other people fishing in Labrador to the Bay of Islands.

In comparison to St. George's Bay the cod catch in the Bay of Islands was high, averaging 30 quintals per fisherman in the late 1850s, 40 by 1870, and 60 in 1872. But partly because of failures in Labrador and the spectacular rise of a commercial herring fishery in areas of the bay, cod production declined sharply after 1875, when average yields dwindled to less than 10 quintals per fisherman (see Appendix 9–3). The total catch ranged from about 1,000 quintals in 1857 to 10,000 in 1874 and then dropped to less than 5,000 despite the rapid increase in population. Towards the end of the century the fishery was based mainly on Woods Island and Lark Harbour at the mouth of the bay.

Throughout the 19th century the development of the cod fishery in Bonne Bay resembled that of the Bay of Islands. Settlement was initially established "inside" the south arm, away from the productive cod grounds at the mouth of the bay. Rocky Harbour and Trout River, the main producers of cod, were the only settlements strategically placed for the exploitation of the fishery. The Bird ledger reveals that some planters fished for cod, but it was a secondary commercial commodity until 1850. With the introduction of larger vessels after 1870 (the number of schooners increased from two to eighteen in 1874) and the consequent expansion of the cod fishery northwards to St. John's Island and Labrador, the catch increased, fluctuating from 2,000 to 5,000 quintals (see Appendix 9–3).[26] There is a widespread oral tradition about this seasonal trek northwards; it was essentially a family migration and most families in Bonne Bay were involved at one stage or other. It is difficult to determine whether these migrations induced or were induced by the influx of east coast and other fishermen via Labrador to Bonne Bay; but the Labrador link was a major force in the peopling of both bays. By 1890 the Labrador fishery had declined, partly because of a series of low catches. Only one schooner left from Bonne Bay in 1891 as opposed to nine in 1884, and the total catch dropped to fourteen quintals per household by the end of the century. As in the Bay of Islands there was a gradual centralization of the fishery in the "outer" settlements such as Trout River, Norris Point, and especially Rocky Harbour, "the premier spot on the coast for cod."[27]

The French Cod Fishery

One of the major themes in the settlement history of the west coast was the special position which migratory cod fishermen from France occupied. The British had agreed by treaty (Utrecht 1713, Paris 1763, Versailles 1783) to allow the French to land and dry their fish on a section of the Newfoundland coast. In Paris the British agreed to prevent their subjects from settling the Treaty Shore and competing with French fishermen, a clause more explicitly stated at Versailles. After 1783 settlement on the west coast was illegal. Another (poorly defined) clause stating that the British could not "interfere" with the French fishery on the Treaty Shore gave rise to French claims of "exclusive" rights to the shore, and British claims to "concurrent" rights to fish there. Throughout the 19th century this conflict between two powerful nations remained a central issue in the development (or underdevelopment) of the west coast.[28]

Despite the application of bounties, the French fishery in Newfoundland began to decline in the last quarter of the 18th century and collapsed completely during the Napoleonic Wars. Bounties were increased after the war and the fishery expanded at a rapid rate. Along the west coast, the infrequency of good harbours and headlands discouraged the French so that their fleet was concentrated overwhelmingly in the Petit Nord. In 1828, for example, only 10 percent of the total migratory personnel operated on the west coast (see Table 9–1).

TABLE 9–1

The French Fishery, 1828

	Men	Merchants	Vessels	Tonnage	Boats[29]
N.E. Coast	9,378	83	228	30,530	1,804
West Coast	1,182	28	32	4,180	249
Banks	1,060	25	53	7,500	—
St. Pierre	900			2,000	200
	12,520			44,210	

They had summer stations or rooms on Codroy Island, on Red Island, Three Rock Cove and Long Point on the Port au Port, at Little Port, Lark Harbour and Tweed Island in the Bay of Islands, and at Point Riche, north of Bonne Bay. Red Island was the most consistently productive station in the study area; it was controlled by a St. Pierrais merchant from 1825–50 who usually placed 150–200 St. Pierrais fishermen there each summer.[30] Fleets of six to ten French ships sometimes fished the waters from Port au Port Bay to Bonne Bay,[31] but the fishery there was poor and the fleet would move north to Port au Choix, the main station for the French on the west coast.

During the war the British gave fishermen permission to prosecute the Treaty Shore and build fishing premises there. The French were faced with a resident British community on their return and conflict over rights arose. Periodically the French tried to appropriate the salmon posts, already alluded to, and threatened to destroy the settlements and confiscate all gear.[32] French-British relationships on the coast, however, were characterized more by co-operation than by conflict. Two distinct ecological zones existed, the residents exploiting the fur, timber, soil, salmon, and herring in the shelter of the arms or inner bays, while the French were located on islands in the Gulf, prosecuting the summer cod fishery. Whenever the settlers interfered with the cod fishery, the French usually retaliated; otherwise there was a record of amity and even commercial exchange between the two groups.

In an effort to avoid British duties on imports, the settlers were willing to risk illicit trading with the French visitors. A French trader from Granville established a store at Sandy Point in 1828, brought out men and provisions each summer from France, and supplied local residents, especially the French-speaking population of the bay.[33] The settlers all along the shore sold herring as bait to the French, and occasionally lumber or produce off their small farms. "From time immemorial it has been the custom of the inhabitants of this shore to barter with the captains of French vessels, exchanging lumber, oars, masts and bait for salt, flour, meat, other provisions, and fishing gear."[34]

Resistance to the French did not stem initially from the residents, who were generally indifferent or ignorant of the political and legal situation, but from mercantile interests now centred in St. John's who were jealous of the illicit but lucrative traffic in bait on the south and west coasts, and were fearful that the French might capture traditional markets overseas. Using the Legislative Assembly in St. John's as their mouthpiece, they complained bitterly about French interloping. Although the British government did not wish to endanger Anglo-French relations, they did eventually legislate against the bait traffic, forcing the French from the south coast to the Treaty Shore where the resident population had been increasing rapidly, and hence intensifying competition for all marine species.

Relations with the residents worsened with the advent of lobster as a commercially exploitable species. Threats to remove the residents from all three bays were renewed and even in Bonne Bay, where the French never had a room, the settlers were warned not to fish beyond the mouth of the bay.[35] As late as 1894, the French had a plan to remove the British settlers from St. George's Bay and replace them with St. Pierrais while retaining the French-speaking Acadians in the bay. At no time, however, was the effort actually made to dislodge the residents, and with increasing support from St. John's and London government officials, and a waning French fishery, the occasional threats to settlers were ineffectual. Indeed, there is little evidence that the French hindered the growth of settlement on the west coast, except perhaps on the headland coves close to the cod grounds. The French presence was only seasonal, Paris was far away, and the settlers too numerous and well-established to be banished. It is likely, in the final analysis, that the French promoted, more than they stifled, settlement growth through trade with the residents; and a number of French fishermen settled on the shore.

However, the legal and political situations did retard the extension of government institutions and other amenities of a sedentary society and in this way impeded settlement somewhat. It was not until after 1850 that schools and churches were introduced (apart from those in Sandy Point) and magistrates appointed. Also there was no political representation until late in the century. The lawless state of the area was a source of worry to settlers and traders alike.

Herring and Lobster

After 1860 herring became the commercial staple in all three bays and was the most important factor in luring people to settle on the coast. Herring was used mainly as

TABLE 9–2

St. George's Bay Herring Fishery, 1847–1901
(Yields given in thousands of barrels)

Year	Yield	Year	Yield
1847	20	1874	19
1848	10	1875	20
1850	26	1883	15
1851	20	1884	22
1857	14	1885	26
1858	14	1888	42
1864	20	1890	20
1866	24	1891	12
1872	30	1901	17

bait, particularly after the introduction of trawls and the expansion of the New England, Nova Scotian, and French banks fleets. Late in the century smoked and pickled herring became significant in the diet of human beings, especially in northeastern, urban America.

In St. George's Bay, the commercial herring fishery dates back to the 1820s and from 1850 on was the principal source of income, following the repeal of the export tax on Newfoundland bait to Nova Scotia (1846) and to America (1854).[36] Yields fluctuated, but the annual catch in the bay normally exceeded 20,000 barrels (see Appendix 9–3). The fishery usually commenced in May and lasted from two to five weeks. The herring was netted almost exclusively in the inner bay, particularly around the settlements near Sandy Point which was itself the centre, accounting for one-third of the total catch in the bay. Herring was rarely caught on the Port au Port, or even on the north coast of inner St. George's Bay.

The rise of the commercial herring fishery in the Bay of Islands and Bonne Bay occurred later but developed more rapidly. Unlike the fishery in St. George's Bay, here the herring could be caught in great quantities through the ice in the arms of the bays; it was the development of this winter fishery that induced summer fishermen in Labrador to settle in these areas. The winter season extended from January to March, but herring could also be taken in May/June and again in October/November. In response to the quickening demand of the American urban market and the banking vessels, herring catches soared after 1860, with occasional annual yields of 50,000–60,000 barrels in the Bay of Islands.[37]

This boom resulted in a spate of applications for land grants, and the governor, touring the area in 1866, predicted a rapid increase in population. At its peak in about 1870, the herring fishery was described as a mine of wealth and the chief support of the inhabitants. At first, it was conducted primarily around the terminus of Humber Arm, but later some settlers moved north each October to meet the herring on its slow migration southwards along the coast and netted them in the northern and middle arms of the bay. As the herring moved south to Humber Arm, the fishermen abandoned their fall camps and factories and continued to pursue the herring from their permanent homes.

Herring migrations, however, were extremely complex, uncertain, and poorly understood. Between 1877 and 1884, the herring stock dropped sharply in the Bay of Islands, and over sixty families were forced on relief.[38] A similar slump occurred in

TABLE 9–3

Bay of Islands Herring Fishery, 1857–1901

Year	1857	1864	1866	1868	1870	1874	1875	1876	1884	1891	1901
Yield (1000 brls)	1½	30	30	50	60	30	20	50	10	18	73

Bonne Bay where production had been the highest of all three bays up to 1875. The sudden decline in herring terminated the inflow of settlers to these areas and initiated out-migration. The herring did return, however, to the west coast before the end of the century; the Bay of Islands, especially, capitalized on the introduction of the railway for fast delivery of herring-on-ice to the Canadian and American urban markets.

Lobster

Late in the 19th century, lobster, formerly used as bait by the French, became a fashionable item of diet, and emerged as an important commercial species on the western shore. It was a Nova Scotian enterprise initially, but the techniques of production were borrowed from America's east coast where the canning of lobster began about 1840. A small amount was canned by the Nova Scotians in the Bay of Islands as early as 1856, but it was not until the 1880s that the industry became commercially sound. No other enterprise on the west coast developed so rapidly: as compared with only twelve canning factories along the entire coast in 1887, four years later there were seventy-six in the study area alone, valued at $30,000 and employing seven hundred persons in the processing sector.[39] These factories ranged from small family-owned structures valued at $100 to mercantile plants worth over $2,000 employing up to 80 persons, and packing up to 2,500 cases in a season. Most factories were valued at less than $400.

Initially Nova Scotian entrepreneurs and capital dominated the industry; skilled personnel and servants or labourers were brought over each season, but Newfoundland merchants were quick to invest and recruited local labour to prosecute the fishery. Entrepreneurs were assigned certain sections of the coast by the government; they supplied local fishermen with the requisite gear to procure the lobster for their factories and hired local labour, including women and children, to process the catch.[40] There were forty such concessions in the study area in 1893, twenty-five of which were operated by resident west-coast traders based mainly in Sandy Point, ten by St. John's merchants, and the remainder by Halifax entrepreneurs.

Gradually the local lobster fishermen began to take over the canning process, purchasing tins and other necessities from the merchants, and a multitude of small family-operated factories sprang up along the shore. The industry also generated some local winter employment involving the manufacture of pots or traps and wooden cases for packing, and the building of factories. Undoubtedly the lobster fishery developed at a propitious time when many families were almost destitute because of the decline of the traditional cod and herring fisheries, a fact reflected by the rapid entry of local labour into the new industry. Relief payments were reduced and in some outports, such as Trout River, a rise in population was related to the commercial exploitation of lobster.[41]

Port au Port isthmus was the most productive lobster area on the coast, processing about one third of the total catch. In 1891 nearly 30,000 traps or pots were set in the study area and over 10,000 cases of lobster (about 200 lobsters per case) were packed and exported. Otherwise the distribution of the enterprise was fairly diffuse, with higher yields in the settlements close to, or facing, the Gulf such as Trout River, Lark Harbour, and Chimney Cove, in the larger outports in Humber Arm, in Sandy Point, and in the Barrisways.

The rapid growth rate of the 1880s was not sustained in the subsequent decade, apart from the Port au Port Peninsula and Bonne Bay. Local tradition attributed the decline in production in the Bay of Islands and especially in St. George's Bay (Appendix 9–4), to a reduction in stocks. The large factories collapsed because some entrepreneurs, worried over French threats and dissatisfied with returns on initial investments, withdrew their support. Often these factories were rapidly taken over by new owners and production managers. One such example was at Highlands where a fully equipped factory was offered for sale after two years in operation.[42]

Because lobster was caught in cod grounds and clashed seasonally with the cod fishery, friction arose between resident cod fishermen and lobstermen and between residents and the French fishermen. The latter disputed the residents' rights to catch lobster and established a few factories on the coast, mainly at Port au Choix and St. John's Island but also on the Port au Port Peninsula and in the Bay of Islands.[43] Rarely were more than sixty men involved in the two latter areas and they combined cod fishing with catching lobster. Three St. Pierre merchants controlled the lobster factories and the personnel were mainly St. Pierrais, but they also recruited local labour. The French were not consistent in their attitude to a resident lobster fishery: on one hand, they threatened the settlers and even destroyed their factories, while on the other, they gave some entrepreneurs permission to build.[44] Opposition to a resident lobster industry was not confined to the French. Resident cod fishermen in Rocky Harbour, for example, initially objected to the commercial lobster fishery on the basis that lobster was part of their traditional bait, the pots were encroaching on their cod nets and the offal interfering with cod and herring migrations.[45] The commercial success of the lobstermen eventually convinced these conservative cod fishermen to enter the industry themselves.

Logging, Farming, and Mining

Writers extolling the attractions of the west coast for potential settlement after 1860 emphasized the wealth of its forest and mineral resources, and the fertility of the soil. This literature emerged at a time when Newfoundland was endeavouring to diversify its economy, which for centuries had relied on the cod fishery. Following the boom in world cod markets during the Napoleonic Wars, the production of cod per capita began to decline and in the course of the century continued to drop at an alarming, if uneven, rate (Ryan, 1973:73). Newfoundland's population quintupled through the 19th century and the long-settled eastern harbours and coves, especially, became overcrowded. The inability of the traditional economy to absorb the increasing labour force caused eyes to turn to the undeveloped terrestrial resources of western New-foundland for economic salvation. There was an intensive political effort in St. John's to develop these resources, an ambition especially articulated in the proposal to build a railway from St. John's to St. George's Bay. This enthusiasm for "western" development was fed by often exaggerated reports from scientific surveys of land resources and by the somewhat visionary viewpoints presented by visitors and residents of the western shore being the new frontier[46] (Brosnan, 1948:56; Hiller, 1972:15–18).

Among the resources most lauded was timber, and there is little doubt that it was of critical importance in the establishment of permanent settlement on the west coast. As elsewhere in the traditional economy of rural Newfoundland, timber was the basic material of the settlers' production technology. The dwelling house and ancillary outbuildings, the fishing premises and other structures on the foreshore were fashioned out of wood, as were most farm tools, fences, fishing gear, boats, schooners, and transport vehicles. Fish was packed in wooden containers for export, and even house furniture and kitchen utensils were mainly wooden.

The forest, of course, was the main source of fuel. In parts of Conception Bay and especially in Labrador, an adequate supply of timber was not always readily available, and oral tradition suggests that the heavily forested areas surrounding the inner arms of Bonne Bay and the Bay of Islands was a factor in the decision to settle here permanently. A greater stimulus developed in the latter areas in 1865, however, with the establishment by Halifax entrepreneurs of a large sawmill, valued at over $40,000, in Corner Brook. Excellent stands of white pine and yellow birch, fir, spruce, and hazel were to be found along the Humber Valley. As early as 1808 a survey of this area and St. George's Bay confirmed the suitability of the timber for shipbuilding, and the viability of a sawmill industry on the Humber was assessed in 1847.[47] Six years later an application was made by two Nova Scotians for exclusive cutting rights $1^1/_2$ miles on either side of the Humber and for a grant of land to provide food for oxen and loggers.

When operations finally got under way in 1865 the logs were cut close to the river, floated to the Sound, and sawn into boards up to 4 feet in breadth, or into spars 60 feet long and $2^1/_2$ feet in diameter.[48] Initially, most of the loggers, carpenters, and other personnel came from peninsular Nova Scotia or from the Restigouche Valley in northern New Brunswick, areas long associated with commercial logging. Over 30 families from Restigouche were brought in by an entrepreneur and settled in the Sound. As the lumber enterprise progressed, up to 100 men were employed, producing from 3–5 million board feet and up to 1,000 tons of lumber annually. The timber was sold mainly in Boston, Halifax, St. John's, Liverpool and Ireland, and was used locally for constructional timbers, shingles, spars, staves, hoops, and even laths for lobster pots. (A smaller mill, established also in the 1860s across the Sound in Summerside, also catered to the local market.)

Despite complaints over the rapid depletion of pine through wasteful cutting techniques, both mills continued to operate, with the Corner Brook plant changing ownership several times before the construction of the paper mill there in 1925. A number of smaller sawmills were established in all three bays before the end of the 19th century. Winter unemployment was one of the major problems in the traditional Newfoundland economy, and since commercial logging was essentially a winter activity it was an important stimulus to year-round settlement.

Because of the abundant supply of good timber, the construction of schooners became a popular activity originating in the early 19th century when Jerseymen built vessels in St. George's Bay. With the rapid growth in the labour force after 1860, vessel construction became important commercially. Between 1873 and 1891, over 80 vessels, averaging 45 tons, were built in the study area (see Appendix 9–5).[49] Over half of these schooners were built in Bonne Bay, but the largest were built in the Bay of Islands (averaging 60 tons). A Nova Scotian trader in Summerside produced vessels of up to 180 tons, employing Nova Scotian labour; Halifax was a major market, but St. John's merchants also became involved in the industry on the west coast.

The only other commercial wood-working operation was the manufacture of wooden containers for provisions and fish. An enormous number of barrels were required for the herring fishery. The settlers not only supplied their own needs, but carried on a brisk trade with the merchants.[50] Barrel-making was a labour-intensive operation carried on in the woods in winter and family migrations inland were associated with this activity from the beginnings of settlement.

On an island where many provisions were imported, and their supply being limited and uncertain, the possibilities for commercial farming on the west coast were widely discussed. Early visitors such as Cormack, Wix, and Jukes were enthusiastic about the climate and the natural fertility of the soil. Cormack described the rich intervale soils in St. George's Bay as suitable for the cultivation of potatoes, barley, oats, and even wheat, while Wix, who had travelled widely in Newfoundland, maintained the west coast had the most cultivable soil on the island. In 1847 the Surveyor General estimated that it cost £15 to clear an acre of land around St. John's, but only one-sixth that amount in St. George's Bay which, he suggested, could support 200,000 persons.[51] Later in the century, as the fishery worsened, farming was seen as the potential keystone of the west coast economy and suggestions for a comprehensive road network along the shore and near interior were proposed.[52] Sears (Brosnan, 1948), for example, maintained that a road from Port au Basques through St. George's Bay area and the Humber Valley to Notre Dame Bay could be built for £10,000 and would bring £60,000 worth of land into agricultural production. Farming remained essentially a subsistence activity, however, a condition predicted by Rev. Jeffrey who cautioned against the exaggerated reports of contemporary observers, pointing out that whatever superiority might exist was as much a result of hard work as a consequence of nature.[53]

The major aim of the settlers was to become as self-supporting as possible in foodstuffs, thereby diminishing their dependence on the merchants for winter provisions. This goal was achieved in St. George's Bay whose extensive intervale soil made farm production more successful than in any other area – in marked contrast to the paucity of agriculture in the two northern bays (see Appendix 9–6). Most families grew enough potatoes, cabbage, turnip, and other small vegetables to last the household for a year, and kept enough cows for milk and butter and an adequate store of cattle, sheep, and pigs for meat.

The volume of farm production was by no means uniform within the Bay and there was considerable internal exchange and sale of produce. The Acadians, especially along the north shore of the inner bay, were good farmers, as were the English and Jersey settlers in the Barrisways who shared with the inhabitants of Codroy Valley the distinction of being among the most productive farmers in Newfoundland throughout the 19th century.[54] Each household here worked an average of 8–10 acres, kept 3–4 cows, the same number of cattle, a horse or oxen, 8–10 sheep, and 2–3 pigs. A local market existed at Sandy Point, where cultivable land was scarce, but farm produce from the Barrisways and elsewhere in the Bay was sent as far away as St. John's.

This agricultural tradition was reinforced by the arrival of the Scots in Highlands (and later in Campbell's Creek) who, in the 1860s, competed for land with the inhabitants of the Barrisways. The Scots eventually cleared more land and raised more farm produce and livestock per capita than any other cultural group in the area. Late in the 19th century, agriculture became important on the Port au Port Peninsula. Many Acadians arrived with the intention of farming, bringing with them their cattle, sheep, and looms. They found they could grow the traditional crops of their Cape Breton homeland, and some observers maintained they were better farmers than the English.[55] Indeed, farming in that region was so successful that towards the end of the century it was suggested that Sandy Point be relocated on the peninsula to avail itself of the produce there, and that the railway be extended to Stephenville to facilitate the export of agricultural goods from the region.[56]

In contrast, farming in the Bay of Islands and Bonne Bay regions was restricted by the sharp rise of the land from the shore. But wherever the slopes inclined gradually, the land was usually improved for farming, with low-lying areas at the head of the arms providing the best sites. Throughout the 19th century, the average household production was about one-fifth that of St. George's Bay. Most settlers worked one or two acres – not enough to support a family over the year. Sheep were fairly plentiful, but few families kept cattle or pigs, especially in Bonne Bay. The absence of animals meant heavy dependence on the merchant. In periods of economic distress, as in the late 1870s when the herring fishery failed, there was a greater emphasis on agriculture.[57] Nova Scotian entrepreneurs in the Bay of Islands introduced some degree of agricultural specialization: one merchant established a farm at Gillams to feed his staff and there was a similar enterprise associated with the mill in Corner Brook. A few Nova Scotian families settled in the Humber Valley, near Deer Lake, and raised a wide variety of crops including potatoes, cabbage, turnip, wheat, oats, corn, peas, beans, carrots, parsnip, lettuce, savoury, parsley, thyme, and asparagus, as well as livestock and poultry.[58] They considered conditions better there than in the homeland, and believed that if roads were built and a proper system of land grants adopted, there would be a major influx of Nova Scotian farmers and loggers to the area.

The colonial government's efforts to diversify the economy after 1860 was best exemplified in its interest in mining. Much of the debate on mineral development focused on the west coast where geologists and others reported important deposits.[59] Coal, limestone, gypsum, and lead were found in St. George's Bay; and coal, iron, limestone, lead, copper, marble, slate, and asbestos in the Bay of Islands. The proposed railway to the west was linked to the concept of industrialization through exploitation of these mineral resources. Politicians predicted that mining would ultimately surpass the fishery as the most important commercial enterprise on the island, and investors applied for mining concessions. A leading St. John's businessman, C. F. Bennett, opened a lead mine near Port au Port, employing thirty men, but the enterprise was discontinued after a few years, probably because of French objections.[60] Towards the end of the century, a copper mine was established at York Harbour, Bay of Islands, employing over three hundred men at its peak, and a company from Swansea, Wales, opened a slate quarry at Summerside. However, neither operation lasted long: the British government's continued reluctance to endorse grants on the Treaty Shore stymied mineral exploitation to some extent, but most deposits were either not exploitable economically, or investors were unwilling or had insufficient capital to invest in mineral development.

One of the major characteristics of resource utilization on the western shore was the multiplicity of resources exploited. Virtually all were exploited seasonally, often in combinations as they became available. Certain resources or combinations were, moreover, segregated spatially and their availability varied through the century. This complex pattern is schematized as follows:

Resources	Location	Time
1. Fur(d)* Game(s)* and Wood(i)*	Interior	Winter
2. Agriculture(s) and Salmon(d)	River mouths	Summer
3. Herring(i)	Inner arms	Fall/Winter/Spring
4. Cod(d) and lobster(i)	Bays, Gulf	Summer

*d (declining after 1850); i (increasing); s (stable 1800–1900)

These resources lay roughly in zones following the coastline: deep in the interior were fur and game, then wood, then agriculture and salmon, followed by herring, then lobster, and cod out in the Gulf. There was also rough summer pasture in the interior, but it required only a modicum of labour. Settlement was strategically located on the shore along the line dividing marine from terrestrial resources. It was accessible to long-distance marine transport and contiguous to the foreshore with its harvest of caplin, squid, and kelp and to the small farms (niche 2) which were vital to survival.

Because of seasonal synchronism and the spatial segregation of resources, settlers could not possibly exploit them all; on the other hand, no single resource could support a family for a year. Certain combinations were chosen which varied not only through time and from bay to bay, but also within bays and even individual settlements. The major discord occurred between niches 1 and 3 and between 2 and 4 (diagram above), although some form of farming figured in all combinations. It was generally not feasible for settlers in the Bay of Islands, for example, to log commercially and fish for herring beneath the ice, or to farm in the Humber Valley and fish for cod, or to prosecute simultaneously the salmon and cod fisheries. In the same way, there was competition between the spring herring fishery in St. George's Bay and the early cod fishery there. Seasonal competition was somewhat diminished, however, because some resources, although exploited at the same time of year, were commercially popular at different times in the 19th century. Fur was declining, for example, when herring was on the rise, and lobster became popular when both salmon and cod were on the wane. It may well be, of course, that the decline of one species was initiated by the rise of another.

The spatial range of resources also restricted or influenced combinations. Although settlers could conceivably exploit both extremities, trapping deep in the interior in winter, planting crops on the coast in spring and then migrating to the headlands and islands in the Gulf, or to Labrador, for the summer cod fishery, such an adaptation was rare. Settlers sought to minimize seasonal movement by exploiting contiguously located resources as much as possible. But because individual resources were often insubstantial and uncertain, settlers were frequently compelled to move temporarily from their permanent homes and exploit distant resources. Sometimes these seasonal shifts resulted in the creation of new settlements, as in the coves and harbours in the Bay of Islands by cod fishermen from Humber Sound; and sites were sometimes occupied for a few years and then abandoned, as in the case of the ephemeral herring settlements in Middle and North Arm.

The complex patterns of resource utilization are matched by the ethnic complexity of the population on the western shore, but there is no clear correlation between them. Certain groups, however, can be associated with particular combinations or niches: the early English and Jersey settlers emphasized salmon and fur with subsistence logging and farming and later they switched to herring; the French dominated the migratory cod fishery, whereas the Micmacs based their economy on trapping. Both Scots and Acadians developed farming and the latter depended greatly on the herring fishery. Most of the loggers and farmers in Humber Sound were Nova Scotians and New Brunswick Scots of Presbyterian background, and the herring and cod fishermen of both Bonne Bay and Bay of Islands came mainly via Labrador.

Even if some groups developed distinctive patterns of resource use initially, many soon lost this identity in the harsh struggle for a livelihood on the frontier. Despite the diversity of exploitable resources and the breadth and vitality of the traditional subsistence sector, the settlers could never become completely self-supporting and it was essential, in order to survive, to continue the commercial economy. The absence of self-sufficiency sustained exogenic trade. Most immigrants adapted quickly to the pre-existing or prevailing pattern of economic production in the areas they settled, and it was the time of arrival, rather than the ethnic background, that influenced the particular combination of resources a pioneer family adopted for exploitation.

Commerce was the mainstay of successful permanent settlement and of economic growth, but the development of the commercial sector was impossible without the support of merchants or traders. The processed staples were forwarded by the traders from the west coast to distant overseas markets and a great variety of goods were collected overseas for the settlers. These traders were as varied in their background and as complex in their aspirations as were the settlers. Several distinct types of entrepreneurial activity evolved, and different relationships developed between settlers and traders which are fundamental to the understanding of the geography of settlement on the coast.

III. SETTLERS AND TRADERS

Even before migrants settled permanently on the west coast, there existed a highly developed and complex system of trade. The British migratory cod fishery was centuries old when it reached the west coast, and the concomitant system of trade was equally established. British merchants hired fishermen in the homeland and brought them out each summer to fish and process the cod in Newfoundland's coves and harbours; the men normally returned home in the fall and the dried fish was usually sent to markets in the West Indies or southern Europe where exotic goods were procured for the homeland markets. Permanent settlement was established when some of these migratory fishermen, or some of the merchants who organized and controlled the fishery, realized that a resident fishery would be more profitable.

A number of Jersey and southwest English mercantile firms were involved with this migratory fishery along the west coast after c. 1750, and some with the initiation of permanent settlement there. One was the firm of T. S. Bird of Sturminster Newton and Poole (see Handcock and Thornton, this vol.) who established a station at Woody Point, Bonne Bay, about 1800 and dominated trade in that area for the next four decades or more. Every spring one or two vessels were dispatched from Poole to Seal Island or Forteau, the firm's headquarters in Labrador, dropping off, *en route*, provisions and personnel to prosecute the summer fishery at Harbour Breton on the south coast, at the Bay of Islands, and at Bonne Bay. This migratory pattern persisted until the commercial demise of the firm. Meanwhile some of the employees took up permanent residence on the coast and while still trading with Bird and relying on him for provisions, became self-employed, independent fishermen. By 1840, for example, there were at least thirty Bird dealers with their own accounts in Bay of Islands and Bonne Bay, the majority of whom were residents.[61] Each spring Bird transported provisions and sometimes young male apprentices to these planters and collected their winter produce: predominantly fur, staves, and barrels. Later in the year ships were sent over from Poole or Liverpool, or down from Forteau, to collect the summer produce of cod, oil, salmon, and less regularly herring, caplin, and trout, which were either shipped back to England or to the Mediterranean market. An agent for the firm was stationed at Woody Point where a store was maintained year-round. He was responsible for the collection of local produce and for the distribution of goods and provisions to the planters.

Some indication of the value of these provisions is revealed in insurance policies on freight. Between 1837 and 1841, for example, the total value of goods discharged from five Bird voyages amounted to almost £12,000, distributed as follows: Harbour Breton £4,200, Bay of Islands £600, Bonne Bay £3,000, and Seal Island £2,000.[62] Profits derived from supplying settlers stimulated mercantile support for a resident fishery. As settlement expanded on the west coast the British merchants adapted more and more to the roles of supplier and exporter for the settlers and consequently were less involved in the old migratory ship fishery. Indeed, it was in their interests to suppress subsistence production on the coast in order to maintain the influx of provisions, the volume of exports, and the profits from such trade. The value of produce exported from the coast was high. In 1841 one Bird sloop of 40 tons, valued at £200, carried £1,000 of produce to Liverpool and another vessel bound for the same port was insured for £1,800.[63]

Prices for provisions and produce were usually set by the merchants who tried to arrange it so that their cost to the fishermen equalled or exceeded the price paid them for fish. Exchange was usually on a non-cash basis, and as a result, the settlers were often in a state of continuous debt to the merchant and rarely in a position to accumulate reserves of capital. In 1840, for example, Bird advanced £532 worth of provisions to fifteen settlers in Bonne Bay and Bay of Islands, but collected only £311 of produce from them in return. That year all but three of the thirty dealers were in his debt, some debts extending back several years. This inability or unwillingness of the settlers to pay off their debts was a major flaw in the trading system from the mercantile point of view. Fishermen in debt and badly in need of supplies sometimes turned to interloping traders willing to pay cash for cargo. Bird repeatedly instructed his agent in Bonne Bay to collect as many debts as possible and cut off all provisions to those dealers who were known to traffic with rival firms or coastal hawkers. Such supervision was difficult, especially in the Bay of Islands where the firm did not have a resident agent. Here Jerseymen had a station and they sometimes secured the produce of Bird's creditors. To avert this traffic Bird tried to set the price of fish slightly above that given by the Jersey traders and such competition was the fisherman's best hope of a just price for his product.

Fluctuating prices for fish and the uncertainty of the catch added to the financial risks undertaken by the merchant in extending credit. With the decline in the migratory fishery it became increasingly difficult to control a business from so remote a location as Poole, despite the presence of an agent and the regular summer visitation of a member of the firm with news of markets and prices. In eastern Newfoundland the English merchants yielded to a rising indigenous mercantile group, based in St. John's, after the Napoleonic Wars, and it was only a matter of time before the power of British merchants waned in the more isolated areas. By 1850 the Birds had abandoned the west coast trade; the Jerseymen, who persisted with the migratory ship fishery, lasted longer, but they also were eventually displaced by new mercantile interests. By contrast, the French migratory fishery and its associated mercantile system endured until after 1900, although it became increasingly centralized in the homeland and received enormous state support.

From the beginning of settlement on the west coast, Halifax merchants competed with those from Britain, and later from St. John's; eventually the propinquity of Halifax to the Gulf meant its dominion over trade along the coast. Actually their chief competitors were the New England fishermen and traders who vied with them for the lucrative West Indies' markets. The Halifax merchants depended heavily on Newfoundland fish and oil for this trade, especially after the Napoleonic Wars when the high cost of wages, insurance, provisions, and salt hindered their own cod fishery. Halifax eventually managed to force the Americans to trade with the British West Indies through her port, and by a series of bounties bolstered her own fishery in the Gulf.

Trade between Halifax and the west coast was prosecuted in basically three ways: (i) indigenous fishermen and traders transported produce to Halifax in locally-built family schooners in exchange for provisions, (ii) traders travelled from Halifax to the west coast with provisions and collected produce there, either from resident traders or directly from fishermen, or (iii) merchant houses in Halifax placed agents on the coast to manage retailing and wholesaling outlets. Initially, the dominant pattern of trade seemed to be carried out by family schooners. In 1808, for example, there were eight vessels between twenty and sixty tons among the twenty recorded settlers, which almost certainly were used for trade. Seven of these settlers, all from St. George's Bay, sent their produce to Halifax, and one of these, a Jerseyman in Sandy Point, owned a sixty-ton vessel. This tradition of sending local schooners, which were owned either by a well-to-do planter or an extended family, to Halifax persisted through the 19th century. It is still recalled by older people in all three bays, but especially in St. George's Bay where cultural contacts with Nova Scotia and relative proximity were important influences.[64] At the peak of this trade 15 to 30 St. George's Bay schooners made 3–4 trips to Halifax each year, each time taking 300 to 900 barrels of produce, mainly herring which, in aggregate, amounted to 80 percent of the catch. As settlement expanded on the west coast Halifax merchants despatched their own vessels to trade there, a pattern stimulated by heavy British immigration to Nova Scotia and the consequent expansion of agriculture in that province. Halifax, heretofore, had had a poor agricultural hinterland and was sometimes compelled to look to New England for Newfoundland provisions. By the 1840s, however, even the Birds at Bonne Bay depended to some extent on Halifax for provisions.

More than any other factor, the rise of the commercial herring fishery intensified and consolidated these lines of trade. From the outset this trade was dominated by Nova Scotian traders, mostly from Halifax. Initially they confined themselves to St. George's Bay, but after 1860 Nova Scotian traders travelled to the two more northerly bays in search of herring.[65] The importance of Halifax in the commerce of St.

George's Bay is reflected in 1850 by the stiff opposition of Sandy Point residents and traders to the imposition by the provincial government of a tax on the import of provisions from Nova Scotia.[66] Residents objected on the basis that their trade was almost entirely with Halifax and they had no political representation in St. John's. This opposition resulted in the withdrawal in 1854 of the first resident magistrate and superintendent for protection of fisheries and collector of customs on the French Shore, stationed since 1850 at Sandy Point. Disaffection with the provincial government did not abate. Settlers continued to complain over the lack of infrastructural facilities and in 1888 secured a direct steamer link with Halifax in place of the inadequate service supplied by Bowrings in St. John's. A Halifax fishing firm, Farquaher and Company, operated the new steamer which visited Sandy Point, Birchy Cove, and Woody Point, the main centres on the west coast, once a fortnight through the summer. The 800-ton vessel accommodated freight and passenger traffic and the Farquaher Company greatly extended its trade with the herring fishermen. Oral tradition and documentary sources claim that prices for produce were higher, and provisions were cheaper in Halifax, and that Nova Scotian merchants and traders were usually willing to deal on a cash basis.[67] Halifax currency was an important medium of exchange on the west coast.

Perhaps more important for west coast commerce in the long run was the number of Nova Scotians who developed independent businesses in the area. By 1890 at least half the non-native resident merchants or traders were of Nova Scotian birth. Some came initially to manage the herring trade, especially in Humber Sound, but the most distinctive Nova Scotian entrepreneurial contributions were the exploitation of lobster and lumber and the development of shipbuilding. Nova Scotians had considerable experience developing these resources in their own province, and on the west coast, where labour was cheaper and overheads less, such resources were under-exploited.

In contrast, fear of the French, the sparseness of settlement, and the distance from St. John's discouraged the Water St. merchants from trading in western Newfoundland. But with the rapid rise in settlement and trade after 1865 the St. John's merchants became anxious to extend their hegemony to this remote part of the island. Efforts were made to establish regular communications with the west by steamer, railway, and telegraph, and eventually firms such as Bowrings, Bairds, Harveys, Jobs, and Munroes established stores in the area.[68] Provisions were exchanged for herring, cod, lobster, salmon, timber, and hay. Jealous of the inroads made by Nova Scotian entrepreneurs, the Water St. merchants accused them of operating without a licence on the French Shore, of avoiding provincial taxes and export duties, and of depleting the resources of the area through wasteful exploitation.[69] Despite the extension of government aid after 1875 through relief payments, the building of roads, public wharves, and schools, the provision of regular winter mail services overland to supplement their improved forms of communication, and above all the establishment of local government in the area and political representation in St. John's, the Water St. merchants did not dislodge Nova Scotian supremacy over trade there. Indeed, until 1875 distant Quebec City probably traded more with the west coast settlers than did St. John's.[70]

Like the Nova Scotians, the New Englanders rapidly expanded their fishery in the Gulf early in the 19th century, sending over one thousand vessels each season under a generous bounty system. It was a diversified fishery, exploiting rich stocks of mackerel, herring, halibut, and cod. There is little evidence, however, of trade between these fishermen and the west coast inhabitants, and none of the former ever settled on the coast. The Treaty of Washington (1871) officially opened the door for American transactions with the settlers and the spiralling demand for bait for New England bankers resulted in a steady stream of American fishermen and traders to Bay of Islands and Bonne Bay during the herring season. Up to sixty schooners would appear in each bay each fall and the residents would load these vessels with fresh herring which were promptly salted in the hold; once loaded, the vessels sailed for New England or the Banks, discharged their cargo and often returned for a second or third load before freeze-up.

Sometimes the visitors supplied the settlers with fishing gear and provisions in exchange for the herring, but more often they paid the settlers in gold and could offer higher prices than the Nova Scotians, or sell provisions at lower cost. In 1870, for example, the poorer fishermen in the Bay of Islands complained because the Americans, who were not allowed to fish, could supply flour and other provisions at a lower rate than could the Newfoundland merchants.[71] Gloucester became the centre for this west coast herring trade, and in 1875 a Gloucester merchant established premises on Woods Island, Bay of Islands, to carry on the trade. Generally the industry waxed and waned according to the supply on the coast, but by the end of the century smoked herring had become a popular item of diet in urban America, thereby increasing the price. Gloucester merchants paid one to two dollars a barrel for processed or semi-processed herring and in peak years up to 60,000 barrels were caught in the Bay of Islands alone.

Mention has already been made of the French trade in bait (largely herring) and other west coast produce, for which the residents were reimbursed in provisions and gear, but often in cash. The illicit bait trade attained enormous proportions along the south coast at the peak of the migratory French cod fishery in the 1850s. In a single season over £56,000 was paid for bait in Fortune Bay by bankers operating out of St. Pierre. The rapid expansion of settlement along the south coast is, in part, attributable to this lucrative trade. Eventually the provincial government, under pressure from the Water St. merchants, managed to suppress the trade on the south coast by means of the Bait Act (1888) forcing the French and St. Pierrais to seek bait on the Treaty Shore. For a few years following the Bait Act, fifty to seventy French vessels visited St. George's Bay each season and paid up to $20,000 to the residents there for herring.[72] It was usually sold unprocessed to the French for 50 to 80 cents a barrel, a price which was considered as good as $1.50 for a processed barrel from the Nova Scotians or New Englanders. Distance from St. Pierre and the Banks, and the decline of the French cod fishery meant, however, that St. George's Bay and the west coast never developed a lucrative bait export trade with the French.

As settlement expanded on the western shore, control over trade by merchant houses in distant centres became more difficult. Under the old migratory mercantile regime, transactions with the fishermen were normally restricted to spring and fall, a pattern which often proved inadequate given the fluctuating circumstances of a fishing economy. Settlers preferred more direct and frequent contacts with the sources of supply, so that after 1860 resident traders came to dominate retail trade. The growth of a resident fishery was paralleled by the growth of independent resident traders. In 1850 the resident magistrate and collector of customs reported seventeen retail stores on the coast,[73] and by the end of the century there were over fifty in operation. Few of these small traders came directly from the ranks of resident fishermen. In an economy where the extension of credit had been the basis for the relationship between producer and wholesaler, and barter the medium of exchange, it was difficult for ordinary fishermen to accumulate the reserves of capital necessary to launch a retail trade. Indeed the small traders were, themselves, often in debt to non-resident merchants who supplied them, a situation responsible for one of the features of the entrepreneurial history of the west coast – the ephemeral careers of so many petty traders. A sharp decline in the catch or of market prices could result in immediate bankruptcy among marginal operators. This instability could also be disadvantageous to the supplying merchant, or wholesaler, as in the example of a Halifax creditor who came to Sandy Point to collect debts from traders there, but failed.[74] One trader, who had been advanced £1,500, declared bankruptcy and on appeal to the naval officer, the only authority, he was informed that it was foolish to extend so much credit in so lawless a place.

Apart from the Bird enterprise, no large-scale monopolistic mercantile operation was ever established on the west coast. Settlement was sparse and isolated from urban centres such as St. John's and Halifax where the major merchant houses were located and where information on demands and prices for produce was more accessible. Moreover, the absence of a fully developed legal system and of local government, coupled with the French threat to the security of property, militated against large-scale commercial expansion on the coast.

The system of exchange between the fishermen and independent resident traders differed little from the old migratory mercantile scheme. Every spring the local trader received supplies from a non-resident merchant, or from coasters, which were passed on to the fishermen in exchange for a promise of his fish and other produce in the fall. Sometimes the small merchant sent a schooner around to collect the fish and deliver supplies, or the fishermen came to the store. If a surplus remained after the fisherman 'paid for' his spring and fall supplies, this amount was usually credited to his account. Like the transatlantic merchants of old, the resident traders tried to fix prices in a way that eliminated the possibility of the fishermen accumulating profits. Despite the proliferation of interloping traders with the rise of the herring and lobster trade, and the concomitant increase of cash as a medium of exchange, the continued use of barter and credit is widely evidenced in oral tradition and in documents right to the end of the century.[75] When the seven leading traders in Sandy Point, for example, threatened to discontinue the extension of autumnal credit to their dealers in 1858, an alarmed resident magistrate explained to the governor that over four hundred inhabitants would become destitute and might starve as a result.

The extension of credit tightened the grip of trader over settler and consolidated the lines of retail trade. In extending credit, however, the trader risked his small reserves of capital, since he depended on the fisherman's word to deliver his produce in the fall: the fisherman might abscond or the fishery could fail. On the other hand, ignorant of external market conditions and price fluctuations, the fisherman depended to an extent on the honesty of the trader in the settling of prices for produce. On the west coast these inherent flaws in the system were sometimes partially offset by local traders relying on agnatic and affinal kin ties or on ties of friendship to conduct their retail trade; and as mentioned earlier a group of fishermen, often kin, might share a schooner and transport their produce directly to the distant merchant, receiving provisions in exchange. Conversely, visiting vessels dealt directly with the settlers, using their schooners as floating stores.

Within each bay there was considerable endogenous trade. For a variety of reasons subsistence production often varied in volume and in range from household to household, encouraging direct exchange of mostly farm and forest products between settlers themselves. These transactions were informal and reciprocal and were based on kin and neighbourhood ties. Sometimes a "nunnyback" walked from settlement to settlement carrying goods on his back which he peddled to local settlers.

The persistence of these decentralized forms of commerce inhibited the emergence of indigenous traders and growth of central places. The distance to *entrepôts* discouraged many fishermen from investing in the carrying trade while the basic unreliability of visiting traders made resident traders indispensable. Rarely were the staples collected by these traders delivered directly to consumers. Instead, they were taken to large merchant houses, primarily in Halifax, where they were assorted for re-export. The west coast traders received provisions for their stores in exchange, and cash for any surplus. In an area where produce and markets were uncertain and traders often numerous, the resident traders could not afford to specialize in any particular commodity or function and availed of every opportunity to trade and to engage in other pursuits. One trader in Humber Sound, for example, collected cod, herring, salmon, lobster, and furs in exchange for imported goods; he also invested in farming, logging, and shipbuilding, ran a hotel, was a Justice of the Peace and Collector of Customs, and was in charge of the Road Board.

The residential location of these small traders or brokers along the western shore was critical to the development of central places. Some traders were scattered through the many outports, especially with the proliferation of settlement late in the century, but most were congregated in four villages: Sandy Point, Birchy Cove, Summerside, and Woody Point. Each of these settlements had a deep harbour, allowing safe anchorage for large schooners, and each was centrally situated in relation to population distribution, affording the least aggregate travel time for trade between settlers and traders.

Sandy Point was the only safe harbour in St. George's Bay. It was in clear view of most settlements in the inner bay and along the south coast of the Port au Port Peninsula. Sandy Point was one of the oldest settlements on the coast and was by far the most populous and prosperous throughout the 19th century. The first resident traders were descendants of 18th century families from Jersey and the West Country such as Messervy, Pennel, and Parsons. Their first clients were mainly relatives, but as settlement grew, the Messervys, at least, expanded their business and remained important traders. With the rise of the commercial herring trade, a number of settlers from diverse areas set up small businesses in Sandy Point, mainly between 1840 and 1870: Garnier, Leroux, and Helbot from northwestern France, Le Grandais and Pieroway from Jersey, Nardini from Italy, McFatridge and Thomas from Ireland, Forrest from New York, and McLean, Alexander, McKay, and Bishop, probably all from Nova Scotia.

It is difficult to trace the social and economic background of these traders, or the circumstances that brought them to the western shore. Some may have entered as agents for distant merchants, as did Henry Forrest who arrived in 1827 to represent a Quebec City firm, but who became an independent trader by 1835. Others may have come with a small amount of capital and with an eye for trade. But most likely several were just fishermen who accumulated enough capital to share or own outright a schooner and build a retail store. The majority of the traders came from traditional source areas for immigrants – Nova Scotia, Jersey, and France – and depended on fellow countrymen for trade. Most remained in business and passed their enterprises on to heirs. Some became quite prosperous, running a substantial store and two-three schooners, while others were only slightly better off than the fishermen, and indeed, often fished to supplement their income. Many other traders appear only fleetingly in the records and it is impossible to measure the scale of their enterprise or the time spent on the shore.

Until the 1880s the Sandy Point traders dominated retail trade in St. George's Bay.[76] Business was brisk. In 1872, for example, the value of exports from Sandy Point exceeded £35,000 and some traders there delivered over £2,500 worth of provisions in the fall. More important, mercantile residence attracted legal, administrative, and cultural services which in turn stimulated commerce. About the middle of the century two churches, one later elevated to the status of cathedral, schools, taverns, a customs house, courthouse, jail and barracks were established, bringing minister, priest, teachers, magistrate, customs officer, and constables to Sandy Point. Subsequently, the village became the focus for communications and transport including a central post office, telegraph station, regular steamer and local ferry service, as well as for the professional services of a doctor and a fisheries supervisor.

The primacy of Sandy Point was not challenged until the rise of the lobster trade (and, briefly, mining) in the 1880s when a number of traders including Hutchings, Bennett, Bairds and their original agents Abbot and Haliburton, set up on the Port au Port isthmus, gradually capturing much of the retail trade of the peninsula. Sandy Point itself, located on a sand bar, was slowly being swallowed up by the sea. A large breakwater was built to prevent tidal flooding in the harbour area and a law was passed to prohibit the cutting of trees which served as a shelter belt behind the village and its harbour. Nevertheless, severe damage through flooding did occur (over $30,000 was spent to repair and maintain the public wharf alone), and as early as 1884 it was proposed to relocate all administrative services across the harbour in St. George's or at Port au Port.[77] At the end of the century the advent of the railway dealt Sandy Point the *coup de grace* by by-passing it and stimulating a migration of businesses and services from there to new centres such as Port au Port, Stephenville Crossing, and especially St. George's. Today Sandy Point is deserted.

Birchy Cove (later called Curling), Summerside in Humber Sound, and Woody Point in Bonne Bay emerged as central places only after 1865 with the sudden rise of the herring trade. Four families from Sandy Point: Bagg, Messervy, Pennel, and Parsons – all affinally related and descendants of early settlers there – began the mercantile career of Birchy Cove. They were joined by some Irish traders from eastern Newfoundland or Ireland such as Murphy, Boland, and Petries and by Anguin from Nova Scotia. Legal, socio-cultural, and communications services followed. A mile across the Sound on the north shore at Summerside were located two of the most prosperous enterprises – Carter from Nova Scotia and Petipas, probably Acadian. They were joined by Pynns of St. John's who operated a small sawmill, and by Barrys and Dunphys of Irish origins who invested in the herring trade. As in Sandy Point, the coming of the railway, with stations established at Humbermouth (Riverside) and Birchy Cove, robbed Summerside of most of its commercial enterprises which then were re-located across the Sound.

Apart from the mill at Corner Brook, with its Nova Scotian entrepreneurs, particularly Fisher and Tupper, this settlement did not engage much in retail trade, mainly because of its extreme location at the head of the Sound. There was competition, however, between Birchy Cove and Corner Brook over the location of both telegraph and railway stations.[78] Other outports also competed for central functions. An American agent or trader established an enterprise on Woods Island and late in the century, several indigenous settlers engaged in petty trading at different locations around the Sound and outer bay.

Woody Point was the collecting and distributing centre for the Birds of Bonne Bay from about 1800 to 1850 when they were replaced by the Jersey firm of De Gruchy, Renouf, Clement and Company. This latter firm was also probably the proprietor of the Jersey room in St. John's Beach, Humber Sound. As in the Bay of Islands, the emergence of the commercial herring and lobster fisheries attracted a number of agents or traders to Bonne Bay, all of whom settled in Woody Point, including Silver, Seely, Muir, Payzant and Frazer, and Haliburton from Nova Scotia; Houlihan, Brown and Whalen from Newfoundland; and Taylor from Ireland. A few native-born settlers such as Roberts and Butt also established stores. Services similar to those in Sandy Point and Birchy Cove were introduced to Woody Point although there was competition from the settlers deep in South Arm who argued that facilities such as the public wharf and steamer terminal, the post office and money-order office, would be more centrally placed at Baileys Point, in full view of the inhabitants of the bay.[79] The inhabitants were strongly supported by the resident magistrate who also managed the North West Trading Company store at Baileys Point. However, Woody Point was more central for the settlers across the arm and around the mouth of the bay to Lobster Cove; the introduction of a regular ferry service confirmed its primacy.

The morphology of all these low-order centres was similar. Throughout the 19th century schooners were the life-line of commerce and the sea was the road. Warehouses and retail stores crowded the waterfront. All resident traders had large wharves, which together ranged in a neat row along the harbour, each projecting finger-like out to sea; they were backed by a tier of warehouses and stores. A street ran parallel to the shore behind these structures, and further back were the residences of the traders, usually more substantial and architecturally pretentious than those of the fishermen, with their ancillary outbuildings. Property lines ran back from the shore, transecting these tiers and forming long rectilinear lots, with each trader enjoying private access to his wharf. This geometry was sometimes disrupted by natural conditions, such as uneven topography or water depth; sometimes the properties and humbler structures of the fishermen were interspersed with the properties of the traders. Indeed the distinction between the morphology of these small service centres and that of rudimentary outports was merely one of scale.

In the past, the peopling of Newfoundland has been interpreted largely in the context of a single staple: cod. Although it is clear that up until the late 18th century this resource was fundamental in the formation of permanent settlement on the Avalon Peninsula and other areas of the east coast, its role in the expansion of settlement beyond these nuclear areas in the subsequent century was considerably diminished. On the south and west coasts, on large sections of the north coast of the island, and in Labrador, a combination of resources, including cod, induced year-round occupancy. Seal, salmon, and fur were significant in the northern areas, while herring, caplin, squid, salmon, lobster, fur, and timber were exploited in the south and west. The growth of the bait trade was of vital importance in the spread of settlement along the south coast and instigated permanent settlement on the western shore. With fur and timber, bait processing provided winter employment, a crucial consideration in the decision to set up permanent homes. This is not to belittle the importance of cod in the traditional west coast economy, but it was generally only an adjunct to these other resources. Finally, the feasibility of subsistence farming was critical in the formation of permanent settlement.

Despite the euphoria about western development and the building of the railway, the west coast fell sadly short of the expectations enunciated by proponents of a new frontier. Commercial agriculture failed to flourish and commercial logging remained confined to a few settlements in Humber Sound. No road network or marketing arrangements developed to encourage the prospective farmer. Stands of white pine, the most desirable timber for export, were limited and soon exhausted. Fur and salmon stocks became depleted early, minerals remained unexploited, and the settlers looked to the sea for their basic livelihood. The west coast is singularly lacking in harbours, having a long, straight, cliff-like littoral, with few places to land and dry fish. With the exception of the Port au Port peninsula, the permanent population was largely huddled in the shelter of the inner arms of the bays, which comprised only a miniscule fraction of the total coast. Here the settlers were poorly situated in relation to the cod grounds and the herring stocks fluctuated widely, often causing economic distress. These pockets of settlement were isolated from the main *entrepôts* and markets, and the absence of strong mercantile links through large-scale operations inhibited the expansion of overseas trade and concomitant economic growth. The west coast remained on the fringe of the hinterlands of St. John's and Halifax, an entrepreneurial backwater in a rapidly specializing and centralizing commercial world.

NOTES

1 Based on census returns for 1857, 1869, 1874, 1884, 1891 and 1901 (Newfoundland, Department of Colonial Secretary, Appendices Journals House of Assembly, St. John's. *Census of Newfoundland and Labrador*). Additional estimates are derived from various published and manuscript sources: (1801) Charles M. Pole, "The Pole Papers, 1797–1802"; (1808) Sir John T. Duckworth, The Duckworth Papers, 1810–12: "Report on the Fisheries in the Gulf by H.M. Sloop 'Avenger' "; (1813) Lt. F. Chappell, 1818:76–7; (1822) W. E. Cormack, 1928:90–1; (1828) *J.H.A.*, 1852:348; (1830) *Society Propagation Gospel: Sermons Preached*, xvi, 1830–4:81; (1830) Newfoundland, Department of Colonial Secretary, Series 2, Incoming Correspondence, 5, July 24, 1830; (1838) Colonial Office 194/101 September 1838: "List of Inhabitants on the Western Shore"; (1841) *J.H.A.*, 1852:350; (1843) Newfoundland Governor's Office, 1, Series 3, Local Letters, September 9, 1843; (1847) *Public Ledger*, St. John's, December 22, 1854; (1851) *J.H.A.*, 1851:141; (1853) G.N.1/3, June 1, 1853; (1865) *J.H.A.*, 1865:624. Most estimates are crude and must be treated with caution.
2 C.O. 194/21 (1788):172, 195/14, May 26, 1794, 194/40, January 10, 1798, 194/49, October, 1810; The Pole Papers, July 31, 1801; F. Chappell, *Voyage*, 1813:76–9, *S.P.G.*, 1830. Their numbers were greatly reduced through intermarriage and out-migration but a distinct Micmac settlement opposite Sandy Point was described by Rev. Lind as late as 1857 and they are still recalled in local oral tradition. Rev. Henry Lind, Diary, July 17, 1857.
3 The Duckworth Papers, 1810–12; C.O. 194/101 (1838).
4 Catholic Parish Register, Sandy Point, 1850–68.
5 *J.H.A.*, 1866:627, *Royal Gazette*, St. John's, January 28, 1873.
6 C.O. 194/23 (1784):332, /36 (1786):194, /37 (1786), /14, May 26, 1794, /40, January 10, 1798; Pole Papers, July 31, 1801.
7 C.O. 194/36:194, /37 (1788):71, /38 (1789):128, /38 September 13, 1789. The salmon fishermen of St. George's Bay had experienced harassment from the Americans during the War of Independence.

8   Pole Papers, July 31, 1801; Duckworth Papers, 1808, 1811; Cormack, *Journey*, p. 92; Newfoundland, Colonial Secretary's Office, Series 1, 32 (1821):74–6; E. Wix (1836:189); C.O. 194/101 (1838); *J.H.A.*, 1848:422, 1851:872, 1857:301–2, 1866:629. Yields were sometimes measured in barrels, especially after 1850, and one barrel is taken to equal half a tierce.
9   Gt. Britain, Chancery, Masters' Exhibits c 108/69–71, Bird Papers, 1839–40. The average price was £4-10-0 per tierce.
10   C.O. 194/58, March 6, 1816.
11   C.S.O. 1/32 (1821):74–76, /34, April 8 (1824):81–90, /8 (1831):191; C.O. 194/65, August 23, 1821; /74, April 8, 1824. For other evidence of French interference see: C.S.O. 1/5 (1830):235–7; Newfoundland, Governor's Office, G.N.1 /3 July 13, 1879, June 10, 1899.
12   *J.H.A.*, 1851:172, 1857:301.
13   C.S.O. 1/37 (1829):125, /87 (1875); *J.H.A.*, 1852:110, 1857:301, 1872:636, 1873:719, 1875:750.
14   *J.H.A.*, 1852:110, 1868:506; G.N.1 /1, 3, July 13, 1879, June 20, 1899; C.S.O. /2, June 10, 1887.
15   *J.H.A.*, 1857:353, 1866:616, 620, 1871:505, 664, 1872:636, 642, 1874:758, 1876:439; C.S.O. 2/87, August 13, 1875, /153, February 7, 1878; G.N.1/3, July 13, 21, 1879. According to local belief the introduction of logging on the Humber had a deleterious effect on yields of salmon and herring: C.S.O. 2/87, July 30, August 13, 1875, /104, January 23, 1880; G.N.1 /3, October 16, 1879.
16   C.S.O. 2/87, August 13, 1875, /153, February 7, 1878, /100, October 31, 1879; G.N.1 /3, July 13, 1879, July 7, 1885, June 20, 1888, September 14, 1893; *J.H.A.*, 1858:438–9, 1865:625, 1866:619, 626, 1868:505, 508, 1876:439.
17   C.O. 194/23 (1733):184–5.
18   C.O. 194/23, February 2, 1733; /26, October 20, 1763; /27, October 22, 1765, October 27, 1766, December 15, 1767; /21 (1788):172; /14, May 26, 1794; /40, January 10, 1798; /47, November 18, 1808; /49, October, 1810; C.S.O. 1/3 (1764):235; /5 (1774):219; The Pole Papers, July 31, 1801; Chappell, *Voyage*, 1813:77.
19   Bird Papers, April 4, 1837, April 21, 1838, September 11, 1838, July 8, 1839, March 26–7, July 24, 1840, August 15, 1841, August 20, 1842, June 9, July 16, August 20, 1843.
20   C.S.O. 2/87, September 4, 1875. A Micmac from St. George's Bay who brought beaver skins to Corner Brook for sale was beaten up by the settlers for encroaching on traditional trapping grounds. See also: S. W. Benjamin, 1884:103–13.
21   W. H. Whiteley, 1973:240–72. Prior to the Treaty of 1783, the French had claimed the entire west coast by maintaining that Point Riche, its southern limit, was at Cape Ray.
22   Pole Papers, July 31, 1801; Census 1808; Cormack *Journey*, 1822:96; Wix, *Journal*, 1836:189; Census 1838; C.S.O. 2/34 (1839):217–9, June 1, 1853; (1847) *Public Ledger*, December 22, 1854; J.H.A., 1851:172, 1852:110, 1857:301, 1858:438.
23   Diary Rev. Lind, July 7, 1857; *J.H.A.*, 1868:506, 1872:490; C.S.O. 2/100, October 31, 1879; G.N.1 /3, July 13, 1881; *Census of Newfoundland*, 1891.
24   Bishop E. Feild, 1850:438; (1859) Rev. W. H. Tucker, 1877:155; *J.H.A.*, 1863:402, 1866:506, 624, 626, 1868:505; 1872:640; (1869) Rev. U. B. Rule, 1927:30; G.N.1 /3, August 19, 1879, June 10, 1887; *Evening Telegram*, July 17, December 21, 1888, May 9, 1891.
25   J.H.A., 1866:626, 1870:490, 1871:761, March 10, 1884; G.N.1 /3, June 27, 1876, June 10, 1887; *Census of Newfoundland*, 1884:156, 1891:242, 248.
26   C.S.O. 2/100, October 31, 1878, /106, September 30, 1881; G.N. 1/3, August 19, 1879, July 13, 1881. The 13,000 quintals recorded in 1874 appears to be an error.
27   C.S.O. 2/135, September 14, 1889.
28   Much has been written on the diplomatic manoeuvres of French and English in the delicate negotiations over the French Shore question. See especially: F. F. Thompson, 1961.
29   C.O. 194/78 (1829):74.
30   (1847) *Public Ledger*, December 22, 1854; *J.H.A.*, 1863:402, 1866:506, 1867:630; G.N. 1/3, March, 1881, July 12, 1890, November 11, 1891, June 12, October 16, 1893, May 11, 1894, May 9, 1900. A firm from Granville, Normandy was also involved with this station.
31   *J.H.A.*, 1858:438, 1863:402, 1877:755, G.N. 1/3, October 9, 1893.
32   C.S.O. 2/19 (1807):223–4, /31 (1819–21):306, /5 (1830):1–13, /8 (1831):191, /34 (1839):217–9; Wix, *Journal*, 1836:189, G.N. 1/3, September 9, 1843; *Public Ledger*, December 22, 1854. Threats to evict the settlers in St. George's Bay at one stage caused panic among the local traders who refused to extend credit to the resident fishermen. G.N. 1/3, August 18, 1858.
33   C.S.O. 2/5 (1830):1–3; *J.H.A.*, 1874:790, 1897:761. One French vessel paid £150 for bait in Bonne Bay.

34 C.S.O. 2/141, April 30, 1891. For further details of this contraband traffic, see: G.N. 1/3, November 27, 1878, March 24, 1879, July 13, 1881, May 10, 1888, June 4, 1889, October 15, 1890, June 26, 1891, April 30, 1892, November 11, 1892; C.S.O. 2/106, July 8, 1881, /114, June 15, 1883, /117, July 8, 1884, /124, September 2, 1884. *J.H.A.*, 1872:641, 1876:750.

35 *J.H.A.*, 1873:718, 1874:758; G.N. 1/3, July 14, 1873, April 21, 1877, May 15, 1879; C.S.O. 2/106, August 22, 1881.

36 Cormack, *Journey*, 1822:92; C.O. 194/74, April 8, 1824; C.S.O. 2/34 (1824):87–90; C.O. 194/101 (1838). Estimates are derived from the censuses of Newfoundland and from the following primary sources: (1847) *Public Ledger*, December 22, 1854; *J.H.A.*, 1848:422, 1851:172, 1852:110, 1857:363, 1858:437. 1866:616m 1872:636, 1875:750; G.N. 1/3, September 17, 1855, June 10, 1856, July 7, 1885, June 4, August 6, 1888, October 15, 1890; C.S.O. 2/114, June 4, 1883; *Evening Telegram*, December 27, 1887, May 22, 1891.

37 *Censuses of Newfoundland*, 1857–1901; J. Hatton and M. Harvey, 1883; *J.H.A.*, 1866:625, 1870:498, 1876:372; C.S.O. 2/87, July 5, 1875.

38 C.S.O. 2/90, December 17, 1877, /153, February 7, November 1, 1878; October 3, 1879, /104, January 23, May 15, 1880, /104, September 30, 1881, /106, November, 1887; G.N. 1/3, December 15, 1876, July 25, 1878, August 19, October 16, 1879; April 8, 1880; *Morning Chronicle*, St. John's, January 13, May 25, November 20, December 6, 14, 16, 28, 1876; Benjamin, *Century Magazine* 1884:108.

39 C.S.O. 2/100, October 31, 1878, /106, August 4, 1881, /128, July 14, 1888; G.N. 1/3, July 15, 1881, June 22, September 28, 1886, June 10–11, 1887; *Evening Telegram*, November 4, 1886, July 27, 1887; *Census of Newfoundland*, 1891.

40 G.N. 1/3, July 11, 1891, August 19, 1893.

41 G.N. 1/3, June 29, July 4, 1887, June 13, 23, 1888, July 11, November 11, 1891; C.S.O. 2/126, September 9, 1887, /130, May 31, 1888, /139, October 14, 1890.

42 *Evening Telegram*, January 10, 1891. In the first season 660 cases were packed, but only 200 in the following year.

43 G.N. 1/3, February, 1891, October 3, 9, 1893.

44 G.N. 1/3, 1881, June 13, 1888, October, 1890, October 3, 1893; C.S.O. 2/138, April 26, 1890.

45 C.S.O. 2/126, June 10, September 9, 1887; /130, May 31, 1888; /135, September 24, 1889.

46 Monsignor Sears of Sandy Point, for example, considered the west coast in 1876 as a "country abounding in natural resources calculated to support a large and thriving population comfortably, a good climate, good soil, minerals as valuable as they are diverse, and fisheries unequalled in any part of the world" (Brosnan, 1948:56). See also Hiller, 1972:15–18.

47 C.O. 194/47, November 18, 1808; Duckworth Papers, 1808; *Public Ledger*, December 22, 1854; C.S.O. 2/68 (1854):1–3.

48 For details of the operation see: J.H.A., 1866:626, 1868:564, 1870:497, 1872:640, 1873:719, 1874:784, 1875:751, 1876:372, 1879:682; G.N. 1/3, July 2, 1874, June 27, 1876, July 13, 1879; C.S.O. 2/87, August 13, September 1, 1875, /100, October 31, 1879, /126, October, 1887, /130, November 12, 1888; *Census of Newfoundland*, 1874:154; *Morning Chronicle*, St. John's, May 4, 1875, June 16, 1887.

49 J.H.A., 1873:472, 1876:572, March 10, 1884, March 16, 1887.

50 C.O. 194/101, September, 1838; Bird Papers, April 20, 1841, April 24, July 21, 1843; C.S.O. 2/87, August 13, 1875; Hatton and Harvey, *Newfoundland*:317.

51 *Public Ledger*, December 22, 1854. See also: C.O. 194/101, September, 1838; G.N. 1/3, April 8, 1880, July 16, 1886; C.S.O. 2/128, April 27, 1888.

52 G.N. 1/3, April 20, 1878, C.S.O. 2/153, February 7, 1878; Brosnan, *Pioneer History*:86.

53 G.N. 1/3, April 8, 1880.

54 Pole Papers, July 31, 1801; Cormack, *Journey*, 1822:91–6; Wix, *Journal*, 1836:159; J. B. Jukes, 1842, 2V:165; J.H.A., 1851:171; Lind Diary, August 4, 1857, August 11, November 12, 1862; G.N. 1/3, June 14, November 12, 17, 1862, October 27, June 14, July 13, September 26, 1879, July 16, 1886; *Censuses of Newfoundland*, 1857–1901.

55 *J.H.A.*, 1851:171, 1866:627.

56 *Evening Telegram*, January 30, 1886; C.S.O. 2/147, September 28, 1895.

57 C.S.O. 2/92, 1877, /126, 1887; G.N. 1/3, July 25, 1878, July 6, 1881, July 4, 1887.

58 C.S.O. 2/87, August 13, 1875; *J.H.A.*, 1875:751, 1879:681.

59 *J.H.A.*, 1870:751; G.N. 1/3, September 14, 1872, July 25, 1878; *Royal Gazette*, January 28, 1873.

60 G.N. 1/3, September 17, October 8, 1873, June 17, 1874; *Royal Gazette*, September 30, 1873; *J.H.A.* 1874:790, 1875:748; C.S.O. 2/92, June 4, 1877.

61 Account Book, Bird Ledger, 1839–40. Others continued to return home with Bird each fall, but were no longer mere servants or labourers for Bird at Bonne Bay.

62 Letter to Insurers, Bird Papers, April 5, 1837, April 18, 26, 1839, April 17, 1840, April 16, 1841.

63 *Ibid.*, August 23, September 15, 1841.

64 Pole Papers, July 31, 1801; Duckworth Papers, 1808; Cormack, *Journey*, 1822:90; C.O. 194/101, September, 1838; J.H.A., 1848:422, 1851:141, 1852:110, 1857:363, 1865:625, 1866:616, 619, 628; Lind Diary, 1857; G.N. 1/3, June 22, 1859, September 25, 1879, July 31, 1881, June 23, 1888.

65 C.S.O. 2/35 (1840):150; *J.H.A.*, 1851:141, 1858:439, 1865:625, 1866:616, 628, 1871:664, 1872:642, March 10, 1884: C.S.O. 2/87, September 4, 1875; *Evening Telegram*, February 15, June 29, August 26, 1882, November 21, December 21, 27, 1888; G.N. 1/3, June 23, 1888.

66 C.S.O. 2/78, December 2, 1865.

67 C.S.O. /2 (1829):10; *J.H.A.*, 1866:628.

68 *J.H.A.*, 1865:625; G.N. 1/3, August, 1874, October 28, 1890; C.S.O. 2/85, October 3, 1874, /117, April 15, 1884, /114, October 9, 1886; *The Newfoundlander*, St. John's, October 13, 1874; *The Times*, August 21, 1875; *Morning Chronicle*, January 13, December 6, 16, 1876; *Evening Telegram*, June 2, 29, 1882, November 1, 1883, February 21, 1885, May 20, 1887, January 4, May 9, November 4, 1891.

69 C.S.O. 2/70, June 16, 1866; G.N. 1/3, July 2, 1874, June 27, 1876; C.S.O. 2/87, July 30, August 13, 1875.

70 C.S.O. /2, September 19, 1829:10; July 14, 1830:5, /87, September 4, 1875; Bird Papers, July 25, 1842; *Public Ledger*, December 22, 1854.

71 *J.H.A.*, 1870:491, 1871:665, 1877:761; *Evening Telegram*, February 17, 1882, December 21, 1888, May 30, 1891.

72 G.N. 1/3, May 10, 1888, June 4, 1889, October 15, 1890, June 26, November 11, 1891, April 30, 1892.

73 G.N. 1/3, March 16, 1850.

74 C.S.O. /2, September 9, 1843.

75 *Royal Gazette*, November 3, 1846; G.N. 1/3, August 18, 1858; *J.H.A.*, 1858:439, 1859:393, 1866:616, 626, 628, 1870:498; Brosnan, *Pioneer History*, 1868:28; C.S.O. 2/153, February 7, 1878; Benjamin, *Century Magazine*, 1884:107–8.

76 C.S.O. 2/59 (1850):39; *J.H.A.*, 1851:175, 1866:619, 1872:636; *Public Ledger*, December 22, 1854. This section is based on extensive documentary sources and wide-ranging field interviews and observation over five years.

77 C.S.O. 2/114, September 5, 1883, /130, October 26, 1888, /147, September 28, 1895; G.N. 1/22, October 14, 1884; *Evening Telegram*, January 30, 1886.

78 C.S.O. 2/147, June 3, August 20, 1897, June 17, 1898.

79 C.S.O. 2/121, January 24, 1883, /123, September 18, November 7, 19, 29, 1885, /128, August 1, 1888.

REFERENCES: SECONDARY SOURCES

BENJAMIN, S. W.
  1884 "The Bay of Islands in Calm and Storm." *Century Magazine*, 6:103–13.
BROSNAN, REV. M.
  1948 *Pioneer History of St. George's Diocese, Newfoundland*. Toronto, Mission Press.
CHAPPELL, LT. F.
  1818 *Voyage of H.M.S. "Rosamund" to Newfoundland and the Southern Coast of Labrador*. London, J. Mawman.
CORMACK, W. E.
  1928 *A Journey Across the Island of Newfoundland in 1822*. London, Longmans, Green & Co.
FEILD, BISHOP E.
  1850 *Journal of a Voyage of Visitation in Newfoundland, 1849*. London, Society Propagation Gospel.
HATTON, J. and M. HARVEY
  1883 *Newfoundland, the Oldest British Colony*. London, Chapman & Hall.
HILLER, JAMES K.
  1972 "Whiteway and Progress." *The Newfoundland Quarterly*, 4:15–18.
INNIS, HAROLD A.
  1954 *The Cod Fisheries: The History of an International Economy*. Toronto, University of Toronto Press.
JUKES, J. B.
  1842 *Excursions in and about Newfoundland, 1839–40*. London, J. Murray.
RULE, REV. U. B.
  1927 *Reminiscences of My Life*. St. John's, Dicks & Co.

Ryan, S.
   1973 "The Newfoundland Cod Fishery in the Nineteenth Century." Paper presented to the Canadian
   Historical Association, Kingston.
Thompson, F. F.
   1961 *The French Shore Problem in Newfoundland*. Toronto, University of Toronto Press.
Tucker, Rev. W. H.
   1877 *Memoir of the Life and Episcopate of Edward Feild*. London, W. Wells Gardner.
Whiteley, W. H.
   1973 "James Cook and British Policy in The Newfoundland Fisheries, 1763–67." *Canadian Historical
   Review*, 54(3):240–72.
Wix, E.
   1836 *Six Months of a Newfoundland Missionary's Journal, 1835*. London, Smith, Elder & Co.

APPENDIX 9–1*

Male Heads of Household

Place of Birth	Total	St. George's Bay	Port au Port Pen.	Bay of Islands	Bonne Bay
Conception Bay	67	2	1	26	38
France	60	29	20	7	4
Southern England	55	9	2	25	19
Cape Breton (Acadian)	33	21	10	2	—
Nova Scotia	31	4	1	22	4
South Coast	26	2	—	7	17
Cape Breton (Scots)	20	13	2	5	—
Jersey	14	8	—	4	2
Labrador	13	—	—	9	4
St. John's	12	4	1	6	1
St. John's Island	10	—	—	—	10
St. Pierre	10	7	3	—	—
Ireland	10	7	—	2	1
Trinity Bay	7	3	1	—	3
Quebec	6	3	—	3	—
Bonavista Bay	6	1	—	1	4
Placentia Bay	5	1	—	2	2
Fortune Bay	4	1	—	3	—
Notre Dame Bay	3	1	—	1	1
Southern Shore	3	—	—	3	—
U.S.	3	2	—	—	1
Scotland	2	—	—	2	—
Wales	2	—	—	2	—
P.E.I.	2	—	—	2	—
Magdalen Islands	1	—	1	—	—
	405	118	42	134	111

*This table is based on parish records, gravestone evidence, private family documents and interviews. The author gratefully acknowledges the work of geography students at Memorial University who carried out investigations of outport communities on the west coast each summer from 1970–74 under his direction as part of the regular undergraduate field camp. Especial thanks to Howard Brown, M.A. student, for extensive archival research.

APPENDIX 9–2
Total Population and Religions

Year	Settlement	Families	Protestant	Roman Catholic	Total Families	Total Protestant	Total Roman Catholic	Total Population
1808	St. George's Bay				17			162
	Port au Port							
	Bay of Islands							
	Bonne Bay							
1838	St. George's Bay				86			423
	Port au Port							
	Bay of Islands							
	Bonne Bay							
1857	St. George's Bay	193	431 (42%)	592 (58%)	231	626 (49%)	656 (51%)	1282
	Port au Port	6	—	39 (100%)				
	Bay of Islands	22	118 (83%)	25 (17%)				
	Bonne Bay	10	77 (100%)	—				
1869	St. George's Bay	226	610 (43%)	804 (57%)	454	1425 (51%)	1349 (49%)	2774
	Port au Port	10	—	77 (100%)				
	Bay of Islands	160	484 (51%)	462 (49%)				
	Bonne Bay	58	330 (98%)	6 (2%)				
1874	St. George's Bay	275	690 (42%)	973 (58%)	718	2299 (54%)	1992 (46%)	4291
	Port au Port	61	25 (7%)	313 (93%)				
	Bay of Islands	208	749 (57%)	567 (43%)				
	Bonne Bay	174	835 (86%)	139 (14%)				
1884	St. George's Bay	369	784 (39%)	1209 (61%)	985	2946 (53%)	2597 (47%)	5543
	Port au Port	118	42 (7%)	582 (93%)				
	Bay of Islands	262	941 (60%)	627 (40%)				
	Bonne Bay	236	1179 (87%)	179 (13%)				
1891	St. George's Bay	460	879 (36%)	1580 (64%)	1205	3421 (52%)	3210 (48%)	6631
	Port au Port	145	90 (11%)	708 (89%)				
	Bay of Islands	346	1173 (62%)	731 (38%)				
	Bonne Bay	254	1279 (87%)	191 (13%)				
1901	St. George's Bay	562	1062 (35%)	1938 (65%)	1609	4384 (49%)	4431 (51%)	8815
	Port au Port	276	235 (15%)	1308 (85%)				
	Bay of Islands	497	1638 (63%)	966 (37%)				
	Bonne Bay	274	1449 (85%)	219 (15%)				

APPENDIX 9–3

Household Production: The Fishery

	Number Houses	Quintals Cod	Average Per House	Barrels Herring	Barrels Salmon
1857					
St. George's Bay	185	800	(4)	14,140 (76)	5
Port au Port	6	550	(91)	—	—
Bay of Islands	22	1,050	(48)	1,400 (64)	138 (6)
Bonne Bay	12	540	(45)	980 (81)	48 (4)
1869					
St. George's Bay	219	No			
Port au Port	10	Data			
Bay of Islands	160				
Bonne Bay	54				
1874					
St. George's Bay	262	3,074	(11)	19,206 (73)	334 (1.5)
Port au Port	61	2,436	(40)	—	46 (.5)
Bay of Islands	202	9,860	(49)	34,325 (170)	958 (5)
Bonne Bay	160	13,322	(83)	33,875 (212)	88 (.5)
1884					
St. George's Bay	339	10,381	(31)	22,118 (65)	339 (1)
Port au Port	116	5,175	(45)	161 (1)	50 (.5)
Bay of Islands	248	5,405	(22)	10,463 (42)	87 (.3)
Bonne Bay	213	7,508	(35)	2,620 (12)	46 (.2)
1891					
St. George's Bay	420	2,356	(5)	11,892 (28)	149 (.4)
Port au Port	137	3,635	(26)	35 (.3)	31 (.2)
Bay of Islands	314	5,476	(17)	17,938 (57)	43 (.1)
Bonne Bay	236	4,334	(14)	1,525 (7)	48 (.2)
1901					
St. George's Bay	600	4,028	(7)	17,105 (28)	240 (.4)
Port au Port	191	4,401	(23)	574 (3)	14 (.1)
Bay of Islands	475	4,825	(10)	73,313 (154)	114 (.2)
Bonne Bay	252	3,465	(14)	6,334 (25)	73 (.3)

APPENDIX 9–4

Lobster

	Number Factories	Value	Traps	No. Men Employed	Women	No. Cases
1891						
St. George's Bay	34	$11,330	11,059	217	44	3,792
Port au Port	17	5,765	4,448	66	18	1,411
Bay of Islands	23	11,850	11,550	203	84	3,995
Bonne Bay	2	600	2,200	51	15	1,100
	76	$29,545	29,257	537	161	10,298
1901						
St. George's Bay	17	$ 2,005	3,723	126	3	851
Port au Port	11	—?	8,210	5?	?	2,838
Bay of Islands	10	6,500	5,862	112	16	1,909
Bonne Bay	37	5,357	9,438	204	57	1,627
	75	$13,862	27,233	447	76	7,225

APPENDIX 9–5

Vessel Construction 1873–91

	Tons					Total
	−25	25–50	50–75	75–100	+100	
St. George's Bay	6	6	1	1	—	14
Bay of Islands	1	11	6	2	7	27
Bonne Bay	15	21	3	5	1	45
Total	22	38	10	8	8	86

APPENDIX 9-6

Household Production: Agriculture

Year		Number Houses	Improved Acres	Tons Hay	Total Cattle	Sheep	Lbs. Butter
1857	St. George's Bay	185	813 (4.5)	430 (2)	550 (3)	507 (3)	942 (5)
	Port au Port	6	22 (3.5)	32 (5)	37 (6)	38 (6)	—
	Bay of Islands	22	33 (1.5)	25 (1)	18 (1)	85 (4)	—
	Bonne Bay	12	16 (1.5)	9 (1)	4 (.25)	40 (3)	—
1869	St. George's Bay	219	1,383 (6)	825 (4)	699 (3)	989 (4)	1,150 (5)
	Port au Port	10	25 (2.5)	31 (3)	26 (3)	67 (7)	—
	Bay of Islands	160	215 (1.3)	58 (.5)	44 (.25)	41 (.25)	—
	Bonne Bay	54	58 (1)	7 (—)	—	—	—
1874	St. George's Bay	262	1,006 (4)	888 (3)	529 (2)	1,444 (5.5)	9,865 (38)
	Port au Port	61	151 (2.5)	180 (3)	103 (2)	300 (5)	2,325 (39)
	Bay of Islands	202	202 (1)	186 (1)	119 (.5)	364 (1.5)	1,380 (7)
	Bonne Bay	160	29	26	11	56	130 (1)
1884	St. George's Bay	339	2,255 (7)	1,263 (4)	744 (2)	1,490 (4)	13,606 (40)
	Port au Port	116	1,473 (13)	298 (2)	236 (2)	594 (5)	2,882 (25)
	Bay of Islands	248	529 (2)	448 (2)	295 (1)	865 (3.5)	6,360 (26)
	Bonne Bay	213	172 (1)	117 (.5)	126 (.5)	227 (1)	2,670 (12)
1891	St. George's Bay	420	2,573 (6)	1,574 (6)	1,192 (3)	2,137 (5)	15,253 (36)
	Port au Port	137	502 (4)	379 (2.7)	293 (2)	662 (5)	4,170 (30)
	Bay of Islands	314	739 (2.5)	729 (2.5)	481 (1.5)	1,590 (5)	5,992 (19)
	Bonne Bay	236	415 (2)	199 (1)	130 (.5)	591 (2.5)	3,020 (12)
1901	St. George's Bay	600	—	2,546 (4)	1,682 (3)	2,413 (4)	38,250 (64)
	Port au Port	191	1,201 (6)	1,139 (5)	711 (3.5)	1,147 (6)	18,070 (95)
	Bay of Islands	475	1,011 (2)	793 (1.5)	649 (1.5)	1,921 (4)	11,520 (24)
	Bonne Bay	252	1,062 (4)	276 (1)	173 (.5)	1,116 (4.5)	1,622 (6.5)

Bibliography: Primary Sources

ABBREVIATIONS

C.O. – Colonial Office; C.S.O. – Colonial Secretary's Office; C.S.P.A.W.I. – Calendar State Papers, America and West Indies; G.N. – Governor's Office; J.H.A. – Journals, House of Assembly; P.A.C. – Public Archives Canada; U.S.P.G. – United Society Propagation of the Gospel.
All primary sources are in Provincial Archives, St. John's (unless otherwise stated).

OFFICIAL

Great Britain, Colonial Office Correspondence.
  Series 1, 1574–1757. 69 vols.
Great Britain, Colonial Office Correspondence.
  Series 194, 1696–1922. 279 vols.
Great Britain, Calendar of State Papers, Colonial Series, America and the West Indies, 1574–1737.
Great Britain, House of Commons, 10 (1785–1801)
  Reports on the State of Trade to Newfoundland, London, 1793.
Great Britain, House of Commons.
  Report from Select Committee on Newfoundland Trade, London, 1817.
Great Britain, British Parliamentary Papers.
  Emigration, 10–14, 1842–1864. Shannon, Irish University Press, 1968.
Great Britain, Parish Record Collections.
  P227/OV11, 1788
  P186/OV22, 1840
  In Dorset Record Office, Dorchester
Great Britain, Privy Council, Boundary Documents, 1923
Newfoundland, Department of Colonial Secretary
  Census of Newfoundland, 1836.
Newfoundland, Department of Colonial Secretary
  Census of Newfoundland and Labrador, 1857.
Newfoundland, Department of Colonial Secretary
  Abstract Census and Return of Population, etc., of Newfoundland, 1869.
Newfoundland, Department of Colonial Secretary
  Census of Newfoundland and Labrador, 1874, 1884, 1891, 1901.
Newfoundland, House of Assembly
  Journals 1833–41, 1843–65.
Newfoundland, Governor's Office
  Outgoing Despatches, Series 1 1820–1934

Newfoundland, Governor's Office
  Incoming Despatches, Series 2 1825–1934.
Newfoundland, Governor's Office
  Miscellaneous, Series 3 1850–1949
Newfoundland, Department of Colonial Secretary
  Registry of Deeds, 1810–
  In Confederation Building, St. John's
Canada, *Census of Canada*, 1861. RG. 31. In National Archives, Ottawa.
Canada, *Census of Canada*, 1871. Ottawa: 1. B. Taylor, 1873. In National Archives, Ottawa.
Canada, *Census of Canada*, 1881. Ottawa: Maclean Roger & Co., 1882. In National Archives, Ottawa.
Canada, *Journeaux de l'Assemble Legislative* (1841–1846). In National Archives, Ottawa.
P. Magnix Collection, 1883. In National Archives, Ottawa.

Newspapers (St. John's, unless otherwise stated)
  Evening Telegram, 1879–
  Carbonear Star, 1833–35
  Harbour Grace Standard, 1862–94
  Harbour Grace Weekly, 1828
  Mercantile Journal, 1816–24
  Morning Chronicle, 1862–73, 1876–80
  The Mercury, 1889
  The Newfoundlander, 1827–84
  The Patriot, 1840–48
  Public Ledger, 1827–82
  Royal Gazette, 1810–
  The Times, 1844, 1849–94
  The Weekly Herald, 1849–56

Accounts, Letters, Diaries, Papers
  Charles M. Pole, Governor. Papers, 1797–1802
  Sir John T. Duckworth, Governor. Papers, 1810–12
  Rev. Henry Lind, Sandy Point. Diaries, 1857–59, 1861–64.
  Canon J. T. Richards, Diaries, 1904–19–   . (Private)
  Lester & Garland Papers, 1761–1815
    In Maritime History Centre, Memorial University
  Great Britain, Chancery 108, Masters Exhibits
    Accounts and Letter Books, Joseph Bird and Thomas Street, 1824–48

PARISH REGISTERS

  Anglican
    Trinity (1757–   )
    Harbour Grace (1776–   )

Bonavista (1786–   )
St. John's (1802–   )
Greenspond (1815–   )
King's Cove (1834–   )
Port de Grave (1837–   )
Fogo (1841–   )
Strait (1848–   ). In Blanc Sablon.
Rose Blanche (1860–   )
White Bay (1864–   )
Hermitage (1867–   )

Roman Catholic
Harbour Grace (1806–   )
Labrador (1847–   ). In Diocesan Archives, Quebec.
Blanc Sablon (1849–   ). In Blanc Sablon and Lourdes.
Sandy Point (1850–   ). In St. George's.
Searston (1867–   ). In Searston.
Harrington Harbour (1873–   ). In Harrington Harbour.

Wesleyan (Methodist)
Carbonear (1793–   )
Bonavista (1822–   )
Brigus (1822–   )
Burin (1850–   )
St. George's (1862–   )
Strait (1866–   ). In Strait.
St. Anthony (1873–   )
Red Bay (1878–   )

Congregational/Presbyterian
St. John's (C) (1802–   )
St. John's (P) (1842–   )

Miscellaneous
Calendar of Letters, United Society for Propagation of the Gospel, 1721–93.
Register of Fishing Rooms, Bonavista Bay, 1806.
Register of Marriages, Roman Catholic, 1825–28.
Marriage Certificates, 1825–79.
E. F. J. Mathews Collection, Poole.

Glossary: Dialect Terms

BYEBOATMAN fisherman and boat owner who moved to his "room" in Newfoundland in spring on a merchant's fishing ship, hired migratory men for the summer fishery and normally returned home in the fall.

CHINTZE to fill up interstices between vertically placed timbers of a wall with various materials.

CLAN (pl. CLOINNE) a territorially-based agnatic descent group in Highland Scottish tradition, comprising a number of major segmented lineages.

CLANN living representatives of a lineage or of one of its segments.

FLOATERS fishermen who moved north to the Labrador coast in spring with their supplies, fished from their schooners through the summer, and unlike "stationers" did not have a base on shore.

LANDSMAN man who trapped seals in winter with special nets attached to the shore.

LINHAY a lean-to shed attached to rear of a dwelling.

LIVEYER(E) settlers; "live here."

PATCH a collection of baby seals on ice floe.

PLANTER fisherman and boat owner who lived year-round in Newfoundland, frequently with family, and often hired on migratory labourers for fishery.

ROOM berth and structures on the foreshore, plus other buildings and property, of a fisherman or merchant.

SLIOCHD a branch or line of descent.

STATIONERS fishermen who moved north to the Labrador coast in spring, often with families, to their "stations" or "rooms" for the summer fishery and usually returned home in the fall.

TACKSMAN the principal tenant of a conjoint farm in Highland Scottish tradition who sublet usually to other members of his kin and received his tenancy from a landowner or chief.

TILT a crude temporary dwelling.

TRUNNEL headless wooden pin or peg used to fasten timbers; tree-nail.

WHITECOATS baby harp seals.

Index

ISER BOOKS

Studies

Papers

Mailing Address:
ISER Books (Institute of Social and Economic Research)
Memorial University of Newfoundland
St. John's, Newfoundland, Canada, A1C 5S7